ENVIRONMENTAL ETHICS AND BEHAVIOURAL CHANGE

Environmental Ethics and Behavioural Change takes a practical approach to environmental ethics with a focus on its transformative potential for students, professionals, policy makers, activists, and concerned citizens. Proposed solutions to issues such as climate change, resource depletion and accelerating extinctions have included technological fixes, national and international regulation and social marketing. This volume examines the ethical features of a range of communication strategies and technological, political and economic methods for promoting ecologically responsible practice in the face of these crises.

The central concern of the book is environmental behaviour change: inspiring, informing and catalysing reflective change in the reader, and in their ability to influence others. By making clear the forms of environmental ethics that exist, and what each implies in terms of individual and social change, the reader will be better able to formulate, commit to, articulate and promote a coherent position on how to understand and engage with environmental issues.

This is an essential companion to environmental ethics and philosophy courses as well as a great resource for professionals interested in practical approaches to environmental ethics. It is also excellent supplementary reading for environmental studies, environmental politics and sustainable consumption courses.

Benjamin Franks is Lecturer in Social and Political Philosophy in the School of Interdisciplinary Studies, University of Glasgow, UK.

Stuart Hanscomb is Senior Lecturer in Philosophy and Communication in the School of Interdisciplinary Studies, University of Glasgow, UK.

Sean Johnston is Professor of Science, Technology and Society in the School of Interdisciplinary Studies, University of Glasgow, UK.

"Urgent environmental problems and the need to change policy and behaviour are explored and tackled with rigorous questioning of conflicting ethical theories. . . . This is a major philosophical contribution to the study of environmental concerns and moral obligations." — Dr David Lamb, Hon Reader in Bioethics, University of Birmingham, UK; Visiting Lecturer in Animal Welfare Ethics, University of Southampton, UK

"Addressing some of the biggest questions confronting humanity, Franks, Hanscomb, and Johnston expertly guide the reader through the complexities of our 'modern' world; and suggest ways in which a command of environmental ethics and behavioural change can produce a truly more inclusive society." — Dr JFM Clark, Director of the Institute of Environmental History, University of St Andrews, UK

"Environmental Ethics and Behavioural Change is an incredibly helpful, clear and rigorous guide for any of us vexed about the rights and wrongs of environmental and ecological policy and practice. It is suitable for practitioners and students across disciplines." — Prof. Simon Sadler, University of California, Davis, USA

"This is an excellent and timely book. It draws on philosophical, psychological, political and other ideas to illuminate today's most urgent environmental issues, such as climate change, fracking and animal welfare. The book is exceptionally clear. It is a valuable resource for students, activists and anyone concerned about the future of our planet." — Richard Smith, Professor of Education, University of Durham, UK

ENVIRONMENTAL ETHICS AND BEHAVIOURAL CHANGE

Benjamin Franks, Stuart Hanscomb and Sean F. Johnston

First published 2018
by Routledge
2 Park Square, Milton Park, Abingdon, Oxon OX14 4RN

and by Routledge
711 Third Avenue, New York, NY 10017

Routledge is an imprint of the Taylor & Francis Group, an informa business

© 2018 Benjamin Franks, Stuart Hanscomb and Sean Johnston

The right of Benjamin Franks, Stuart Hanscomb and Sean Johnston to be identified as authors of this work has been asserted by them in accordance with sections 77 and 78 of the Copyright, Designs and Patents Act 1988.

All rights reserved. No part of this book may be reprinted or reproduced or utilised in any form or by any electronic, mechanical, or other means, now known or hereafter invented, including photocopying and recording, or in any information storage or retrieval system, without permission in writing from the publishers.

Trademark notice: Product or corporate names may be trademarks or registered trademarks, and are used only for identification and explanation without intent to infringe.

British Library Cataloguing-in-Publication Data
A catalogue record for this book is available from the British Library

Library of Congress Cataloging-in-Publication Data
A catalog record has been requested for this book

ISBN: 978-1-138-92404-8 (hbk)
ISBN: 978-1-138-92405-5 (pbk)
ISBN: 978-1-315-68461-1 (ebk)

Typeset in Bembo
by Swales & Willis Ltd, Exeter, Devon, UK

CONTENTS

List of illustrations ix
Preface xi
Acknowledgements xiii

1 Rationale: ethics for guiding environmental behaviours
 and practices 1
  1.1 Reasoning through ethics 1
  1.2 Environmental values 2
  1.3 Reframing contemporary environmental issues 5
  1.4 Broader perspectives 7
  1.5 Psychological insights and sustainable practices 8
  1.6 Social power and environmental actions 9
  1.7 Behavioural change 10
  1.8 The whole picture: an integrated approach 11

2 Ethical reasoning 14
  2.1 The domain of ethics 14
    2.1.1 Meta-ethics 15
    2.1.2 Normative ethics 17
    2.1.3 Applied ethics 17
  2.2 Utilitarianisms 19
    2.2.1 Challenges to utilitarianism 20
    2.2.2 Concluding comments on utilitarianism 27
  2.3 Rights-based ethics (deontology) 27
    2.3.1 Criticisms of deontology 32
    2.3.2 Environmental justice 35
    2.3.3 Concluding comments on deontology 36

2.4 Virtue theories 37
    2.4.1 Criticisms of virtue theory 41
    2.4.2 Concluding comments on virtue theory 43
2.5 A defence of ethics 44

3 Conflicting values: anthropocentric, biocentric and
  ecocentric ethics   48
  3.1 Anthropocentric ethics 49
      3.1.1 The Western tradition of anthropocentrism 49
      3.1.2 Immanuel Kant and secular arguments for valuing
            other species 52
      3.1.3 Transforming anthropocentric values into behaviours 54
  3.2 Biocentric ethics 56
      3.2.1 Questioning biological hierarchies 56
      3.2.2 Albert Schweitzer and reverence for life 59
      3.2.3 Popular expressions of biocentrism 62
  3.3 Ecocentric ethics 65
      3.3.1 Aldo Leopold and the Land Ethic 66
      3.3.2 Popular expressions of ecocentrism 70

4 Shallow, deep and social ecologies   75
  4.1 Arne Naess and notions of 'shallow' and 'deep'
      environmental ethics 76
      4.1.1 Shallow ecology 77
      4.1.2 Deep ecology 79
      4.1.3 Challenges and critiques of deep ecology 82
  4.2 Murray Bookchin and social ecology 85
      4.2.1 Challenges and critiques of social ecology 88
      4.2.2 Popular expressions of biospherism 90
  4.3 Appropriate and inappropriate technologies 93
      4.3.1 Ernst Schumacher and 'intermediate' technologies 93
      4.3.2 Appropriate technologies and the biospheric view 94
      4.3.3 Technological fixes as alternatives to behavioural change 95

5 Environmental behavioural change and the psychology
  of influence   102
  5.1 Some fundamentals of attitude and behaviour change theories 104
      5.1.1 Dual process theory 105
      5.1.2 Framing 108
      5.1.3 Framing and narrative in An Inconvenient Truth 109
      5.1.4 Framing, biases and heuristics 112
  5.2 Psychosocial barriers to environmental behaviour change 114
      5.2.1 Knowledge 114

        5.2.2 Emotional engagement 120
        5.2.3 Existing attitudes, values and wants 123
        5.2.4 Psychological denial 127
        5.2.5 Social influence: norms, authority and trust 133
        5.2.6 Enablers 139
        5.2.7 Habits 139
    5.3 Conclusion 144

6 The practical and moral limitations of the psychology
    of influence   152
    6.1 Social marketing and nudge 152
        6.1.1 Social marketing 152
        6.1.2 Nudge 156
    6.2 Challenges to using psychological influence (I): the
        ethics of nudge 159
        6.2.1 Undermining autonomy in everyday choices 159
        6.2.2 Undermining self-development 162
        6.2.3 Undermining the individual's relationship
              with government 163
        6.2.4 Issues of fairness 164
    6.3 Challenges to using psychological influence (II):
        'Common Cause' 164
        6.3.1 Message tailoring 165
        6.3.2 Spillover 168
        6.3.3 Segmentation 172
        6.3.4 Ideology 172
    6.4 Conclusion: The case for collectivist frame 173

7 Economic change: corporations and environmental
    responsibility   179
    7.1 Introduction 179
    7.2 Capitalism: a brief introduction 181
    7.3 The corporation 185
    7.4 Milton Friedman and the rise of corporocentrism 187
    7.5 Critics of Friedman 189
        7.5.1 Friedman, CSR and the role of stakeholders 189
        7.5.2 Corporations as non-virtuous agents 191
    7.6 Corporate citizenship 194
    7.7 Corporate environmentalism 195
        7.7.1 Monetarising the environment: carbon credits 196
        7.7.2 Ethical consumption 197
    7.8 Ecologically responsible alternatives 198
    7.9 Conclusion 200

8 Constitutional political change: Green votes and
   Green representation   204
   8.1 Introduction 204
   8.2 Politics and the state: the basics 204
   8.3 Green politics and state institutions 206
   8.4. State effectiveness and legitimacy 213
   8.5 Constitutional green politics 214
   8.6 Specialist green parties 217
   8.7 Democratic state methods of behavioural change 220
   8.8 Non-democracies and environmental policy 222
   8.9 Evaluating constitutionalism 224
   8.10 Constitutionalism and non-constitutionalism 227
   8.11 Conclusion 228

9 Non-constitutional political change: Green direct action,
   civil disobedience and symbolic activity   232
   9.1 Introduction 232
   9.2 Green direct action and civil disobedience 234
       9.2.1 Diversity 237
       9.2.2 Immediacy and empowerment 238
       9.2.3 Satisfaction 239
       9.2.4 Demoi-cratic 240
       9.2.5 Criticism and replies 240
   9.3 Combining direct action and constitutional action 242
   9.4 Symbolic action 243
   9.5 Eco-terrorism 246
   9.6 Organisation: social networks and electronic communications 250
   9.7 Lifestyles 253
       9.7.1 Ecological communes 253
       9.7.2 Lifestyles and the community 254
   9.8 Conclusion 255

10 Conclusion: integration without reduction   261
   10.1 Coexistence at every scale 261
   10.2 Virtues and empowerment 263
   10.3 Promoting economic and political change 267

Appendix: reflections on teaching   269
Index   274

PREFACE

Environmental Ethics and Behavioural Change takes a practical approach to environmental ethics that focuses on its transformative potential for students, professionals, policy makers, activists and concerned citizens. Proposed solutions to issues such as climate change, resource depletion and accelerating extinctions have included economic and technological fixes, national and international regulations, social marketing and the personal integration of green values in lifestyles. This volume examines the ethical features of a range of communication strategies and technological, political and economic methods for promoting ecologically responsible practice in the face of these crises.

The central concern of the book is environmental behavioural change: inspiring, informing and catalysing reflective change in the reader, and in their ability to influence others. By making clear the forms of environmental ethics that exist, and what each implies in terms of individual and social change, the reader will be better able to formulate, commit to, articulate and promote a coherent position on how to understand and engage with environmental issues.

Reflecting the multiple factors affecting our environment, *Environmental Ethics and Behavioural Change* adopts a multidisciplinary approach that draws from a range of academic specialisms. It provides a clear introduction to the main ethical theories; explains how different constellations of principles that shape the main environmental philosophies and movements have developed over time; and, how these relate to contemporary political philosophical views. Just as importantly, it explores the spectrum of current and proposed methods for addressing environmental sustainability; how they can be applied to contemporary social issues and professional practices; and, how these can be communicated effectively to stakeholders such as businesses, local communities, consumers and government. These techniques range from principles supporting wise technological choices to the psychology of behavioural change and the politics of individual, group and societal choices.

Ethical theories outlined and discussed include utilitarianism, deontology and neo-Aristotelianism, and the spectrum of green philosophical paradigms include anthropocentric, ecocentric and biocentric value systems, deep ecologies and social ecologies. Examples and case studies are drawn from contemporary issues such as fracking, windfarms, geo-engineering and transition towns; and the approaches to communication and behaviour change examined include strategies and tactics associated with technological fixes, free markets, ethical consumption, constitutional politics, community-based initiatives, symbolic actions and direct action; and tactics such as social marketing and practice theory.

For each ethical paradigm our analysis involves:

- An exploration of the behaviours that it requires of individuals and organisations.
- An examination of the practical possibilities and barriers associated with communicating its principles, and with communicating the forms of attitude and behaviour change it demands.
- An assessment of the limitations that its principles place on the types of communication and behaviour change strategies and tactics that can be employed, and whether or not they might be seen to be effective.

Yet the book is more than a compendium of techniques: throughout, it stresses the ethical implications of environmental action, explaining why practitioners need to be sensitive to issues of power and inequality, autonomy and collective responsibility, in order to promote workable, resilient and morally defensible revisions of current social practices.

Benjamin Franks, Stuart Hanscomb and Sean Johnston
Dumfries, Scotland, June 2017

ACKNOWLEDGEMENTS

We thank our current and former students and colleagues, who have inspired and helped shape this book, in particular Drs David Borthwick, Bettina Bluemling, Steven Gillespie and Mhairi Harvey and Prof. Joseph Murphy. We would also like to acknowledge the continuing support of our families.

1

RATIONALE

Ethics for guiding evironmental behaviours and practices

This chapter introduces the scope and principal topics of the book by posing big questions for readers, individually and collectively. What are the major environmental problems we face? What are our fundamental values and how do they affect our attitudes concerning the environment? What makes ethics particularly relevant to questions of how we humans inhabit and manage our environments? What should be done – and by whom? What behaviours and practices have to change and how should this be accomplished? What ethical issues are raised by the proposed solutions? How can these insights be combined and applied successfully, and where do they lead?

1.1 Reasoning through ethics

At the heart of this book is the grounding of environmental actions in defensible ethical principles. Chapter 2 introduces ways of identifying and analysing dilemmas about judging notions of right and wrong and deciding our priorities of concern.

Reasoning about ethics has developed into consistent frameworks from the ancient Greeks. Complementary approaches have been constructed over the past 250 years during the periods known as the 'Enlightenment', 'Industrial Revolution' and 'modernity'. The oldest of these theories embeds moral thinking and behaviour in *virtues* or qualities of character. By contrast, Humanists – including some of the supporters of the French and American revolutions – developed an ethical system founded on rights and duties (so-called *deontology*). Also, suiting a period of burgeoning commerce, a third system of ethical principles became popular from the nineteenth century. The best-known version, *utilitarianism*, judges morality by a kind of accounting procedure: the best action is one that provides the maximum return of happiness.

The jostling values introduced in subsequent chapters can be fitted to one or another of these frameworks. These rigorous systems provide guidance. They identify constraints on certain actions and motivate others. As will become evident through our coverage, the authors find virtue ethics to be the most compelling basis for environmentally-sound practices.

Our aim in this book is to demonstrate how these approaches to ethical reasoning can be applied consistently to a range of activities relevant to understanding and changing environmental behaviours. These frameworks place challenging constraints on acceptable human activities and encourage new practices that have been relatively uncommon in modern societies. Our intent is to critically discuss the broad variety of methods available to change behaviours and to produce sustainable practices. The book consequently addresses readers ranging from professionals to managers to concerned citizens, and from working contexts stretching from companies to governments to environmental organisations.

1.2 Environmental values

The moral judgements we make are based on values, but there are other kinds of values as well. We value a very wide range of things, sometimes based on a moral evaluation, but also based on their practical use, their aesthetic qualities, or because we like them for other varied and unspecified reasons.

'Value' is such a basic idea that it is hard to define without being circular: we value X because X is valuable; and X is valuable because we value X. However, it is possible to offer some indication of what makes something valuable, even if it is in a rather abstract way. For instance, what we consider valuable has some connection with needs, wants and, broadly speaking, what matters to us. Other things being equal, we desire what we find valuable, and the desiring of something is conceptually related to having emotional responses towards it; e.g., happiness when in its presence, anger if someone unjustifiably harms or interferes with it.

It can also be said that the worlds we as individuals and communities inhabit are defined by values as much as they are by their physical features. Natural science aims to discover truths about the material world – truths that exist whether we know about them or not – but we first have to be motivated to find out about the world in order for the practice of science to exist or flourish. In other words, we have to first find valuable the sorts of truths that science can provide. This need to care applies to the generation and continuation of all human activities, whether it is playing *Scrabble* or voting in a democratic election. We do not primarily live in a physical world, but in a world shaped by values.

It is possible for only one person to find a particular thing valuable, but more typically, because of common instincts or social norms, values tend to be shared. In order for societies to function, however, various moral (and other) values must be shared – either because they are held to have inherent value, or because of a recognition of their practical necessity. For example, for many it is simply seen as a good thing to be honest with other people under most circumstances; honesty is valued for its own sake. For some though there may be no such regard for the fundamental value of honesty, but nevertheless a recognition that for valuable goals to be achieved (such as successful teamwork) being generally an honest person is a requirement and, in this instrumental sense, valuable.

This distinction between inherent (or intrinsic) values and instrumental values is a vital one for both ethics in general and for environmental ethics. For example, is species extinction and biodiversity loss wrong just because of its negative consequences for human well-being, or also because these things are valuable in their own right?

This book is primarily about moral (or ethical) values, and the nature of these will be explained in Chapter 2. However, other kinds of value become important as well, not least because one approach to understanding ethical value (known as consequentialism) is in terms of the effects our actions have on what people care about. For this reason, an accurate appreciation of what matters, and to how many, is essential for making moral decisions. Moreover, moral values will often come into conflict with other types of values; for example, those associated with economics, political power and lifestyles that are environmentally unsustainable. In order to fully appreciate the importance of environmental ethics and how it can analyse and influence approaches to behaviour change, we must also understand the challenge it faces from other important types of value.

Chapters 3 and 4 explore and assess distinct moral worldviews: different ways of perceiving and valuing environments. Their bottom line is that people in Western cultures have traditionally expressed (and often still do) only passing concerns beyond their own interests, and base this orientation on a variety of arguments. In fact, the term 'environment' itself, coined in the mid-nineteenth century, did not then have its current focus on nature and other forms of life, but instead on the differing local contexts affecting human lives.

The two chapters sketch how ethical sensibilities have adapted to new knowledge and to growing human powers and insights. Over the most recent five centuries, human activities have been characterised by expansion: new territories (such as European conquest of the Americas), larger groupings (creation of expanding urban environments, nation-states and empires) and exploitation of new resources (such as the transatlantic slave economy, iron production, gold fever and hydroelectric power). This growth brought experiences of fresh geographical contexts and active efforts to manage them to suit human needs. How have these expanding activities relied on a shared ethical vision? What consequences have they entailed for other human cultures, species and ecosystems?

By the twentieth century, two environmental contexts had risen to prominence. On the one hand, modern cities became increasingly artificial environments. Working animals were replaced by machines, and for some urban residents the opportunities to experience non-human life were minimal. On the other hand, nations increasingly defined 'wilderness areas' to be regions that are reserved or conserved (in other words, either protected intact or managed wisely as a resource). In distinctive ways, these contrasting environments embodied human values alone: modern cities became island enclaves dedicated to a single species, while conservation areas managed those aspects of the non-human world that were particularly valued by people, such as hunting, fishing and scenic beauty. Today, more than half the world's population lives in urban areas. Few genuine wildernesses remain, although some regions (such as the deep oceans) remain relatively free of human activity. To what extent does such segregation of interests succeed in ensuring sustainable environments?

While these novel human experiences largely consolidated ethical sensibilities that focused on human interests (so-called 'anthropocentric' or human-centred ethics), there has been a gradual broadening of sensitivities from opposing voices regarding the varieties and contexts of life that are worthy of moral concern. These historical roots are just as pertinent today as members of modern societies continue to grapple with distinct systems of value. What do these past episodes reveal about human behaviours and how they can change?

As discussed in Chapter 3, changing attitudes concerning ethical principles such as compassion, justice and freedom have extended notions of kinship and community. Through the nineteenth century there were social movements to dismantle the European and American slave economies, to extend voting rights to non-land-owning residents and to reduce legal barriers to women's participation in society (such efforts continue in numerous contexts today, particularly in combatting wider ethnic and gender inequalities). Although the 'correct' moral judgement and actions may appear obvious today, these issues have provoked intense disagreement along political, religious and economic lines for individuals, groups and entire nations. These topics were 'wicked problems' (see Chapter 5) in the sense of requiring multiple forms of intervention. In that respect, they are analogies of our present quandaries about sustainable environments.

These transitions of attitude gradually extended the ethical landscape to considerations of humans in general. A handful of voices suggested that other species might be considered worthy of similar moral attention. At the centre of such claims were reassessments of value: should non-humans be understood as mere resources for human benefit, or do they have worth in themselves? Certain non-Western theological traditions recognise other life forms as having intrinsic rather than instrumental value.

Into the twentieth century, these concerns were most often expressed by actions to prevent specific cases of suffering (more recently dubbed life-centred or 'biocentric' ethical concerns). Humane organisations increasingly opposed the physical mistreatment of animals, particularly in urban settings. Questions of inclusiveness remain: which animals should be our focus and which qualities (of them or us) justify this protection? Are all forms of life worthy of human concern, and how should this realisation affect our activities? Also, in what ways should humans be altering their behaviours in order to respect these values?

The science of ecology reveals more abstract qualities of life to be considered. Interactions between forms of life suggest interdependence; harming one component of an ecosystem may have effects elsewhere in the system (an insight inspiring what is now known as an 'ecocentric' ethical perspective). If such symbiosis is delicate or fragile, it may place constraints on acceptable human actions. Since these new ethical sensitivities emerged during the mid-twentieth century they have become important components of environmentalism. Even so, this growing abstraction – from people, to certain animals, and then to complex ecosystems – can be disorienting and baffling. Where should human attentions be focused and what should we do to wisely manage our actions?

These questions remain as vital now as they were a half-century ago, and they continue to produce new thoughtful perspectives. These are attentive to larger scales of place and time. Environmental ethics today – as hinted in widespread concern about anthropogenic (human-caused) climate change – considers the global scale and the many ways that our biosphere may be harmed or potentially helped by human activities. An historical perspective on the environment has been important, revealing the effects of past human activities on our shared present. The changes to ecosystems around the world have been profound, and in some regions disastrous for the loss of once-common species, habitats and ways of life. Given this human aptitude to transform environments, what effects are current activities setting up for our descendants (often referred to today as 'future generations', and sometimes consciously including other species and ecosystems)? What can or should we do to avoid predicted dangers?

Modern environmental ethics has inherited these multiple concerns, and is expressed along a spectrum of value systems. Each of them considers the ethical dimensions sketched above, but in contrasting ways. Chapter 4 explores more recent environmental values, which demand considerable reorientation of human activities. So-called 'deep ecologies' call for longer-term analysis of human activities and individual responsibilities; so-called 'social ecologies' focus on reconfiguring human and social relations in ways that assure a sustainable existence for all forms of life and the planet as a whole. These are demanding stances that identify extensions to our sense of duties, and may identify broader virtues to guide our behaviours.

1.3 Reframing contemporary environmental issues

This book is motivated by the proliferation of environmental quandaries. Awareness has grown over just the past few generations of the widespread environmental harms caused by humans. Accumulating concerns have been triggered by specific events. Cases of toxic waste dumps, oil spills, species extinctions and agricultural mismanagement have become more frequent in modern societies and more frequently reported by mass media.

These concerns extend not just to accidents, but also to potential harms caused by human innovation. New policies, technologies and modes of life periodically raise concerns from publics that have become mistrustful of the unplanned consequences that seem to accompany modern practices. For instance, wind turbines, an alternative to the burning of fossil fuels for energy production, have been criticised for potential harms to birds, nearby residents, tourist enjoyment of natural landscapes and national economic competitiveness; legislation to curb industrial pollution may be challenged because of its negative effects on company profits and employment.

This focus on the here-and-now and on first-hand implications is a common feature of human problem-solving, and arguably has proven to be a highly effective technique for rapidly advancing science and engineering. Direct experience and experimentation can often reveal precise cause-and-effect relationships. This knowledge can identify immediate problems, and its reapplication often can solve those problems speedily and efficiently. Indeed, this approach is at the centre of 'modernity', the beliefs, attitudes and ways of life that now describe most human societies.

This mind-set nevertheless has drawbacks: it may limit our vision about complex and unfamiliar situations. Human activities and human powers have scaled up dramatically in recent times. The pace of change has obscured important features: the range of unanticipated consequences and the nature of their implications for pre-existing systems and future options can be difficult to assess. Human-made systems have grown dramatically in complexity over the past century, particularly socio-technical systems such as transport (rail, road and aviation networks and their corresponding leisure and commerce offshoots), communications (from telegraphy and the telephone to radio, television and the internet), food production (from mega-farms to refrigerated distribution to microwave meals) and a global scale for economics. Each has come to be managed by cohorts of specialists who may nevertheless neglect the interactions with other systems.

Among the most complex natural systems overlooked by this short-sighted attention are ecosystems and the global climate. Environmental issues have too often been approached by subdividing complex problems into more easily understandable but inadequately assessed portions.

Common problem-solving approaches have relied on attention from individual disciplines, with each approaching or 'framing' the issues in distinct but narrow terms. Problems may be identified alternately as 'essentially' poor engineering design, inappropriate corporate behaviours or inadequate public awareness. Consider, for example, a hypothetical case of water pollution resulting from a consumer washing product. An engineering solution might recommend the installation of processing equipment in water treatment plants to remove the problematic chemicals before the effluent reaches waterways and reservoirs. Alternatively, a technological solution might focus on the manufacturers' conversion to less polluting chemical products. A policy response might apply penalties via fines, or incentives via reduced taxation, to encourage chemical companies' adoption of cleaner chemical processes and products, or alternatively focus on providing public funding for treatment plant conversions. Yet another approach might be to educate consumers about the undesired effects of their washing products on life forms in the affected waterways, with the aim of encouraging their use of other products. A hedonistic frame, on the other hand, would not see it as a problem at all unless the ecological damage had an identifiable personal impact.

> **Framing**: a way of understanding and acting in accordance with a concept or issue that emphasises and prioritises certain features of it in a manner that will inevitably (though not always deliberately) obscure alternative perspectives or paradigms.

1.4 Broader perspectives

On the face of it, each of these solutions is motivated by a degree of ethical awareness. Professional engineers, for example, have traditionally received some training in appropriate conduct during their careers. Their dealings with customers, superiors, peers and authorities must conform to laws, but also to higher standards of behaviour in being fair, honest and helpful. Similarly, the notion of a 'good corporate citizen' – a company actively responsible and responsive to its community – is commonly assumed. Legislators, policy-makers, public committees and other organisations also are assumed to adopt norms of responsibility and ethical standards beyond legal requirements. Individual consumers, too, may be motivated by personal convictions to alter their individual lifestyles.

Yet such solutions tend to over-simplify complex problems, both technically and ethically. They may focus on discrete events and causes. They may identify single agents for blame and correction. Having an attention misdirected to a particular time and place, they may not be analysed adequately to reveal more general, long-term or subtle harms and their more complex causes. Lessons learned by one designer, company, maintenance engineer, consumer group or local council may not be passed on to inform other contexts. To make matters worse, the ethical judgements are likely to be weakly applied and narrowly constructed.

Environmental attentions have typically been limited in scope and scale, and this misdirected view carries deeper implications. Technological solutions usually require reliance on experts (an approach to problem-solving and governance dubbed 'technocracy'). This may unjustly off-load excessive responsibilities and unrealistic expectations onto a particular party, and at the same time limit the voice and decision-making power of others. Trust in engineering approaches, a feature of modern societies, may also promote false confidence in the technical resolution of environmental problems. Such faith in analysis, innovation and step-by-step progress can inspire inaction by non-experts, who include not just passive publics but other varieties of decision-maker and professional as well. How far can we rely on technological solutions to environmental issues, and what ethical assumptions and implications do they involve?

Another dimension of group short-sightedness is the neglect of wider harms. This was famously noted in what has become known as the 'tragedy of the commons'. During the late eighteenth century, landowners in Britain began to enclose grazing land that had previously been a shared resource for their communities. They identified specific harms in sharing: every individual livestock owner sustained their animals on the common land and caused minor degradation as a result, but collectively their actions caused the resource to be unsustainable. On the other hand, the introduction of hedgerows and fences by landowners deprived their communities of sustainable livelihoods. The human tendency to act from self-interest rather than community interest has numerous more recent examples: transnational industrial air pollution; the near-extinction of blue whales during the 1960s; the failure of the Grand Banks fishery during the 1990s. At the heart of environmental problem-solving is a fundamental and ancient ethical issue: what are the benefits of competition and cooperation, and under what circumstances should one be chosen rather than the other?

In the economically-integrated modern world, actions of one community or organisation may have far-reaching effects on people and other life forms elsewhere. More subtly, the interconnectedness of human cultures, ecosystems and global phenomena have generally been under-valued or ignored. The biggest problem is also the most recently recognised: the reality and pace of anthropogenic climate change have been conclusively demonstrated only in the past generation. Preceding it were over two hundred years of industrial revolution and the explosive development of the entwined systems of modern societies.

A key question for environmental ethics, then, is how to integrate this growing knowledge about interconnectedness, and to generate a holistic sense of values and practices. The chapters explore techniques that support a *principled* approach to problem-solving. The term 'integrity' is particularly apt to describe this book's theme. It has been used by environmental ethicists to describe the functional characteristics of sustainable ecosystems and of the biosphere as a whole. The word also describes behaviours that are consistent and cohesive, and that express clear personal convictions. Integrity in this sense is arguably a crucial characteristic (or virtue) for all professionals and citizens active engaging with environmental and social concerns.

1.5 Psychological insights and sustainable practices

In subsequent chapters we explore how environmental issues are perceived and acted upon. Chapter 5 is founded on theories of cognitive bias and the psychology of influence that have informed the rapidly growing fields of environmental psychology and environmental communication. The notion of framing highlights the need to tailor messages to audiences' existing beliefs and values, and 'dual process theory' claims that effective communication appeals to both our 'fast' or emotional mode of decision-making, as well as to our 'slow' or reflective mode. With a particular emphasis on climate change communication, the chapter considers how psychological insights can be used to help explain and overcome barriers to personal environmental behavioural change such as lack of emotional engagement, the presence of conflicting values, an absence of social norms, and the habitual nature of human behaviour. Continuing an important theme of the book, Chapter 5 also considers the potential of this area of research for identifying relevant virtues of environmental behavioural change. Among those highlighted are resilience, virtues of cooperation and a willingness to take responsibility in the context of a problem that demands a collective solution.

Chapter 6 takes a critical look at methods used to influence environmental attitudes and behaviours that are based on the knowledge and techniques of commercial marketing. Controversy in this area tends to stem from the tendency to target the relatively unconscious modes of decision-making that are discussed in Chapter 5. Social marketing is the application of this form of expertise towards socially beneficial outcomes. Its success in the field of public health has to some extent been replicated for environmentally relevant behaviours, but there are good reasons to think that this is far from the complete answer to the problem. More importantly for our purposes, some serious ethical concerns have been raised about its employment by governments and other institutions. These include the perpetuation of a consumerist frame of mind that obscures the severity of the problem we face, and that fails to engage relevant collectivist values.

A growing branch of ethical debate addresses the subdivision of social marketing known as 'nudge'. This is the method of manipulating select features of everyday practices (such as the default settings on thermostats) in order to encourage individually or socially desirable behaviours. Environmental, or 'green', nudges have been criticised for, among other things, undermining autonomy and their potentially exaggerated impact on already disadvantaged sections of society. Nevertheless, with due transparency, broad public consent and the contextualising of these methods among more deliberative and values-based approaches to behavioural change, a case can be made for their ethical legitimacy.

1.6 Social power and environmental actions

Throughout the book we trace how the power to alter environments is distributed in modern societies. Power to harm, hinder or help may be shared unequally between governments, commercial enterprises, opposition groups, technological innovators and individuals. These shifting hierarchies and opportunities are inherently political. Examination of the politics of environmental action – and its ethical dimensions – are fundamental to our coverage.

The worldview of corporations is particularly important to contemporary environmental problems and solutions, and is explored in Chapter 7. In the developed world, corporations play a highly influential role in the economy, and their power is something many environmentalists seek to harness. However, economic solutions carry their own implicit assumptions, such as the ability to assign a monetary value to the quality of life, or to the relative importance of other beings. Corporate actors and market activity rely on particular types of social relationship and institutional arrangement that normalise attitudes and behaviours that can be counter-productive from an ecological perspective.

Chapter 8 looks at how established political solutions, through policy-making, legislation and regulation, may exert power in ways that address wider environmental harms only indirectly. It identifies and ethically evaluates the types of behaviour needed to influence legislators and policy makers to make environmental change. In doing so it discusses the ambiguous and contested position of electoral politics in environmental movements. The strength of the commitment to, or rejection of, representative politics foregrounds the differences in the philosophical positions within the wider green movement. As a result, Chapter 9 explores the potential of non-constitutional approaches to alter environmental practices. It examines the multiple forms of political change, from the wide diversity of tactics covered by descriptors such as 'civil disobedience', 'direct action' and 'eco-terrorism', to constructing green communes and supporting sustainable community housing. It highlights the justifications that prioritise some methods over others and critically assesses the arguments for these unconventional tactics. The strengths of non-constitutional action include their diversity, immediate practicality and accessibility, but there are also weaknesses in consistency and impact.

The ways in which ethical values are grouped, prioritised and put into practice identifies different environmental, philosophical and political positions. For instance, those that prioritise property rights interpret ecological problems, identify viable solutions and carry out their programme in different ways to those who prioritise the welfare of non-human animals. The ethical is intimately and unavoidably connected to the political.

1.7 Behavioural change

At this juncture it is important to clarify what we mean by 'behavioural change';[1] a term that has tended to have a fluid meaning and that describes an evolving area of study. For example, John B. Watson's recasting of psychology as behaviourism, from the 1910s, understood behaviours merely as reflexes that could be altered by external stimuli. Watson and his followers did not consider people's internal mental states or the wider cultural context to be relevant for understanding or predicting behaviours. More recently, behavioural change is a term that has been adopted by niche policy-makers such as the UK government's Behavioural Insight Team. Its aim is to meet government targets with respect to health and the environment by altering individual behaviours via the manipulation of psychological biases. The unconscious or automatic influence of the 'nudges' they employ shares features of behaviourism, but underpinning these techniques are the insights of cognitive psychology and thus a more developed understanding of the mind and its functions.

The term 'behavioural change' in this book, however, is used in a much broader sense. It includes attention to people's psychological motivations, both reflective and automatic, but also to the social context of human activities, the physical resources they involve, and the norms and values embedded within them. The meaning of behavioural change employed here is thus quite holistic, and can be aligned with the notion of 'social practices'; a concept derived from influential traditions in twentieth- and twenty-first-century philosophy and sociology. Practices are relatively resilient combinations of *material resources* such as human physical labour and technologies, *competencies* such as intellectual capabilities and other psychological strengths, and *shared meanings*, in particular identities and values. For instance, being a member of an allotment society (a subdivided community vegetable plot, the British equivalent of a North American 'community garden') means that there are materials (land, tools, a meeting room), a stable set of rules by which the society operates, some shared goals, some shared values about what makes a good allotment (well-maintained and productive) and what makes a good allotment member (a regular attender who maintains their plot and good relations with other members). The members also tend to develop particular types of shared identity, terminology and particular ways of viewing their activity and the wider world in which it takes place. Engaging in a social activity also provides opportunities for challenging, changing and even transcending that practice as well as endorsing and extending it. Stable (but reflective and adaptable) practices develop into what are variously described as 'traditions' or 'social structures'. It should also be noted that alongside more complex activities, simple everyday routines – such as showering, line-drying of laundry, and cycling to work – can also be regarded as practices.

By understanding human behaviour in terms of practices, the interplay between the individual and the social is clarified. Individuals are not seen as totally autonomous irrespective of the social context or entirely determined by their social circumstances, but choices and viewpoints instead arise out of particular productive activities (those that are satisfying to perform and/or have a useful product at the end). Achieving behavioural change combines attention to both large-scale institutional action, including governments and international organisations, and the everyday activities of individuals or small groups. Thus it looks at both smaller-scale actions such as consumption habits and lifestyle choices, and larger-scale structures for social change such as governmental prohibitions and state structure. The individual and social are treated as being interdependent. Individual actions, such as a particular voter's electoral choice, require the social structures of a democratic state and a meaningful constitution. Similarly, large-scale social structures, like a market economy protected by legal institutions and general laws of contract, develop out of, and are maintained by, the individuals connected with these institutions.

Engaging in a social practice involves making choices. Participants develop an evaluative process for assisting decision-making. For instance, the allotment society might have to make a choice as to who should be allowed a scarce plot from the waiting list of applicants, and correspondingly develop a formal and informal set of criteria for making a selection. Those with a vegetable patch decide what to grow, whether to use pesticides, and how to distribute the harvest. Formal and informal norms assist in these decisions.

1.8 The whole picture: an integrated approach

This chapter identifies the important disciplinary perspectives applied in this book: ethical theory as a rigorous and rational approach to sound decision-making; historical insights and analogy to guide actions; the psychology of influence to understand barriers and enablers of environmentally-responsible action; and political philosophy to identify constraints and opportunities for behavioural change.

Each approach – applying lessons from the past, shaping behaviours and influencing the exercise of power – needs to be acutely sensitive to wider social, cultural and temporal consequences of the adopted solutions. Ethics is the touchstone throughout this book for wielding these tools cautiously.

As introduced in this chapter, ethics can be an effective tool for wise decision-making and action to address complex contemporary problems, and particularly questions of environmental engagement.

The history of ethical concerns is admittedly a patchy one. This chapter has suggested that it is possible to trace a gradual extension of human sensitivities from narrow definitions of 'who counts', to extending considerations of what the 'worthy community' includes. This faith in moral improvement and philosophical foundations has been cited by several of the key thinkers discussed in later chapters, and parallels other widely-shared beliefs: faith in scientific progress; faith in growing engineering expertise; faith in the scaling up of economic systems; and – as this book attests – faith in contemporary understandings of human behaviours.

Yet this trust or tendency can be challenged, as subsequent chapters will explore. The growth of knowledge, for example, seems obvious in certain domains, but may be more sporadic and partial than we commonly recognise. Moreover, the ethical dimensions may be overlooked in our eagerness to know more (genetic engineering and nanotechnology being examples of recent research fields that have raised continuing ethical concerns). Human powers to engineer the planet are also unquestionably growing, but there is increasing controversy about the ecological side-effects and community harms of such applications. Similarly, the scale and sustainability of global economic activity are increasingly questioned.

Ethical positions continue to mutate as social science, technology and scholarship evolve. As hinted above, what could be called a 'philosophical ecosystem' of environmental ethics exists today. Understanding the variety of these interacting forms and competing values is a fundamental aim of this book, and the first stage to dealing with the diversity of contemporary ideas about environmental issues.

Despite the discord in behaviours, the uneven historical record suggests that the range of discourse about environments and ethical actions has broadened considerably for modern audiences. The popular centre-of-mass has shifted, or at least lurched episodically, from solely human-centred towards more inclusive life-centred, ecosystem-centred or even biosphere-oriented considerations. Individuals and groups are thinking, talking and acting in ways that were uncommon a generation ago.

While there is no convincing evidence of a cultural evolution towards environmental wisdom, this book argues that ethics and corresponding behavioural change provide a viable route. Its interdisciplinary approach raises questions that transcend individual fields of scholarship and restricted professional remits. Based on our experiences with students from a wide spectrum of backgrounds, national origins and career contexts, we expect that engineers, policy-makers and economists around the world will find the coverage as relevant as do citizens and activists.

And the implications of environmental ethics and behavioural change affect far larger audiences, particularly those without a voice: communities (both human and non-human) marginalised in modern societies.

Second, ethics constructs intellectual foundations as bases for wise action. As discussed in subsequent chapters, traditional frameworks of ethics (described as virtue, deontological and consequentialist approaches) can be linked with contemporary environmental paradigms (often labelled anthropocentric, biocentric, ecocentric, deep and social ecology) to address the perspectives introduced in this chapter.

Just as fundamentally, the book relates behaviours and behavioural change to such ethical frameworks. This linkage provides sound motivations and pragmatic drivers to guide the solution of environmental issues. In a manner that is consistent with certain forms of what has been called 'environmental pragmatism'[2] it is argued that we need to better understand how behavioural change comes about in individuals and collectives; we need to ethically assess these options and the practices that utilise them, and we need to consider the degree of coherence between models of behavioural change and the ethical orientation of the individual or organisation promoting that change.

The overarching perspective of this book is one of optimism. Environmentalism does not have to be doom-laden. Alongside the discouraging examples of narrow prejudices, technological errors and abuses of power, we cite encouraging evidence of the rapidity and scale of profound change. We argue that social, cultural, technological and scientific transformations are within grasp and, with some care, are controllable. In a fraction of a single human lifetime, for example, some modern societies have witnessed substantial improvements in racial and gender inclusiveness, generated more democratic human interactions, dramatically transformed awareness and sensitivities about other species and ecosystems, adopted empowering technologies and identified many of their insidious side-effects to make them safer. None of these changes were fast enough for their supporters, but the fact that all of them occurred in the face of substantial opposition is good reason to be hopeful. This book is intended to ground that hopefulness in understandings that can be applied effectively to improve contemporary environmental issues and human practices.

Notes

1 Note that this term is generally regarded as interchangeable with 'behaviour change'.
2 An approach to environmental ethics that emphasises the need for environmental activists and academics to open-mindedly engage with people's existing environmental attitudes and behaviours if they are to have any influence over them. (See Hourdequin, M. (2015) *Environmental Ethics*. London: Bloomsbury, 197–202, for an excellent overview of the varied and complex set of views that comprise this school of thought.)

2
ETHICAL REASONING

2.1 The domain of ethics

In a chapter specifically about the theoretical basis of environmental ethics, in a book aimed at promoting informed reflection on, and promotion of, morally defensible behavioural change, it is necessary first to explain terms like 'ethics' and 'morals'. In some philosophical traditions, 'morals' (*Moralis*), refers to the principles that distinguish 'right' from 'wrong' that exist independent of the agent. 'Ethics' (*Ethikos*) by contrast refers to the character of the subject. However, as discussed later, these two are intimately connected, and the terms are used interchangeably in this book.

The philosopher Peter Singer, who was a major influence on the development of animal rights and promoter of environmental ethics (as well as a representative of one of the schools of moral philosophy this chapter addresses) points out that ethics is primarily concerned not just with our own self-interest (egoism) but with the question of how we treat others:

> The crux of ethics is the ability to detach oneself from one's own standpoint and take an impartial perspective. This is impossible for a creature that lacks all reasoning ability; but once we can discuss moral issues, it becomes impossible to avoid seeing a situation as others see it. I am only one among others, and their interests ought to count as mine do.
>
> *(Singer 1987, 150)*

Singer's description highlights three significant features of moral consideration. First, it concerns the choices we make. Moral reasoning is redundant where action is wholly causally predetermined or any chance of agency is impossible. If a person is slipped a drug that makes them incapable of thinking rationally, reducing them to an automaton, then such a person, whilst still a subject of moral worth (that is to say we care about what happens to them), is not at present a moral subject (an entity capable of making a moral decision). Creatures that act purely on instinct, who are incapable of considering and acting on alternatives, are incapable of making moral judgements. Thus a moral agent is one capable of identifying right action and has the ability to act on this judgement.

Second, the choices are based on principles, rules, or norms that are explicable to others. These are guides to how one should act, how to live, the main goals we ought to concentrate on and what sort of person we should be. In short, as Singer identifies, ethics deals with determining comprehensible guides for action when our behaviour impacts on others.

Third, for Singer these decisions are 'rational'. Since the Enlightenment, reason and science have replaced commitment to the teachings of a single religious text as the basis for ethics. The role of reason is different in particular types of ethics (as will be discussed below). For Singer reason might be less important for defining a set of moral principles and more about providing clear, consistent and impartial justifications for one's choices.

At the end of the section quoted above Singer (1987, 150) presents a challenge, asking 'But who are "the others"?'. In other words, who is it that morally-informed decision-makers should be concerned about? Too often it is just the interests of those above us in the workplace or wider social hierarchy that take priority when we weigh up decisions, or else just colleagues, suppliers or customers. As a supporter of utilitarianism (a term explained below), Singer argues that we need to expand the circle of concern further, to include not just wider members of our community but the global citizenry who can be impacted by actions and inactions. In addition, Singer includes in his category of 'others' non-human sentient animals and entities who do not currently exist: i.e., future generations (Singer 2011, 48–70 and 242–5).

Ethics as a discipline is usually divided into three interconnected sub-disciplines: 1) meta-ethics, 2) normative ethics and 3) applied ethics. For the most part this book concentrates on applied ethics, and this chapter is on normative ethics, but as these are not discrete categories it is worth outlining them, indicating their importance to the evaluation of social and environmental policies and activities.

2.1.1 Meta-ethics

Meta-ethics explores the foundations of, scope and status of ethical statements, asking questions like: what is right? Are moral claims like the conclusions of natural scientific or mathematical formula or are they closer to the 'truths' of poetry and visual art? Are ethics the product of an individual's consciousness or do they have an independent existence? Some common meta-ethical positions reduce moral theory to simply emotional utterances (emotivism) or statements about individual preferences (subjectivism). Take the example of an environmentalist who argues that coal-burning power stations should be replaced because the greenhouse impacts of their carbon dioxide emissions damage habitats for multiple species and the life chances of vulnerable groups. A subjectivist might accept the environmentalist claim, but undermine its status by claiming that, whilst true, it is just a statement of personal preference. This is a position which, problematically, can also be extended to attitudes to racism, genocide and infanticide – 'you think barrel bombing your own citizens is wrong, I think it's right, we just have different preferences'.

Another popular position is cultural relativism. A cultural relativist reduces moral statements to sociological statements about what is socially approved in different societies. In some parts of the world consensual premarital sex is not subject to moral censure; in other parts it is deeply rejected. Rather than saying one culture has the right answer, the cultural relativist simply responds that the action is acceptable in one cultural context and wrong in the other. Similarly, environmental concerns are subject to the same cultural consideration. Where they are embedded features of that society they should be respected, where they are not that too should be respected. Cultural relativism is a popular and in some ways pertinent response, as it rightly identifies that in real life there are communities based on different moral positions and traditions. It rightly indicates that casting moral judgements without intimately understanding the operations of different social surroundings is both arrogant and leads to dangerous meddling. A prohibition against nakedness might be a useful taboo in freezing climates, but less significant in temperate ones. The imposition of the taboo in the wrong circumstances can generate bad health outcomes and ignores how the two communities are probably acting under the same principle – dressing appropriately for the climate.

Cultural relativism has many problems. First, it would mean approving or tolerating all sorts of pernicious practices just because they are in accordance with that culture's dominant values. Second, it views cultures as homogeneous, but this is rarely the case since people have disagreements about ethical values in even the most rigid societies. To side with the dominant cultures might be merely to support a particular grouping within that society (and not even the majority grouping). Third, cultures are not discrete and separate but instead are permeable and overlap. Nevertheless, challenging unacceptable behaviours based on inappropriate values in one social setting will generate responses in other settings. Environmental behavioural change has to be sensitive to different economic and cultural circumstances. Blanket prohibitions against private motor cars might work in large urban centres with a well-developed and well-funded public transport system, but would cause enormous hardship and social and economic breakdown in post-industrial rural communities with dispersed populations.

There are also problems with meta-ethics that assume that moral values are universal. First, proving that they are universal is a difficulty. Second, even if there are universal values, how they operate, or are interpreted, in different contexts will still lead to differences. As the philosopher Mark Rowlands explains (2015), with reference to the work of Ludwig Wittgenstein, 'there are no rules for the interpretation of rules'.

This text assumes that ethical principles are at least inter-subjective (shared between people), knowable, stable but not necessarily fixed, and the product of – and produced by – actual social practices. That is to say, every social activity, in order to be sustainable, has implicit and explicit norms that guide practitioners, and these can be identified, evaluated and, on some occasions, challenged and transformed.

2.1.2 Normative ethics

Normative ethics seeks to identify, clarify and assess for consistency the rules by which we choose our actions. Where different principles come into conflict, such as non-maleficence (avoiding causing harm) and respecting autonomy (the right of the individual to choose their own destiny), normative ethics attempts to provide a non-arbitrary basis for prioritising norms and resolving the disagreement. It thus explains the place of environmental principles in wider moral theories. For some environmental principles might be core, whilst for others they are peripheral. Much of the discussion in this chapter deals with normative ethics.

2.1.3 Applied ethics

Applied ethics, on the other hand, makes up most of the rest of this book. In applied ethics, moral principles are related to more precise questions of procedure and practice. What appear to be perfectly consistent, coherent and rigorous normative principles, when put into practice might lead to perverse outcomes or procedures. For instance, an environmentalist might encourage the reuse of waste materials in the most efficient and socially benevolent way: repairing consumer durables to extend their workable life and to cut down on resource depletion or finding new uses for discarded items are often examples of benevolent and environmentally desirable practice. However, when the waste products are tissue samples from dead infants, held without parental consent, as was done at Alder Hay hospital in the UK (see Evans 2001; Chouhan and Draper 2003), these apparently sufficient and desirable principles are found to produce distressing and controversial practice. Applied ethics from some traditions can give the impression that ethical principles are first identified in isolation and then applied to real-world situations. This approach seems problematic on a number of grounds, not least because it assumes a questionable meta-ethical position; that isolated reason can identify universal moral principles. What constitutes 'the rational' is influenced by the particular activity one is engaged in. In an academic debate, it would be irrational to act in a partisan and disrespectful way to opponents, whereas in a lively football crowd to be non-partisan and too willing to agree with opposing supporters would undermine the sporting rivalry. Even moral philosophy is also a social activity with its own forms of social organisation, discourse, materials and norms, which therefore is prone to focus on particular topics as most valuable and generate particular types of values (such as rigour, rationality and conceptual clarity) and as such might have been slow to react to ecological concerns and acknowledge environmental principles.

Ethical enquiry is already core to many social activities even if it is not always identified as such. Social and medical researchers, in most professional contexts, will require formal ethical clearance for their activity and will similarly be involved in ethical assessment of other research protocols. Professional and many corporate institutions have formal ethical guidelines and codes of practice by which members and employees are – at least minimally – expected to adhere. More informally, colleagues interpret the behaviours of their co-workers and employers in recognisable but looser ethical terms, referring to upholding or violating rights, respect (or disregard) for dignity and gaining or losing good outcomes.

Although there is a clear distinction between the 'legal' and the 'moral', ethical analysis and its corresponding discourse have been a way of analysing legislation, promoting alternatives and guiding public engagement. The justification for particular policies and legislative programmes appeal to a considerable number of moral norms, such as protection of individual liberty, general utility, reciprocity, fairness, and assistance to the vulnerable. Environmentally motivated law is frequently discussed in this way.

Other major political issues are wholly entwined with ethical terminology. As we will see, contentious political issues dealing with ecology invariably raise issues of morality. Take for instance controversies around protests to ensure oil companies dismantled their deep-sea platforms on land, with the additional expense of decommissioning, rather than dumping at sea. These cover issues of good outcomes (economic or ecological) and for whom (shareholders, customers, competitors, eco-systems). Issues of rights and autonomy include whether dumping in an unowned part of the ocean constitutes a violation of property rights, whether prohibitions on deep-sea disposal are an illegitimate interference with a corporation's liberty or are necessary to ensure the right of sea creatures to have a habitable environment. They also touch on the character of the corporate entity: is it entirely self-interested, economically responsible or compassionate?

This book concentrates on environmental action for a sustainable biosphere. This involves raising questions about the types, extent, intensity and distribution of harms from climate change caused by human behaviours; the ethical issues raised by various strategies of prevention, amelioration and mitigation, and how these might protect or violate the rights of particular entities, fairly or unfairly redistribute resources, or encourage vice-like or virtuous behaviour.

Climate change is important partly because it raises questions about what should be the focus of our individual well-being, and that of those close to us, our nations, the whole human community, and non-human animals too. As explored historically in the following two chapters, responses have prioritised various scales ranging from individual members of species, to protection of viable species even at the expense of individual members (such as culling weaker members) and, more recently, the protection of ecosystems and the whole biosphere. There are a range of political, legislative, commercial, technological and communicative approaches available to reduce the amount of atmospheric carbon and respond to the current and imminent harms. Each raises questions of priority and symbiosis, with some developing into coherent mutually supporting strategies, whilst others – which appear to be equally attractive – are not easy to mutually accommodate. Such choices are the subject of moral consideration.

In order to assess these different strategies for behavioural change more systematically, this chapter is devoted to the three main ethical theories, highlighting their pertinence to the main ecological issues. Our coverage highlights some of the main themes of this book, as it identifies the types of social relationship, main social institutions and accounts of agency these ethical approaches are either predicated on, challenge or sustain and reinforce. The first of these – utilitarianism – is perhaps the most pervasively used in debates around climate change as it privileges the reduction of bad social outcomes as well as the promotion of good social outcomes.

2.2 Utilitarianisms

Utilitarian ethics is the most well-known form of consequentialist moral reasoning. What all consequentialist theories share in common is the priority they give to achieving a particular outcome, rather than concern for the particularities of the method used or the character of the person or nature of the social practice that generates the desired outcome. For utilitarianism, the desired outcome is greatest social utility or happiness.

> **Utilitarianism**: A form of consequentialism, or way of judging actions according to their consequences, specifically in relation to the amount of satisfaction gained by all concerned. The aim is to maximise happiness for the greatest number.

John Stuart Mill (1999, 55), the great nineteenth-century proponent of utilitarianism, describes it as holding:

> [T]hat actions are right in proportion as they tend to promote happiness, wrong as they tend to produce the reverse of happiness. By happiness is intended pleasure, and the absence of pain; by unhappiness, pain and the privation of pleasure.

Pleasure can be derived from multiple sources, from playing games and watching a favourite television show to conducting a difficult orchestral piece or raising a contented family. Similarly, pleasure can be eroded by living amongst pollution and environmental degradation.

There are, for Mill, different kind of pleasures; 'higher' pleasures, which he associates with intellectual activities and 'lower' ones, which are baser and more physical (57–8). Jeremy Bentham, who along with John Stuart's father, James Mill, was one of the founders of utilitarianism, provided in his book *An Introduction to the Principles of Morals and Legislation* a seven-point algorithm for assisting in making utilitarian decisions. He devised a 'hedonic calculus' for choosing between rival options. Given a choice, one should, according to this calculus, consider the outcome of each option in terms of intensity of the happiness (or pain), how long the outcome lasts (duration), the probability that the desired end result occurs (certainty), the immediacy or otherwise of the desirable outcomes (propinquity), its ability to generate other actions likely to produce positive outcomes (fecundity), the likely negative outcomes (purity) and the number of people impacted (extent).

Like Bentham, John Stuart Mill's account is a social one. It is about overall general happiness amongst all people, not individual happiness; although frequently, argues Mill, encouraging each other to pursue our own happiness will generate positive social outcomes. For utilitarians, the goal is to maximise the generation of pleasure and minimise the sensation of pain across society. Thus, avoiding ecologically damaging outcomes becomes important to utilitarians because of the potential risks to general happiness. For some utilitarians, such as Singer (2011, 254), the happiness of non-human animals is also of moral significance, so habitat degradation to extract resources for human satisfaction, but at significant expense to non-humans, is not acceptable.

Not all consequentialisms are utilitarian: Hedonism, for example, argues that what matters is individual not social happiness. An odd paradox is that a society of mutually competing hedonists is unlikely to be very satisfying, as each is ambivalent about others' personal happiness and can often regard each other as hostile rivals. Productivism is also different to utilitarianism in that it prioritises increases in economic output. If an act frustrates efficient production it is wrong. This is sometimes conflated with utilitarianism, as the assumption is that the more commodities are available, the more people will consume and the greater number of consumers will lead to greater satisfaction. But the two are not synonymous. The pursuit of ever-increasing acquisition could lead to disastrous ecological outcomes, but also generate types of self-interested institutions and individuals. People could be conditioned to think of themselves only as consumers whose worth is based on their immediate access to consumer goods and who are unlikely to develop fulfilling social relationships.

2.2.1 Challenges to utilitarianism

There are problems for utilitarians of most varieties, also shared by most other major consequentialist theories, which raise significant questions about the use of such goal-orientated reasoning for the formulation and justification of environmental and social policy. This section will end with a brief account of just seven of them: 1) efficiency of calculating outcomes, 2) the efficacy of calculating outcomes, 3) unfairly enhancing inequality, 4) impersonal relationships, 5) problem of agency, 6) violations of autonomy and 7) demandingness. Other issues, such as integrity and the meta-ethical status of utilitarianism, are not directly addressed here.

2.2.1.1 The efficiency problem

The efficiency problem concerns the practicality of utilitarianism. Bentham, the great Enlightenment thinker, saw ethics in almost engineering terms. His hedonic algorithm was to facilitate scientifically precise ethical answers. However, imagine someone is walking through a moorland in which a small fire breaks out. They could choose to run away from the fire and flee to safety, leaving the forest to burn, or they could pick up the fire flapper (also known as a beater) to quickly extinguish the fire. A utilitarian would argue that they should calculate the likely benefits and costs of each option: how intense, certain and immediate are the harms of allowing the fire to burn, how long will they last, what other harms will arise and what entities will be hurt. Then there is the question of the regenerative benefits of forest fires, their certainty, purity and extent as well as the pleasure to any pyromaniac in the near vicinity. By the time the walker has made the calculations the fire has engulfed them and the moorland. Thus, most contemporary utilitarians propose 'rule utilitarianism' as a solution to this problem.

Rule utilitarians suggest that rather than judging the moral value of each individual action by its consequences (standard act utilitarianism), instead people need good general rules of conduct to live by, such as 'put out easily extinguishable fires if there is no risk to yourself, otherwise leave the area quickly'. These general rules of conduct are chosen on the basis that if this rule is generally adhered to, it will generate greater happiness than any easily understood alternative. It is a simple device for quick, sometimes automatic, decision-making. (See System 1 thinking and heuristics in Chapter 5.) Rule utilitarianism can thus justify important principles like respecting autonomy because, on the whole, respecting the desires of people on how they wish to live their own lives, so long as they are not interfering with others, generates more positive social outcomes than continual external (or heteronomous) interference.

Act utilitarianism involves calculating the utility and disutility of every choice. **Rule utilitarianism** suggests that 'act utility' is impossible, or at least highly undesirable, and instead general rules of conduct are drawn up to which everyone abides. The rule is selected on the basis that, if adhered to, it will produce the best overall consequences.

However, as might be expected, rule utilitarianism meets some rather severe objections. The question arises: what should a rule utilitarian do if breaking the rule in a particular instance generates greater happiness than keeping to the rule? If one violates the rule, then it is no longer a general rule of conduct, and we are left with act utilitarianism. If instead one keeps to the rule regardless of the consequences – what J.J.C. Smart (1973, 10) calls 'rule worship' – then one is privileging something else rather than the maximisation of happiness and thus it is not properly utilitarianism. There may be solutions to this problem generated by positing additional rules, such as 'break the rule if it produces extremely bad outcomes'. But this potentially leads to the continuation of rule worship at the expense of some social utility.

2.2.1.2 The efficacy problem

The efficacy problem concerns the usefulness of utilitarianism. It is not altogether clear what it is that utilitarianism should measure. Is it happiness, absence of pain, or satisfaction of desires? This leads to different types of utilitarianism, some suggesting that the goal is to maximise the satisfaction of particular mental states, with 'negative utilitarianism' prioritising the limitation of unhappiness and pain, rather than the maximisation of happiness, to avoid accusations of sadism. Others, like 'preference utilitarians', argue that we should concentrate on meeting individual desires even if it causes that individual pain. For instance, someone training for a marathon is likely to suffer significant discomfort, but a preference utilitarian would still help to satisfy the runner's ambition.

Despite these different forms of utilitarianism, it is not altogether clear how one measures happiness or satisfaction of desires against other alternatives. Is the most important pleasure that of a driver using good roads, or listening to uninterrupted birdsong on a summer's evening walk through a sun-speckled woodland, or enjoying an organically grown fruit grown in your own allotment? It is doubtful that these can be reliably measured and quantified, and they are so different in kind that reducing them to a shared standard is bound to lose something of significance. Without a shared standard, however, utilitarianism cannot prioritise when conflicts arise.

Too often policymakers and others use simple quantifiable targets, not because the goals are ethically justifiable but because it is easier to find evidence to judge performance based on these benchmarks. Simple easily measurable targets have the benefit of providing a clear basis for assessing performance. However, these targets are often inappropriate for judging complex activities and attempts to meet these targets (such as financial profitability) can produce disastrous outcomes and undermine otherwise benevolent activities. In the oft-quoted words of an Abenaki film-maker Alanis Obomsawim: 'When the last tree is cut, the last fish is caught, and the last river is polluted; when to breathe the air is sickening, you will realize, too late, that wealth is not in bank accounts and that you can't eat money'.

2.2.1.3 Unfairly enhancing inequality

Roger Crisp (1997, 169–70 and 1998, 32) points out that utilitarianism faces a number of problems with the issue of equality and fairness. Although Mill and other utilitarians, like Singer, have been advocates of equality, recognising that sexist or racist behaviour and customs are irrational and cause immense harm, nonetheless it is possible to see how utilitarian policy formation can lead to unfair outcomes. It can justify the generation and maintenance of a perpetually disadvantaged minority whose welfare is significantly lower than the majority population, but whose subservient position significantly raises the utility of the rest. An example might be a slave population that has to perform all the unpleasant work for the majority who are delighted at the reduction of their drudgery. Rectifying the situation might reduce overall satisfaction as the majority population are now burdened with the undesirable tasks performed by the minority and they suffer from the loss of esteem as a result of the eradication of their elite position. Liberation from servitude has many benefits for the minority population but these good outcomes extend to a much smaller population. Similar outcomes arise in environmental settings; pollution and toxic waste might be targeted for dumping on the same small community as their disutility only decreases marginally with each new delivery, whilst fairer even distribution would generate greater disutility. Similar reasoning can be applied to dam building projects in China since the 1950s. More than 20,000 have been built with (in theory) national interests in mind, but a number of these – most notably the 'Three Gorges' scheme in Hubei province (completed in 2008) – have proved highly controversial. There are various reasons for this, but perhaps the most prominent is the displacement of millions of people and the subsequent failure of the Chinese government to adequately compensate many of them (Boyd 2013). Thus utilitarianism, a theory predicated on the egalitarian principle of taking the interests of each entity as seriously as any other entity, nonetheless can generate gross unfairness. The ability to impose a utilitarian decision across an entire population also suggests a hierarchical and coercive political structure (see also 2.2.1.6 below).

Singer (2011, 49–52) argues that utilitarianism is in fact radically egalitarian: utilitarianism challenges sexist and racist behaviour because what matters is maximising the happiness of individuals, regardless of the gender or ethnicity of that individual. Sexism, argues Singer, is when the interests of a person or group are overlooked or minimised simply because they are a member of a particular gender. Similarly, racism occurs when someone has their interests ignored or marginalised simply because they are perceived to be a member of a particular ethnic group. As a utilitarian, for Singer, the main interests are avoiding pain and living a happy life. Singer then goes on to identify another form of prejudice: speciesism. A speciesist society is one in which the interests we consider important for humans are overlooked or considered unimportant for non-humans, simply because they aren't of our species.

For Singer almost all examples of humans eating meat is speciesist. Humans can live healthily on a vegetarian diet. Enjoying a steak, jerk chicken or *gefilte* fish is a minor interest for a human but for the cow, chicken or fish, not being caught and slaughtered is a major interest. One should, argues Singer, prioritise meeting major interests over minor interests. Singer's account explains that on most occasions prioritising the lives of humans over non-humans is justified: the cognitive abilities of humans make them more prone to stress and they have richer social connections, thus their pain and loss is more deeply felt than that of, say, a cow, but nevertheless a cow should not be killed or severely hurt simply to satisfy a human's whim. Thus, for Singer, utilitarianism's radical egalitarianism provides the basis for compassionate consideration of non-humans.

2.2.1.4 Impersonal relationships

The next criticism is that utilitarianism's radical egalitarianism undermines the value of close relationships. For utilitarians, one individual's happiness matters as much as that of any other individual (Mill 1999, 105) and regardless of species (Singer 2000). The characteristics of a specifically ecological utilitarianism is that it concentrates on the relationship between individuals and groups of plants and animals (including humans) on the generation of the health and well-being of the biosphere (Van Buren 1995, 265) and, as such, it informs the ecocentric and biocentric philosophical movements (see Chapters 3 and 4). This radical impartiality, argue critics, might be destructive to all sorts of personal relationships that give lives meaning. It would mean that a parent would have to cut their time spent with their own children if greater social utility could be generated by babysitting for someone they have never met. All practices that require a degree of partiality, such as romantic attachments or team loyalty, would be eroded by the requirement to cut such ties on every occasion if it produces general utility.

Mill (1999, 90–1) responds to these criticisms by arguing that maintaining close relationships produces better outcomes, so that there are utilitarian grounds for partiality. A society is generally happier and psychologically secure if children know that on many occasions their parents will prioritise their interests. This seems a strong counter-argument and explains why a parent can treat their child in a partial manner, but not make their offspring's interests supreme in all cases. It points to different responsible parties saving different priorities and rules as these will generate best social outcomes. We would expect parents to act partially, but government policymakers not to favour their families (an expectation which is not always met). However, Mill's response is not entirely satisfactory as it still suggests that parental love is only justified because it generates greater good, not because it is a good in itself. It would seem odd to protect a diverse habitat only because it was likely to lead to better outcomes for human society.

2.2.1.5 The problem of agency

The famous libertarian (or more properly 'propertarian')[1] theorist Robert Nozick provides a telling criticism of utilitarianism in his thought experiment, the 'experience machine'. Nozick's objective is to show that the internal mental experiences of people, whether it is the sensation of having desires satisfied or just straightforward happiness, do not provide the proper basis for determining what is fundamentally important. Imagine, says Nozick (1974, 42–3), that a neuropsychologist could manipulate a person's brain so they felt that they were engaged in all sorts of positive experiences – such as writing the great contemporary novel, embarking on exciting new relationships or exploring new worlds – but really they were unconscious in a tank with electrodes stuck to their head (a scenario similar to that used in the sci-fi trilogy *The Matrix*). The person is even woken up occasionally so they can choose a new satisfying experience to leave the machine, thus satisfying preference utilitarianism. Nozick asks, why would someone reject the opportunity to be plugged into the experience machine designed to maximise inner experience?

The answer for Nozick is that something else is much more important, namely that those plugged-in are not active agents in the world, influencing and being influenced by the world around them. He also explains that utilitarians have their moral theory back to front. Inner experiences, like happiness, usually matter because they are a product of our interactions with the world; contentedness is important when it is the result of having done something worthwhile, not as a stand-alone feeling. Further, as Nozick points out, by acting in the world individuals develop into particular types of person (maybe heroic or generous or collegial). A comatose manipulated brain is not a model of what people aspire to be. Nozick's conclusion that '[W]e prefer to live (an active verb) ourselves, in contact with reality' (45) is also shared by many who reject his deontological position. It is this ability to engage in and shape our destinies and social relationships that matters, not just our inner experiences. Environmental behavioural change involves being an active rounded agent in the world, rather than living an imagined ecological good life.

Nozick's intriguing thought experiment has particular resonance with environmentalists. Facing up to social and ecological dilemmas is often deeply uncomfortable and there is an understandable tendency for many of us, encouraged by social structures that encourage compliance, to prefer the illusion that all is well, rather than face up to upsetting realities and significant challenges (see Chapter 5). However, to be a properly acting agent in the world means being critically aware and involves dealing with some of the unpleasantness that constitutes parts of social and ecological environment. In engaging with the world, critical agents can not only change themselves but the arenas which they inhabit.

2.2.1.6 Violations of autonomy

From Nozick's account of agency there is the additional problem of a persistent conflict between pursuing desirable goals and respecting individual freedom. It is this conflict that shapes many disputes in public policy such as the ownership of handguns, legal drinking age, compulsory wearing of crash helmets and seatbelts, smoking bans, drug prohibition and taxation of carbon-based fuels. Proponents and opponents of bans and restrictions on harmful products and activities are involved in weighing up the social benefits that result from constraints of individual freedom to choose against the costs of violations of autonomy. For Nozick no social benefit is sufficiently strong to justify interfering with individual liberty. This places his libertarianism at odds with many ecological strategies as these often prioritise protecting unowned ecological entities at the expense of consumer's freedom of choice.

Many social activities are predicated on protecting individual liberty (a concept discussed in more detail in the next section) against consequentialist pressures. Patients have the right to choose or refuse treatment, retailers may buy and sell goods to their preferred client rather than the one who will bring greatest social benefit, and individuals have the freedom to speak truths that may be socially unpleasant. Mill is aware of these significant challenges to utilitarianism, but argues that respect for autonomy can be incorporated into utilitarianism. Autonomy is the individual acting without interference to pursue their own goals, so long as it is reciprocal. It is, argues Mill (1985), only through allowing individual freedoms such as 'liberty to form opinion' and to 'express opinion' that we are able to determine good policies and meet the vast array of people's interests. Allowing people to dissent and act on their own inclination, so long as they do not restrict others from doing the same, is the best way to develop responsible knowledgeable citizens and a happier society, unencumbered by wasteful prohibitions.

Mill's defence of autonomy, however, appears to fall foul of the criticisms of rule utilitarianism raised above. If respect for autonomy is justified because it generates good social outcomes, what about those cases where it doesn't? If the rule is breached, then it no longer operates as a general rule. If it is kept regardless of outcome, then it is guilty of 'rule worship' and is no longer a utilitarian principle.

2.2.1.7 Demandingness

The final problem with utilitarianism is that of its demandingness and it is an objection that many environmentalists will be familiar with. All moral theories (except ethical egoism) make demands on us, as they all require some deviation from pursuing self-interest alone (see Hooker 2009). Some make greater demands than others. Some might be relatively modest demands, such as declining to wear the pelts of endangered animals. Other ethical demands require substantial changes to our lifestyles. For utilitarians, especially green utilitarians, the objection is that it demands too much from each of us as moral actors. Every action we take has to be calculated to maximise greatest utility even at great expense to ourselves (so long as that the expense is offset by greater advantage to others). We can never treat ourselves if there is a person or sentient creature who is in avoidable need elsewhere. Climate change with its profound negative outcomes would impose significant changes to our individual behaviours; for example, foregoing all unnecessary consumption and abandoning carbon-reliant transport in order to reduce the harms caused by raised levels of atmospheric carbon. Such substantial change to lifestyle and life-plans, especially when outcomes occur to people not yet born, seem to be too challenging.

To some green critics, the apparently excessive demands of utilitarianism are not an objection to the theory but simply highlight the extent to which social institutions and accepted norms have to change. Failure to fully live up to the demands do not make them invalid but act as guidance for ideal action, in the same way that other ethical principles such as egalitarianism cannot always be achieved but nevertheless provide a basis for demarcating desirable from less desirable options.

2.2.2 Concluding comments on utilitarianism

Despite the problems with utilitarianism, it does have a great deal to recommend it as a useful ethic for analysing and defending environmental action. Many of the key critiques of existing policies, technologies and behaviours that contribute to climate change employ a form of utilitarian reasoning. The Intergovernmental Panel on Climate Change (IPCC), journalists like George Monbiot, activists like Mark Lynas (2007) and filmmakers such as Franny Armstrong (writer and director of *The Age of Stupid*) all highlight the myriad devastating negative impacts; the great disadvantages (sometimes called 'disutilities' by utilitarians) that are arising and will inevitably arise from increasing carbon consumption and emissions if changes are not made. To ignore, or downplay, the consequence of human actions is to be deeply and indefensibly negligent. However, there are dangers with consequentialisms in general and utilitarianisms in particular. Identifying which goals to pursue and how and when to measure them not only raises questions of methodology but ethico-political ones too.

Any system for calculating and weighing up rival options, playing off one set of preferences against another, requires particular types of bureaucracy and specific forms of governance. In addition, even individual choices are either made within formal organisational settings or are influenced by the wider social context in which they are made. Effecting good ends privileges the norms and structures of efficient management and that usually reduces the autonomy of individuals and undermines other values and the practices in which these values are formed. Environmental projects need to identify the consequentialist norms at work, how they shape institutional, social and personal behaviours. It requires sensitivity to the problems of consequentialism, even when ecological goals are so clearly desirable.

2.3 Rights-based ethics (deontology)

As discussed in Chapter 3, the main challenger to utilitarianism emerged at about the same time. It is known as deontological moral theory, or rights-based ethics. Most of the great ethical debates have been between advocates of deontology and utilitarianism or between rival forms of deontology. So too in relation to climate change, disputes arise over whether its main harms in damaging habitable zones undermines the very ecological basis necessary for individuals to have rights, or whether environmental policies that arise to reduce carbon emissions are themselves violations of fundamental economic freedoms and produce unnecessary social harms (see, for instance, Lawson 2014, 12–13).

> **Deontology**: A way of judging actions according to whether they obey particular rules, in particular respect for rights, rather than on producing particular outcomes.

At the core of deontology is the principle of respecting rights and keeping to one's obligations and duties, regardless of outcome. It is thus a foil to consequentialist ethics. The major and most influential forms of deontology emanate from the works of John Locke and Immanuel Kant, who argue that there are foundational and universal rights, and these are found through reason (or natural law). Ethical behaviour is consciously chosen rather than instinctive or habituated behaviour (see system 2 thinking in Chapter 5). In addition, it is this ability to reason – a uniquely human characteristic for the Enlightenment deontologists – which gives an entity rights. So rights are not only discovered through abstract reasoning, but also apply only to those capable of reason. It is this account of what constitutes a morally significant entity that has led to deontology, in its classical form, being perceived as the most anthropocentric of the three main ethical theories.

The concept of autonomy, although a term with many interpretations, is closely linked to the notion of rights. Autonomy and rights figure together in political and ethical debates, whether on reproductive control, anti-colonial or national independence movements, or rights to a healthy and clean environment. The different versions of autonomy share the key characteristic that a moral being is 'an end in itself' (Kant 2005, 108). The worth of the rational moral subject is not dependent on how they are useful to others or act as an instrument to some predetermined goal. In utilitarianism, it is the achievement of the goal – social utility – that is more important than the means. People can be used in whatever way necessary to achieve that goal, reducing them from being sovereign subjects to slaves. Deontologists argue that rational people have to be free to choose their own goals and be allowed to pursue them, so long as they do not interfere with other people's freedom to do the same. However, non-rational, and therefore non-autonomous creatures, like most non-human animals, only have value in so far as they are useful to rational beings.

There are different meanings of autonomy. Some describe it as 'freedom from interference' and 'freedom to determine one's future'; others as 'the ability to identify one's interests and plan to achieve it', 'recognition from self and others of one's uniqueness, dignity' and 'independence'. Rights are the areas of freedom for the moral subject to do things (in the case of positive rights) or to be free from interference (in the case of negative rights). So anti-smog campaigners appeal to negative rights: they demand that heavy industries do not foist pollutants onto their bodies and private property (like laundry drying on their own land). By contrast, campaigns for access to water would be a positive right. It is a demand to have something.

Appeals to rights, and the corresponding obligations for others to respect those rights, concern protecting and extending an individual's freedom. Deontology's core concepts of individual autonomy, freedom, reason, rights and duties make it one of the cornerstones of liberal political and economic thinking (and is discussed in Chapters 7, 8 and 9).

The apparently slight distinctions in the identification of what it means to be an autonomous agent have significant impacts on the interpretation of freedom and the account of rights and duties required to protect and enhance such freedoms. Locke has a relatively simple account of autonomy; having rights means being able to develop your own thoughts and views and use your own body as you see fit, so long as it does not limit the freedom of others to do the same. For Locke (1988, 287–88), because an individual's body is their own property, no one has prior rights over the individual's labour produced by their body. From this, he argues that any previously unowned objects that are produced by that labour are also the legitimate property of the individual. A person might do with their private property, whether it is their body or an external object they have produced, as they please, so long as they do not violate anyone else's rights over their property or lives. So consenting to having one's face tattooed to appear like a skeleton (see Figure 2.1. below) violates no rights and thus, for classical deontologists, raises no substantive ethical issues.

What an individual chooses to do with their property (including their own bodies) does not have to be rational or consistent. A person might buy and wear all sorts of offensive and politically contradictory apparel, or even mindlessly destroy their own possessions, but if they are not interfering with others then there are no grounds for intervention. Medical consent works largely in terms of basic autonomy. Doctors may think that the person's decision to forego treatment is unwise, but if they are competent to make a decision, have been properly informed and are not acting under coercion, then the patient's decision is usually legally and morally binding. Similarly, much consumer behaviour, which critics point out is frequently irrational and self-destructive, is posited on and defended by Lockean notions of freedom.

Kant, by contrast, has a more sophisticated and restrictive account of rights. Autonomy for Kant is based on self-regulation. Individuals are autonomous not just because they are capable of reason but because they use reason to make their decisions. Non-humans are not rational and act on instinct. They cannot make choices, and thus they are non-moral entities. Humans who cannot act rationally, like children or those with severe mental-health problems, are not moral agents. Similarly, people who can act rationally, and thus are sovereign moral entities, but who opt to act selfishly or in contravention to rational norms, are behaving immorally. Thus, for Kant, autonomy is a form of self-regulation. Individuals are free to act, but their freedom is predicated on their ability to reason, to escape being a simple slave to passion or instinct. The sovereign subject is moral because they are choosing to act in accordance with binding moral principles. These principles are themselves rationally deduced and universal.

Some lesser principles of conduct are hypothetical; they are required in order to reach a particular goal. Take, for example, someone who wishes to live a long healthy life. In such a case it would be advisable if that person avoided smoking cigarettes. 'Don't smoke cigarettes' is a hypothetical rule based on a particular goal. Binding moral rules, however, are universal. These apply to all sovereign individuals whatever the outcome. These universal or categorical principles, which include for Kant prohibitions against lying, breaking promises and killing

FIGURE 2.1 Rights over your own body. (Nora Lives photo, Wikipedia Commons license: https://tinyurl.com/y9sopeob

(even self-killing), are deduced by reason and apply to everyone regardless of the consequences. In contrast to Locke, Kant's deontological ethic demands more than simply acting in accordance with one's wishes without interfering with or interference from others.

Categorical moral principles can be logically deduced, claims Kant, by application of the 'categorical imperative'. Although there are three slightly different versions of the categorical imperative formulated by Kant, the most cited version states: 'Act only on the maxim through which you can at the same time will that it should become a universal law' (Kant 2005, 97). The categorical imperative requires two steps from the rational moral actor. The person facing a moral dilemma needs to identify the rule or maxim that determines the choice they made, and then consider whether that rule can be applied universally without contradiction. If it can be universally applied, then acting on that rule is morally acceptable, if it cannot, then to choose to act in that way is partial and illegitimate (Kant 2005, 99).

Kant (2005, 98–100) gives a number of examples that illustrate the categorical imperative. Amongst them is the prohibition against breaking a promise on the grounds that keeping it is difficult and inconvenient. If someone acts in this way, argues Kant, they are acting on the maxim that it is acceptable for them to break a promise out of self-interest. In such a case, consistent with the categorical imperative, they have to agree that anyone and everyone can break a promise whenever it suits them. In which case, the very purpose of promising becomes impossible, since no one would ever have trust in such a promise. It is thus logically inconsistent to break a promise and thereby immoral.

Kant's notion of autonomy, and thus of right, is more restrictive than the neo-Lockean one. For instance, for Kant, committing suicide, as it is a killing done out of self-interest, falls foul of the categorical imperative as it would allow anyone to kill themselves or anyone else if it meets their interests. For neo-Lockean libertarians (or propertarians), by contrast, a person's body and life are their own and they should be free to do with them whatever they please, so long as there is no interference with anyone else. Destroying one's garden to create an asphalt parking lot violates no property rights. However, a Kantian might consider littering in public spaces to violate the categorical imperative for although, on an individual basis, dropping a single greasy chip wrapper causes little or no harm on its own (and thus on a utilitarian basis has little to concern us), the perpetrator would have to logically allow anyone to litter anywhere, making public spaces so inaccessible and hazardous to health that littering would be impossible. Thus, littering falls foul of the categorical imperative.

Other accounts of autonomy recognise that free decision-making takes place within material contexts; that, without sufficient resources such as food, a healthy environment and adequate socialisation, a person is not in a position to make autonomous decisions. Similarly, the extent to which people have access to resources influences their ability to formulate life plans. It is this account of liberty, based on freedom to do things, that demarcates modern liberals from classical liberals.

Core evaluative principles shape political strategies and movements. They highlight specific issues as ones of particular importance and similarly marginalise others, whilst also directing attention to particular policy solutions as practical and desirable over other options (Freeden 1996). Thus, the classical liberalism of Robert Nozick, F.A. Hayek, Ayn Rand and Isaiah Berlin is identifiable by its giving a core position to negative rights and thus seeing the most significant problems as those of violations of property rights, solutions to be based on maintaining these freedoms, and giving little space to political issues concerning non-rights-bearing entities. It is Berlin (1969) who most famously popularised the distinction between positive and negative freedom. Negative rights are rights of non-interference. An individual is free in so far as no one is impeding them in acting in the way that they wish (whether the motivation is based on desire or reason). Thus, 'freedom of speech' is usually described in terms of negative freedom. It means that no one should prevent someone uttering their views. It does not mean that anyone has to assist the speaker. Classical liberals prioritise social arrangements based on actual consensual agreement. Such agreements – or contracts – protect negative liberty. No one can be interfered with unless they consent to it, and thus autonomy is always respected. As people will not make contracts unless it is in their interests to do so, such contractual arrangements will also foreseeably have utilitarian benefits as both parties to the deal gain from the contract, and thus it generates greater social happiness. Hence Adam Smith's (2012) notion of the invisible hand – that the best social outcomes are achieved not by directly aiming to manipulate social affairs to produce the best social results, but by allowing individuals the freedom to pursue their self-interest with their rights properly protected. So by prioritising negative rights, utilitarian ambitions can be met.

2.3.1 Criticisms of deontology

Some deontologists consider negative rights to be insufficient. Robinson Crusoe, after all, was not subject to any interference on his desert island, but his freedom was severely curtailed. These liberal critics of negative freedom argue that liberty is not just the absence of interference, but the positive ability to plan and choose one's destiny. However, to be autonomous in the sense of being able to identify and choose between different potential destinies and to have the intellectual resources to plan for how these might be achieved in order to make a sensible choice, requires some psychological and social resources (Rawls 1972, 204). Those in dire poverty or who have significant educational and psychological disabilities are less able to foresee potential opportunities or to achieve them. Through the mere misfortune of where and when they are born, they have their autonomy curtailed. John Rawls and other modern liberals, such as T.H. Green and John Maynard Keynes, emphasise liberty as the freedom to do things. So some interventions are justified if they extend this positive freedom. For instance, someone born in a deprived urban centre surrounded by post-industrial decline may not have the opportunity to visit woodlands and might never be aware of pleasures of countryside walks or that there are fulfilling jobs in forest stewardship. Their freedom to make informed life choices is limited. Rawls suggests that just principles can be discovered by people making political decisions without knowing where they will be within a society and what skills or attributes they might have. Given this, a person might initially think a slave society is beneficial as slave owners are freed from menial duties, but then realise they might be a slave. Similarly, a complete free market society in which people are free to live according to their saleable skills might be initially considerable desirable, but from behind the 'veil of ignorance' you don't know if you would have marketable attributes. Rawlsians consider that parties behind the veil of ignorance will not make self- or class-interested decisions but impartial moral ones. This would mean ones that give prominence to the interests of the least powerful, because they might turn out to be the least powerful.

Classical liberals who privilege negative freedoms view the notion of justice as simply respect for these negative rights regardless of outcome. Modern liberals, who moderate negative rights with respect for positive freedom, see justice more in terms of 'fairness' ensuring that the opportunities of the most disadvantaged are the focus of attention.

Many of the main debates of the post-war period have been between modern liberals and classical liberalism, and since the leaderships of Margaret Thatcher and Ronald Reagan the latter has been in the economic and political ascendancy. Classical liberals are critical of modern liberals, utilitarians and other consequentialists who would interfere with the liberty of others in order to reach predetermined goals, such as protecting vulnerable eco-systems or extending the freedom of others. Consistent classical liberals also reject paternalistic interventions, where the violation of a person's autonomy was not done for the social good, but to benefit the particular individual being constrained. Hence they reject legislation that compels the wearing of crash helmets on motorcycles or seat-belts in cars as they are a limit on individual choice and undermine personal responsibility. Such interference also produces over-powerful and oppressive redistributive structures that do not achieve their desired goals. Thus classical liberals often attack environmental policies that interfere with freedoms such as imposing taxes or limiting opportunities for contract making, and regard effective solutions to social and ecological problems as coming from prioritising negative freedoms.[2] Modern liberals, by contrast, are critical of classical liberals' limited account of freedom and how it allows for, and indeed celebrates, the generation of economic inequalities that result from free contracts. Inequality reduces the negotiating power of weaker parties in future 'consensual' contract negotiations for vital resources.

There are additional problems with privileging principles of private property and contractual relationships as the core principles for ideal social relations. Because they give supreme priority to negative freedom, such individual contractual relationships can lead to bad social outcomes, especially for those who are not capable of forming contracts, such as environmental entities. For a classical liberal an owner of property is under no prior obligation to take into account the impact of how they use their private property except if it violates the property rights of others. Under classical liberalism a landowner who deliberately obliterated a rare and valuable ecosystem which gave aesthetic pleasure and knowledge to many who interacted with it would have committed no offence, unless there was a prior contractual arrangement stating that they would protect it. Indeed, to interfere with the landowner by preventing such destruction would be a violation of the owner's supreme property rights.

Criticisms of the stricter Kantian deontological principles cover not just the dangers of being blind to consequences, which tend towards the negligent, but the problems with his categorical imperative. As it stands, a liar might be able to escape from the restrictions of universalisability by describing the maxim they were acting under, in a way that was so specific to their situation that it leads to no possible contradiction if universalised. To return to the littering example, a violator might claim that the rule they were operating under was that 'one should not litter unless it is to protect a Versace jacket from a grease stain'. The violator might claim they would support this rule being applied to any other high-fashion wearer under similar circumstances. To avoid the construction of self-serving maxims additional stipulations are required as to what counts as a morally relevant feature of an action. But this condition is absent in Kant's account. If one was brought in, the stipulation either runs the risk of circular reasoning or requires bringing in non-deontological ethical principles.

An early academic eco-philosopher William T. Blackstone (1973) argued, *contra* standard liberal positions, that a healthy environment was a fundamental right rather than a merely desirable outcome on the basis that it is a prerequisite for fulfilling all other obligations (65). Thus, Blackstone argues, property rights should be secondary to the protection of this ecological right (67). As will be seen in Chapter 7, classical liberals disagree, arguing that there are no such superior rights to property rights, and that property rights are the best guarantor for producing a healthy environment. It is noteworthy, however, that Blackstone's argument still places specifically human interests at the centre of concern; protection of the environment is predicated on the protection of other, almost exclusively human, rights.

As discussed in more detail in Chapter 3, environmental thinkers have increasingly challenged the deontological view that only rational beings have unconditional worth and that non-rational entities have only instrumental value. This casts sentient, but non-rational, creatures as mere tools for the satisfaction of rational beings' interests. Much environmental theory and practice, as discussed in later chapters, is critical of institutional behaviour based on the liberal approach to nature.

> **Instrumental value**: the evaluation of a living or non-living thing as a tool or instrument to achieve some end.

Some ethicists, like Tom Regan (1980, 1998), argue that animals have rights based not on rationality, but sentience; it is the ability to experience the world in their own way that gives them intrinsic value. Regan's defence of rights based on sentience rather than rationality is intuitively appealing. Ecological theorists from a range of perspectives have adopted the view that an environmental entity has intrinsic value. That means it is good in itself, and not just valuable because it assists in achieving some particular goal, often an objective that is centred on human benefit.

> **Intrinsic value**: the inherent, rather than instrumental, value of an entity.

Intrinsic values (sometimes referred to as immanent values) are a feature of deontological and virtue theory (see below), being of particular relevance to ecologists who are critical of those who see the natural world solely in terms of instrumental values. More radical environmental philosophers see a value in biotic entities that does not depend on how useful they are to achieving human ends, but as valuable in themselves.

Deontology concentrates on humans as rational beings. Yet such an approach is criticised not just because it marginalises non-rational creatures but distorts the account of human agency; we are also sensual and emotional. Someone who acted solely on pure reason would not be fully developed. A parent might recognise that they have rationally deduced duties to their child, but we would think their actions were missing something if the only reason they gave sustenance to their offspring was because it was dictated by rationally deduced duty. Similarly, someone who did not feel awe at their first glance of the Grand Canyon or sadness at the destruction of the Great Barrier Reef might be considered deficient in some vital respect.

Prioritising rights as the supreme value generates institutions and norms based on contractual relationships. Yet privileging these norms above all others can damage important and useful institutions and behaviours. The complex uncodified norms and social relations that protect commons in pre-industrial, industrial and post-industrial societies start to become undermined when they are subject to contract (see Chapter 7). (See, for instance, Caffentzis and Federici 2013; Graeber 2012, 98–126.) Entities like eco-systems, biospheres and individual members of non-human species are marginalised as they are unable to make contracts.

2.3.2 Environmental justice

The concept of 'environmental justice' has increasingly come to the fore in recent years in response to the global impacts of ecological crises and the recognition of the wickedness of the problems (see Chapter 1 and Chapter 5) of responding to climate change. The term, as environmental theorists like John Dryzek and David Schlosberg (2005) and Paul Harris (2016) identify, has diverse and evolving interpretations. A similar concept of 'climate justice' has also developed, which largely refers to the development and application of environmental justice to the specific areas of climate change (Schlosberg 20 utilitarian maxim 13, 45). In many ways environmental justice and climate justice attempt to incorporate features and insights from deontology and utilitarianism.

Like utilitarianism, it acknowledges the importance of social outcomes and the ways in which many current practices have negative consequences across the global population, including groups usually marginalised in decision making (Harris 2016, 39–41). For some advocates of environmental justice, these marginalised groups and interests include those of non-human animals. Like deontology it also concentrates on the principles that govern the fair formulation of policy – the protection of rights. Basic environmental resources, like clean air and water, are seen as a necessary basis for having and maintaining rights (47). As Harris (2016, 43–45; 108–10) discusses, the human rights, especially of those who are distant from the policymakers, need to be protected. He suggests that the impartiality that is often associated with Rawls' veil of ignorance becomes a feature of environmental policy, especially as it gives prominence to the interests of the least advantaged groups and individuals.

36 Ethical reasoning

Issues of equity, participation and fair dealing associated with notions of social justice (and common to modern liberalism) are also a feature of environmental justice. Those who have gained most from ecological degradation, claim proponents, should have most responsibility and provide more resources for mitigation and reduction of climate change, often embodied in principles like the 'polluter pays' or 'clean up your own mess' (Gardiner 2004, 579). In addition, principles of (at least minimal) equality of welfare have become features of environmental justice. Environmental justice is thus centrally concerned with modern liberal consideration for healthy human development.

Because of the complexity of environmental justice, it sometimes runs the risk of being theoretically abstruse. How is equity measured? Is a coal miner, who through labour organisation has achieved a relatively good income but suffers severe health problems, a beneficiary who should 'pay'? Can ignorance of the impacts of carbon release count as a mitigating factor? Does having a fair impartial process for deciding policy, which is often more time-consuming, take precedence over taking clear effective policy decisions to minimise harms?

Borrowing from MacIntyre (1991), it is likely that there is no single dispassionate account of environmental justice, but there are specific, if overlapping, versions that develop in and through particular types of social practice. In the context of community struggles against an industry that produces consumer durables, which, to lower costs, dumps toxic waste into local environments damaging aquifers, there is significant correspondence between the social justice principles and the ecological values of environmental justice. However, where pollution may be an unavoidable feature of a vital health treatment, a more subtle rearrangement of principles might be required.

2.3.3 Concluding comments on deontology

Despite these problems, rights-based theorists correctly identify important shortcomings in consequentialist ethics, in particular that it can undermine people's autonomy and reduce them to mere instruments to achieve predetermined goals. It highlights the importance of individual freedom to determine the direction of one's ambitions. Being in control of one's destiny is an important part of living a worthwhile, if not necessarily happy, life. As discussed in relation to rule utilitarianism, it may be possible to reconcile respecting autonomy and promoting good ends. Guaranteeing individual rights might meet the criteria for a good rule utilitarian maxim. Deontologists, following Adam Smith, have claimed that a happier more sustainable society is a foreseeable outcome for respecting rights, even if it is not the ultimate motivation for that principle. Nevertheless, the reconciliation is only provisional: for a consequentialist it is ultimately about good ends and rights must be violated to achieve the best outcome, whilst a deontologist must ultimately allow great suffering if that is the only way to protect supreme rights.

Various forms of political action seek to either draw from the strengths of liberal deontological institutions or alternatively find them damaging and seek ways to respond, limit and replace them (as discussed in Chapters 7, 8 and 9). Many of the alternatives draw on features of virtue theory, as providing a robust response to the weaknesses of deontology.

2.4 Virtue theories

Virtue ethics draws on the works of classical virtue theorists such as Aristotle and Plato and on that of contemporary advocates such as G(ertrude) E.M. Anscombe, Roger Scruton, Martha Nussbaum and Alasdair MacIntyre. Because it was largely associated with the ancient cultures and then with religious ethics and theocratic institutions, as traced in Chapter 3, virtue ethics declined as an apparently empirical (utilitarian) or rational (deontological) basis for morality took prominence, sweeping out ideas associated with superstition, theology and oppression. Indeed Adam Smith's more virtue-based *Theory of Moral Sentiment* (originally published in 1759) has been historically overlooked for his more deontological *Wealth of Nations* (published in 1776).

There has been an understandable and unfortunate association of virtue theory with pre-modern tyranny, to which contemporary virtue advocates respond (see, for instance, Driver 2006, 141; MacIntyre 1988, 88–90). This is largely due to its connection with Aristotle (1992), who supported dictatorship, the necessity of gender-division and slavery. Virtue theory has been identified with non-Western traditions, such as Confucianism, and these too have been perceived as backwards-looking and oppressive because of their association with feudalism (e.g., Yu 1998). In the West, virtue theory started to attract attention again by the late 1950s, and was progressively shorn of its commitments to illegitimate hierarchy, as associated with Aristotle and the Christian virtue tradition. Hence it adopted the label neo-Aristotelian ethics.

Virtue theory's rediscovery was initially due to Anscombe (1958) whose essay 'Modern Moral Philosophy' points to some of the main problems of utilitarian and Kantian deontological ethics (2) and the importance of other ethical values, such as friendship and integrity, which are not formally part of these traditions (10). She indicates that the solution to the problems lies in a reconsideration of virtue theory (16–19).

> **Virtue ethics**: concentrates on the types of person or the kind of inter-personal relationship engaged in the action rather than on strict duties or consequences. It gives guidance on the sorts of characteristics that make an admirable person or a flourishing activity.

Whilst there are differences within the distinct strands of virtue theory, the main features are stable. Virtues are types of character trait, or attributes of interpersonal relationships, that are good in themselves. Characteristics like bravery, integrity, wisdom and compassion are admired not just because they can bring about good outcomes, but because they are considered (all things being equal) better than their opposites. That is to say, virtues are intrinsically valuable as well as having an extrinsic or instrumental use.

Opposing each virtue are (often) two corresponding vices, which are considered undesirable in themselves, as well as likely to bring about bad outcomes. For instance, the two corresponding vices to the virtue of bravery are rashness and cowardice. To be brave means avoiding the extremes of running away whenever danger appears and taking risks for no good reason. Thus a virtue is seen as being in the middle of two opposing tendencies (Aristotle 1976, 101). That is not to say that it is a mathematical average between the opposing vices, but that this account of virtue is a heuristic to appropriate responses, as it is one that avoids under or over-reaction (Hughes 2001, 62–3).

For neo-Aristotelians, the virtues work in unity. To be brave is to pick the correct person and the right occasion to fight (wisdom); to battle in order to resist a bully, not to act as a tormentor (compassion); to use no more than sufficient force to resist intimidating force (moderation); not to be carried away into humiliating a foe (self-discipline). If one is fearlessly attacking someone for no good reason, or for unjust reasons, then the attacker is not courageous or heroic, but reckless. According to Aristotle (1976) the more people practice virtuous behaviour the easier it is to act virtuously: it is an in-built part of one's character. For MacIntyre (1985, 273–4) the more virtues are embedded into social activities, the more these practices flourish. In neo-Aristotelian ethics, unlike Kantian philosophy, a morally good person might no longer be rationally-deducing correct action, as it simply becomes part of their ingrained personality.

Anscombe was joined by a range of contemporary ethicists such as Michael Slote, Rosalind Hursthouse and Julie Driver. Virtue ethics takes in a broad range of political and social positions, with Anscombe and Roger Scruton associated with conservative brands of virtue theory, Nussbaum from more overtly feminist and socially-liberal positions, and Paul Blackledge and Kelvin Knight from radical socialist ones. Alasdair MacIntyre has been associated with both conservative and radical positions. Virtue theory, as Hursthouse explores, has become embraced and developed by environmental thinkers such as Aldo Leopold, Arne Naess and Holmes Rolston III.

One of the main differences is that between collective and individualistic virtue theory. Individualistic virtue theory concentrates on developing each person's moral character and their individual emotional training. It focuses on ensuring that people respond to events in the most appropriate way – for example, not giggling at others' misfortunes but instead showing controlled sorrow and compassion. As each individual develops the right attitudes and traits, they are more likely to flourish. In its more individualistic form, virtue theorists seek guidance by asking 'what would a model of virtuous behaviour do?' This role model, however, changes depending on the virtue theorist from Jesus or Mahatma Gandhi to Benjamin Franklin or even Al Gore (see Chapter 5).

In more collectivist virtue ethics, like those of MacIntyre, the emphasis is on developing social practices and traditions that are rich in these intrinsic goods. Thus, engaging in virtuous practice is a potentially transformative enterprise. The more virtuously people act, the more their character develops and transforms. Virtues, for MacIntyre (1985), develop within rule-governed social settings, which produce internal and external goods. The types of norms and the values they generate change over time, as do the participants' identities. For instance, a novice might learn chess, a rule-governed activity, solely for instrumental goods (pleasing a parent or teacher), but as they become engrossed in the pastime they develop patience, good sportsmanship, and come to identify themselves as a chess player (188). As they become more skilled, like the truly expert players, they develop strategies and styles that alter the practice itself. These rule-governed activities intersect with other similar activities, which have related virtues.

Different practices will have different combinations of virtues to the fore. Field hockey might prioritise physical bravery more, and patience rather less, than chess but neither is wholly lacking in these practices. To develop a rounded character usually involves having access to, and participating in, more than one set of activities. These activities can be corrupted by unvirtuous behaviour. A chess player who intimidates her opponents or succeeds in cheating in order to win the game (and gain the external goods of acclaim), makes people less willing to participate in that activity and thus the practice withers.

The differences between individualist and collectivist virtue theorists are not too great. Individualist virtue theorists, like Aristotle, accept that for a person to fully develop and flourish (what he calls *Eudaimonia*), helps to develop a flourishing society, and that people prosper most where there are other virtuous people and virtuous activities to engage in. Similarly, if corrupt practices develop, then the whole of society can be corrupted to the detriment of each individual, as described of ancient Greece:

> So the condition of the cities was civil war. [. . .] And in self-justification men inverted the usual verbal evaluations of actions. Irrational recklessness was now considered courageous commitment, hesitation while looking to the future was high-styled cowardice, moderation was a cover for lack of manhood, and circumspection meant inaction, while senseless anger now helped to define a true man, and deliberation for security was a specious excuse for dereliction. The man of violent temper was always credible, anyone opposing him was suspect. The intriguer who succeeded was intelligent, anyone who detected a plot was still more clever, but a man who made provisions to avoid both alternatives was undermining his party and letting the opposition terrorize him. Quite simply, one was praised for outracing everyone else to commit a crime – and for encouraging a crime by someone who had never before considered one.
>
> *(Thucydides 1998, 3.81, 169–70.)*

In a wholly corrupt society such as that undermined by civil war, the ability to carry out meaningful ethical analysis is undermined as the terms themselves are debased. Just as virtue encourages the production of other virtues (a virtuous circle), so vice is likely to produce more malignant activities (a vicious circle). Such outcomes are not guaranteed; a virtuous society might be defeated by an unjust one, and vice could provoke virtuous responses, but for virtue theorists, developing the virtues is more likely to produce positive outcomes (*Eudaimonia*).

Some differences between virtue theorists are unproblematic and are consistent with this ethical approach. Some neo-Aristotelians are going to concentrate on particular constellations of virtues that are specific to their practice or sphere of interest and these are going to differ according to the activity or historical epoch. In some practices or epochs, some virtues may come to the fore. Similarly, some character traits or inter-personal values are no longer pertinent. For instance, sexual fidelity, an important Christian virtue, might be justified by neo-Aristotelians in the circumstances of 12th-century Europe, when childbirth was a major killer of young women and contraception and other sexual health and pregnancy knowledge was largely non-existent. Ensuring women did not need to undergo unwanted and under-supported pregnancies would allow for other virtues to thrive. However, in the light of medical advances, chastity has rightly become a more marginal virtue. Similarly, as environmental crises have arisen, new ecological virtues are required. Some virtue theorists, such as Paul W. Taylor and Thomas Hill, have concentrated on describing and promoting what Hursthouse (2007, 162–3) identifies as 'concern for nature'.

Hursthouse (2007, 163–70) clarifies what is meant by 'concern for nature'. It involves having the right attitude and response to the natural world that is consistent with the other virtues like wisdom and compassion. The more people act respectfully towards nature, the more they change their personalities in a positive way. Rather than being repulsed by the unusual scurrying movements or unfamiliar life-cycles of other beings, we develop a sense of wonder and respect at their differing ways of engaging within the world. Such engagement not only benefits humans but the natural world too. By contrast, having the wrong attitude towards animals, or acting on poor information about human relationships to natural ecology harms us and the wider biosphere. It is not enough simply for it to be a set of feelings or attitudes; virtues have to be put into practice.

Amongst virtue theory's greatest strengths are its diversity and flexibility. It has a richer and more varied moral discourse for identifying and evaluating moral problems. Whilst utilitarianism reduces all morals to evaluations of 'good outcome' versus 'bad outcome', or deontology to simple questions of meeting duties and respecting rights, virtue theory encompasses a diverse range of ethical concepts: courage, temperance, liberality (friendliness), patience, appropriate self-regard and truthfulness to name just a few of the dozen initially identified by Aristotle (1976, 104).

Whilst Aristotle's initial description of the virtues barely mentions the ecological environment, they can be easily applied to ecological entities. Wisdom and benevolence involve treating non-human animals in the right way, and because of their different biologies this means treating them differently to humans. Dressing a pet dog in human clothing and feeding it chocolate is a form of self-interested foolishness. Contemporary virtue theory also recognises that old virtues change their meaning and new ones emerge as different types of social activity develop. Prudence, for instance, takes on new meanings in times of ecological scarcity and has helped in developing other contemporary green virtues like sustainability and resilience. Some attributes – or inter-personal characteristics – have been identified as being particularly pertinent to the generation and transmission of knowledge. These 'epistemic virtues' (Brady and Pritchard 2003), like attentiveness, integrity, practical and theoretical wisdom and compassion, are vital for the generation, transmission and reception of environmental science and social research on the impacts of climate change (see Chapter 5).

Certain virtues are compatible with utilitarianism and deontology. For instance, concern with the virtues of integrity and justice would incorporate concepts such as 'respect for rights', whilst charity, concern for the interests of others and so on incorporates utilitarian considerations. However, unlike its Enlightenment-based ethical rivals, virtue theory does not universally prioritise one value over all others. This flexibility is underlined by the emphasis it places on virtues that allow us to reach wise decisions across a wide variety of contexts. Practical wisdom (*phronesis*) is often seen as pre-eminent (Aristotle 1976; Sandler 2013, 8).

Practical wisdom is needed when more than one course of action presents itself to us, either via a dilemma we ourselves perceive, or via a difference of opinion among experts and other authorities. Under such conditions, we need to be able to make decisions on the basis of relevant ethical principles and unique features of the situation in question. The virtuous person is thus a good deliberator in a landscape of ethics and other values where abstract rules can at best take us only part of the way to deciding on the right thing to do. This means they will be able to think sensitively and critically; listening fully, identifying and examining arguments, and being reflectively aware of the types of reasoning errors and biases people are vulnerable to (see Chapter 5). Also, since so many decisions involve committees, boards and other collectives, 'group-deliberative virtues' (Aikin and Clanton, 2010) such as 'deliberative wit' (facilitating constructive dialogues) and 'deliberative temperance' (managing our emotions in situations of disagreement) are increasingly seen as important.

2.4.1 Criticisms of virtue theory

One of the main criticisms of virtue theory is that it is too vague to provide meaningful guidance. It is after all a theory that seems to unite deep conservatives, like Scruton (2000) who sees virtues exemplified in the aristocratic pursuits of fox hunting and, by contrast, MacIntyre and Blackledge who consider the radical versions of socialism, so detested by Scruton, as potential places were virtue might flourish. One reply might be to point out that there are rival versions of utilitarianism and deontology too. These rival schools are clearly demarked (say between more modern liberalism and classical liberalism in deontology), so too rival versions of virtue theory can be clearly distinguished and a preference made on the basis of how consistently and coherently they apply the theory.

A more significant problem is that many want as simple a moral code as possible. Clear formulas for guiding or overseeing professional practice (for instance) are regarded as more desirable than complex ethical charters comprising multiple and fluid concepts. Thus, deontology with its simple account of respecting rights, and utilitarianism with its clear commitments to prioritising good outcomes, have an advantage over virtue theory in the market-place of competing moral theories. Indeed virtue theory goes further by proposing that good moral practice is more than just simply following the rules (even if the norms are rationally deduced) as even a robot can obey instructions. Sometimes ethical practice means challenging and transcending existing moral codes. Such an approach is, though, inconsistent with, and represents a challenge to, many institutional procedures, thus generating hostility to virtue-centred approaches.

Perhaps the most important critique of virtue ethics from an environmental perspective is that virtue theory is still primarily concerned with human flourishing and thus is anthropocentric. We should care for other species, their habitats and the wider biosphere because, argues Hursthouse (2007, 169), it helps humans to flourish. Such anthropocentrism, as Chapters 3 and 4 discuss, have come to be seen as detrimental to developing ecologically sound perspectives and practices. One way around this problem is an account of *Eudaimonia* that includes the flourishing of all living things as well as human thriving. One of the problems here is that some living things are highly detrimental to human flourishing (such as the malaria-carrying *Anopheles* mosquito) or to other species such as pests and parasites. As raised in Chapter 3, being concerned for the well-being of the whale means placing the lives of krill at risk. Opting for some living creatures over others is usually based on anthropocentric considerations.

Finally, virtue ethics is said to suffer from the problem of essentialism. Most ethical theories and political positions assume an account of what human subjects are 'really like'. Classical liberal deontology, found as a guiding set of principles within much Western governance since the late 1970s and early 1980s, assumes that we are, at heart, self-interested egoists. Kantian liberalism is predicated on an account of individuals as fundamentally rational beings, whilst utilitarians believe we are pleasure-seeking calculating beings. Similarly, most virtue theory rests on an account of a human essence. Every creature has a good that is its proper goal (*telos*) in life, and for Aristotle we understand that creature by its pursuit of this goal. So, for instance, a flourishing elephant is one that has healthy strong tusks, does not attack other elephants, looks after its young, is not frightened of water, and so on. Elephants are not free to follow this goal, they simply following it through instinct. Humans too have an ultimate goal, determined by their essence. The practice of the virtues is to create a better person, 'man-as-he-could-be-if-he-realised-his-essential-nature', out of the raw material of what the individual is currently made (MacIntyre 1985, 52). However, humans are rational and capable of acting other than on instinct, thus what is virtuous for humans is to fulfil our natures, both rational and emotional.

These essentialisms are problematic in a number of ways. First, they are unprovable; as yet, no one has determined a test for identifying the fundamental character of all humanity. Second, they are ethically limiting; if human subjects are predetermined by a biological or spiritual essence, then they are not free to choose what constitutes the good. Finally, it casts some human beings as 'moral monsters', namely those who are deficient in whatever is declared the true basis of their nature.

A more benign way of interpreting virtue theory's apparent essentialism is that it merely takes into account that we are particular types of animal with psychological and physical traits. Behaviours and expectations must take these into account, such that humans can develop. Where humans are physically or psychologically different the types of resources and institutional norms necessary for them to flourish need to be recalibrated.

2.4.2 Concluding comments on virtue theory

Virtues are those personal or inter-personal traits that are good in themselves and help to generate further good practices and traits. There are multiple irreducible virtues, which each help to mutually define the others. They are based in social practices that develop into traditions over time. The strength of virtue theory, which is why it is given greater emphasis in this text, is that it incorporates many of the key insights of utilitarianism and deontology into its contemporary expression. Virtues like compassion and benevolence take into account utilitarianism's concern for the well-being of others; justice and integrity are similarly sympathetic to deontology's commitments to protecting rights and meeting obligations. Virtue theory also introduces other important values like fairness and courage, which are marginalised in the other two theories but help to moderate the other key virtues. An additional advantage of virtue theory is that it does not make any single virtue supreme in all circumstances. It recognises that in different practices some virtues are more prominent than others. A lifeboat rescue operator requires physical courage and particular technical skills, whilst concern for nature is relatively minor (though not entirely absent). By contrast, an organic arable farmer will require less physical courage, different technical knowledge, but concern for nature is more prominent.

The notion of environmental justice, which similarly assimilates utilitarian and modern liberal principles, can also be adopted into virtue theory. Its location next to other values highlights how environmental justice requires people to act fair-mindedly and thoughtfully. Environmental justice assists in *Eudaimonia* – the developing of flourishing individuals, human communities and ecosystems.

Many virtue theories are resistant to a single account of good, as these can disrupt and deform benevolent social practices. For instance, Aldo Leopold describes how, when industrial productivity became the over-riding goal of farming, it led to soil erosion and the undermining of a community ethic (see Chapter 3). The virtues of a particular social activity might not be immediately apparent to those not engaged in it. For example, if one knows nothing of card games like bridge, it might be that one only sees negative traits in the participants (sedentary behaviour or lack of sociability); while those engaged in it see patience, development of mental capacities (memory), good sportsmanship and, in the intermissions, opportunities for collegiality. Virtue theory, thus, stands in opposition to many contemporary approaches to shaping behaviour that are based on the imposition of universal norms through supervisory instruction and legislation. For instance, environmental legislation, which is justified on utilitarian grounds, requires a communications framework for informing the whole citizenry and for surveillance and sanction against miscreants.

When it comes to promoting wider political action, whilst virtue theory does not easily boil down to a clear single guide for action, which more popular utilitarian and any deontological traditions are able to do, it can nonetheless inspire practitioners to reflect on and revise their practices to embody environmental concerns. As practices intersect, virtuous reflection on one set of practices can impact on those activities they interact with, prompting further ethical reflection and change. Virtue considerations are found in everyday discussions and analyses of events, whether in the criticisms of untrustworthy politicians, condemnations of greedy financial institutions or resistance to thoughtless and unwise executive decisions. Notions derived from virtue theory such as integrity, compassion and fair-mindedness are also found alongside ethical principles from rival traditions in many codes of professional practice.

2.5 A defence of ethics

Ethics is a critical discipline. It opens up often widely accepted social activities and norms to analytic evaluation. It is hardly surprising that it can generate negative reactions and resistance. Some people dismiss moral evaluation of current practices as merely 'moralism'. Such complaints are legitimate where the account of 'moralism' refers to inappropriate ethical principles being used or inadequate methods for applying these principles to the practical situation; however when the complaint of 'moralism' refers to a total rejection of ethical enquiry then it becomes problematic.

Where ethical considerations are wholly rejected this is often due to misconceptions about the status and purpose of moral enquiry. Part of the misconception might be due to ethics being mistaken for theological pronouncement or dogma, because for centuries moral discourse, like all language pertaining to human action, was under the control of religious authorities. Whilst not ignoring the influence of people of faith and religious ethics on the development of the field, this book takes a largely secular approach to identifying, describing, applying and evaluating ethical responses to environmental issues. Following Enlightenment figures such Kant, John Stuart Mill, David Hume and others discussed in the following chapter, these secular approaches to ethics attempt to ground the identification of rules of conduct in scientifically-observable phenomena (Mill) or principles deduced by reason (Kant) or comprehension of what makes humans empathetic (Hume), rather than appeals to a supernatural entity or exegesis of a particular religiously-ordained text.

Another reason for rejecting moral discourse is because it presents a challenge to existing practices and attitudes and offers – perhaps quite radical – alternatives. It asks critical questions about how and why certain actions take place; who should take responsibility; who is impacted; and how they shape individual and collective identities and future prospects? Those who are threatened by such challenges and the potential rise of alternatives might wish to forestall these enquiries by marginalising the discourse in which it is formed and expressed. But even people or institutions that claim to reject moral principles are nonetheless still using them, even if they are not conscious of it. Take, for instance, those who understand climate change as a technological problem requiring a quick efficient scientific solution rather than a matter for ethical deliberation (discussed in Section 4.3.3). This appears to reject ethical reasoning but is instead promoting a rather narrow – and dubious – consequentialist moral position: that the goal of overcoming climate change is the supreme value and no other principle or combinations of principle can take precedence.

Few, if any, meaningful statements are without some ethical component. This could mean they have an implicit or explicit ethical preference (e.g., support for scientific evidence or scepticism of political authority). Meaningful explanations – those that regulate behaviour – are also generated within social activities that themselves require particular types of norms in order to operate. Social and scientific research, for instance, generates important forms of knowledge pertinent to environmental debates. Such research requires commitments to integrity, transparency and, for social research, respect for participants' autonomy. Without these, research and knowledge construction will deteriorate. Ethics is not an add-on to debates about climate change; moral principles are deeply embedded in the social practices that cause and respond to it. Analyses of ethical principles provide an avenue for critical analyses of important social behaviours and institutions, and assist in refining or radically transforming our everyday social practices.

One of the key ways in which different ecological philosophies and environmental movements are identified is through their different constellations of ethical principles. Apparently similar moral concepts change their meaning depending on the ethical concepts that surround them and their priority amongst other values. For instance, classical liberal deontology gives absolute primacy to negative rights and these are seen to apply only to humans, understood in terms of property owners. Modern liberal deontologists, by contrast, seek a balance between negative and positive rights and view human freedom in terms of self-development rather than of property rights. As will be seen in the next two chapters, the degree to which human interests take priority over the non-human and the ways in which the human and biotic inter-relate, shape distinctive ecological philosophies, and guides their analysis of environmental problems and shapes their responses to them.

Notes

1 'Propertarian' is used as a synonym for 'libertarian', a political and ethical position that prioritises rights of non-interference and property rights. See Chapter 7 for a discussion of the term.
2 See Koch Industries, an opponent of regulation of greenhouse gas emissions, which produced an advertisement arguing that social divides will be eliminated by greater commercial freedom (www.ispot.tv/ad/AGih/koch-industries-its-time-to-end-the-divide).

References

Aikin, S. and Clanton, J. (2010) 'Developing group-deliberative virtues'. *Journal of Applied Philosophy* 27 (4): 409–24.
Anscombe, G.E.M. (1958) 'Modern moral philosophy'. *Philosophy* 33 (124), 1–19.
Aristotle (1976) *Ethics*. Harmondsworth: Penguin.
Aristotle (1992) *The Politics*. Harmondsworth: Penguin.
Bentham, J. (2000) *An Introduction to the Principles of Morals and Legislation*. Available online at: https://socserv2.socsci.mcmaster.ca/econ/ugcm/3ll3/bentham/morals.pdf.
Berlin, I. (1969) 'Two concepts of liberty', in I. Berlin, *Four Essays on Liberty*. London: Oxford University Press.
Blackstone, W. (1973) 'Ethics and ecology'. *The Southern Journal of Philosophy* 11, 1–2: 55–71.
Boyd, O. (2013) 'The birth of Chinese environmentalism: key campaigns', in Geall, S., ed., *China and the Environment*. London: Zed Books.
Brady, M. and Prichard, D. (2003) 'Moral and epistemic virtues'. *Metaphilosophy* 34, 1/2. 1–11.
Brand, S. (2009) *Whole Earth Discipline*. London: Atlantic.
Caffentzis, G. and Federici, S. (2013). 'Commons against and beyond capitalism', *Upping the Anti: A Journal of Theory and Action* 15: 83–97.
Chouhan, P. and Draper, H. (2003) 'Modified mandated choice for organ procurement', *Journal of Medical Ethics* 29.3: 157–62.
Crisp, R. (1997) *Mill on Utilitarianism*. London: Routledge.
Crisp, R. (1998) 'Introduction', in J.S. Mill, *Utilitarianism*. Oxford: Oxford University Press.
Driver, J. (2006) *Ethics: The Fundamentals*. Oxford: Blackwells.
Dryzek, J. and Schlosberg, D. (2005) 'Environmental justice', in J. Dryzek and D. Schlosberg, eds, *Debating the Earth: The Environmental Politics Reader*. Oxford: Oxford University Press, 427–8.
Evans, H. (2001) 'What's wrong with "retained organs"? Some personal reflections in the afterglow of "Alder Hey"', *Journal of Clinical Pathology*, 54.11: 824–6.
Freeden, F. (1996) *Ideologies and Political Theory: A Conceptual Approach*. Oxford: Oxford University Press.
Gardiner, S. (2004) 'Ethics and global climate change', *Ethics* 114.3: 555–600.
Graeber, D. (2012) *Debt: The First 5,000 years*. New York: Melville House.
Harris, P. (2016) *Global Ethics and Climate Change*, Second Edition. Edinburgh: Edinburgh University Press.
Hooker, B. (2009) 'The demandingness objection', in T. Chappell, ed., *The Problem of Moral Demandingness: New Philosophical Essays*. Basingstoke: Palgrave Macmillan, 148–62.
Hughes, G. (2001) *Aristotle on Ethics*. London: Routledge.
Hursthouse, R. (2007) 'Environmental virtue ethics', in R.L. Walker and P.J. Ivanhoe, eds, *Working Virtue: Virtue Ethics and Contemporary Moral Problems*. Oxford: Oxford University Press.

Jonsen, A.R. (2000) *A Short History of Medical Ethics*. Oxford: Oxford University Press.
Kant, I. (2005) *The Moral Law: The Groundwork to a Metaphysics of Morals*. Routledge: London.
Lawson, N. (2014) *The Trouble with Climate Change*. Npl: Global Warming Policy Foundation.
Locke, J. (1988) *Two Treatises on Government*. Cambridge: Cambridge University Press.
Lynas, M. (2007) *Six Degrees: Our Future on a Hotter Planet*. London: HarperCollins.
MacIntyre, A. (1985) *After Virtue*, Second Edition. London: Duckworth.
MacIntyre, A. (1988) *Whose Justice? Which Rationality?* London: Duckworth.
MacIntyre, A. (1999) *Dependent, Rational Animals*. Chicago: Open Court.
Maynard, M. (1991) 'Developing the health care market', *The Economic Journal* 101: 1227–86.
Mill, J.S. (1985) *On Liberty*. Harmondsworth: Penguin.
Mill, J.S. (1999) *Utilitarianism*. Oxford: Oxford University Press.
Nozick, R. (1974) *Anarchy, State and Utopia*. Oxford: Basil Blackwell.
Rawls, J. (1972) *A Theory of Justice*. Oxford: Oxford University Press.
Regan, T. (1980) 'Utilitarianism, vegetarianism, and animal rights', *Philosophy and Public Affairs* 9.4: 305–24.
Regan, T. (1998). 'The Radical Case for Animal Rights' in Louis Pojman, ed., *Environmental Ethics: Readings in Theory and Application*. London: Wadsworth.
Rowlands, M. (2015) *A Good Life: Morality from Birth to Death*. Granta Books.
Sandler, R. (2013). 'Environmental Virtue Ethics'. In H. LaFollette, ed., *The International Encyclopedia of Ethics* 1–9. Oxford: Blackwell.
Schlosberg, D. (2013) 'Theorising environmental justice: the expanding sphere of a discourse', *Environmental Politics* 22.1: 37–55.
Scruton, R. (2000) *On Hunting*. Yellow Jersey.
Singer, P. (1987) 'A covenant for the Ark?', in O. Hanfling, ed., *Life and Meaning*. Oxford: Blackwell, 141–152.
Singer, P. (1990) 'Introduction', in P. Singer, ed., *Ethics*. Oxford: Oxford University Press.
Singer, P. (2000) *Animal Liberation*, Second Edition. London: Pimlico.
Singer, P. (2011) *Practical Ethics*, Third Edition. Cambridge: Cambridge University Press.
Smart, J.J.C. (1973) 'An outline of a system of ethics', in J.J.C. Smart and B. Williams, eds, *Utilitarianism; For and Against*. Cambridge: Cambridge University Press.
Smith, A. (2010) *Theory of Moral Sentiment*. Harmondsworth: Penguin.
Smith, A. (2012) *The Wealth of Nations*. Ware: Wordsworth.
Steiner, G. (2010) *Anthropocentricism and its Discontents*. Pittsburgh: University of Pittsburgh.
Thucydides (1998) *The Peloponnesian War*, trans. by Steven Lattimore. Indianapolis: Hackett.
Van Buren, J. (1995) 'Critical environmental hermeneutics'. *Environmental Ethics* 17.3: 259–75.
Wolff, J. (2006) *An Introduction to Political Philosophy*. Oxford: Clarendon.
World Food Programme (2016) 'Hunger statistics'. *World Food Programme*. Available online at: www.wfp.org/hunger/stats.
Yu, J. (1998) 'Virtue: Confucius and Aristotle', *Philosophy East and West* 48.2: 323–47.

3

CONFLICTING VALUES

Anthropocentric, biocentric and ecocentric ethics

The ethical reasoning introduced in Chapter 2 may contrast with our personal environmental concerns and actions: often impassioned but impressionistic and inconsistently applied. Moral values – for individuals, communities and entire societies – can evolve to become more consistent over time. How, then, have such heartfelt ethical sensitivities come to be expressed, extended and employed systematically to motivate corrective actions?

Across human history, the relationship between people and their environments has varied from culture to culture. Over the past century, recognition of environmental concerns has become more explicit, and distinct frameworks of ethical consideration have been explored. Each of these frameworks defines a system of values, and the different rankings of values means that they yield dissimilar guidance about appropriate behaviours. Present-day understandings are still diverse and yield conflicting beliefs and practices.

Chapter 2 introduced the frameworks of moral theory at the heart of this book. This chapter takes a different tack, stepping back to sketching the historical roots and contemporary expressions of these distinct moral traditions, and illustrating how new perspectives have been based on fresh combinations of shifting philosophical values, scientific insights and growing human powers to alter environments. While our environmental sensitivities and behaviours continue to jostle and evolve, this chapter traces distinct value systems that broadly encompass popular contemporary perspectives. Over the past generation or two, they have sometimes been identified by the labels 'anthropocentrism', 'biocentrism' and 'ecocentrism', which refer to human-centred, life-centred and ecosystem-centred foci, respectively. Chapter 4 extends consideration to more recent global perspectives on environmental ethics. Subsequent chapters detail how such values and attitudes can be harnessed to methods of behavioural change linked to ethical reasoning, psychology, communication strategies and political action.

3.1 Anthropocentric ethics

Moral values in the Western world traditionally have prioritised human concerns.[1] Consideration of human wellbeing nevertheless ranges across a spectrum of possibilities and may take into account other life forms and environments in particular circumstances. Anthropocentrism is not one worldview, but many.

> **Anthropocentrisms**: ethical perspectives that privilege human well-being over the well-being of other species.

3.1.1 The Western tradition of anthropocentrism

Valuing people as the primary or sole entity worthy of consideration is the most widespread and popular paradigm today. It informs most laws, government policies, and individual decision-making. Even so, there are nuances. The intensity of values may vary along various scales. An early example of this spectrum of importance was the ancient ranking of life forms known in Latin as the *Scala Naturae*, or Ladder of Nature. Plato, Aristotle and later Greek philosophers envisaged a hierarchy of beings in which those above relied on those below as a resource.

The scheme was absorbed and popularised in early European Christian tradition as the 'Great Chain of Being', which converted the natural philosophy of the Greeks into a theological scale of perfection or goodness. A sixteenth-century illustration by Diego Valadés, a Mexican-born cleric, makes the relationships graphic, showing a chain extending downward from heavenly angels to link people successively to flying, swimming and land-based creatures, and then to plants and, finally, to non-living things (Figure 3.1).

From such depictions comes the everyday language of 'higher' and 'lower' forms of life. Valadés positioned each entity according to its theological value: angels were superior to saints, saints to kings, and kings to common people, all of whom were vastly more important in the greater scheme of things than were other creatures. But it also raised the question of how to incorporate the indigenous peoples and exotic animals being encountered beyond Europe and in the New World. According to this game, anthropocentrism was anything but a level playing field.

The American historian Lynn White Jr (1967) argued that the history of anthropocentrism can be traced to particular biblical interpretations by Christian scholars. Reading the account of origins in Genesis as a prescription for how humans are meant to prosper, he suggests that 'nature' was typically understood as a backdrop or mere resource for human affairs. God had given his creations Adam and Eve domination over all living things. Humankind had co-existed with animals in Eden, but when Adam and Eve sinned, they had to rely on the natural world for survival.

Extending the Greek view of a hierarchy of beings, mediaeval Christian scholars argued that other species were created to serve human needs and were meant to

50 Anthro-, bio- and ecocentric ethics

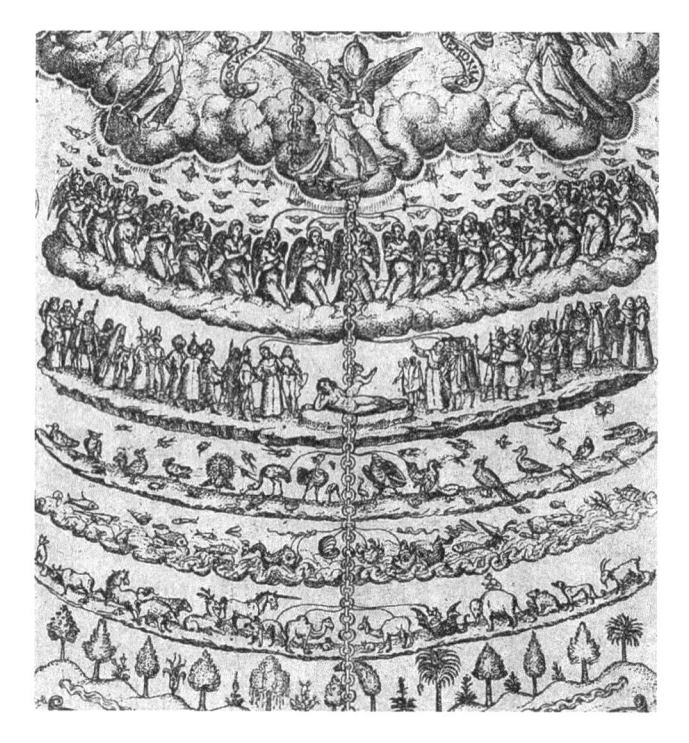

FIGURE 3.1 A depiction of the Great Chain of Being. (Valadés 1579, Wikipedia Commons license: https://upload.wikimedia.org/wikipedia/commons/b/b7/The_Great_Chain_of_Being_%281579%29.jpg.)

be subordinate to human wishes. Their low ranking on the Great Chain of Being explained why it was appropriate that a cow or chicken should serve to feed a nobler creature.

The moral logic was persuasive. Where Aristotle had argued that 'Nature made nothing in vain', a seventeenth-century minister could argue that human lice had been provided by the Creator to teach their hosts habits of cleanliness. The utility of animals, plants and minerals relied on their identification as resources that had been created to be used.

Such views informed not only the harvesting of animals (Figure 3.2), but also justified the exploitation of the seemingly endless resources of the New World. This human focus, and consideration of the environment as a setting for human affairs, was enduring. The first usage of the term 'environment', by the Scottish philosopher and writer Thomas Carlyle in 1828, hinted at this limited meaning (Jessop 2012).

The ranking of living things provided other benefits from the human perspective. Animals could provide not merely material products – meat, milk, eggs, leather, fur, and so on – but could also serve as amusement and entertainment. Bear-baiting and fox hunting – popular from classical times until the present day in

FIGURE 3.2 Animals to serve human needs: butchering a whale in the Faroe Islands, sixteenth century. (Gessner 1558, out of copyright.)

some human environments – generally avoided consideration of the ability of animals to suffer, or else judged it to be subordinate to the enjoyment of the spectators or to wider human interests such as management of the numbers of hunting stock.

Other uses of animals, justified according to an anthropocentric argument, have aspired to a higher and humane purpose. Caged animals in zoos, increasingly popular for royalty from the Middle Ages, spread to wide audiences in the nineteenth century as a recreational and educational pastime in many cities.

Vancouver, Canada, was typical of many. The young city founded a large civic park and zoological garden, Stanley Park, in 1905, scarcely twenty years after its foundation as a west-coast railway terminus. The first inhabitants of the zoo were locally-captured animals, but the exhibits expanded to include exotic species: polar bears, monkeys, penguins and tropical birds housed in concrete pens and metal cages which, to modern eyes, would appear relatively stark and comfortless. Indeed, in 1994 a city referendum voted to close the facility owing to growing public dissatisfaction with the living conditions of the zoo's residents.

It is notable, however, that these sentiments and actions were not universally applied. The zoo included an aquarium that, in 1964, had been the first facility in the world to hold an orca ('killer whale') for public display and research, and over the following decades it was home to other whale species.[2] Growing public and scientific familiarity with the whales undoubtedly altered sensitivities to the quality of their lives in captivity and raised moral questions that did not extend to some of the other aquatic residents of the aquarium such as alligators and sharks. During the 1990s the aquarium was expanded to improve the conditions for the whales. The building programme faced opposition from some citizens concerned about the welfare of the marine animals, but also from others decrying the loss of the park's trees.

3.1.2 Immanuel Kant and secular arguments for valuing other species

Such cases suggest changing values for modern audiences. Why are whales more worthy of our concerns than, say, jellyfish and conifers? Which living things deserve human compassion, and on what grounds should we provide it?

While a theological basis of ordering has faded from prominence, the concept of a hierarchy of life forms worthy of moral consideration remains culturally embedded. There are distinct secular arguments for ranking forms of life. Even though they usually place humans at the top, they may lead to different ordering of the scale of importance. Consider, for instance, a common 'scientific' criterion of the nineteenth century: the complexity of organisms. Giraffes are more complex biological systems than earthworms are, for example. This criterion is not entirely satisfactory, though, because it depends on which characteristics we assess: the DNA of birds consists of fewer genes than that of some flowering plants, and onions have much more genetic material than humans do.

As introduced in Chapter 2, the eighteenth-century German philosopher Immanuel Kant advanced such moral reasoning. He was a key contributor to the fertile period of intellectual development in the eighteenth century known as 'The Enlightenment'. Its participants vaunted reason and individual intellectual freedom as the means to human betterment. By developing a rational basis for beliefs and actions, they argued that social progress could replace tradition and dogma. Kant argued for three distinct reasons to guide our treatment of other living things: utility, reflexivity and sentience.

The utility argument is the most obvious and familiar one: how useful is the life form to our needs? Farm animals such as sheep provide food and clothing; pet dogs may provide companionship or protect a household; horses (at least until the past century) provided the muscle-power for human transportation. And, as mentioned above, animals may also be employed to amuse and educate. On the other hand, distant and exotic species may not intersect at all with human affairs, and so do not generate a moral value.

There is also a flip-side to the utility argument: some other forms of life oppose human interests. Mice and birds eat stores of grain; foxes kill small farm animals; and, in certain locales, bears or elephants may endanger human settlements. This negative utility, or harm, encourages a reconsideration of how humans should treat such animals.

Kant's second argument for valuing other species was reflexivity. He suggested that we should treat animals humanely because this reflects on our treatment of other humans and demonstrates our refined moral values. Kind treatment of a suffering cart-horse or lame dog will have the beneficial effect of teaching others not to be cruel, and to extend these considerations to human relations. Our status as compassionate and reasonable beings is reflected in the ways we act towards less powerful creatures. As Kant put it,

Any action whereby we may torment animals, or let them suffer distress, or otherwise treat them without love, is demeaning to ourselves.
(Kant 1997, 434.)

> **Reflexivity**: for Kant, the reflection of human moral values through our treatment of non-humans.

It is important to emphasise that this still prioritises human interests: the aim is ultimately to improve human behaviours rather than to benefit non-humans. An illustration of this nuance relates to the topic of vivisection. From the nineteenth century, experimentation on animals extended scientific knowledge. In an age without effective pain relief or anaesthesia (and without moral consideration of the animals' suffering) such vivisection (literally 'live-cutting') experiments were, for many audiences then and now, cruel and inhumane. Kant's ethical stance, however, justifies such harm to the animal subjects if human benefits may follow from the resulting knowledge. In such an extreme case, direct human utility would take precedence over the reflexivity argument. Such 'enlightened anthropocentrism' illustrates the gulf between human and non-human interests.

Kant also discussed a third consideration to guide human behaviours regarding other forms of life, and it is relevant to the case of biological experiments. Today (and, to a lesser extent, during the nineteenth century) certain species are employed in such experiments while others are not. We are increasingly aware of (and sensitive to) the potential suffering of primates, rabbits and 'laboratory' mice, but probably very little concerned about experimentation on fruit flies and corn plants. Is there an ethical principle or an ordering of the 'Great Chain of Being' behind this?

We might entertain various reasons for our implicit choices. One consideration might be our personal engagement with certain species: small furry mammals, for instance, are usually more appealing, and more compassionately treated, than scaly crawling creatures. A second related reason may be that certain life forms seem more like humans in their behaviours, sentiments and suffering. Yet that similarity may be hard to pinpoint. Small monkeys are demonstrably human-like in many ways (and, indeed, the first Victorian audiences, as well as modern-day television viewers, were captivated by the enchantingly familiar traits of chimpanzees and gorillas). Yet dolphins have a body shape and living environment alien to human experience; why do we now value them so highly?[3]

Kant argued that this third consideration for valuing other forms of life related to 'sentience'. 'Intellectual capacity' has been an intuitive and popular criterion for moral consideration. Kant argued that different species exhibit different capacities of understanding and suffering. In particular, they are distinguished by rational abilities and self-awareness.

Rationality was a highly-valued quality for Enlightenment philosophers, and remains so in modern culture. The ability to observe, learn and reason is the essence of modern science, and may inform our preferences for dolphins over sharks and lemurs over lizards. From the standpoint of eighteenth-century knowledge, Kant argued that no other species was rational in the human sense, but that some had limited degrees of understanding.

Related aspects of ability to reason concern self-awareness and autonomy (i.e., independence or self-direction). Kant claimed that other forms of life do not have the human capacity for self-consciousness, a capacity to anticipate future events and plan their actions accordingly. Acting by instinct rather than by conscious choice, non-humans are incapable of appreciating or intentionally altering their state of being. Both enjoyment and suffering, he suggested, are closely linked with sentience.

Kant's arguments provide guidance and boundaries for moral consideration of other forms of life. We should take account of species when they are useful to us, and treat them in ways that reflect our higher human standing, but only in rather limited circumstances should we consider their capacity to appreciate harms. This is a firmly anthropocentric perspective. It argues that most animals, and certainly plants, are a means to an end rather than having moral standing themselves (Hughes 2002).

3.1.3 Transforming anthropocentric values into behaviours

The various flavours of anthropocentrism guide environmental behaviours. These usually lead to actions that can be justified by moral arguments and extended to novel situations. The arguments generally are framed according to the distinct ethical approaches in Chapter 2: by basing actions on outcomes (consequentialist ethics), on rights and duties (deontological ethics), or by emphasising moral character (virtue ethics).

Theological guidance, for example, is often framed in terms of human duties or religious virtues. Biblical interpretations commonly have motivated audiences to appreciate their responsibility to act in particular ways, for instance to prosper from God's creation (e.g., to engage in mining, forestry and fur-trading). Alternatively, they may prioritise the need to act as wise custodians or stewards to maintain these resources sustainably and to respect the Creator by avoiding waste. Or, yet again, such understandings may highlight the need to act in ways consistent with virtues of compassion and beneficence towards less-powerful forms of life.

Kant's ethical prescription is equally fertile in motivating environmental actions. It defines the species deserving special consideration to be mainly those similar to humans, or directly serving human interests as a living resource. Apes may be seen by human populations as having little utility, but they are commonly deemed worthy of moral consideration because of their similarity to us; cows are of great value not because of their (limited) sentience, but because of the products they supply. They should be treated in a humane fashion to reflect the moral sentiments of their owners, but just as importantly to wisely protect them as productive animals.

This consideration of utility is the most widely applicable and almost universally accepted factor, and may supersede other concerns when making anthropocentric judgements. Thus the intelligence of rats is (generally) a trait to be abhorred rather than celebrated: homes and food supplies are universally defended from these clever competitors. For similar reasons, orcas were sometimes hunted by fishermen until the 1960s in order to protect salmon stocks and their families' survival.

Such actions are based on consequentialist problem-solving, as they are carried out to produce (or avoid) a particular result. From Kant's time through the nineteenth century – a period of fertile invention and rapidly growing human powers applied in novel ways – the principle of utility was expanded into a complete framework for ethics. Utilitarianism (as developed by Jeremy Bentham and his successors), converted ethical decision-making into moral arithmetic. Seeking 'the greatest good for the greatest number' is equally familiar in economics and policy-making.

Utilitarianism (discussed systematically in Chapter 2) is a reliable and popular ethical approach for guiding actions because, like arithmetic, it yields a clear decision based on the factors that define the goals. Yet it is also highly sensitive to how these factors are identified. During Bentham's lifetime and today, 'the greatest good' has usually been defined in terms of human interests; the 'greatest number' is usually defined as a subset of 'humans'. In a particular situation, the human interests may focus, for example, on optimising stockholders' profit, the productivity of a farm, or regional standard of living.

The application of ethical frameworks is strongly affected by underlying values. Within the laudable utilitarian approach to ethical decision-making are traces of the hierarchy described in the Great Chain of Being. Inclusion in the 'greatest number' requires that the entities being counted are recognised as alike and deemed worthy of being counted. This is not a fatal flaw, but it does require particular attention when utilitarianism is applied to environmental concerns. Anthropocentric versions of utilitarianism generally prioritise human interests. More inclusive versions may include consideration of other life forms, but only as far as they influence human interests and reflect human values. Thus, for example, decision-making about building a shopping mall is likely to take into account the benefits to potential shoppers and business people, but may devote less weight to farmers in the region, to indigenous wildlife, or to the long-term sustainability of the local ecosystem.

A more subtle difficulty is that utilitarian approaches may prove to be inadequate for considering qualities that are important to humans but difficult to quantify. Taking into account the aesthetic beauty of a landscape or the enjoyment of a dog-walker (not to mention the well-being or contentment of her dog) can be challenging.

Singer's account of equality of interests can provide a justification for prioritising human well-being over lower animals, based on humans' higher intellectual capabilities (2011, 51–2), However, Singer himself says that our knowledge of other animals' capabilities has advanced, with self-awareness being identified in many other species. Regan (1980) advances a more compelling criticism of anthropocentric ethics, arguing that Singer's utilitarianism is inadequate as a basis of animal rights as it is possible for human interests to always trump non-humans: for instance, mass enjoyment of a barbecue of a single cow. Instead, Regan argues for rights of animals based on the intrinsic value of being alive and experiencing the world.

3.2 Biocentric ethics

As discussed above, some versions of anthropocentric ethics consider the well-being of certain animals, but generally in relation to human interests only. There are, nevertheless, other moral positions that recognise other species in their own right. Pet owners, for example, may identify the animals they care for as companions or friends, rather than merely as creatures that provide them with comfort. Pets may be recognised as having innate qualities often associated with humans such as empathy, loneliness or joy. Indeed, the term 'pet' has been challenged by the term 'companion species' (Haraway 2003). This acknowledgement of similarity transforms these human to non-human relationships from a mere living resource to a degree of kinship.

3.2.1 Questioning biological hierarchies

There are earlier examples in Western thought of a wide appreciation of the similarities and value of living things. At a time when discussion of moral behaviours was the remit of theologians, botanist-philosopher John Ray published *The Wisdom of God Manifested in the Works of Creation* (1691). The book drew upon his work as a naturalist to classify plants and animals according to similarities and differences, an approach that became familiar to subsequent scientists. But he also explored 'natural theology', an attempt to understand the purpose of different forms of life, and whether they should be considered solely as resources for people:

> It is a generally received opinion that all this visible world was created for Man; that Man is the end of the Creation, as if there were no other end of any creature but some way or other to be serviceable to man . . . yet wise men nowadays think otherwise.
>
> *(Ray 1691, 175.)*

Indeed, Ray had concerns beyond non-human creatures and living things in general. He expressed his doubts about 'minerals, salts and earths' (98) being intended merely for human use, a perspective that foreshadowed later ethical positions discussed in Chapter 4. Ray concluded that the existence of these non-human components of the world must be 'to enjoy their own Beings' (Ray 1691, 367). In essence, he was arguing for the intrinsic value of living and non-animate things, a perspective that was uncommon then, and still relatively uncommon today.[4]

The development of ideas concerning inherent and instrumental values was linked to associated advances in scientific knowledge, especially in the natural sciences. New species were being discovered, new worlds were being explored and science was involved in new scales of investigation via newly-invented instruments. For some species, the instrumental value for human affairs was obvious: beaver pelts, for example, empowered a fashion industry and international trade. But other newly encountered life-forms were difficult to assign to the Great Chain of Being: their inherent and instrumental values were unclear. These explorations pointed towards the idea that humanity was not so much the master of nature, but merely one of the members of the natural community. They also supported a view of creation as being too complex for incautious human meddling.

Ray's conclusions provided ethical guidance on how to engage with the non-human world. He was suggesting that the worth or significance of living things should not be defined solely in terms of their utility to humans. Actions based on human benefits could not adequately ensure their appropriate treatment. Considerations of human responsibilities also appeared insufficient here. If all living things have inherent worth, they must also have rights to exist. How should humans determine their corresponding duties?

Reassessments of the natural world and the place of humans within it were part of the scientific revolution occurring during Ray's lifetime, but some later influences were closer to home. An important parallel for later environmental thinking was the issue of human slavery, one of the most profound social debates of the nineteenth century. Although difficult for modern audiences to appreciate, the kinship of humans in newly-explored locales raised moral and scientific questions that divided audiences. Also, like more recent debates concerning global environmental questions, these intellectual positions were also wrapped in economic and political considerations.

As noted in Chapter 2, the equality and fairness objection to utilitarianism is that it provided potent utilitarian arguments in favour of slavery. The capture and provision of slaves had been an established and profitable trade, not only for European traders but also for certain African elites for over three centuries. From the sixteenth century, the Atlantic slave trade provided a labour force that was considered essential for profitable agricultural colonies in what are now the USA, West Indies, Cuba and Brazil.

In the decades following American independence from Britain, voices against the Atlantic slave trade rose in several countries. Promoted actively by the Quaker sect in Britain and reform politicians, the transportation of slaves was prohibited by law on British ships from 1807, and in the same year the US Congress outlawed the importation of slaves. Brazil was the last country in the Americas to ban imports in 1853.

These legal measures were a compromise that restricted, but did not end, slavery in the Americas. In the USA, internal slavery remained lawful in most states and territories, and became increasingly reliant on the offspring of enslaved people born into slavery to sustain the labour force. The economic cost of relying on a paid rather than an enslaved workforce, and the dismantling of the plantation system of agriculture in the southern states of America, was widely deemed to be prohibitive. The threat of rising production costs and declining international market competitiveness was a significant factor in the secession of seven of the thirty-four American states and the resulting Civil War during the early 1860s. Nevertheless, a growing anti-slavery movement pressured politicians and shifted public opinion. Slavery within British colonies was finally abolished in 1833, in the USA in 1865, and in Brazil in 1888. Such constitutional measures and campaign tactics were a model for environmental actions that have been pursued in our generation, as explored further in Chapter 8. It is worth noting that slave revolts and the underground railway (helping runaway slaves reach northern states) can also be seen as precursors to anti-constitutional direct action discussed in Chapter 9.

What might today be labelled social marketing (discussed in Chapter 6) was an important element of the anti-slavery movement. The changing of attitudes relied not just on careful theological and secular arguments and gradual economic accommodations, but also on the portrayal of the plight of enslaved persons and the rising empathy that this evoked in wider publics. Ethical evaluations were greatly influenced by campaigns to inform, explain and argue.

Medallions were distributed to promote the abolition of slavery. The first, named 'The Seal of the Slave' (1787), was adopted by the Society for the Abolition of the Slave Trade. One of the earliest examples of mass media symbolism, the iconography was imprinted on men's clay pipes, women's bracelets and wall hangings the nineteenth-century equivalents of T-shirts, buttons and posters. Alternate versions appearing on tokens and pamphlets depicted a female slave, extending the visual impact two generations later (Figure 3.3).

In the following generation, a handful of writers extended these notions of human equality. The English teacher and activist Henry Stephens Salt championed opposition to vivisection (recall section 3.1.2 above) by arguing for the similarities across the animate world in rhetoric that hints at earlier abolition debates:

> If we are ever to do justice to the animals we must get rid of the antiquated notion of a great gulf fixed between them and mankind, and must recognise the common bond of humanity that unites all living beings in one universal brotherhood
>
> *(Salt 1894, 4.)*

Salt's ethical perspective and actions will appear familiar to modern audiences. He founded the Humanitarian League in 1891, arguing for vegetarianism and against hunting for sport. The anti-vivisection movement, to which he contributed, influenced public opinion in some of the ways that had been used a century earlier for the abolitionist campaigns. Illustrations, pamphlets and essays depicted the plight of laboratory animals. Salt's value system, and the duties that followed from it, no longer corresponded to anthropocentrism.

FIGURE 3.3 Antislavery medallion, c. 1830. (British Museum, Wikipedia Commons license: https://commons.wikimedia.org/wiki/File:SisterSlave.jpg.)

3.2.2 Albert Schweitzer and reverence for life

Born a generation after Henry Salt, German theologian and medical doctor Albert Schweitzer extended these philosophical considerations further. In his early career, Schweitzer wrote and preached on the disparities produced by colonialism, arguing that it promoted two-tier values of 'civilised' and 'native' peoples. He spent most of his career as a medical missionary in Africa motivated in part, he suggested, as personal atonement and reparations for the historical injustices of slavery (Schweitzer 2005).

Alongside his concerns for human inequities, Schweitzer developed an ethical principle that he disseminated through numerous popular writings (e.g., Schweitzer 1931, Schweitzer 1933, Schweitzer 1965). His ethics of 'reverence for life' provided a justification and guidance for individuals' behaviours towards all living things. Schweitzer's framing of values was increasingly influential during the first half of the twentieth century and led to the Nobel Peace Prize in 1952, although his views on African problems were increasingly criticised as out of step with contemporary realities.

Schweitzer sought to express his values in deep but simple ways (Seaver 1955). One of the best known is a general principle expressed as a single-sentence epigram:

> It is good to maintain and encourage life; it is bad to destroy life or obstruct it.
> *(Schweitzer 1987, 309.)*

Schweitzer's perspective on values is a form of virtue ethics, and is based on what has been described as a 'nature-centred' ideal that promotes an individual's active engagement with the world beyond our species (Martin 2007). We will use the term 'biocentrism' to describe such broad sensitivity towards all human and non-human life.

Biocentrism: considerations that focus on the well-being of individual living things of all varieties.

In his book *The Philosophy of Civilization*, an unfinished four-volume treatise, Schweitzer explained that his ethic of reverence for life was inspired by threads from several philosophical traditions, including Greek virtue ethics, Christian ethics of love, Buddhist teachings about the links between forms of life, and Daoist philosophy emphasising a spiritual element of all things.

The ethic is radical in at least two respects. First, it is demanding, requiring scrupulous attention to our immediate environment to avoid harm to other living things around us:

> A man is truly ethical only when he obeys the compulsion to help all life that he is able to assist, and shrinks from injuring anything that lives . . . He tears no leaf from a tree, plucks no flower, and takes care to crush no insect. If in summer he is working in lamplight, he prefers to keep the window shut and breathe a stuffy atmosphere than see one insect after another fall with singed wings upon his table.

These demands also have an active component: individual people should not just avoid harming other individual life forms, but also should try to promote the welfare of these creatures by specific acts:

> If he walks on the road after a shower and sees an earthworm that has strayed on to it, he bethinks himself that it must get dried up in the sun if it does not return soon enough to the ground into which it can burrow, so he lifts it from the deadly stone surface and puts it on the grass. If he comes across an insect that has fallen into a puddle, he stops a moment in order to hold out a leaf or a stalk on which it can save itself.
> *(Schweitzer 1987, 310.)*

The second radical dimension of Schweitzer's position is that it does not acknowledge any hierarchy of life at all. He calls for 'constant regard for everything that lives, down to the lowest manifestations of life', and singles out tree leaves and irritating insects as typical, but seldom considered, examples deserving our individual compassion. This is a far cry from Henry Salt's moral prescription to treat animals as our kin. Instead, the reverence for life requires every 'instance of life' to be considered in equal terms.

Schweitzer's biocentrism is individualistic in every sense. It concerns how individual people should behave towards other individual creatures, and does not focus on groups of people (such as social groups and societies) or on communities of other forms of life (such as local populations and species). In fact, he argued that a personal sense of ethics should always override an 'ethics of society', which he thought imposed inappropriate obligations on individuals by creating allegiances to concepts such as 'the common good' or 'nationalism' (Schweitzer 2009, 135–6). Schweitzer argued that such affiliations, and their utilitarian perspective, prevent genuinely egalitarian behaviours.

Schweitzer pays relatively little attention to interactions between life forms, and the conflicts that these produce. Humans are 'life which wills to live, in the midst of life which wills to live' (Martin 2007, 5). Should individual people become involved in conflicts in nature, simultaneously protecting prey while preserving life for predators, for instance? Admitting that such conflicts were frequent and inevitable, Schweitzer counselled 'resignation', or recognition of our inability to alter events beyond our control. Yet more active engagement with suffering animals raised further dilemmas. Describing how a person should care for an injured heron, for example, he noted that he would have to sacrifice the lives of many fish over the weeks or months that the bird healed. The ethical guidance became a riddle: in such a case, Schweitzer suggested, 'we can show mercy only if we act without mercy at the same time' (Schweitzer 2009, 153). Elsewhere, he noted,

> Whenever I injure life of any sort, I must be quite clear whether it is necessary. Beyond the unavoidable, I must never go, not even with what seems insignificant. The farmer who has mowed down a thousand flowers in his meadow as fodder for his cows must be careful on his way home not to strike off in wanton pastime the head of a single flower by the roadside, for he thereby commits a wrong against life without being under the pressure of necessity.
>
> *(Schweitzer 2009, 144.)*

Yet the more fundamental ethical criterion for the relative significance of cows over flowers remained elusive. Jason Kawall's (2016, 204–5) development of Schweitzer's position does, however, present a way to do this. His argument is that, as well as life itself, other features of entities, such as rationality, compassion and the capacity to love, have inherent value too, and these should also figure in decision-making. This view has intuitive appeal – where killing is unavoidable, the virtuous person would take into consideration other intrinsically valuable characteristics of the organisms in question. A problem with his approach is that it is vulnerable to a variation of an uncomfortable argument put forward by Singer: once we are prepared to weigh up these qualities, if someone should be in the position of having to kill (or let die) either an orphaned mentally subnormal human infant or a more intelligent or sympathetic chimpanzee, they ought to save the chimpanzee.

Schweitzer's ethic of reverence for life expresses an extreme form of biocentric view that is quite different from the anthropocentric perspectives discussed in Section 3.1. Its fundamental principles are that:

- human individuals should recognise that they live among a multitude of other individual life-forms;
- each individual organism, as an independent centre of life, has the right to pursue its own good in its own way;
- individuals should be sensitive and sympathetic to the needs of all other life forms, and act in ways that help the lives of those individuals to continue well.

3.2.3 Popular expressions of biocentrism

The more demanding aspects of Schweitzer's framework of reverence for life lie well outside prevailing Western traditions, and encourage radically unfamiliar behaviours. Yet his biocentric ethic provides guidance and promotes some values that have been widely recognised over at least the past couple of centuries.

Schweitzer argued that sympathy for living things beyond ourselves is a natural psychological trait of humans, and probably other living things too. He argued that this extends naturally to compassion for lives that may initially seem dissimilar to ours but can be recognised as kin.

This notion of kinship and brotherhood was at the heart of Schweitzer's writings, but also those of Henry Salt and of the anti-slavery campaigners a century earlier. An even more widely shared sentiment is compassion for suffering. This focus on specific cases appears to be almost universally compelling. The Society for the Prevention of Cruelty to Animals, for example (later the Royal Society for the Prevention of Cruelty to Animals, or RSPCA), was founded as early as 1824 by a group of British Members of Parliament. It was a model that spawned numerous regional and national organisations and local branches having similar aims through the twentieth century.

The charities' early actions focused on cruelty towards working animals such as overloaded or malnourished cart-horses. Later campaigns highlighted the suffering of other urban animals frequently in the public eye such as abandoned or mistreated pets. Public support for the organisations, increasingly known as 'animal protection leagues' and 'humane societies', grew decade by decade, supported by popular information campaigns via print media and exhibitions (Figure 3.4).

FIGURE 3.4 SPCA poster by Morgan Dennis, 1934. (Local History Department, Onondaga County Public Library, Syracuse, NY, by permission of the American Humane Association.)

These widely-shared concerns and activities generally focus on specific cases of suffering caused by human cruelty or neglect. They encourage individual interventions to identify, prevent or remediate cases of harm to animals. Such concerns cannot be identified as anthropocentric. There is seldom an obvious direct human interest in curtailing animal cruelty, except for the effect of reducing anguish for the sympathetic observers. On the other hand, such cases often focus on favoured forms of life such as cats and dogs at most branches of the RSPCA, horses for the World Horse Welfare Society (1927) and, more recently, cetaceans at the Whale and Dolphin Conservation Society (1987), the Chinese Animal Protection Network (2004) and organisations dedicated to snow leopard conservation. Schweitzer's universal compassion is seldom a feature of such campaigns, perhaps because of the difficulty in recognising cases of avoidable harm to species that are distant or unfamiliar, or else the dilution of practical action that would result from casting the net of attention too broadly. Such animal protection campaigns often centre on the harms inflicted by humans on other species. In practice, priority of attention also is usually given to types of animal that have close relationships with humans. Familiarity, affection and loyalty, if not utility, are factors supporting such concerns.

For the most recent animal protection campaigns, the rhetoric of compassion and kinship is often overt. Donations may be framed as 'adoption' of particular animals, allowing a family identity and personal responsibility to be imagined. While attention is sometimes given to endangered species, information campaigns frequently highlight vulnerable individuals (e.g., orphaned pandas or stranded polar bears on ice floes). As discussed in Chapter 5, this method of identifying a shared concern to promote a change of behaviour is both effective and sound. It supports Schweitzer's claim that the psychology of sympathy is a pervasive human trait and a firm basis underlying ethical practices.

Such organisations suggest a diluted form of biocentrism, but others lie closer to the ideals of Henry Salt and Albert Schweitzer. The anti-vivisection movements of the late nineteenth century were radical and active in their opposition to animal cruelty. They sought to prevent experimentation on animals by generating vocal opposition to research practices of their day.

Today, biocentrism provides an ethical justification for vegetarian and vegan practices. An argument for not eating meat, poultry and fish is that the lives of the animals were sacrificed to become sources of food for humans. The more subtle argument for a vegan diet is that the consumption of milk, eggs and similar products requires living animals to be dedicated to serving as subordinate species to humans. In effect, the vegan argument is that the use even of animal by-products relegates animals to slavery. In both cases, harm and potentially suffering are likely to be inflicted on the animals concerned.[5]

So-called 'animal liberation' movements carry this advocacy further. Identifying affinities between oppressed humans and caged animals, their actions seek to publicise and counteract cases of cruel or unnecessary treatment. Targets have included laboratory animals subjected to painful experimental trials or harms for purposes that may be considered trivial (such as to test allergic reactions to human cosmetics) or those concerning inhumane commercial practices (such as egg-producing hens subjected to inadequate living space). In some cases, animal liberation groups use direct action, as discussed in Chapter 9.

Schweitzer's radical and demanding biocentrism, and more popular expressions of it that prioritise certain animals, cannot be identified primarily as 'environmental ethics' any more than early anthropocentrism can be. However, both biocentrism and anthropocentrism may provide a component of more environmentally-focused ethical guidance. Schweitzer's emphasis on 'instances of life', compassion for specific cases of suffering, and personal engagement to promote the 'will to live' make it particularly relevant for nearby, short-term ethical actions.

FIGURE 3.5 Radical biocentrism: animal liberation. (Ekinez Sortu photo, Creative Commons license: http://tinyurl.com/ybflhy5y.)

3.3 Ecocentric ethics

Albert Schweitzer's ethic, focusing on individual cases of suffering and personal actions to prevent or correct them, expresses some of the concerns of more recent environmental attitudes. It argues for kinship between all life forms and, more subtly, for a degree of interdependence. As a powerful species, for example, humans have great power to affect the prospering, as well as the eradication, of badgers, trees and ants.

Yet the complexities of such interactions are not the focus of the ethic of reverence for life. A deeper sense of this interconnectedness was developed over Schweitzer's lifetime in the science of ecology. There are traces of the concept in the ancient views of the Great Chain of Being, as 'more important' forms of life are dependent on those below them as resources. The term 'food chain' is a popularised version of this notion. More generally, this new interdisciplinary science sought to study the diverse elements of nature as a totality or whole – an approach known more generally as holism.

> **Reductionism**: an alternate approach, breaking down a complex problem into more easily explainable separate parts.
>
> **Holism**: the approach of attempting to understand a situation as a whole, rather than part by part.

The holistic approach is generally more challenging than the conventional reductionism that is common and effective in scientific investigation. Rather than reducing a problem to a set of simpler sub-problems, holism demands consideration of the multiple scales and interconnected contributions making up an effect. There are practical difficulties to this: complex systems may interact in ways that obscure understanding or make prediction problematic. In the case of consequentialist ethical considerations, this may make it difficult to decide whether 'a good deed' is genuinely beneficial after all. In such circumstances, Schweitzer's examples of caring for individual creatures may be difficult to scale up to wider environments. This complexity consequently challenges utilitarian decision-making: how can different alternatives be traded off to discover the optimal solution if the effects of the trade-offs are difficult to anticipate?

3.3.1 Aldo Leopold and the Land Ethic

Ecology provided a basis for extending ethics based on new scientific understandings. A key contributor to this approach was Aldo Leopold, an American forester, ecologist and writer. Leopold's attentions and activities highlighted a wider perspective on non-human life than Schweitzer's approach, and grew to become the first modern expression of an environmental ethic. His orientation encouraged consideration of a value system that prioritised not humans or instances of life, but ecosystems of interdependent species.

> **Ecocentrism**: ethical considerations that focus on the well-being of ecosystems, i.e., interacting communities of lifeforms and the physical environments that they inhabit.

Leopold's career experiences chronicled newly identified problems that had been created by human activities in what once had been sparsely inhabited environments. After obtaining a graduate degree in forestry before the First World War, he worked for the United States Forest Service in New Mexico, where he developed a natural management plan for the Grand Canyon. Leopold popularised the term 'wilderness' to describe regions free of roads, buildings and commercial activities such as mining, agriculture and logging. This ambition to preserve the variety of sublime natural settings and to protect them from degradation or eradication was an early aim of American legislators, although precisely what was to be conserved, and how, proved to be contentious. In 1864, for example, Abraham Lincoln's government granted the State of California public ownership of the Yosemite Valley, and eight years later Yellowstone became the first National Park. These and subsequent protected enclaves provoked public controversy over the restrictions that they imposed preventing development.[6] Conservation organisations such as the Sierra Club (founded 1892 by Scottish immigrant John Muir) played an increasing role in the public debate (Muir 1901). Less widely discussed was the precise definition of 'nature' and which elements within it were to be conserved. Protection focused on areas of spectacular scenery or sites of unique phenomena (such as geysers, primeval forests and vast canyons). Yet prior human occupants were not always treated inclusively. For example, early in the century Native Americans living in some of these regions were resettled elsewhere.

In the early 1920s, Leopold proposed the Gila Wilderness Area as a conservation region devoted to recreational hunting, fishing and hiking. His early responsibilities included hunting natural predators such as mountain lions, bears and wolves, which attacked local livestock as well as the deer favoured by recreational hunters. However, he later came to see these species as necessary parts of such environments, and wrote about these sentiments under the title 'thinking like a mountain' (Flader 1974). Describing how he mistook an old wolf for a deer and 'pumping lead into the pack' of mature cubs that accompanied it, he reasoned that 'no wolves would mean hunters' paradise'. Over the following seasons, though, he saw the longer-term effects of eradication:

> I have watched the face of many a newly wolfless mountain, and seen the south-facing slopes wrinkle with a maze of new deer trails. I have seen every edible bush and seedling browsed . . . to death. I have seen every edible tree defoliated to the height of a saddlehorn.
>
> *(Leopold 1968, 130.)*

Leopold argued that deer could be even more threatening to mountains than wolves were to deer, producing ecological changes that could require decades to recover. By considering a non-human perspective and non-human scale of geography and time, he argued, the relationships between forms of life could be reassessed more wisely.

Leopold's earliest ecocentric views have been widely shared by subsequent environmentalists, ecologists and wider publics. The Canadian nature writer Farley Mowat, for instance, wrote of wolves as human kin, and part of a network of interdependent communities and species in the far north (Mowat 1952, 1963). Philosopher Stephen Clark argued more recently that to consider nature management from a human perspective, and serving human interests, leads to unworkable solutions: 'We may find ourselves shooting Indian wild dogs to preserve deer, and simultaneously shooting deer to preserve trees' (Clark 1983).

Leopold's career was also closely linked to commercial realities. From the mid-1920s he was a director of the US Forest Products Laboratory, a government organisation researching and developing wood products as a sustainable resource. A decade later, appointed Professor of Game Management at the University of Wisconsin, his attention shifted from plant to animal life as a sustainable resource to be wisely managed. Leopold suggested that protected wildlife refuges and hunting laws were not adequate to protect ecosystems. Instead, he increasingly argued for landowners and government to responsibly manage habitats in ways that would encourage interdependence of diverse species, including humans themselves.

Leopold's professional activities were paralleled by experiences chronicled in a series of essays about his 'weekend refuge'. He had purchased some thirty hectares of barren land in central Wisconsin, an environment entirely logged of trees and overgrazed by cattle to leave little but sand. On this 'sand farm, first worn out and then abandoned by our bigger and better society', he said, 'we tried to rebuild, with shovel and axe, what we are losing elsewhere' (Leopold 1968, vii–viii). The collection, *A Sand County Almanac*, was published in 1949, the year after his death.

The final section of the book ('The Upshot') develops what Leopold called 'the Land Ethic'. He prefaced it with what he identified as growing environmental threats from modern development: landscapes transformed by car tourists and outdoor recreation, conservation organisations 'striving . . . to give the nature-seeking public what it wants', and 'a whole gamut of techniques toward the artificial end'. To safeguard trout, he complains,

> The Conservation Commissions feel impelled to kill all herons and terns visiting the hatchery where it was raised, and all mergansers and otters inhabiting the stream where it is released.

While fishermen may be content 'with this sacrifice of one kind of wild life for another', he observes, ornithologists are likely to be angered (Leopold 1968, 170). Leopold notes similar failures of ecological mismanagement elsewhere: tree damage by rabbits in England, where pheasants have been over-cropped, or the destruction of local flora and fauna by goats on numerous tropical islands.

Leopold argued that ethical values were being extended by growing scientific knowledge and human innovation. He noted that an ethic was, in ecological terms, 'a limitation on freedom of action in the struggle for existence', but that there had not yet been an ethic focused on humans' 'relation to the land and to the animals and plants which grow upon it'. Leopold's 'Land Ethic' enlarged the sense of community beyond co-operating people to include 'soils, waters, plants and animals, or collectively: the land'.

Leopold summarised this collection of entities as a 'biotic community'. This sense of community was considerably broader than Albert Schweitzer's scope of attention. Not only did it include living things such as water bugs and trees, but also soil, water and air. Leopold argued that these components of the environment were more than mere resources and had an intrinsic right to existence, 'at least in spots', in 'a natural state' (Leopold 1968, 202–4). This hints at a virtue ethic. Just as Schweitzer had a single-sentence summary of his reverence for life, Aldo Leopold summarised the principle of his Land Ethic compactly:

> A thing is right when it tends to preserve the integrity, stability, and beauty of the biotic community. It is wrong when it tends otherwise.
> *(Leopold 1968, 224–5.)*

The key terms of 'integrity', 'stability' and 'beauty' are admittedly difficult to define. In scientific terms, 'integrity' and 'stability' appear to translate, at least in part, into 'maintenance of biotic diversity' and 'long-term sustainability or viability'. These mappings onto biological science are not adequate to fully capture his intended meaning, though, and the term 'beauty' is even more problematic. Leopold's *A Sand County Almanac* dedicates a chapter to a 'conservation aesthetic' that discusses how we define and interact with wider natural environments. He uses the phrase 'love and respect' to appraise things that are 'natural, wild and free' (Leopold 1968, vii–viii). Authenticity of experience is important to him, and overly artificial or simplified management of wildlife (such as the trout fisheries described above) are criticised. Leopold argued for ethical and aesthetic appreciation of environments, and to resist considering land use merely in economic terms.

Yet alongside these holistic and intangible dimensions, Leopold also argued for considering the likely consequences if we are not sufficiently cautious about our treatment of environments. These utilitarian ethical considerations are emphasised later in his essay:

> The ordinary citizen today assumes that science knows what makes the community clock tick; the scientist is equally sure that he does not. He knows that the biotic mechanism is so complex that its workings may never be fully understood.
> *(Leopold 1968, 205.)*

The American expansion across the continent, he suggested, should be understood not as people taming nature, but as land, native species and different peoples co-existing in symbiotic relationship, shaping each other as members of a larger community.

> **Symbiosis**: mutually beneficial interdependence.

The American southwest had been transformed over the previous century by ranchers and over-grazing livestock towards 'a progressive and mutual deterioration, not only of plants and soils, but of the animal community subsisting thereon', something not expected by the early American settlers (Leopold 1968, 206).

Leopold argued that similar situations were happening even more frequently in his time. The 'dust bowl' catastrophe of the 1930s, when the fertile topsoil of much American pastureland was lost, had not been redressed over a decade later because poor grazing and deep ploughing practices had not been altered. Instead, Leopold argued, farmers had over-used new technologies (small tractors and combine harvesters) and focused on immediate production and economic gain for themselves, rather than on a community ethic. The historical evidence appeared to indicate that human-made changes have often been ecologically violent and 'of a different order than evolutionary changes, and [having] effects more comprehensive than is intended or foreseen'. This practical fact, he argued, should make human behaviours much more cautious and long-range (Calicott 2010).[7]

3.3.2 Popular expressions of ecocentrism

Leopold's writings made relatively little impact between his death and the mid-1960s, during a period when the Western world was rapidly innovating and expanding toward modern consumer culture (consumerism). The petrochemical industry was revitalised by large-scale adoption of plastics; electrical appliances and electronics expanded as electrical power became ubiquitous; road quality, car ownership and mobility co-evolved in many countries. Widespread confidence in scientific research and material progress was unshakable as standards of living improved in many countries.

While Leopold had given brief examples of bad environmental outcomes produced by misplaced optimism, the first prominent support for his views came from a biologist, Rachel Carson. Her book, *Silent Spring*, was an investigation of the effects of a synthetic pesticide, DDT, on birds and the wider environment (Carson 1962). The chemical had been widely used as an insecticide since the Second World War and increasingly was being employed in agriculture. Carson's findings were first published as a series of articles in *New Yorker* magazine and were attacked initially by the chemical industry. However, her findings were defended by a network of scientists and the principal American conservation organisation championing the well-being of birds, the Audubon Society (founded 1905). In the two years before her premature death from cancer, her findings were largely verified by a Presidential Science Advisory Committee, and celebrated by a number of American scientific organisations. Carson's activities are credited with triggering American public concern about pesticide usage and with the growth of the environmental movement (Lytle 2007). An indirect consequence of growing public concerns was the creation in the USA of the Environmental Protection Agency in 1970.

More generally, Carson's research questioned popular faith in technological progress, an attitude that grew alongside growing awareness of declining natural environments. Coupled with this faith was unfounded confidence in environmental management and to anthropocentric perspectives in general. 'The "control of nature"', she noted, 'is a phrase conceived in arrogance, born of the Neanderthal age of biology and philosophy, when it was supposed that nature exists for the convenience of man' (Carson 1962, 261). Her important case mapped onto Aldo Leopold's more general perspectives, and their shared field of ecology grew rapidly in popularity from the 1960s.

By identifying specific contexts where human activities have caused environmental harms, both Leopold and Carson influenced wide audiences. For some, Leopold's most effective criticisms concerned contemporary examples such as the overflowing car parks surrounding stocked-fishing lakes, which transformed personal communion with nature into a mass consumer experience. There is a hint of anthropocentrism here, even if Leopold's broader critique was firmly ecological.[8]

For others, Carson's carefully documented trail of ecological effects was most keenly absorbed when specific examples of suffering were revealed: thin eggshells resulted from high DDT levels in earthworms and, as a result, left many eagles' nests empty of offspring. The widely shared affection for birds played an important role in creating public awareness of chemical pollution and of ecological discoveries such as 'bioconcentration' of chemicals accumulated in successive species in a food chain. This public sensitisation to environmental harms consequently owed much to the sentiments for the suffering of individual animals that are prioritised in biocentrism.

From the time of Carson's work, popular environmental sensitivities have been heightened by a combination of anthropocentric, biocentric and ecocentric concerns. For the first environmentally-sensitive audiences these ecological concerns were combined with broader contemporary issues. An early example was the celebration of 'Earth Day' at American colleges and schools in 1970 to raise awareness of issues such as air pollution, famine, depletion of oil reserves, species extinction and global conflicts. The event was marked by speeches from scientists, mainstream politicians and activists, and by peaceful demonstrations across the country. Two decades later, similar clusters of concerns were marked in annual Earth Day events around the world. Similar communication strategies are discussed in Chapters 5 and 6, and in Chapter 9 as an example of symbolic action.

The first modern 'environmentalist' organisations (as opposed to earlier 'conservation' organisations) were initially focused on the nuclear arms race and its potential effects on human survival. Friends of the Earth (1969) and Greenpeace (1971) were founded in North America, but quickly spawned independent branches in other countries. Both organisations emerged from former members of the Sierra Club, and adopted protest and direct action (addressed in Chapter 9) to influence growing publics and to alter practices. An initial campaign for Greenpeace focused on underground nuclear testing and the possibility of environmental consequences of explosions near tectonic faults; later confrontations concerned atmospheric nuclear testing by France in the South Pacific. Related issues concerned the harms of unsafe storage of nuclear waste and operation of nuclear power reactors. While nuclear issues remained important, some members oriented towards more explicit environmental issues such as commercial whaling, which threatened to cause the extinction of several species during the 1970s, and then to public campaigns against commercial seal-hunting and the dumping of toxic wastes in international oceans.

Specific pollution events have underlined the rhetoric of environmentalist organisations and expanded public awareness of harms to individuals, human communities, other species and, in some cases, to ecosystems. Landmark cases (both legally and ethically) included revelation of the pollution of Love Canal (1976), a neighbourhood in New York State affected by leakage from toxic chemical wastes dumped there by a local company during the 1940s and 50s, and the Chernobyl nuclear accident (1986). Public concern focused initially on consequences for humans (such as displaced families and the medical consequences of toxicity) and subsequently on other species. Extreme oil spillages comprise another class of concern, such as the *Amoco Cadiz* disaster (1978) in the waters off Brittany, France; the *Exxon Valdez* tanker spill (1989) in Prince William Sound, Alaska; and the *Deepwater Horizon* ocean-drilling platform spill (2010) in the Gulf of Mexico. Such technological traumas depict specific victims (often sea-birds and marine mammals) to communicate a sense of the magnitude of ecological effects, but often frame these disasters in terms of the long-term human harms of despoiled beaches, falling tourism, costs and responsibilities for clean-up and economic hardship (see Chapter 5).

Such events evoke concerns for other beings, but judging appropriate actions may still be difficult. The three value systems explored in this chapter – anthropocentric, biocentric and ecocentric – provide divergent guidance about appropriate behaviours. They identify diverse justifications and strategies based on value systems that may be incompatible in some circumstances. As discussed above, there are dilemmas in prioritising either people, individual life forms or more abstract concepts such as ecosystems or biotic communities.

A case that illustrates this confrontation of values concerns the farming of mink for their fur pelts. From a narrowly anthropocentric stance, this practice may appear entirely reasonable. If the animals are bred and raised to maturity, and then sacrificed humanely, the principal concern would be to ensure that farmers can make adequate profit from the activity and thereby provide benefits to their family, and also benefits to the other people involved as fur traders, fashion designers, garment producers and eventual purchasers.

A biocentric stance may yield dramatically different guidance. It would argue that captive mink will live constrained lives unlike their experiences in the wild. In extreme cases, small cages and barren environments could make existence a misery; in the best cases, where the welfare of the animals might be considered so as to ensure their excellent physical condition until adulthood, the mink would still ultimately be exploited for their valuable fur. This more humane treatment, increasingly protected by laws, also may be encouraged according to Kant's concept of reflexivity, in which appropriate virtues in mink farmers serve as examples for wider communities. Yet, in either circumstance, a biocentrist might argue for the closure of mink farms, or even for the immediate release of all captive mink. While this is likely to challenge a business practice or actually break a law, it would satisfy the radical biocentric position of ensuring what Schweitzer called 'the will to live' and prevent suffering.

A third guide to action could be argued from an ecocentric stance. On the one hand, the captive mink are not experiencing a natural life as part of an ecosystem and ideally would be offered this opportunity either in an altered farming context or in the wild. On the other hand, to release captive mink into the neighbouring environment can cause unexpected and negative consequences. Released mink are effective predators and have dramatically reduced the population of water voles and altered river ecosystems.

This example echoes Leopold's concerns about the eradication of wolves in national parks, and how they jostled with the interests of recreational hunters, deer and mountain ecosystems. Such cases are all around us, and encourage a closer examination of how ethical values can be marshalled to reshape our practices.

Notes

1 'Western heritage' refers here to traditions transmitted from ancient Greek and Roman cultures, and subsequent Judeo-Christian-Islamic-humanist interpretations initially on the European and American continents, and more widely valued in the modern world.
2 The captive (male) whale was dubbed 'Moby Doll', suggesting its cultural transition from being understood as a terrifying sea monster (Moby Dick) to a cuddly companion.
3 It is worth noting that the cultural appeal of orcas rose after a single whale was available in captivity and widely witnessed by global publics through television news reports and documentaries, and before the complexities of the social habits of the species were well understood. The case suggests the power of popular education in rapidly transforming ethical sensitivities, as developed in Chapter 5.
4 An example hinting at this perspective about inanimate things is the discouragement by some outdoors organisations of the use of sharp metal crampons and walking sticks, which can scar or damage rocks on trails during hiking or hill-climbing pursuits, and the similar disparagement by some rock climbers of the overuse of 'camming devices' in cliff fissures.
5 It is worth noting the counter-argument that, by requiring more crops, veganism destroys habitats that are useful for other animals. The reply is that meat- and dairy-dependent diets use more grain and agricultural land than vegan diets do.
6 Examples include the flooding of the Hetch Hetchy Valley in Yellowstone National Park to create a water reservoir for San Francisco (1920s and 30s) and more recent efforts to legalise strip mining for coal in National Parks (1990s).
7 An early expression of what was later referred to as the 'Precautionary Principle'.
8 It should be noted that this chapter introduces several flavours of anthropocentric thinking. These range from the instrumental view of nature that was summarised by Lynn White Jr, to the more subtle biases towards human interests that are expressed in some versions of ecocentrism.

References

Calicott, J.B. (2010) 'The conceptual foundations of the land ethic', in C. Hanks, *Technology and Values: Essential Readings*, 431–53. New York: Wiley-Blackwell.
Carson, R. (1962) *Silent Spring*. Boston: Houghton-Mifflin.
Clark, S.R.L. (1983) 'Gaia and the forms of life', in R. Elliott and A. Care, eds, *Environmental Philosophy: A Collection of Readings*, 182–97. Milton Keynes: Open University Press.
Flader, S.L. (1974) *Thinking Like a Mountain: Aldo Leopold and the Evolution of an Ecological Attitude toward Deer, Wolves, and Forests*. Columbia: University of Missouri Press.
Gessner, C. (1558) *Historiae Animalium*. Zurich: C. Froschauer.

Haraway, D. (2003) *The Companion Species Manifesto: Dogs, People, and Significant Otherness*. Chicago: Prickly Paradigm Press.
Hughes, J.D. (2002) *The Environmental History of the World: Humankind's Changing Role in the Community of Life*. London: Routledge.
Jessop, R. (2012) 'Coinage of the term environment: a word without authority and Carlyle's displacement of the mechanical metaphor', *Literature Compass* 9.11: 708–20.
Kant, I. (1997) 'Vigilantius', in P. Heath and J.B. Schneewind, eds, *Lectures on Ethics*. Cambridge: Cambridge University Press.
Kawall, J. (2016) 'Reverence for life as a viable environmental virtue', in L.P. Pojman, P. Pojman and K. MacShane, (eds), *Environmental Ethics: Readings in Theory and Application*, 202–15. Boston: Cengage Learning.
Leopold, A. (1968) *A Sand County Almanac*. Oxford: Oxford University Press.
Lytle, M.H. (2007) *The Gentle Subversive: Rachel Carson, Silent Spring, and the Rise of the Environmental Movement*. New York: Oxford University Press.
Martin, M.W. (2007) *Albert Schweitzer's Reverence for Life: Ethical Idealism and Self-Realization*. Aldershot: Ashgate.
Mowat, F. (1952) *People of the Deer*. Toronto: Little, Brown.
Mowat, F. (1963) *Never Cry Wolf*. Toronto: McClelland and Stewart.
Muir, J. (1901) *Our National Parks*. Boston: Houghton Mifflin.
O'Neill, J. (1992) 'The varieties of intrinsic value', *The Monist* 75.2: 119–37.
Ray, J. (1691) *The Wisdom of God Manifested in the Works of Creation*. London: R. Harbin.
Regan, T. (1980) 'Vegetarianism and Animal Rights', *Philosophy and Public Affairs* 9.4: 305–24.
Salt, H. (1894) *Animals' Rights Considered in Relation to Social Progress*. London: Macmillan & Co.
Schweitzer, A. (1931) *The Primeval Forest*. New York: Macmillan.
Schweitzer, A. (1933) *Out of My Life and Thought*. Baltimore: Henry Holt.
Schweitzer, A. (1965) *The Teaching of Reverence for Life*. New York: Henry Colt & Co.
Schweitzer, A. (1987) *The Philosophy of Civilisation*. New York: Prometheus Books.
Schweitzer, A. (2005) 'Sermon, 6 Jan 1905', in J. Brabazon, ed., *Albert Schweitzer: Essential Writings*, 76–80. Maryknoll, NY: Orbis Books.
Schweitzer, A. (2009) 'Reverence for Life', in P. Cicovacki, ed., *Albert Schweitzer's Ethical Vision: A Sourcebook*, 135–52. Oxford: Oxford University Press.
Seaver, G. (1955) *Albert Schweitzer: The Man and His Mind*. London: Adam and Charles Black.
Singer, P. (2011) *Practical Ethics*, Third Edition. Cambridge: Cambridge University Press.
Valadés, D. (1579) *Rhetorica Christiana*. Perugia: Petrus Jacobus Petrutius.
White Jr, L. (1967) 'The historical roots of our ecological crisis', *Science* 155 (3767): 1203–7.

4

SHALLOW, DEEP AND SOCIAL ECOLOGIES

The previous chapter introduced three value systems that consider environmental dimensions: anthropocentrism, biocentrism and ecocentrism. The differences between these perspectives can be understood as both a shift of attention and a change of scale. And, to varying degrees of satisfaction, these rankings of values can be expressed according to any one of the three ethical frameworks introduced in Chapter 2 (virtue ethics, deontology or consequentialism) to work out solutions to ethical quandaries.

Anthropocentric ethics focuses on people, and often on those 'nearest and dearest': we may favour local persons over distant people, and probably favour the welfare of our kinship group over the welfare of the wider community, or may consider the well-being of our business stakeholders over national interests. From the discussion so far, it should be evident that human-centred actions can be described in terms of virtues, duties or outcomes.

By contrast, biocentrism widens attention to non-humans and – potentially – to a very wide range of non-human interests. Biocentric ethics may call upon either virtues or responsibilities (deontology). As formulated by Albert Schweitzer, a virtuous person would show reverence for life and behave in ways that consider the well-being of other life forms, whether or not those creatures are capable of reason, consciousness of a 'will to live' or even able to sense harm. On the other hand, consideration of duties frames biocentric principles in a different way: values can be reflected in the recognition of rights of other living things, or alternatively as a set of responsibilities that can be defined for people, and perhaps for other species having a degree of sentience. By contrast, a consequentialist version of biocentrism is difficult to conceive: if all instances of life have intrinsic value, then how can they be traded off in any meaningful way? We might consider quantifying instances of life, but would quickly realise that human interests would have negligible influence in an environment that includes an incomparably greater number of termites and microbes. Assuring opportunities for all life forms would seem to break down in any attempt to assess their relative values.

Ecocentrism shifts attention even further from humans, considering all living things but also the inanimate aspects of the environments that support them. Again, as introduced in Chapter 2, the stance is commonly framed either in terms of virtues or duties. Its values may be expressed in terms of desirable outcomes, but this takes some work.[1]

Besides the greater inclusiveness of each of these successive value systems, there are at least hints of a change of physical scale. As suggested above, anthropocentric attention is often biased towards local circumstances. Schweitzer's orientation still emphasised personal encounters and actions, but ecocentrism generally considers scales beyond direct human experience. Aldo Leopold, for example, described regional sensitivities, according ethical and ecological consideration to mountain valleys, deserts and large single-crop farms.

This expansion of physical scale and broader sense of kinship is central to the environmental ethics discussed in this chapter. Two important formulations, so-called 'deep ecology' and 'social ecology', consider not only regional or national scales, but global scales. Their planet-wide attention characterises them as variants of biospheric ethics (not to be confused with 'biocentric' ethics).

Biospherism: ethical considerations that focus on the well-being of the biosphere and its constituents.

The biosphere is the thin layer near the surface of the Earth capable of sustaining life, and includes the rocky crust and soil (lithosphere), bodies of water (hydrosphere) and air (atmosphere). The constituents and physical extent of this global ecosystem are being extended steadily by scientific research as the interdependences of newly discovered and more physically distant life forms are identified. This evolving relationship between scientific knowledge and moral sensitivities has been a feature of environmental ethics over the past century and is one reason that recent proponents have named their variant forms of ethics as extensions of the science of ecology.

4.1 Arne Naess and notions of 'shallow' and 'deep' environmental ethics

From the 1970s, the Norwegian philosopher Arne Naess criticised contemporary environmental ethics and developed broader philosophical arguments for guiding environmental actions and lifestyles. His approach challenged conventional attitudes and practices by highlighting aspects of modern culture that were contributing to growing environmental harms.

4.1.1 Shallow ecology

Naess summarised his early views about environmentalism in a 1973 issue of *Inquiry*, a philosophical journal that he had founded fifteen years earlier. While praising the emergence of ecology as a scientific study, he argued that responses to ecological problems were inadequately conceived and targeted. In the short essay, he contrasted two contemporary approaches for dealing with environmental issues, characterised as 'shallow' and 'deep' respectively.

The 'shallow' movement, Naess argued, had 'twisted and misused' the message of scientific ecologists. Its major failing was that it wrongly prioritised environmental concerns. His two-sentence description observed that the proponents were focusing on the 'fight against pollution and resource depletion', and had the central objective of ensuring 'the health and affluence of people in the developed countries' (Naess 1973, 95).

> **'Shallow' ecology**: a term coined by philosopher Arne Naess for ethical considerations of well-being focusing on local environments, short-term contexts and human-centred concerns.

Naess argued that this first wave of environmentalism, although inspired by Rachel Carson's work and the rediscovery of Leopold's writings, was too often diluted and biased towards immediate concerns and human interests. This attention is superficial and insufficient.

Naess suggested that the shallow ecological approach failed to examine environmental questions holistically, and instead reduced them to particular local harms to be corrected by short-term tactics. In effect, he criticised the attention merely to immediate consequences. By identifying environmental issues according to utilitarian criteria, he hinted, problem-solvers and their communities tend to focus on the well-being of 'the greatest number' in narrow terms: concerns might be limited to company stockholders or residents of a neighbourhood, for example. Such attentions obscure recognition of larger implications affecting the well-being of other human communities and other life forms, especially those far away.[2] In short, 'shallow ecology' bends ecocentrism towards anthropocentrism and localism.

Similarly, the utilitarian notion of maximising 'the greatest good' is commonly conceived as a sharply-targeted action to speedily or inexpensively resolve a problem. The best solutions, Naess argues, are wrongly identified as simple actions that leave other aspects of human life intact. His examples suggest that this prejudices the evaluation of outcomes in favour of the aspects of life that we are unwilling to sacrifice (such as standard of living and personal convenience) or consider too difficult to alter (consideration of harms to other peoples or species). Just as Leopold's evocative writing criticised rising consumerism, and Carson's work challenged faith in technological progress, Naess is concerned with issues that meld scientific knowledge, political policy and individual behaviours.

Consider, for example, Naess's point about pollution: how can the 'fight against pollution' be considered shallow? First, this fight often focuses on specific local events without satisfactorily considering 'the bigger picture'. For example, it may identify the leakage of a chemical by-product into local waterways, but not question the need for such chemicals by wider society. Second, it may encourage actions that obscure or cover up these deeper issues. Thus civic clean-up campaigns may collect litter and improve the aesthetics and hygiene of a community, but fail to address the more fundamental causes of littering. These may include, for example, the manufacture and sale of disposable packaging, or cultural disdain for personal responsibilities, or ignorance of the longer-term environmental effects of plastic packaging and pull-tabs from canned drinks. In the same way, recycling campaigns – while achieving important benefits of efficiently reusing some materials and limiting the growth of waste dumps – may fail to recognise the social, cultural, economic and political factors that encourage continued (and unsustainable) wasteful production. In the worst case, recycling may encourage companies and consumers to expand wasteful practices with the confidence that the problem of pollution can be dealt with successfully. Instead of encouraging frugality, these innovations may promote increased consumption.

Similarly, Naess's implied criticism of a focus on 'resource depletion' is that it particularly threatens the lifestyle of Western countries (for example the OPEC oil crisis of 1973 illustrated, for his contemporary audiences, the dependence of Western economies and individual lifestyles on the embargoed supply of crude oil by the Organisation of Petroleum Exporting Countries). The unasked question in such discussions is 'resources for whom, and for what purpose?' This limited awareness, he suggests, camouflages harms to environments and forms of life not valued within modern societies.

More recent examples can also illustrate this view of shallow ecology. Energy-saving appliances, on the one hand, are a great improvement over the wasteful devices of past decades. They may, however, encourage consumers to continue to buy, and eventually discard and recycle, even more such 'labour-saving devices'; we may ask whose labour is being saved. Similarly, the installation of 'eco-friendly' light bulbs, or participation in Earth Day events, may encourage individuals to feel that they are positively contributing to sustainability, while leaving the preponderance of their lifestyles unquestioned and intact.

In short, Naess identifies that 'shallow' environmental considerations opt for:

- focusing on human interests first;
- focusing on the local scale;
- identifying the best environmental solutions as those which will cause the least disruption to the status quo;
- encouraging superficial 'band-aid' solutions to problems.

Naess's critique classifies shallow ecology as environmental consideration that is poorly targeted, unfairly focused and ineffective in the long term. It identifies the inadequacy of self-interest for motivating environmental ethics, and a need to establish deeper ethical principles to guide actions. It also suggests that a focus on consequences is an unworkable ethical framework, and that judgements about good environmental practices require a clear sense of duty or virtue.

4.1.2 Deep ecology

While the label is useful in identifying a cluster of questionable environmental actions, it must be admitted that no-one accepts being labelled a 'shallow ecologist'. The term was adopted by Naess as a pejorative label to mark out what he identified as unsatisfactory attitudes and practices, and to differentiate them from his preferred ethical stance, which he called 'deep ecology'.

> **Deep ecology:** a term coined by Naess for ethical considerations focusing on the well-being of individuals, communities and ecosystems based on personal adoption of a global and egalitarian perspective.

The concepts are not entirely novel. Naess's first summary article described ideas that he acknowledged as circulating within a contemporary 'deep ecology movement'. These have recognisable threads in numerous earlier writers, including Carson, Leopold, Schweitzer and Salt, but are more carefully distinguished and merged by Naess. By attempting to characterise these attitudes and principles, he hoped to shift attention from the 'presently rather powerful movement' that promotes shallow actions towards the 'deep, but less influential movement' that could challenge them (Naess 1973, 95).

In his earliest writing on the topic Naess devoted most attention to identifying discrete values that defined the 'deep' expression of environmental ethics (Naess 1973, 96–8):

1. Rejection of the man-in-environment image. This requires giving up notions of humans (or other species) considered against an environmental backdrop. In its place, Naess calls for consideration of 'the relational, total-field image'. This demands an extension of the commonly accepted limits of the science of ecology to consider the moral relations between all elements of the shared ecosystem. Humans, other species and their inanimate living contexts are mutually interdependent, and so must be considered simultaneously and in combination in any situation that would previously have considered them independently. This point is relevant to the criticism of mediaeval Christian views made by Lynn White Jr (Section 3.1.1), but also applies to anthropocentric and biocentric thinking more widely.

2. Biospherical egalitarianism. This rather intimidating term involves seeking close partnership with other forms of life at all planetary scales. By contrast, Schweitzer's 'reverence for life' ethic and Leopold's Land Ethic were expressions of 'biological egalitarianism', focusing on individual lives or regional ecosystems, respectively, rather than a sense of global equity. This demanding virtue (discussed further below) can be defended by considering its utilitarian consequences as well. Naess suggested that such relationships provide humans with 'deep pleasure and satisfaction' and, by assuring life-equality for mammals, we are likely to improve the lot of humans.
3. Principles of diversity and symbiosis. In effect, co-existence and interdependence of dissimilar things are to be encouraged, and 'richness of forms' and 'new modes of life' may have intrinsic value in themselves. These principles illustrate how dramatically Naess extends ethical considerations. He refers not just to biological diversity such as varieties of potato, but also diversities of human ways of life. This position can also be defended by considerations of its outcomes. As Naess observes, diversity enhances the potentialities of survival. However, which entities survive requires further explanation: genetic diversity does not necessarily result in greater opportunities for each variant form, but may ensure that one or more of those forms survive environmental pressures. Thus a species or a local ecosystem (or indeed a company, a cultural practice or human occupation), may survive even if constituent parts prove unable to continue sustainably. These principles argue for a reorientation of attention, supporting 'the fight against economic and cultural, as much as military, invasion and domination', and 'opposed to the annihilation of seals and whales as much as to that of human tribes or cultures' (Naess 1973, 96).
4. Anti-class posture. This position is a refinement of the second point about egalitarianism, and the third concerning symbiosis. It seeks to avoid 'exploitation and suppression' in cases of 'conflict between groups' (Naess 1973, 97). This argues against conventional categories and attitudes that express inappropriate forms of control, such as notions of social class, 'developed' versus 'developing' nations, and ethnic or gender identity.
5. Fight against pollution and resource depletion. As discussed above concerning the weaknesses of shallow considerations, Naess argues that responsible professionals should resist collaborating in their work with 'institutions or to planners with limited ecological perspectives', and particularly those who deliberately flout the wider perspectives (Naess 1973, 97). He equally counsels citizens and activists to adopt and promote these principles in their own environmental actions.
6. Complexity, not complication. Naess notes that the science of ecology demonstrates the astonishing complexity of the natural world, as illustrated by the bewildering variety of life forms, interactions between them, and environmental contexts in which ecosystems are configured and adapt. One reaction, he suggests, is recognition of profound human ignorance about these systems, and the caution that should limit attempts to disturb them

(this point foreshadows the *Precautionary Principle* that counsels us to avoid taking actions that have unclear potential for causing negative effects).[3] The wider theme here is of the value of holism as a means of understanding and valuing these interconnected aspects on a global scale. There are strong hints of Leopold's Land Ethic and recognition of the need for interdisciplinary approaches and the virtue of (epistemic) humility. Naess observes,

> It is the global character, not preciseness in detail, which distinguishes an ecosophy [ecological philosophy]. It articulates and integrates the efforts of an ideal ecological team, a team comprising not only scientists from an extreme variety of disciplines, but also students of politics and active policy-makers.
>
> *(Naess 1973, 100.)*

7. Local autonomy and decentralisation. Naess argues that forms of life are more vulnerable when they are highly dependent on distant influences. His claim is that small-scale systems are inherently more stable than large-scale hierarchical systems. One reason, he suggests, is ecological equilibrium founded on a network of nearby interdependencies. The presumably rapid and direct connections between these elements permit a more robust, responsive and sustainable existence than does control from afar that is subject to different forces. A related argument was raised by Aldo Leopold in his discussion of the 'biotic mechanism' (Leopold 1968, 214–20). He describes the cycle of energy flow through 'biotic pyramids' of interdependent species, waters and soil. Such ecosystems may be relatively isolated by geographical differences, making them regionally distinct. They may also be perturbed by human activities. For example, megafarms may be designed according to an artificially simple biotic pyramid (e.g., cows, manufactured feed and water supply from deep aquifers). Because these systems are heavily reliant on external supplies of feed and export markets, they are neither self-sufficient nor stable. Similarly, human manipulation of natural biotic pyramids can be short-sighted and disastrous. Leopold describes how international transportation of farm products short-circuits such cyclical and sustainable activities, 'pooling on a world-wide scale . . . the formerly localized and self-contained circuits' (Leopold 1968, 218). Naess's support for local autonomy and decentralisation carries political dimensions (by encouraging self-governance, for example) and also characterises biospherical views concerning appropriate technologies (discussed in Section 4.3 below).

The choice between 'deep' and 'shallow' ecology, Naess implied, was a choice of prioritising either principles or the proximate. That is, deep ecology was founded on applying ethical principles in ways that could be widely recognised as consistent and equitable while shallow ecology focused on immediate and nearby problems.

Naess's criteria for deep environmental ethics seek to combine scientific knowledge with heightened ethical sensitivities. He describes the role of science as inspiring and fortifying the perspectives of the movement. Naess emphasises, however, that deep ecology requires adoption of intuitions and ethical principles that may not be obvious or defensible from known science alone (Naess 1973, 100). Instead, deep ecology defines new norms of behaviour and an extended system of values (just as biocentrism and ecocentrism do). Naess sought to extend his discipline to an ecological philosophy and to make it the basis for guiding human behaviours. This unified framework has global implications, but Naess emphasised that it would have local variants based on specific contexts, values and individual priorities. His later formulation of what he dubbed 'Ecosophy T' has been described as his personal framework of environmental ethics, developed during his Norwegian mountain excursions. The 'T' relates to the name of his mountain hut, 'Tvergastein', or alternatively to the Norwegian word *tolkning*, meaning 'interpretation' (Naess and Drengson 2005).

Over subsequent decades, and particularly in association with environmental philosopher George Sessions and sociologist Bill Devall, Naess refined his 'platform', or shared worldview, of deep ecology through several iterations (Drengson, Devall, et al. 2011). The later versions identified themes common to diverse philosophical, religious and cultural traditions, rather than defining a rigid set of precepts (Sessions 1987). Broad but inclusive, such reformulations combined general statements with hints of the forms of action required (Table 4.1).

TABLE 4.1 Reformulation of deep ecology 'platform principles'. (Devall 2002.)

1. All living beings have intrinsic value.
2. The diversity and richness of life has intrinsic value.
3. Except to satisfy vital human needs, humankind does not have a right to reduce this diversity and richness.
4. It would be better for human beings if there were fewer of them, and much better for other living creatures.
5. Today the extent and nature of human interference in the various ecosystems is not sustainable, and lack of sustainability is rising.
6. Decisive improvement requires considerable change: social, economic, technological and ideological.
7. An ideological change would essentially entail seeking a better quality of life rather than a raised standard of living.
8. Those who accept the aforementioned points are responsible for trying to contribute directly or indirectly to the realisation of the necessary changes.

4.1.3 Challenges and critiques of deep ecology

Expressions of deep ecology evolved from a set of intuitions to a 'platform' meant to unite diverse traditions into a movement or alliance for wise environmental actions. Yet Naess recognised ambiguities and potential problems in defending his set of perspectives. We may ask, for example, whether it is possible to genuinely treat all forms of life as equal. This requirement is at the centre of Schweitzer's ethic, and Naess's call for 'biospherical egalitarianism' reiterates it. He nevertheless qualified his original statement by admitting that it held 'in principle', noting that 'any realistic praxis necessitates some killing, exploitation, and suppression'. It raises the questions of 'how much?', and 'in what circumstances?' While this appears to provide a vaguely-worded 'get-out clause' for the ethical principle, Naess echoes the quandaries addressed by Schweitzer and Leopold when they discussed favouring herons over fish, or wolves over deer. Adopting the concepts and terminology favoured by these predecessors, he says:

> The ecological field-worker acquires a deep-seated respect, or even veneration, for ways and forms of life . . . *the equal right to live and blossom* is an intuitively clear and obvious value maxim.
> *(Naess 1973, 96.)*

This intuition is not equally shared by all individuals and societies; Naess downplayed the overt egalitarian emphasis from later versions of the deep ecology ethic. However, the essence of these ideas is still represented in the first two principles listed in Table 4.1, although the phrase 'vital human needs' in the third principle similarly defies precise formulation. Naess noted,

> My intuition is that the right to live is one and the same for all individuals, whatever the species, but the vital interests of our nearest, nevertheless, have priority . . . The greater vital interest has priority over the less vital. And the nearer has priority over the more remote – in space, time, culture, and species . . . The terms used in these rules are of course vague and ambiguous. But even so, the rules point toward ways of thinking and acting which do not leave us helpless in the many inevitable conflicts between norms.
> *(Naess 1995, 222.)*

For instance, the hunting of endangered species for food or clothing might be vital for the survival of some nonindustrial human communities, but certainly not for affluent societies. In fact, members of rich societies should assist poor communities in ways that avoid their need to exploit threatened species.

A difficulty for Naess's explanation is that concepts such as 'reverence' and 'veneration' draw upon religious or spiritual sensitivities that have been neglected in modern societies. Schweitzer and Leopold had made headway with such writing when it was directed towards the sublime natural environments experienced by naturalists, hikers and wilderness tourists, but deep ecology directs attention to the myriad contexts making up the planetary scale. Are there additional bases for respecting varied forms of existence – from humans to all living things, and even to more abstract biotic communities?

For some expressions of deep ecology, this sense of inclusion or kinship has been justified by considering the biosphere itself as a living organism. Such an identification may encourage an extension of the guidance of biocentric ethics: if the earth is thought of as a delicate and threatened lifeform, should we not actively protect it from harm? As a theological and cultural idea it is, of course, an ancient one, and revived in some contemporary environmental contexts (e.g., the magazine *Mother Earth News* (1970)). But, as with other aspects of environmental ethics, scientific knowledge has contributed to new interpretations of ethical values. From the 1980s, the British engineer James Lovelock and collaborators experimented with computer simulations that suggested the ability of planets to self-regulate temperature, atmospheric composition and other physical variables via interdependent chemical, physical and biological feedback loops. In effect, biospheres adapt and evolve in ways that may maintain the sustainability of the constituent parts. The research also indicated that such stability could ultimately fail if these mechanisms were perturbed too far. Their body of work, named Gaia theory after the primal Greek goddess of the Earth, did not hint at biospherical 'sentience', but instead revealed how complex systems involving living and inanimate constituents can stabilise conditions on a global scale. Evidence of this co-evolution of life forms and their non-animate environments supports the global perspective of deep ecology, and suggests the co-dependence of the living and inanimate systems that make up the biosphere.

> **Gaia theory**: a term coined by James Lovelock to describe how biospheres adapt to maintain stability.

Critics have also challenged the philosophical principles inherent in deep ecology. American philosopher Richard Watson, for example, argues that deep ecology is inherently unjust because it wrongly encourages a 'hands off' attitude towards nature. Rather than being egalitarian, he claimed, the ethic demands that humans as a species must control their innate capabilities and curtail their activities (Watson 1983). This denies the free exercise of human powers, and counters the values expressed by Naess and collaborators. For example, the deep ecology ethic appears to encourage unreasonable compromise: the abandonment of aspirations for higher standards of living, restrictions on the use of other species as resources and the reduction of human populations (Table 4.1). Instead of defending egalitarianism, Watson suggested, deep ecology singles out humans to carry the burden of harsh responsibilities.

By contrast, he argued that the best strategy for a sustainable biosphere is based on the human-centred perspective. By solving problems that affect human interests, Watson argued, other species and their environments will automatically be protected.[4] He concluded with a consequentialist anthropocentric argument: 'there is very good reason for thinking ecologically, and for encouraging human beings to act in such a way as to preserve a rich and balanced planetary ecology: human survival depends on it' (Watson 1983, 255).

The political implications of deep ecology – for example, the ways in which its guidance would alter individual freedoms or the collective exercise of human powers – have been challenged across the political spectrum. Among the most vociferous critiques came from the American writer and social philosopher Murray Bookchin. One of his criticisms focused, like that of Watson, on the unfairness of deep ecology, but identified the victims differently:

> Deep ecology . . . preaches a gospel of a kind of 'original sin' that accurses a vague species called humanity – as though people of color were equitable with whites, women with men, the Third World with the First, the poor with the rich, and the exploited with their exploiters. (Bookchin 1988, 12.)

Bookchin argued that humans were not all equally responsible for environmental harms. Most, in fact, had little if any power to alter their mode of life. He criticised the notion of 'vague and undifferentiated humanity' identified 'essentially as an ugly "anthropocentric" thing' (Bookchin 1988, 12).

A second target for Bookchin's criticism was the eclecticism and incoherence of the deep ecology 'platform', which seeks to bring together distinct traditions for concerted action. He bluntly characterised the movement as 'a black hole of half-digested, ill-formed, and half-baked ideas', observing that

> Deep ecology has parachuted into our midst quite recently from the Sunbelt's bizarre mix of Hollywood and Disneyland, spiced with homilies from Taoism, Buddhism, spiritualism, reborn Christianity, and in some cases eco-fascism.
> *(Bookchin 1988, 13.)*

Bookchin employed the incendiary phrase 'eco-fascism' to label a contentious thread of environmental discourse that had surrounded questions of population, food supply and means of addressing them (including laws, immigration policies, economic measures or other constraints imposed by governments to alter the behaviours of their citizens and other peoples), and which, he argued, were implicit in expressions of deep ecology (such legislative dimensions are discussed in Chapter 8). In its place, Bookchin suggested that an integral philosophical framework, consistently applied, was the only means of generating viable actions and outcomes in the long term. His alternative, 'social ecology' is, he argued 'avowedly rational' (Bookchin 1988, 25).

4.2 Murray Bookchin and social ecology

Bookchin shares a number of sentiments with Naess. What Naess pejoratively referred to as 'shallow ecology', Bookchin identified as 'vapid environmentalism' (Bookchin 1987):

> As our forests disappear due to mindless cutting and increasing acid rain, as the ozone layer thins out because of the widespread use of fluorocarbons, as toxic dumps multiply all over the planet, as highly dangerous, often radioactive pollutants enter into our air, water, and food chains – all, and innumerable other hazards that threaten the integrity of life itself, raise far more basic issues than any that can be resolved by Earth Day clean-ups and faint-hearted changes in existing environmental laws.
>
> *(Bookchin 1988, 9.)*

In its place, Bookchin and Naess separately advanced a biospheric orientation, scaling up ethical considerations to global proportions.

Both identify common enemies in modern cultures: the economics and appeals of consumerism, which encourage perpetual and unsustainable growth; hierarchies of control and centralisation; and, the applications of technology in ways that undermine ethical considerations. But where Naess highlights the role of personal virtue, Bookchin emphasises the need for fundamental social reorganisation as the route to achieving environmental sustainability. He argues that the ultimate causes of environmental crises can be traced to modern societies' hierarchies of power, noting that 'the domination of nature by man stems from the very real domination of human by human' (Bookchin 2005, 65).

Bookchin contrasts the 'vague, formless, often self-contradictory, and invertebrate thing called deep ecology' with 'a long-developing, coherent, and socially oriented body of ideas' of social ecology (Bookchin 1988, 11). His ethic reassesses earlier concerns and adopts an explicitly social orientation:

> Social ecology rejects a 'biocentrism' that essentially denies or degrades the uniqueness of human beings, human subjectivity, rationality, aesthetic sensibility, and the ethical potentiality of this extraordinary species. By the same token, it rejects an 'anthropocentrism' that confers on the privileged few the right to plunder the world of life, including women, the young, the poor, and the underprivileged. Indeed, it opposes 'centrism' of any kind as a new word for hierarchy and domination – be it that of nature by a mystical 'man' or the domination of people by an equally mystical 'nature'.
>
> *(Bookchin 1988, 26.)*

Social ecology: the term adopted by Murray Bookchin for ethical considerations focusing on ecosystems in the broadest sense, and from a global perspective that emphasises the need for societal transformation.

Advancing the claim of its being a sound philosophical stance, Bookchin argues that social ecology represented the most recent and inclusive version of ethics, which had been advancing since the Enlightenment some two centuries earlier.

He cites waves of moral progress that had been achieved by social and intellectual movements:

- the decline of ethnocentrism, or race-oriented hierarchies, as a result of nineteenth-century opposition to the Atlantic slave trade, national Abolition movements, 1960s American civil rights and 1980s South African anti-apartheid campaigns;
- the decline of androcentrism, or male-oriented hierarchies, as a result of feminist campaigns of the late nineteenth and early twentieth centuries, and more recently as the target of feminist theory during the 1970s;
- the decline of anthropocentrism, or human-oriented hierarchies, as a result of a growing variety of 'Green' and 'Gaian' movements from the 1970s;
- the consolidation and promotion of these anti-hierarchical perspectives in social ecology from the 1980s.

Bookchin argues that this was the culmination of the Enlightenment project to rationally explore the nature of human capabilities and goals, and responsible for generating gradually broadening understandings, more inclusive ethical considerations, and more successful templates for human society.

Recognising the social dimension of environmental problems is crucial to addressing them, he claims, citing contemporary examples such as the Exxon Valdez oil spill, environmentally unsound clearcutting of Californian redwood forests, and the James Bay hydroelectric project that flooded large areas of forest and altered indigenous land use in northern Quebec (Bookchin 1993). Each is an example, Bookchin notes, of social worldviews, economic mechanisms and political environments that create catastrophic but avoidable environmental and societal harms.

More broadly, he suggests that nature and society are intimately linked and co-evolve:

> people create an environment that is most suitable for their mode of existence. [This is] no different from the environment that every animal, depending upon its abilities, creates as well as adapts to, the biophysical circumstances – or ecocommunity – in which it must live. On this very simple level, human beings are, in principle, doing nothing that differs from the survival activities of nonhuman beings – be it building beaver dams or gopher holes.
> *(Bookchin 1993, 361.)*

Yet humans appear uniquely powerful, equipped to disastrously alter their environments, and alternatively to apply technical foresight, experience, cooperation and reasoning to their physical and social environments. The result is rapid social evolution alongside slower biological adaptation. These generate communities, institutions, social structures and pragmatic ethical frameworks. Bookchin's aim is to promote the reconfiguration of these social elements to accommodate wider non-hierarchical perspectives, which in turn will provide a clearer vision of how environmental problems are created, identified and solved. Ecological conflicts will be resolved by a holistic consideration of economic, cultural, ethnic, gender and other conflicts.

Generally expressed in terms of duties or responsibilities, social ecology seeks to ensure social justice in the broadest sense for entities that are not considered adequately, or consistently, by other ethical frameworks. Given the scale of injustices, it is pragmatic to prioritise attention to:

- all humans, particularly the powerless;
- all species, particularly the most threatened;
- aspects of the inanimate world such as natural resources, particularly the most scarce.

Social ecology argues for the transformation of human affairs from market-driven societies into non-hierarchical and cooperative communities. This reconstruction requires careful integration, incorporating social, political, ethical and scientific insights (Bookchin 1994, 2007). He identifies a route towards this reconstruction of social relations by countering competition by collaboration. Focusing initially on the organisational dimensions of people, Bookchin proposes a step-by-step process, based on cooperative social organisation, in which human communities identify common interests. Such communities or municipalities would successively be knitted together, or confederated, into ever-larger networks that gradually would overtake the responsibilities of nation-states.

The result ultimately would be an 'ecological society' composed of a 'commune of communes' with property belonging to the community as a whole, rather than to individual producers or a nation-state (more recent views on this are discussed in Chapter 9). For the individuals in such a society, he envisages an embedding of social concerns in which 'the collective interest is inseparable from the personal, the public interest from the private, the political interest from the social' (Bookchin 1993, 372). Bookchin argues that this form of decentralised direct democracy can provide timely responses to emerging environmental issues, or avoid them in the first place by wise and shared decision-making.

4.2.1 Challenges and critiques of social ecology

While social and deep ecology share certain perspectives and goals, they are constructed on distinct foundations. Naess sought to identify and coalesce shared ideas from multiple disciplines – sometimes with competing criteria and dilemmas for action – while Bookchin sought more fundamentally to create an internally-consistent framework. As a result, some of the critiques (and defences) of these biospheric ethics are different. Naess's deep ecology ethic highlights shared intuitions, but may appear less coherent, precise and defensible than that of Bookchin; on the other hand, social ecology makes bold claims that demand empirical confirmation and commitment.

Bookchin's primary assertion – that hierarchies necessarily generate environmental crises – requires careful verification, because his solution is radical and demanding (i.e., the reorganisation of human societies along cooperative 'communitarian' lines). While hierarchies are evident throughout modern societies and can be blamed for numerous examples of misdirected attentions and unjust consequences, it is not immediately obvious whether positive examples of non-hierarchical communities can be identified. Bookchin suggests that biological ecosystems represent such horizontally-organised and mutually dependent networks, but an equally common (and possibly valid) interpretation stresses the competition between life forms, for example in the Darwinian concept of 'survival of the fittest' (Light 1998).

Human history and archaeology can reveal numerous cases of mutual aid in human interactions. Indeed, a mid-twentieth-century view of native American life was that indigenous peoples had a keener sense of their interdependence with other species than European settlers did.[5] Their co-existence with the animals and plants of their environments varied across the geographical regions they shared, and tribal groupings confederated or faded as mutual needs or opportunities were identified.

Taking such claims further, the socio-political view of 'anarcho-primitivism' argues that early human hunter-gatherer societies were relatively free of social hierarchies, and consequently were more free, cooperative and ecologically sustainable than modern societies. Its proponents, such as John Zerzan (but not, notably, Bookchin), identify primitive social groupings as the model to emulate, encouraging a turning away from 'civilisation' (literally, society and culture based on city life, and particularly on technologies that enable this).

On the other hand, subsequent environmental historians have highlighted the frequent confrontations between indigenous communities over food, water and material resources in some environments, and the ample availability – and sometimes profligate wastage – of resources in other places and times (e.g., salmon and wood on the northwest Pacific coast, and bison on the Great Plains) (Hughes 2002; Penna 2010).

A second important critique of social ecology concerns the feasibility of its recommended course of action. Given the present state of human societies and individual preferences, is it conceivable that an 'ecological society' founded on mutual support and egalitarian relations can be achieved? Key questions relate to how the transition could be effected, and whether each stage in the process would allow a degree of stability and social confidence to extend cooperation further.

A third dimension of criticism concerns potential alternatives to communitarianism as a viable approach to dealing with ecological problems. Free market economies and international policy agreements have evolved rapidly to address some contemporary environmental concerns. For instance, discovery during the 1980s of an 'ozone hole', or depletion of ozone concentration in the upper atmosphere, led to national legislation in developed countries to ban the use of certain chemical aerosols that had contributed to it. The Montreal Protocol (1985) also agreed trade barriers combined with grace periods to restrict the use of chlorofluorocarbons (CFC) in 'developing countries'.[6] Note that, along with evident cooperation associated with such agreements, there is a degree of hierarchical imposition of constraints and penalties on at least some parties. As with all the cases we cite in this book, the ethics of such problem-solving requires careful scrutiny.

There are numerous examples of legal restrictions on environmentally-damaging activities as the principal tactics of ensuring ecological sustainability. These include whole classes of constraint that oppose the freedoms of individuals, companies and other organisations to do as they wish: legislation to prevent disposal of dangerous chemicals into rivers, waste dumps or atmosphere; safety criteria for production, transport and consumption of foods; laws to restrict sales of energy-intensive light bulbs, or to encourage construction using low-insulation materials; and international participation in 'carbon trading' as a means of monitoring and capping the world-wide production of carbon dioxide, the highest-volume 'greenhouse gas'. Supporters of such measures argue that, while sometimes too little and too late, they can in principle respond adequately to unexpected crises, while causing relatively little disruption to modern economic organisation and ways of life. Challenges to this complacency are the focus of Chapter 7.

4.2.2 Popular expressions of biospherism

Both deep ecology and social ecology identify features of modern societies as causes of environmental degradation. In this respect, they both support a spectrum of activities that have shared cultural, economic and social targets.

The cultural dimensions focus on popular confidences and trusts. Belief in guaranteed technological progress, for example, is nearly universal in modern societies (Marx and Mazlish 1996). A related target for deep and social ecologists is the reliance of economics on continued growth, which they argue is unsustainable: products, markets, and resources to supply them, cannot expand indefinitely. Encouraged by continual evolution of consumer products, this trust nevertheless systematically neglects the side-effects or 'externalities', particularly when they affect environments or lives that are distant in time or place. Consumerism, an expression of these confidences, consequently is a perennial target of a biospheric perspective.

Biospherical concerns also identify free-market economics as a powerful force that works against human and environmental well-being. Globalisation, they argue, reinforces economic and political hierarchies that rely on 'marginal' communities, and tend to disempower these minority interests (Klein 2014). As discussed in Chapter 7, the role of corporate ethics consolidates such injustices.

The social critique by biospheric ethicists centres on the complacency and self-interestedness of individuals, groups and organisations. Altering lifestyles is demanding, and tends to resist adequate environmental measures.

In their place, biospherism promotes a degree of cooperation in contesting these aspects of modern society, if not necessarily in achieving more sustainable

FIGURE 4.1 a) Anti-globalisation protest at G8 meeting, Heiligendamm, 2007. (Creative Commons license.); b) World Climate March poster, Paris, 2015. (John Englart photo, Creative Commons license: http://tinyurl.com/ycjymj7n.

human activities. Active discussion, opposition and protest are important features of contemporary biospherically-motivated activities. Examples of popular opposition to established ways of life have proliferated since the early 1970s. Friends of the Earth and Greenpeace attracted wide popular support for protests that steadily moved toward environmental issues (Section 2.3.2). The global perspective increasingly has seeded more recent campaigns such as anti-globalisation protests, which have grown since the late 1980s, and especially since the turn of the twenty-first century. The various means of expressing this opposition, and implementing the aims of biospherism towards effective environmental solutions, are discussed in the following four chapters.

There are abundant examples of biospheric actions that go beyond education, dialogue, rhetoric and protest, however. In terms of individual guidance, deep and social ecology cannot be cleanly demarcated, but we might argue that the 'deep' perspective promotes examples of ecologically sound individual attitudes and behaviours, while the 'social' perspective is illustrated by actions and initiatives that in some respect encourage egalitarian cooperation or at least social participation and cooperation.

Exemplary behaviours are common in the 'Green' movement – a vague term that arguably includes both deep and social perspectives, as well as more limited ecocentric and enlightened anthropocentric orientations. Consider the individual self-sufficient organic farmer, the flat-dweller who installs energy-efficient technologies, or the enthusiast who builds her own wind turbine from scrap materials. All are examples of personal actions that have a negligible overall effect on resolving environmental problems but which, in combination, can be profound. They can be justified by a version of Kant's reflexivity argument: serving as examples of good behaviour, these individuals can encourage others to do the same or more.

Community-oriented actions and initiatives map more closely, perhaps, onto the social ecology perspective. The distinction may be minor and unrecognised, but 'green' activities that foster cooperation and mutual dependence may grow from individual zeal. The examples above have equivalents that rely on social interaction: a neighbourhood or apartment community that installs shared solar panels or water-conservation equipment; an organic farm allotment, in which surpluses feed not just the collective farmers, but a wider receptive community; or, a 'maker' community, in which techniques of repurposing old equipment are disseminated to other enthusiasts online or in shared working spaces. More extended experiences of communalism may also be scaled up. So-called 'eco-communities', although often promoted by local government, land developers or builders, can also be fostered and sustained by residents. Such developments may incorporate ethical principles in their design and operation, such as having positive local environmental outcomes (for example, promoting species and habitat diversity), and creating accommodation for residents of different income levels and household size.

4.3 Appropriate and inappropriate technologies

So far, the question of technology and its role in environmental problems and solutions has appeared between the lines of this text. Chapter 3 addressed it indirectly. The discussion of anthropocentrism hinted that human innovation created new problems, but also powers to solve those problems. By contrast, the chosen life's work of Schweitzer took place in African environments devoid of modern conveniences and even high-quality medical tools. By implication, technology was not an essential feature of his reverence for nature, or of the life well lived. Leopold's Land Ethic confronted the negative aspects of technology more directly. He bemoaned the growing dependence on technologies for human convenience, especially when they affected natural environments. He extended this criticism to environments that were human-managed or human-designed, particularly the practices of large-scale American farming enterprises.

This section, however, addresses technological questions more critically. Both deep ecology and social ecology extend the concerns of Leopold and Carson. Where those voices hinted at negative economic and political dimensions of technologies, Naess and Bookchin make more overt links. Some deleterious environmental aspects of technology, they argue, relate to how it is conceived and the purposes for which it is employed. They also suggest that technological solutions are improperly framed and assessed.

4.3.1 Ernst Schumacher and 'intermediate' technologies

Ernst Schumacher, a British economist who spent most of his career as an economic advisor to the country's National Coal Board, developed sensibilities that had much in common with those of Leopold, Naess and Bookchin. A period in Burma had suggested to him that human lifestyles could not be reduced to economic criteria. His use of the phrase 'Buddhist economics' highlighted his view that quality of life required a more holistic and spiritual sense of fulfilment. Schumacher's influential book *Small is Beautiful* argued for this broader perspective on social, environmental and economic issues (Schumacher 1973). As suggested by the title, he presented the case for a rescaling of human activities to better serve human and environmental needs. Both modern economics and technological development, he argued, needed to be recast.

Schumacher identified two flawed models of technology: 'the super-technology of the rich', on the one hand, and 'the primitive technology of bygone ages, but at the same time much simpler, cheaper and freer'. The first was seductive, but also wasteful and poorly distributed. The second was back-breaking and inefficient, but readily available. Drawing on the work of Gandhi, he defined 'intermediate technology' between these two extremes:

> The technology of production by the masses, making use of the best of modern knowledge and experience, is conducive to decentralisation, compatible with the laws of ecology, gentle in its use of scarce resources, and

designed to serve the human person instead of making him the servant of machines ... One can also call it self-help technology, or democratic or people's technology – a technology to which everybody can gain admittance and which is not reserved to those already rich and powerful.

(Schumacher 1973, 128.)

His perspective mirrored views growing in the counterculture (Kirk 2001), and provided a coherent alternative view of how morally defensible technologies should be conceived and valued. Intermediate in cost, complexity and sophistication, they would rely on people of intermediate know-how, and might consequently trade off these attributes by being of intermediate usefulness, rather than hi-tech. Schumacher identified key attributes as small scale, small harm; mixed technologies and design adapted to local circumstances. Examples would include small wind generators similar to those used on American farms between the wars, which could be repaired or even built from scratch from readily-available materials such as wood and wire, or equivalent power-sources reliant on flowing streams.

4.3.2 Appropriate technologies and the biospheric view

Schumacher's notion of intermediate technologies spawned local initiatives and government policy, and was mirrored in the development of the ideas of deep and social ecologies. The term 'intermediate', however, evoked for some audiences connotations of technology unsuited for the affluent world, while the label 'alternative technology' only has currency while a particular example is new and not-yet-popular (it was coined during the energy shortages of the 1970s in America and Europe, when electric cars and solar panels were first identified as alternatives to petroleum–based technologies). The term 'appropriate technology' has proved to be more neutral and longer-lived.[7]

> **Appropriate technology**: a technology adapted to the needs, skills and resources of its users and environments, and that tends to emphasise local autonomy, egalitarianism and sustainability.

The characteristics of appropriate technology, as defined by Schumacher and others, link closely with biospheric perspectives.

First, appropriate technologies support local autonomy and self-sufficiency by encouraging local expertise in design, production and repair. By avoiding reliance on centralised skills and authority, they consequently reduce hierarchies and potential injustices.

Second, such a locally-oriented scale encourages responsive and responsible innovation. Operating on a small scale may make designers of appropriate technologies more alert to users' genuine needs and contexts, and to immediate side-effects.

Third, appropriate technologies encourage diversity, identified by both Naess and Bookchin as an abstract principle or virtue to be promoted. The concept grows from the scientific principle identified by earlier scientific ecologists such as Leopold: species diversity tends to produce more robust ecosystems which can adapt to unexpected perturbations. The idea is also compatible with the notion of 'technological momentum', which argues that the ferment of nascent technologies offers more adaptiveness to social needs than do mature, large-scale technological systems (Hughes 1998). There is, however, a counter-argument against appropriate technologies: by adapting locally to suit context, they are unlikely to benefit from economies of scale, and so may prove more expensive to develop and maintain (Rybczynski 1991).

Fourth, appropriate technologies are likely to be more sustainable in resource usage. By seeking to employ locally-sourced materials, they encourage clever innovation and adaptation to suit local contexts. This principle of having a 'closed loop' system involving production, consumption and recycling was first identified as a basis for sound ecosystems by Leopold.

More pointedly, Naess and Bookchin criticised a particularly seductive understanding of technology as a 'short-cut' to bypass more demanding social change, a notion dubbed 'the technological fix' (Etzioni and Remp 1972).

4.3.3 Technological fixes as alternatives to behavioural change[8]

Reliance on technological approaches for resolving social, political and cultural issues has been a long-standing human strategy and arguably a human trait, but it became a key feature of modern culture over the past century. Rapid innovation generated widespread appreciation of the potential of technologies to improve modern life and modern societies.

The term 'technological fix' was popularised in the 1960s to label a general approach to problem-solving. Its originator, Alvin Weinberg (1915–2006), was a Manhattan Project physicist and engineer whose career was dedicated to developing nuclear reactors and energy policy. As he recalled,

> I began to look upon nuclear energy as a symbol of a new technologically oriented civilization – the ultimate 'technological fix' that would forever eliminate quarrels over scarce raw materials. I coined the phrase 'technological fix' to connote technical inventions that could help resolve predominantly social problems.
>
> *(Weinberg 1994, 150.)*

Technological fix: a term popularised by physicist Alvin Weinberg for a technological solution to a problem traditionally dealt with by social, cultural or political approaches.

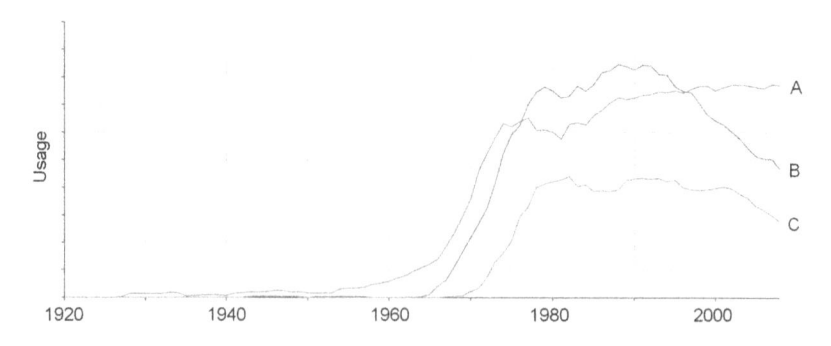

FIGURE 4.2 Modern problem-solving rhetoric: English-language usage of the terms A) 'technological solution', B) 'technological fix' and C) 'technical fix' according to n-gram analysis (Michel, Shen, et al. 2011).

Weinberg's optimism reflected confidence in science and technology, according to which rational direction and technological innovation are the drivers of societal progress. Rather than requiring social transformations or political movements, he claimed, 'the brilliant advances in the technology of energy, of mass production, and of automation have created the affluent society' (Weinberg 1966, 8).

The contentious dimension of technological fixes, however, is the assertion that such solutions may be superior to other means of problem-solving, particularly moral considerations and behavioural adaptation. Indeed, its starkest version suggests that an engineering approach is not only suitable for tackling technological problems but more generally is the most effective technique for diagnosing and resolving social, political and cultural issues. This confidence, or hubris, concerning the relevance of technological solutions to human concerns has been particularly popular for policy-makers, engineers and their organisations in proposals for remediating climate change (Brewer 2007).

The origins of the concept and critiques of the social implications of technology nevertheless pre-dated Weinberg's promotion. From the Great Depression, an American organisation, Technocracy Inc., publicised examples of technological fixes as a general replacement for government. A range of more critical views of the power of technologies to alter societies was expressed in the writings of Lewis Mumford, Jacques Ellul and Herbert Marcuse (Mumford 1934; Ellul 1964; Marcuse 1964).

Weinberg, for instance, acknowledged potential criticisms and admitted that, while technological fixes are simpler than social changes, they tend to create new social problems and sometimes technological side-effects as well. He nevertheless championed technological solutions as 'quick fixes' that would at least buy time for slower-paced and more pervasive social changes. Weinberg cited two examples to suggest the success of the concept: the H-bomb as a means of stifling major wars (if not providing the guaranteed assurance of peace), and the relief of hunger and inequity by the provision of inexpensive and efficient food supplies, distribution and consumer products. Both issues had traditionally been addressed by political policy, education or social transformation, which Weinberg argued produced less predictable outcomes than did technological innovation.

Other claims, drawing upon Weinberg's specific expertise, encouraged optimism among not just technologists but wider publics too – for example, that nuclear technologies could ensure clean and efficient power and avoid longer-term pollution and climate change, a notion later revived by some proponents of climate policy. Broadly similar assertions have been voiced more recently by technology optimists such as Stewart Brand (2009).

On the other hand, Weinberg encouraged an initial dialogue by adopting a diffident stance on such fixes. He distanced himself in his first speeches and articles from examples that others interpreted alternately as either a slippery slope or provocatively naïve: for example, the notion of providing free air conditioners to literally cool down urban tensions in American cities of the late 1960s; or the general provision of *soma* pills to relieve unhappiness, as introduced in Aldous Huxley's *Brave New World*; or even to highlight consumer campaigner Ralph Nader's contention that safer car engineering by corporations might provide quicker reduction of traffic deaths than attempting to change driving behaviours (Weinberg 1966, 9).

As discussed in Chapter 3, a growing cross-section of modern publics became environmentally aware over Weinberg's lifetime. Mass media played an important role in both environmentalism and also in support for technological fixes. While media accounts of pollution episodes increasingly pinned responsibility on short-sighted industries and fuelled public debate about societal reliance on large-scale technological systems, they also promoted confidence in quick solutions such as double-hulled supertankers, plastic packaging that decomposed in sunlight or humidity, and pollution-digesting microbes.

Criticisms of technological fixes became increasingly common while both Naess and Bookchin were developing their deeper social interpretations of environmentalism. Sociologists Eugene Burns and Kenneth Studer (1976) characterised Weinberg's notions of technological fixes as an insupportable faith in the methods of science, and an incremental and myopic approach to problem-solving. Ethicist Max Oelschlaeger (1979) described the notion as a dangerous myth accepted by large companies as much as by the general population.

For an even wider range of environmental theorists, the technological fix was portrayed as hubris, or excessive confidence, regarding human abilities to adequately understand and manage nature through rational means (Uekoetter 2004). As a 'band-aid' solution to problems involving sophisticated systems, technological fixes were argued to both underestimate, and inadequately solve, complex problems. Philosopher Alan Drengson, for example, explored the moral values and religious underpinnings of these wider critical perspectives (Drengson 1995).

The environmental ramifications of technological solutions were more centrally addressed by Naess and Bookchin. Both suggested that the seeming reasonableness of these solutions was largely determined by the framing of the problem (a technique discussed in the next chapter) and, in effect, failed to explore the cultural presuppositions about the nature and potency of technologies. Identifying technological fixes as 'shallow ecology' that values a rapid, targeted solution to a narrowly-defined problem, Naess argued that they promote unrealistic assurance and environmental inaction (Naess and Rothenberg (transl.) 1993).

This criticism about misdirected confidence is central to arguments against so-called geo-engineering, which can be identified as a planet-wide technological fix for anthropogenic climate change. Notional approaches have ranged from the plausible to outrageous, and suggest the spectrum of confidences that underlie these putative solutions. Some geo-engineering approaches are tentative and experimental, such as painting roofs white to reflect sunlight, or cloud-seeding from commercial aircraft to reduce planetary temperature, or to seed oceans with iron powder, which could allow phytoplankton to proliferate with a consequent sequestering of carbon dioxide. These initiatives could be scaled up at relatively low cost, if successful. More ambitious proposals have considered space-borne large mirrors to deflect incoming sunlight, or to convert farmland to 'bright field' crops that reflect sunlight.

> **Geo-engineering**: the intentional human manipulation of environments by technological interventions which have effects on the global scale.

Supporters of the biospheric view argue that such approaches are ethically indefensible.

First, from a consequentialist stance, 'correcting' parameters such as the mean temperature of the Earth, or its average concentration of atmospheric carbon dioxide, is inherently risky. Growing scientific knowledge has revealed the complexity and interdependence of planetary systems involving oceans, atmosphere, land and ecosystems. Even with sophisticated modelling, the effects of planned large-scale perturbations are difficult to predict.

A second point against such technological fixes is that, when applied indiscriminately on a large scale, they are likely to have unequal and unfair effects. Manipulating global temperature, for example, might be particularly deleterious for marginal farmlands, impoverished populations or endangered species. Large-scale technological fixes threaten the deontological principle of justice (see Chapter 2).

A third ethical criticism is that over-confidence in technological solutions may encourage a lessening of individual and collective effort to solve environmental problems, and thereby perpetuate unsustainable practices. For example, if hybrid cars reduce the need for petroleum-based fuel, they may encourage further expansion of vehicles, road networks and car-based lifestyles.

A central concern for biospherical viewpoints is that technological fixes relegate responsibility for solutions to an elite of engineers or planners. This hierarchy of knowledge and power generally endangers weaker parties (e.g., relatively voiceless human populations or other species) and reduces their autonomy. It may concentrate power in the hands of particular social actors (e.g., policy-makers, companies, designers) or regions (e.g., countries) rather than being equitably shared. This pragmatic outcome of placing trust in experts also has implications for individual lifestyles, affecting our personally-adopted virtues and individual sense of responsibilities. In contrast, the biospheric stances of deep and social ecology argue in favour of profound alteration of social organisations, individual attitudes and lifestyles. It suggests that the promises of technological fixes bypass these multiple requirements and provide both unreliable self-confidences and a defusing of moral responsibility.

Given the conflicting attitudes, beliefs and goals concerning our shared environment, the question addressed in subsequent chapters is: how can a shared perspective be promoted and how can a sustainable environment be achieved?

Notes

1 As illustrated by Aldo Leopold's work in game management, it is possible to extend utilitarian consideration beyond human interests alone (e.g., those of hunters and tourists) to include other species (e.g., wolves, deer and trees). Ecological management since the turn of the twenty-first century has extended these sensitivities systematically by identifying 'ecosystem services', i.e., specific benefits exchanged between components of an ecosystem. This may attempt to quantify and optimise, for example, the multiple uses of a forest for wood production, human recreation, deer habitat and carbon capture.
2 One expression of this personal orientation of environmental concerns is the so-called NIMBY (Not In My Back Yard) perspective. Our struggle to acknowledge and act upon climate change is another (see Chapters 5 and 6).
3 The term entered German (*Vorsorgeprinzip*) and then English usage from the 1970s.
4 This claim has similarities to popular notions of the 'trickle-down' approach of supply-side economics implemented, for example, in policies of the Reagan administration in the USA and the Thatcher government in the UK: it argues that by favouring powerful and innovative (and even, perhaps, narrowly self-interested) entities, benefits will nevertheless accrue to those less able to alter their shared living environments. Corporate perspectives and ethics are explored in Chapter 7.
5 For instance, a well-known television and print advertisement campaign, known as the 'Crying Indian', popularised the problem of littering by consumers. It was produced by a non-profit organisation, 'Keep America Beautiful', founded in 1953 by a consortium of US corporations. The campaign was launched on Earth Day in 1971, and was disseminated by public service advertising. The example supports Bookchin's contention that the effects and deeper causes of environmental harm are often inadequately assessed.
6 Note that the term 'developing countries' implies a tendency, or even a moral imperative, towards economic and technological change in the style of the Western model.
7 The term 'sustainable technology' has grown in popularity since the 1990s to challenge it. The phrase has been appropriated by companies and policy-makers as often as by grassroots environmentalists, and arguably is sometimes employed as a form of 'greenwash' to label restricted examples of 'sustainability', as discussed in Chapter 7.
8 Portions of this section are developed further in an article, Johnston, S.F. (2018) 'Alvin Weinberg and the promotion of the technological fix'. *Technology and Culture* 59(2), in press.

References

Bookchin, M. (1987) 'Social ecology versus deep ecology: a challenge for the ecology movement', *Green Perspectives: Newsletter of the Green Program Project*, nos. 4–5.

Bookchin, M. (1988) 'Social ecology versus deep ecology: a challenge for the ecology movement', *Socialist Review* 18 (July–Sept.): 9–29.

Bookchin, M. (1993) 'What is social ecology?', in M.E. Zimmerman, ed., *Environmental Philosophy: From Animal Rights to Radical Ecology*. Eaglewood Cliffs NJ: Prentice Hall, 354–73.

Bookchin, M. (1994) *The Philosophy of Social Ecology: Essays on Dialectical Naturalism*. Montreal: Black Rose Books.

Bookchin, M. (2005) *The Ecology of Freedom: The Emergence and Dissolution of Hierarchy*. Oakland: AK Press.

Bookchin, M. (2007) *Social Ecology and Communalism*. Edinburgh: AK Press.

Brand, S. (2009) *Whole Earth Discipline: An Ecopragmatist Manifesto*. London: Atlantic.

Brewer, P.G. (2007) 'Evaluating a technological fix for climate', *Proceedings of the National Academy of Sciences of the United States of America* 24: 9915–16.

Burns, E.M. and Studer, K.E. (1976) 'Reply to Alvin M. Weinberg', *Research Policy* 5: 201–2.

Devall, B. (2002) 'The deep, long range ecology movement: 1960–2000', *Ethics and the Environment* 6.1: 18–41.

Drengson, A., Devall, B. and Schroll, M.A. (2011) 'The deep ecology movement: origins, development, and future prospects (toward a transpersonal ecosophy)', *International Journal of Transpersonal Studies* 30, 1–2: 101–17.

Drengson, A.R. (1995) *The Practice of Technology: Exploring Technology, Ecophilosophy, and Spiritual Disciplines for Vital Links*. Albany: State University of New York.

Ellul, J. (1964) *The Technological Society*. New York: Knopf.

Etzioni, A. and Remp, R. (1972) 'Technological "shortcuts" to social change', *Science Magazine* 175.4017: 31–8.

Hughes, J.D. (2002) *The Environmental History of the World: Humankind's Changing Role in the Community of Life*. London: Routledge.

Hughes, T.P. (1998) 'Technological momentum'. In M.R. Smith and L. Marx, eds, *Does Technology Drive History?*, 101–114. Cambridge MA: MIT Press.

Johnston, S.F. (2018) 'Alvin Weinberg and the promotion of the technological fix', *Technology and Culture* 59.2 (in press).

Kirk, A.G. (2001) 'Machines of Loving Grace: Appropriate Technology, Environment, and the Counterculture'. In M. Doyle and P. Braunstein, *Imagine Nation: The American Counterculture of the 1960s and 1970s*. London: Routledge.

Klein, N. (2014) *This Changes Everything: Capitalism Versus the Climate*. New York: Allen Lane.

Leopold, A. (1968) 'The Land Ethic'. In *A Sand County* Almanac, 201–26. Oxford: Oxford University Press.

Light, A. (Ed.) (1998) *Social Ecology After Bookchin*. New York: Guildford Press.

Marcuse, H. (1964) *One-Dimensional Man: Studies in the Ideology of Advanced Industrial Society*. London: Routledge.

Marx, L. and Mazlish, B. (Eds) (1996) *Progress: Fact or Illusion?* Ann Arbor: University of Michigan Press.

Michel, J.-B., Shen, Y.K., Aiden, A.P., Veres, A., Gray, M.K., The Google Books Team, Pickett, J.P., Hoiberg, D., Clancy, D., Norvig, P., Orwant, J., Pinker, S., Nowak, M.A. and Aiden, E.L. (2011) 'Quantitative analysis of culture using millions of digitized books', *Science* 331.6014: 176–82.

Mumford, L. (1934) *Technics and Civilization*. New York: Harcourt, Brace and Co.
Naess, A. (1973) 'The shallow and the deep, long-range ecology movement. A summary', *Inquiry* 16: 95–100.
Naess, A. (1995) 'Equality, sameness, and rights'. In G. Sessions, *Deep Ecology for the 21st Century: Readings on the Philosophy and Practice of the New Environmentalism*, 222. Boston: Shambhala Publications.
Naess, A. and Drengson, A. (Eds) (2005) *The Selected Works of Arne Naess*. Dordrecht: Springer.
Naess, A. and Rothenberg, D. (transl.) (1993) *Ecology, Community, and Lifestyle: Outline of an Ecosophy*. Cambridge: Cambridge University Press.
Oelschlaeger, M. (1979) 'The myth of the technological fix', *Southwestern Journal of Philosophy* 10.1: 43–53.
Penna, A.N. (2010) *The Human Footprint: A Global Environmental History*. Chichester: Wiley-Blackwell.
Rybczynski, W. (1991) *Paper Heroes: Appropriate Technology: Panacea or Pipe Dream*. New York: Penguin.
Schumacher, E.F. (1973) *Small is Beautiful: A Study of Economics as if People Mattered*. London: Sphere Books.
Sessions, G. (1987) 'The deep ecology movement: A review', *Environmental Review* 11.2: 105–25.
Uekoetter, F. (2004) 'Solving air pollution problems once and for all: the potential and the limits of technological fixes'. In L. Rosner, *The Technological Fix: How People Use Technology to Create and Solve* Problems, 155–74. New York: Routledge.
Watson, R. (1983) 'A critique of anti-anthropocentric biocentrism', *Environmental Ethics* 5.3: 245–56.
Weinberg, A.M. (1966) 'Can technology replace social engineering?' *Bulletin of the Atomic Scientists* 22.10: 4–7.
Weinberg, A.M. (1994) *The First Nuclear Era: The Life and Times of a Technological Fixer*. New York: American Institute of Physics Press.

5
ENVIRONMENTAL BEHAVIOURAL CHANGE AND THE PSYCHOLOGY OF INFLUENCE

Whereas the previous three chapters have concentrated on the varieties of environmental ethics that have emerged since The Enlightenment, the next five are concerned with different approaches to environmental behavioural change and their ethical implications. Chapters 5 and 6 address the psychological principles, strategies and tactics which governments, non-governmental organisations (NGOs), businesses and other organisations employ in their attempts to influence environmental attitudes and behaviours. With particular reference to climate change, Chapter 5 identifies barriers to environmental behavioural change based on recent research in fields such as environmental psychology and environmental communication. For each of these barriers, the ways in which we might overcome them are discussed, along with a consideration of virtues that could help individuals and communities to achieve these goals. This culminates in a distinctive subset of environmental virtues which complements those – such as reverence for life and respect for nature – that have so far emerged in the book. Chapter 6 looks at ethical issues associated with the psychology of influence, with a specific focus on the practices of social marketing and what is known as 'nudge'.

To begin with, it is helpful to be clear about the meaning of 'communication'. There should be no mystery surrounding this concept, at least not in the sense it is employed in this context. Borrowing from Harold Lasswell (1948) and Carl Hovland et al. (1953), several key questions identifying the basic features of communication can be articulated:

> **Who?** Who is communicating? What is the source of the message? Examples include news media, governments, corporations, NGOs and pressure groups, political parties, academics or other researchers, artists, teachers, religious leaders, community leaders, and people directly affected by environmental problems.

Why? What is the purpose of communicating? What does the communicator hope to achieve? If a distinction can be drawn between messages intended to inform and messages intended to persuade then this question is more nuanced than a first glance might suggest. Information will change beliefs and changes in beliefs will sometimes change behaviours, and persuasion is similarly an attempt to change beliefs and behaviours. The term 'persuasion' does though imply the partial presentation of information and deliberate use of disempowering tactics, and more will be said about the ethical significance of this distinction in the next chapter. In this book our interest concerns communication that aims to change behaviours and/or attitudes.

What? What is the meaning of the message being communicated? As well as the general subject matter of the argument, explanation, story and so on, a message's meaning refers to how the topic in question is being framed. (Roughly speaking 'framing' means the aspects of an issue the communicator chooses to emphasise – a more precise definition and a discussion of the importance of framing in environmental communication will follow shortly.)

How? How is this meaning being communicated? This covers style and genre, as well as the channel or medium. Examples of genre include stories, examples, personal testimonies, images and sounds; and aspects of style include figurative language, vocabulary, use of slogans and tone (tragedy, comedy, horror). Examples of channels are books and articles (academic and popular), documentaries, fiction (novels, films), other art forms, letters, blogs, websites, advertisements (and other marketing), press releases, speeches/lectures/sermons, meetings and negotiations, dialogues, debates, displays (e.g., in museums), posters, protest banners, leaflets/flyers/business cards, tattoos and clothing, and non-verbal communication. Of course, genre, style and channel all carry meaning as well, and, as will be discussed, can themselves be employed as framing devices.

Who? What audience(s) is the message intended for, and what unintended audiences might receive it? Examples include demographic groupings (including geographical, cultural, religious beliefs, political beliefs, gender, age and income), and different settings in which the communication takes place (one-to-one interactions, small groups, organisations, communities, formal settings (such as education), national level (via mass media), and also 'intrapersonal' – communicating with ourselves).

A further pair of questions can be added to highlight something important for assessing the effectiveness or potential effectiveness of an act of communication:

When? Where? What's the broad context of the communication?

In most respects, however, answers will have been provided already by the other questions. For example, persuading the American right (as opposed to American

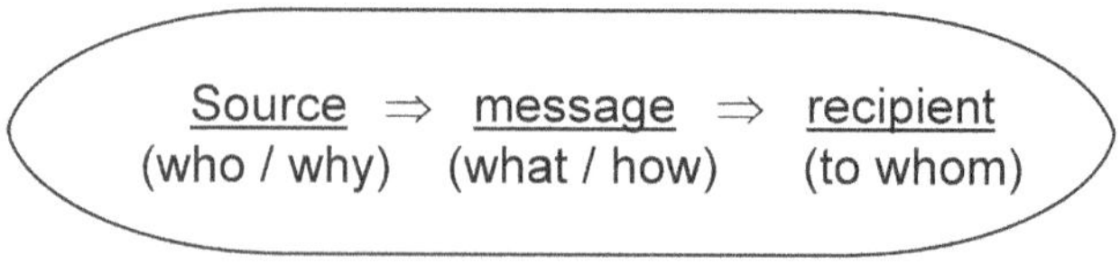

```
  Source   ⇒  message   ⇒  recipient
(who / why)  (what / how)   (to whom)
```

FIGURE 5.1 A basic model of communication. (Original by authors.)

moderates) of the value of policies mitigating climate change will require distinct content, style and channels, and will also be dependent on who is delivering the message. A consideration of these variables should, to all intents and purposes, fill in the contextual detail – the 'where and when'.

Environmental communication – a subdivision of applied communication – subsumes these questions under an umbrella question: is it effective? What degree of success does the communicative act in question have in achieving its goal of changing the behaviour and/or attitudes of its intended audience? The simple model of communication provided helps cement an initial assumption: that effectiveness is a function of the right match between these elements: source, purpose, content, form, channel and intended audience.

To summarise, the socio-psychological principles of behavioural change discussed here serve three purposes. First, in the broad context of a book about environmental ethics and behavioural change they are important to know about. Second, they inform the discussion of the ethics of social marketing and nudge found in Chapter 6. Third, they add psychological depth to other ethical and behavioural change perspectives introduced and analysed in this book, perhaps most notably by contextualising some of the virtues emerging as central to contemporary environmental ethics.

5.1 Some fundamentals of attitude and behaviour change theories

Since the end of the Second World War, numerous theories of, and approaches to, the psychology of influence and persuasive communication have been developed. Examples include: the 'message-learning approach' (Hovland et al. 1953); Cognitive Dissonance Theory (Festinger 1957); the Theory of Planned Behaviour (Ajzen 1991); and the Elaboration Likelihood Model (Petty and Cacioppo 1996). Also important to mention are theories of social power and leadership (for example, French and Raven 1959; MacGregor Burns 1978). The influence of these ideas on the theory and practice of environmental communication is of course huge, and details of some of them will be explored as we begin to address barriers to environmental behavioural change. Initially though, the importance of two foundational ideas emerging from the rich history of research in this area will be explained: dual process theory and framing.

5.1.1 Dual process theory

Dual process theory has become widely accepted in recent decades. Its basic claim is that individuals process information at two levels: one that is quick, implicit and intuitive, and another that is slow, explicit and reflective. What Amos Tversky and Daniel Kahneman (1974; see also Kahneman 2012, 20–1) call 'System 1' is experienced as automatic and fairly effortless, while 'System 2' is self-conscious, experienced as under our control, and involves effort and concentration (see Chapter 2.2.2). In terms of our personal experiences it is easy enough to understand the difference between these two processes. For example, contrast the experience of responding to the questions 'What is 2 + 2?' and 'What is 23 × 48?' Or consider the difference between a habitual action like buying your usual brand of coffee at the supermarket and weighing up price and quality variables after having decided to try something new.

Tversky and Kahneman's System 1/System 2 division is one among several theories that are variations on this theme,[1] and the ethical and practical implications of this duality are reflected in the Ancient Greek distinction between rhetoric and dialectic. In the 1980s Richard Petty and John Cacioppo argued that divergent twentieth-century theories such as Carl Hovland's message-learning approach (1953) and Leon Festinger's Cognitive Dissonance Theory (1957) have not been discredited, but can co-exist because they are situation-specific. As a 'framework for thinking about' an array of credible approaches they identified 'peripheral' and 'central' routes to attitude change. The difference between them

> has to do with the extent to which the attitude change that results from a message is due to active thinking about … the issue. According to the central view, thinking about issue-relevant information is the most direct determinant of the direction and amount of attitude change produced. On the other hand, according to the peripheral view, attitude change is the result of peripheral "*persuasion cues.*" Persuasion cues are factors or motives inherent in the persuasion setting that are sufficient to produce an initial attitude change *without any active thinking about the attributes of the issue or the object under consideration.*
> (Petty and Cacioppo 1996, 256.)[2]

'Persuasion cues' include what are known as 'heuristics', and some of the most influential work on these has also been carried out by Tversky and Kahneman. A heuristic is a simple decision-making procedure that enables speed of thought and action. In place of a thorough appraisal of the available information to inform a decision, attention automatically alights on highly selective variables that experience has shown to have particular relevance to the issue at hand.

Heuristic: A simple procedure – similar to a 'rule of thumb' – whereby decisions are made quickly in accordance with a limited range of familiar situational features.

Through investigating typical errors in our thinking (Tversky and Kahneman 1974; Kahneman 2012); biases in our social behaviour (Janis 1982; Milgram 1974); the role of emotion in decision-making (Epstein 1998; Damasio 1994, 2000; Brady 2013), or through long-established rhetorical ploys (Aristotle 1991), and sales and marketing techniques (Levine 2006; Cialdini 2007), a wide range of heuristics and other biases has been identified. It has been argued that an understanding of as many of these as possible is important for the development of epistemic virtues (see Chapter 2) and therefore for our personal development (Facione et al. 1995; Hanscomb 2017), but for the purposes of this book a selection will be explained – including the 'confirmation bias', the 'contrast effect', 'social proof', the 'default bias' and heuristics based on liking and forms of authority – as they become relevant to barriers to environmental behavioural change.

Before moving on to a discussion of framing, two further points about dual processing models will be made. First, theorists tend to be divided on the value of System 1 thinking. Tversky and Kahneman focus on it as a source of predictable cognitive errors to be avoided, and Hank Davis (2009) sees our automatic employment of heuristics as a deep-seated and dangerous impediment to, in particular, causal reasoning. On the other hand, an appropriate application of heuristics in everyday decision-making is seen by some to 'make us smart' (Gigerenzer et al. 1999). Decisions based on them are, after all, better than chance, and they are themselves capable of being educated through experience and reflection (Epstein 1998).

However, even if System 1 does, in a sense, 'make us smart', its inflexibility and habitual non-voluntary nature can make us highly vulnerable to being unconsciously influenced by professional persuaders (in commercial marketing and politics for instance). These people understand our dominant heuristics and how to manipulate them. As will be discussed in the next chapter, manipulation of this kind, especially when applied to social issues, creates a tension with the deontological emphasis on autonomy, and can be seen to undermine virtues such as critical thinking and good judgement.

The second point to make about dual processing is that more or less any example of communication will include System 1 appeals, no matter how rational or direct it is attempting to be. Consider these two passages:

Passage 1:
   Continued emission of greenhouse gases will cause further warming and long-lasting changes in all components of the climate system, increasing the likelihood of severe, pervasive and irreversible impacts on people and ecosystems. Limiting climate change would require substantial and sustained reductions in greenhouse gas emissions which, together with adaptation, can limit climate change risks.

Passage 2:
   … emissions are rising so rapidly that unless something radical changes … 2 degrees now looks like a utopian dream. … We don't know exactly what

a 4 degree Celsius world would look like, but even the best-case scenario is likely to be calamitous. Four degrees of warming could raise global sea levels by 1 or possibly even 2 meters by 2100 … This would drown some island nations such as the Maldives and Tuvalu, and inundate many coastal areas from Ecuador to Brazil to the Netherlands to much of California and the northeastern United States, as well as huge swathes of South and Southeast Asia … Meanwhile, brutal heatwaves that can kill tens of thousands of people, even in wealthy countries, would become unremarkable summer events … The heat would also cause staple crops to suffer dramatic yield losses across the globe … this at a time when demand will be surging due to population growth … When you add ruinous hurricanes, raging wildfires, fisheries collapses, widespread disruption to water supplies, extinctions, and globe-trotting diseases to the mix, it is … difficult to imagine that a peaceful, ordered society could be sustained.

The first is from the IPCC's Synthesis Report (2014, 8), the second from Naomi Klein's book *This Changes Everything* (2015, 13–14). They contain roughly the same message, but clearly Klein's style is more detailed and emotive, employing terms such as 'calamitous', are 'brutal' and 'ruinous', and conjuring images of ravaged coastlines, drowning islands, starvation, burning homes, pandemics, social and economic chaos. Emotional responses, such as guilt and, in this case, fear, involve an automaticity that epitomises System 1 processing, and indeed emotions have sometimes been explicitly characterised as types of heuristic (Damasio 2000). There is little doubt about the System 1 appeal being made in this extract and, by contrast, the IPCC quotation is making no such appeal. The message is just as serious, but the language and tone academic and does not distract us from the direct meaning of the information provided. However, a person reading this is likely to be aware (or wanting to become aware) of its source, and this knowledge will influence how they engage with it. Many will accept the authority of the IPCC and all that it represents, and some will not. In either case, the message will not be read in a neutral manner but will instead be biased by the reader's perception of the author's credibility.

Maybe we can imagine substantially neutral pieces of information (such as an instruction manual), but for the most part messages will contain elements that appeal to both System 1 and System 2. Advertisements tend to be weighted towards System 1, scientific and other academic writing towards System 2, but to suggest in the latter case that System 1 has no part to play is to overlook the communicative context in which all messages are located, and the extraordinary extent to which knowledge is contested. Implicitly or explicitly the majority of information forms part of an argument rather than simply being an uncontroversial explanation. An argument is a claim (or series of claims) supported by a set of reasons for why we should believe that claim. Arguments, in that case, imply arguers, and arguers have agendas, biases and are prone to error. If an issue will affect us in some way we want to be sure we are being presented with the truth, and in the absence of personal expertise (as is the case for most people on complex issues like climate change), we will look to the context of the claim – including its source – in an attempt to judge what we should and should not believe.

Amidst the complexity of everyday or non-expert decision-making, heuristics will play some kind of a part for most of us most of the time. They are a simplistic response to contextual cues, and at the very least will function quite automatically as guidance for how we should be prioritising our attention.

5.1.2 Framing

The important notion of framing was introduced in Chapter 1, and hinted at via examples in previous chapters. According to Robert Entman (1993, 52):

> to frame is to select some aspects of perceived reality and make them more salient in a communicating text, in such a way as to promote a particular problem definition, causal interpretation, moral evaluation, and/or treatment recommendation for the item described.[3]

To frame something is to take a particular angle on it, and in a sense it is hard to imagine how any piece of communication could not involve some kind of framing (see Sunstein 2015, 512–13). Especially with respect to complex entities or events, any definition, explanation or argument will be selective to some degree, and so 'framing' can simply be understood as referring to the partial and provisional nature of knowledge. Initially, then, the importance of being familiar with the term 'framing' is as a reminder of the value of questions such as: 'What agenda or bias does the message source have?' and 'How will this message be received by its audiences?'

This broad use of the term can be contrasted with Entman's more specific meaning. For Entman, framing refers to a, usually deliberate, attempt to educate or manipulate specified audiences by the tailoring of messages. Framing is often discussed in the context of news media: referring to political and other biases (held by news agencies and target audiences) determining the angle for reporting on a story; and to the background 'agenda setting' that determines which stories are considered newsworthy at all, and how much coverage they receive.

Anti-vivisection campaigns have been an important expression of biocentric ethics since the late nineteenth century, as explored in Chapter 3. Then and now, an advertisement for an anti-vivisection movement usually frames the issue in terms of needless cruelty and animal suffering. However, environmental communication concerned with, say, wilderness preservation or restoration, tends to employ a variety of frames. This can widen the message's reach to a range of audiences with various sensitivities and principles – for example, biocentric or ecocentric values – or it can build an argument by providing multiple reasons for supporting a cause. A recent flyer produced by the Woodland Trust (a UK-based charity), asking for donations towards restoration work on the Loch Arkaig Forest in North West Scotland, describes it as 'steeped in history, teeming with wildlife, and under threat'.[4] The copy focuses on three features of the forest: its animals, its trees (along with lichens and mosses) and its cultural history (the ancient home of Clan Cameron, Bonnie Prince Charlie's missing gold and sightings of kelpies are mentioned). A broad frame of the forest containing secrets, being mysterious and undiscovered, links all three of these, but it is noteworthy that several perspectives are taken in what is a relatively brief piece of communication.

Ancient woodland is important to people for a number of reasons, and this is typical of environmental issues. We are now familiar with there being a wide range of environmental ethics, and if we add to this the considerable variation in the degree to which people will be engaged by even those ethical issues that they agree with, we can see why framing takes on particular importance in environmental communication.

5.1.3 Framing and narrative in An Inconvenient Truth

Framing in this more specific sense, however, is widespread and not just a phenomenon of news media. Messages transmitted by all of the communication channels previously listed will often be self-consciously framed and, as mentioned, there is a pronounced need for this with environmental issues. The best known and most influential climate change documentary to date – *An Inconvenient Truth* (Guggenheim 2006), essentially Al Gore's global warming lecture – skilfully employs a variety of heuristics and takes meticulous care with its frames. Unlike other documentaries on the topic (such as *The Age of Stupid* (Armstrong 2009), *No Impact Man* (Gabbert and Schein 2009), or *Demain* (Dion and Laurent 2015)), radical solutions to the problem are downplayed or ignored. Global warming is 'inconvenient' for government, industry and citizens, but the implication is that things can carry on more or less as normal so long as a collective effort is made to curb emissions. *An Inconvenient Truth* primarily appeals to that part of the American public willing to recognise a problem they were ignorant of or have been avoiding, but less willing to see global capitalism and consumer culture as part of the cause. Abolition of slavery (as discussed in Chapter 3), the suffragette movement and overthrowing apartheid are sources of hope for positive large-scale societal change that will be familiar to the film's audience, as will the technological triumph of the Apollo programme. Through these analogies, a response to climate change is framed as progressive rather than revolutionary, as a source of national pride rather than collective guilt, and as something to which changes in some patterns of use and consumption (combined with some technological fixes) rather than a significant reappraisal of our values is an appropriate response.

In contrast, the New York-based anti-consumption activist Reverend Billy (Talen 2016, 15–16) calls for interventions analogous to the brave direct action and civil disobedience (a form of behavioural change discussed in Chapter 9) of people such as Rosa Parks.[5] Unlike Gore, Reverend Billy is advocating a profound shift from consumerist lifestyles to a more spiritual orientation, making demanding and dramatic actions a more suitable frame.

An Inconvenient Truth explicitly frames global warming as a 'moral issue', but far less explicit is the anthropocentric nature of the morality Al Gore has in mind.

Social stability and the well-being of future human generations play a large part in his argument. Polar bears are primarily used to illustrate melting icecaps rather than to highlight the impact of climate change on other species, and in light of the conservative nature of the film this is to be expected. *An Inconvenient Truth* is well made and has been a hugely influential eco-documentary, but along with demonstrating its persuasive powers, analysing the frames it employs also reveals its limitations.

Gore employs the language of deontology and utilitarianism, but virtue theory, though often implicit, is the film's most prevalent ethic. Important for the documentary's impact is Gore's trustworthiness: as a politician, as someone familiar with the science, and as someone like us. Global warming is carefully framed in relation to each of these. It is shown to be real and man-made, as something demanding a political response, and as something demanding a personal response. Each of these features is then embodied in Gore's character and biography, and a significant part of the film's appeal can be credited to how seamlessly it manages this. Thomas Rosteck and Thomas Frentz (2009) have argued that this achievement is the upshot of a particular narrative structure known as the 'monomyth' or 'hero quest'. It is a plot that sees the individual called away from familiar territory and then confronting various dangers, challenges and temptations before reaching his goal and finally returning home. Endings vary but importantly involve some kind of transformation of the hero, his community, or of the world as a whole. The journey undertaken is usually geographical, but is psychological as well, and can be taken as a metaphor for psychological and philosophical growth.

Mythologist Joseph Campbell (1949) claims there are versions of the hero quest story in most cultures, and hypothesises that it is revealing of something fundamental about the human condition. Consciously or unconsciously this is a narrative form many of us are familiar with (for example, the stories of Jesus, Buddha, Jonah, Heart of Darkness, Lord of the Rings and Toy Story), and one that facilitates a dramatic sequencing of events. Rosteck and Frenz claim that in *An Inconvenient Truth* an otherwise straightforward lecture on science and politics becomes something altogether more engaging through employing this 'larger frame'. The particulars of Gore's personal life (upbringing, family tragedies, values) are intimately woven into his scientific learning and his political career. Like Hilary Clinton in 2016, his failure to be elected in 2000 was a personal blow as well as an enormous setback for American environmental policy. To this and to other challenges Gore responded in ways that deepened his appreciation of the meaning and urgency of our environmental crisis. The lecture tour that became *An Inconvenient Truth* could be viewed as his return to the world with a transformative tool for communication and behaviour change. Alternatively, we can view him as still in the underworld fighting ignorance, inaction and corruption. Either way, we are presented not only with the (mostly accurate) facts about global warming, but with an example of a person whose life has been committed to this cause. In subsequent deliberations, we are encouraged to ask questions about the science and politics of climate change, but also to ask 'What would Al do?' His embodiment of integrity, fortitude, wit and wisdom are plain to see, quite deliberately portrayed, and serve as a role model for a certain type of environmentally motivated person.

Virtue ethics, we might conclude, through its links to narrative, is a potent means of environmental behavioural change. Stories of struggle are engaging and revealing of the qualities needed to choose and acknowledge our values, to stay committed to them in the face of pressure and temptation, and to try to change the world in accordance with them. In their different ways, environmental documentaries – such as *The Age of Stupid* (2009), *Gasland* (2010), *Project Wild Thing* (2013), and *Demain* (2015) – often enact this type of dynamic, and it is easy to see why. In their successful 1995 Brent Spar campaign Greenpeace evoked a 'David and Goliath' narrative frame that helped win public support (Bennie 1998, 398). Their subsequent, more mainstream approach – involving dialogue with big business rather than just direct action – meant that they lost some of this appeal, but it is an appeal that has its limitations in any case. The problem with these types of story is that, unlike David, the small guy doesn't usually win, and this will be off-putting for many. People might support a heroic battler from the sidelines but not be willing to get involved in what could be a lost cause, or they could simply be suspicious that environmental protesters enjoy being the underdog. Audience response can be finely balanced and frames will often be double-edged. The 'little guy' who fails to gain momentum can give the impression of being flawed; of being too fundamentally out of step with social norms, or just generally a loser. If mainstream acceptance is claimed, as in the case of Greenpeace, they lay themselves open to charges of abusing their unelected power, or even of being (as BP attempted to reframe them during 1997's Atlantic Frontier campaign concerning the expansion of drilling off Shetland) the 'Goliath of environmental groups – wealthy, internally undemocratic and unaccountable' (Bennie 1998, 404).

Finally, it is worth noting how Entman's definition of framing includes a narrative sequence. 'To frame', let us recall,

> is to select some aspects of perceived reality and make them more salient in a communicating text, in such a way as to promote a particular problem definition, causal interpretation, moral evaluation, and/or treatment recommendation for the item described.
>
> *(Entman 1993, 52.)*

The final clause of this sentence conforms to an intuitive and scholarly account of basic narrative features (Kearney 2002): what has happened (or is happening)? What has caused it? Is it good or bad? How should we respond? These are the questions associated with most problems we face, most news stories, and most works of fiction. It is, then, no wonder that they are foregrounded in such an influential definition of framing, and form a dominant theme in Chris Rose's *How to Win Campaigns* (2010) – one of the most respected handbooks of environmental campaigning.

5.1.4 Framing, biases and heuristics

A feature of framing that is emerging from this discussion is how it can be intended to educate audiences or manipulate them (Nisbet 2009). Whatever the intention, however, frames are unavoidably manipulative. They are persuasive because they encourage us to see an issue in a certain way through an emphasis on particular interpretations of its content, but their potency is added to by an inflexibility that typifies human thought. Once a way of seeing is established it tends to develop momentum and gain a cognitive dominance beyond what is justified by its content. We are inclined to be less fluid in our thinking than we might be; to not entertain ideas that are too far removed from our current beliefs, and to underestimate the uncertainty inherent in so many of our claims. In a way this is analogous to a perceptual feature of ambiguous forms like the duck-rabbit (see below).

In these types of cases, we can see one or other of the options (either a duck or a rabbit in this instance), but we are unable to see both of them at the same time. Most of us, however, can switch quite easily between one and the other. In the case of framing though, psychological biases can make this far harder. Someone raised in a conservative and religious culture, in the habit of being suspicious of liberal views, and overwhelmingly told (through family, education or media) that anthropogenic climate change is uncertain, or exaggerated, or a conspiracy, will be unable to engage with the opposite view anything like as easily as one can switch to the alternative perspective in an ambiguous figure. There will be an emotional bias generated by deeply held values, norms and empirical beliefs, and looming practical problems associated with placing oneself outside conventions that shape everyday relationships and routines (Boykoff 2011, 149).

FIGURE 5.2 Duck-rabbit illusion. (*Fliegende Blätter*, 23 Oct 1892, Wikipedia Public Domain.)

Established frames of mind are subject to what is called the 'confirmation bias', our (often unconscious) tendency to attend to, seek out and remember evidence and arguments that confirm existing beliefs, while ignoring or dismissing that which conflicts with them. The art of framing a controversial issue becomes one of finding a relevant and non-antagonistic connection between it and your audience's pre-existing beliefs and values, so that the point of view you are aiming to communicate is not immediately rejected. Endless attempts have been made to frame complex global environmental issues such as climate change so as to 'break through the communication barriers of human nature, partisan identity, and media fragmentation . . . [and] trigger a new way of thinking about the personal relevance of climate change' (Nisbet 2009, 2). Examples – some of which will be discussed in this chapter and the next – include physical, mental and spiritual health frames (Louv 2009; Talen 2016); religious frames (Wilson 2006); social progress and quality of life (e.g., the 2009 documentary *No Impact Man*); local independence and security (e.g., Transition Towns Network); local events and crises frames (Shome and Marx 2009); economic frames (e.g., the Stern Report); intergenerational ethics (e.g., *An Inconvenient Truth* 2006); global justice frames (Klein 2015), and the survival of the haggis as a national dish (Nicol 2015).[6]

Confirmation bias: the tendency to selectively engage with information in a way that supports and maintains our existing beliefs.

However, if framing is to be effective it needs to be integrated with a deep, relevant, broad and sustained set of interventions. Deep frames engage emotions and values, and the audience needs to be able to recognise the relevance of these emotions and values to the issue in question. Breadth refers to the requirements for frames to be manifest in multiple practices and modes of communication, and their associated behaviour-change levers – including the motivations for learning new skills or joining community or workplace initiatives, and the reasons given for policy and other infrastructural changes. These frames then need to be sustained and gather momentum. This requires the frame itself being sustainable because it has clear relevance, an authentic depth and breadth of appeal, and is associated with policies that remain credible, and movements that do not wither when initial funding runs out or charismatic leaders move on.

The features of attitude and behaviour change that have so far been discussed have limitations. Dual-process theories are a profoundly important advance on information deficit models, but both are confined within the model of communication outlined at the start of this chapter. More expansive models of behavioural change are less focussed on the individual as a decision-making entity of limited rationality, and instead include variables such as skills and infrastructure as part of a more holistic perspective. (A good example is the ISM (Individual, Social and Material) tool recently adopted by the Scottish Government (Darnton and Evans 2013)).

5.2 Psychosocial barriers to environmental behaviour change

The list of barriers, and suggested responses, that make up the rest of this chapter is original in its organisation, but its items and some of the analysis are based on a couple of decades of research in environmental communication and environmental psychology. These, then, necessarily overlap with the numerous environmental behavioural change recommendation lists that currently exist in the academic and applied literature.[7] The on-going inquiry into virtues that have particular relevance for environmental behavioural change is a more distinctive endeavour. 'Environmentally productive virtues' as a class of environmental virtues has been discussed by Ronald Sandler (2007), but not in such close proximity to the social scientific behavioural change literature as is attempted here. Our investigation is biased towards climate change and encouraging lower carbon behaviours and lifestyles, but the barriers discussed – 'knowledge', 'emotional engagement', 'existing attitudes, values and wants', 'psychological denial', 'social influence', 'enablers' and 'habits' – can usually be applied to other environmental issues as well. Also, it will become clear that these subheadings are all significantly interconnected and often interdependent, such that an understanding of one will typically shed light on several of the others.

5.2.1 Knowledge

Most people know that climate change is happening (Swim et al. 2009, 37; Leiserowitz et al. 2013), accept that it is anthropogenic, and view it as a 'very' or at least 'somewhat' serious problem (Swim et al., op cit.). In the USA there is a sizable minority – informed by political or religious orientation and media bias – who remain sceptical (Leiserowitz et al. 2013), but this type of case, notwithstanding an absence of knowledge about the existence and nature of climate change, is not the problem it once was. However, there is a critical distinction between shallow abstract knowing and the kind of knowing that motivates concernful action; and it is one thing to appreciate something's existence, and quite another to know how to respond to it.

In many respects, it is from these qualifications concerning the question of public knowledge that the rest of the barriers to climate change engagement stem. That action does not necessarily result from knowledge, no matter how rational it would be to act on that knowledge, is now well known (Kollmuss and Agyeman 2002; Kellstedt et al. 2008; Moser and Dilling 2011).[8] The insufficiency of the 'information deficit model' or of the 'rationality assumption' in economics (Jones et al. 2013) – which assumes that possession of the relevant information is enough to change behaviours – has become a cliché. Information, presented in the right way, is usually a requirement for behavioural change, but other things are also needed. What those other things appear to be are explained in the sections that follow this one and in the subsequent chapter.

The theme that runs through the remainder of this subsection is that of 'uncertainty'. Uncertainty with respect to climate change (and other environmental problems) comes in many forms, and from a behavioural change perspective it has a devastating impact. Cognitively it is a cause of confusion and a mental paralysis that, if the issue is not felt to be urgent, will divert our attention to more immediate and solvable matters. Emotionally it contributes to a sense of helplessness which is unpleasant to endure and profoundly demotivating. The negative emotions seen as being associated with climate change are normally fear, guilt and helplessness, but as we will argue in this chapter and the next, there are good reasons for regarding helplessness as the most damaging of all.

The meaning of 'uncertainty'

In scientific practices 'certainty' denotes and connotes something different to what it does in other areas of life. Evidence and theories carry a provisional quality for scientists no matter how well established they are, whereas in many other practices any suggestion of uncertainty indicates an absence of evidence or significant theoretical disagreement. In an absurd piece of argumentation in August 2016 Australian senator and climate change conspiracy theorist Malcolm Roberts (of the One Nation party) latched on to the word 'consensus' as employed by Brian Cox in an Australian TV debate. Consensus, he claimed, is 'not science', even though Cox was merely stating that there is consensus among climate scientists (rather than some popularist position, which is the spin Roberts wanted to give the term).[9]

An increasing number of guidelines and training packages exist to help scientists overcome misunderstandings based on terminology when communicating with the public (e.g., Shome and Marx 2009; Corner et al. 2015). In their recent reports and other communications the IPCC have made considerable efforts to align their vocabulary with that of non-scientists. For example, in their *Fourth Assessment Report* (IPCC 2007) they used the term 'very likely' to mean 90–99 per cent certain, but for the public it was found that 'very likely' typically translates as 65–75 per cent certain. In the *Fifth Assessment* (IPCC 2013) they adjusted accordingly, using 'extremely likely' to refer to claims that are 95–100 per cent certain, and 'virtually certain' to mean 99–100 per cent certain (Painter 2013).

A further impediment to the public's engagement with climate change – in the USA and UK in particular – has been the disproportionate voice of climate sceptics and deniers. Perceived disagreement among experts has been shown to be a 'gateway issue' for the public (Painter 2013, 24; see also Boykoff 2011, 53–76) and unfortunately media preference for debates along crude binary divides ('duelling experts'), or (in the case of the BBC) to ensure balanced reporting, has created the impression that belief in anthropogenic climate change remains controversial among scientists. This was nicely illustrated in 2014 by US-based satirist John Oliver. In a piece called 'a statistically representative climate change debate', rather than one sceptic and one climate scientist putting forward their views, he fills the studio with ninety-seven scientists wearing lab coats and three sceptics.[10] The main point is an abstract one about how this debate should not still be happening in the media, but the purely visual impact of this weight of numbers (and expertise) is also noteworthy (see also Cook and Lewandowsky 2011, 6). To the uncritical eye, media creates powerful illusions.

In recent years the situation has been improving in the UK,[11] but in the US organised climate change denial remains influential and even, at time of writing, at the highest levels of government (Sidahmed 2016). Even as it becomes increasingly hard to deny the scientific evidence, the focus is shifted to other aspects of the problem, such as what can be done about it, and simple media-manipulation tactics can be remarkably effective in a culture looking to confirm its dogmatic political and religious positions or its subconscious need to preserve normality (see the 'confirmation bias' above). For example, faced with limited time and viewer attention span, a denier demanding that a scientist in a TV or radio news item explains how they know a certain (well-known) fact can have a diversionary impact and uses up time so that the debate is unable to reach a conclusion. For those seeking to maintain the status quo this works well since the main aim is to prevent the opposition putting forward a convincing argument and to reinforce the pointlessness of the public entering the discussion. (For further examples and discussion of the strategies and tactics of organised deniers see Oreskes and Conway 2010; Dunlap and McCright 2011; Washington and Cook 2011; and Greenpeace 2013.)

Dual processing

If System 1 and System 2 are providing conflicting responses System 1 tends to win the day, meaning that 'it is entirely possible to know about climate change and yet not to fully believe in it' (Marshall 2014, 234). Climate scientists are more concerned about climate change than are government officials and the general public (Swim et al. 2009, 36–7), not simply because they know more, but because this analytical knowledge is better integrated with System 1 than it is for non-scientists. In part, this is due to greater first-hand experiences of evidence for, and the effects of, climate change; and it has also been hypothesised that their training and education leads them to habitually take abstract evidence more seriously (Swim et al., op cit.). This appears to mean that, short of vast numbers of people being educated as climate scientists to quite a high level, climate change will retain the kind of psychological distance implied by the phrase 'not fully believe it'. As the American Psychological Association's report on the 'interface' between psychology and global climate change puts it:

> Because climate change is so hard to detect from personal experience, it makes sense to leave this task to climate scientists. This makes climate change a phenomenon where people have to rely on scientific models and expert judgment, and/or on reports in the mass media, and where their own

personal experience does not provide a trustworthy way to confirm the reports. For most people, their exposure to and experience of "climate change" has been almost entirely indirect and virtual, mediated by news coverage and film documentaries of events in distant regions (such as melting glaciers in Greenland) that describe these events in relation to climate change.

(Swim et al. 2009, 34.)

The point here is that most people's understanding of climate change is that it might be regarded as every bit as 'certain' as evolutionary theory but that this is not the same thing as understanding it. All things being equal it is this lack of understanding that makes it too easy to forget about, and that contributes to an absence of personal conviction.

Uncertainty about what to do: complexity

Even if we were able to keep the climate change issue nearer the front of our minds, there remain many other uncertainties, in particular with respect to what can or should be done about it. The range of solutions is indefinite, it is unclear how feasible many of these options are, and the situation is made more complex by competing views on the economic and social desirability of the available options (whether or not they are feasible). This is a problem because, as Oliver Payne (2012, 89) puts it:

> The human mind likes simple, local, immediate and linear situations that have some certainty and are easy to 'bring to life'. Climate change is almost the opposite – complex, global, delayed, and with non-linear effects of carbon outputs, the total picture creates uncertainty.

Moreover, disagreement among experts and other commentators with respect to solutions will be off-putting for the public, not just because of the lack of clarity that results, but because they can also lose faith in their leaders' ability to agree on a solution.

In contrast to fixing the hole in the ozone layer, climate change has been characterised by several thinkers as a 'wicked problem' (Rayner 2006; Hulme 2009). In a sense, this is rather an empty descriptor because, according to the originators of the term – urban planners Horst Rittel and Melvin Webber – 'nearly all public policy issues' are 'wicked', including building roads, reducing poverty, improving educational standards, and confronting crime. Their most fundamental point is that social problems should not be treated like scientific problems, and the error of doing so is a 'serious one' (1973, 160).[12] In a sense, then, this is obvious enough (although maybe it was less obvious forty years ago), but some of the characteristics of social problems they subsequently outline are enlightening and provide a helpful frame for understanding the problem of climate change.

> **Wicked problem**: in contrast to a 'tame problem', a wicked problem is one that is complex and changing, and that doesn't lend itself to a simple or optimal solution. Most or all social problems are 'wicked', and according to, e.g., Mike Hulme (2009) climate change (unlike, for instance, the hole on the ozone layer) is helpfully characterised in this way.

Unlike their 'tame' or 'benign' counterparts, wicked problems cannot be approached in a linear manner, but instead require a wide range of interventions guided by a holistic and fluid perspective on the issue. Moreover, they are each what Rittel and Webber call 'essentially unique'. Prior problems will usually have some similarity (although notably not in the case of climate change), but inductive reasoning is significantly limited because the complexity is such that each new problem will have 'distinguishing' features of 'overriding importance' (op cit., 164). Those engaging with wicked problems therefore need a high degree of tolerance for various forms of uncertainty, including the impossibility of finding an optimum solution, solutions being judged as 'good-or-bad' rather than 'true-or-false' (op cit., 162), and the changing profile of the problem itself. Rittel and Webber suggest that wicked problems are often indeterminate, meaning that the definitions of the concepts they employ, its causes, or how the problem should be framed, are continually contested by different groups and voices. There are, for example, multiple definitions of environmental injustice, and multiple theories of its causes and consequences, and therefore of what solutions to it would look like. The best that policymakers can hope to achieve is a 'judgement' – derived in part through argumentation and negotiation – as to the approaches to be taken, rather than something that can be termed a 'solution' to a clearly defined problem.

The mistake with wicked problems is to reduce them, conceptually, to tame ones. This will not work because as human social problems they are inherently complex, and even addressing them as a discrete set of simpler problems will be inadequate because of the interconnectedness of these strands. As soon as a solution is emerging for one it will alter the nature of the others; and responses from the others will have similarly wide-reaching effects. With respect to climate change, a focus on biofuels will decrease biodiversity, and carbon pricing can adversely affect small farms in the developing world (Hulme op cit., 339); windfarms reduce our reliance on coal and gas, but alter landscapes and interfere with ecosystems, and money saved through fuel efficiency is often then spent on emissions-intensive consumables.

We can understand the temptation to tame the issue though, and from the perspective of a particular individual or group wanting to know how to respond to climate change, something more tangible than a shifting complex whole is required. According to climatologist Mike Hulme – author of the influential book *Why We Disagree about Climate Change* (2009) – the answer is to frame climate change as something symbolic of various values and concerns rather than a 'problem to solve'. This way it is not simplistically recast, but instead given life and form that is relatively non-reductive whilst being something individuals and communities can engage with. Specifically, he suggests finding motivating frames that have deep and widespread emotional resonance (2009, 342–55), for example: the nostalgia associated with protecting and restoring nature's wildness ('lamenting Eden'); the fear caused by future extreme impacts of climate change ('presaging apocalypse'); and our 'instinct for justice' that results from viewing climate change as 'an idea around which . . . concerns for social justice can be mobilized' ('celebrating jubilee'[13]).

Hulme, then, recognises that when it comes to climate change (and the same can be said of many other environmental issues), shallow frames are inadequate. His point is that they can only distort and rapidly create a demotivating muddle because climate change is at once profoundly complex and something that requires a response from all of us. Several of the headings that follow develop this insight and discuss how emotions, values, psychological denial and social norms are relevant to the framing of climate change and to environmental behavioural change more generally.

Climate change as 'uncanny'

In many respects climate change really is an extraordinary thing; genuinely mind-bending. We cannot 'see' climate change – only some of its effects – so unless people understand the science well – which they don't – the idea that mere human activity has managed to alter the planet's climate is hard to conceive of. It has a fanciful quality (Norgaard 2009, 33), like a science fiction plot, or for some (it seems) a conspiracy.

Climate change's invisibility in this sense, combined with its magnitude and the magnitude of its future impacts, contribute to it being experienced as 'uncanny' (Marshall 2014); a state in which 'everyday familiarity collapses' (Heidegger 1962, 233). What are otherwise routine activities become entwined in a series of causes that can result in profoundly damaging and irreversible changes to the planet. It is a series of causes we only partially understand but which we are told in good faith is real. We are further told that changes are needed – urgently – but it is not clear what our responsibilities are, and we have no basis for being confident that institutions and individuals are able or willing to do the right thing. The picture is confusing, to say the least, but it is also revealing of some fundamental features of the human condition that are inherently disturbing or anxiety-provoking, including contingency, mortality and the limits of agency. More than most other crises and dilemmas facing our species, there is a whiff of death about climate change that has the potential to draw our attention to our reasons for wanting to continue to exist. Hulme darkly, but rightly, asks us to consider a 'fundamental question that is rarely addressed' in climate change debates: what is the 'ultimate goal' of humanity? There will, of course, be many ways of interpreting and answering this question, but what is important here is the asking of it (or the avoidance of asking it). In a sense, it is a disturbing question because it highlights how carrying on is not a given but a choice, but it also has the potential to empower through animating responsibility and hope.

Climate change provokes an existential crisis. As will be discussed further under 'Psychological denial', there is a limit to the extent we can endure such an ontological disturbance, and without the appropriate social, cultural and political vision and momentum, retreating from this dizzying exposure to an approximation of 'business as usual' is understandable. Courage and resilience enabling us to authentically confront this anxiety becomes an important environmental virtue; one that is supported by a more general recognition that climate change and other environmental crises present an extraordinary opportunity for virtuous self and social development.

Know-how

The final point to mention before moving on to discuss emotional engagement is another form of ignorance that can often impede environmental behaviour change – an absence of skills or the right 'know-how'. This can range from knowing how to influence change through democratic and other means through to everyday skills such as recycling, composting, maintaining a bike, and food and water efficiency. Further consideration of this type of knowledge can be found below under 'Enablers' and 'Habits'.

5.2.2 Emotional engagement

As already mentioned, emotions can be viewed as types of heuristic. The onset of a particular emotion (fear, anger, disgust and so on) is triggered by a happening and the emotion then serves as a rough guide to what to pay attention to in our surroundings (and our memories), as well as readying us for action through various physiological changes. The fearful person is especially tuned in to possible threats, the angry person into injustices, the sad person into loss, the jealous person into rivals, the guilty person into signs of their own transgressions and possibilities for making amends (Damasio 2000; De Steno et al. 2004). Emotions, in short, frame our world.

One thing that pretty much all theorists agree on is a conceptual link between emotions and needs or desires. We feel angry because we care about justice; feel afraid because we want to preserve whatever it is that is being threatened. Emotions are responses to things that matter to us. Emotions personalise the world. As Aristotle knew, emotional responses can be changed by changing our desires (or at least how we prioritise them), but there is a limit to what we can change in this respect. Can we choose to have a different sexual orientation? Choose not to love our children? Choose not to want the esteem of relevant others? Choose not to want friendship?

Current thinking in evolutionary psychology is that our motivational system, and in particular our emotional range, is strongly socially directed (Keltner et al. 2013). In other words, our survival during the era of evolutionary adaptation (roughly one million to ten thousand years ago) was significantly dependent on our ability to recognise and respond to social hierarchies, potential mates, deception, norm transgressions, in-group and out-group membership, kin-relations, and contexts in which competition or cooperation are most advantageous (Ostrom 2014; Workman and Reader 2014, 182–228). Our sensitivity in these respects is clearly translated into the laws, ethics and norms of our cultures, and our strong emotional responses to unlawful killing, fraud and other kinds of deception, insults, sexual infidelity, and kin and filial disloyalty are plain to see. Again we can inspect our experiences of ourselves and others to appreciate this, and we can also analyse what makes a story 'newsworthy' (or have 'news value'). For example, stories of moral and sexual transgression – particularly involving local or well-known people – fascinate us (Rose 2010).

It has also been suggested that we have evolved to be highly sensitive to sudden changes in our surroundings (rather than slow, incremental ones) (Kollmuss and Agyeman 2002, 253–4), and to what is immediate and proximal (rather than what is temporally and geographically distant) (Swim et al. 2009, 33–76). These biases are also reflected in newsworthiness, which typically privileges the local over the international, and stories that are both happening now and that have a neat and compressed narrative arc (Cox and Pezzullo 2015). In other words, a dramatic event (involving death, children, or some other human interest angle) happens and is immediately reported. Its causes are analysed, its consequences assessed, blame attributed or some other resolution reached, and the attention of cameras and reporters moves on. Terrorist attacks in our own country or places we identity with are highly newsworthy for all these reasons. Also, for all these reasons, climate change and many other environmental issues, are not.

Climate change is incremental; for many it is perceived as not a local problem and as temporally distant; its human interest stories lack the drama of wars or political scandals, and its narrative arc is anything but short and neat.

The final characteristic to consider is our dislike of things both perceived as threatening while at the same time being intrusive. Pretty much by definition novelty and peculiarity have news value, and this relates to our watchfulness and suspicion of sudden change. An odd and negative event that happens elsewhere will engage our interest, and if it directly affects us it is likely to engage our emotion and action as well. Marshall (2014, 52) recounts the uproar and direct action in his local community when T-mobile planned to erect a cell phone tower in the area, and contrasts this with the same educated liberal people's response to climate change. The conclusion he reaches is that things that are familiar (including alcohol and smoking), even though far more dangerous than a cell phone tower could ever be, do not feel dangerous. In the absence of signals of visible and novel threat and harm being caused, we are not alarmed by that which ought to be alarming. In their report on the psychology of climate change the American Psychological Association concluded:

> Global climate change appears to be an example where a dissociation between the output of the analytic and the affective system results in less concern than is advisable, with analytic consideration suggesting to most people that global warming is a serious concern, but the affective system failing to send an early warning signal.
>
> (Swim et al. 2010, 38.)

Environmentally unfriendly objects and activities like cars, holidays and leaving electronic equipment switched on fail to feel threatening or wrong. Familiarity implies safety, and from the point of view of our hunter-gatherer ancestors it is easy enough to see why. If you have experienced repeated encounters with someone or something without trauma or death there is a reasonable chance that it is benign.

As things stand, most environmentally unfriendly behaviours tend not to make us feel threatened or guilty, and this helps us keep the reality of climate change psychologically suppressed. On the other hand though, attempts to generate fear and guilt around climate change and other global environmental issues need to be handled very carefully. These can fail because of the uncomfortable juxtaposition of negative feelings and the immediate perception of being able to do little or nothing to tackle what is causing them. The result is typically to suppress or benignly reframe the cause and carry on as before: 'the maintaining of habits and routines' say O'Neill and Nicholson-Cole (2009, 39) 'is a crucial bulwark against threatening anxieties'.

A common criticism of *An Inconvenient Truth* as a piece of environmental communication has been the contrast between its apocalyptic message and its lack of emphasis on solutions. In particular, it is short on ideas for collective responses on a scale matching the size of the problem. The French-made documentary *Demain* (Laurent and Dion 2015), on the other hand, is far more cogent in this respect. Like Klein's contemporaneous *This Changes Everything*, *Demain* pulls no punches in its presentation of how climate change has been affecting, and is likely to affect, the world. But its emphasis on more radical solutions and alternative forms of life – such as massive investment in renewables, transition towns, alternative currencies, anti-growth economic models, and changes to democratic and educational systems – also present a suitably dramatic response. Moreover, for the purposes of the present discussion, mostly credible and digestible examples from around the world are provided by the film that demonstrate how an environmentally sustainable world is not an alien and improbable reality. Through case studies such as the successful adoption of renewable energy in Denmark, a clear bridge is made between where many developed countries are now and where they could be. An imaginable future is presented that brings with it a sense of collective efficacy that leaves us less likely to be overwhelmed and demotivated by fear.

Virtue theory is distinct from deontology and utilitarianism in its basic requirement for an integration of actions and feelings. The virtuous person not only acts in ways that are just, generous and so on, these actions are also the result of spontaneously experienced desires and their associated emotions. It is these emotions that play a vital role in communicating to us right and wrong conduct, and in this respect emotions can be understood as 'intelligent' (Nussbaum 2001; Brady 2013). However, in the case of climate change and other psychologically distant environmental problems, emotions are currently less trustworthy than they typically are in response to more traditional moral issues. The right kind of environmental education might be able to play a mitigating role, but for most of us it is perhaps the virtue of self-knowledge – insight into the seemingly hardwired limitations of this aspect of our psychology – that could make the greatest difference.

5.2.3 Existing attitudes, values and wants

A person might understand climate change well enough, what needs to be done about it, and even know how to do some of these things, but this still does not mean they will.

An individual's life involves multiple pressing concerns that will typically be prioritised over environmentally friendly behaviours, and sometimes come into other forms of conflict with them. It is not so easy to switch from driving to public transport or cycling, or to give up overseas holidays. If we have children we maybe have an enhanced sense of responsibility to consider the future state of the planet, but we also want to get them to school safely, couldn't live with ourselves if anything happened whilst they were roaming the local countryside instead of interacting with a screen, and want to provide the kinds of experiences that only foreign travel can. Through little fault of our own we might find that we are addicted to shopping, and that we have no clue as to what could replace visible material wealth as a sign of social status (or indeed how we might become less concerned about social status). We find nature at best boring, and at worst dangerous, and cannot relate to the kind of people we perceive (on TV, at the town hall, or the PTA) as espousing environmental values (even though we understand the importance of some of those values). Moreover, the conservative church we belong to seems to have no interest in environmental issues, and people we are otherwise on friendly terms with bristle should the conversation look like turning in that direction. Their line seems to be that the Earth is a temporary home and that one's moral and spiritual focus should be on the afterlife. And they might have a point. In fact, from what can be gathered from the media, even the scientific experts don't all agree that global warming is man-made, so if we commit to doing something about it are we jumping on a liberal bandwagon, failing to think for ourselves, and generally risking looking like a bit of a sucker? And what if we end up making ourselves and our dependents less fulfilled and more unhappy as a result? Why should we make this sacrifice when so many others aren't, including those far wealthier than us?

This vignette illustrates four ways in which existing non-environmental attitudes, values and wants can impede the adoption of environmentally friendly behaviours. The first is the immediate, automatic and habitual nature of these motivators and the decisions resulting from them. They are firmly entwined, not just with System 1 processing and emotions, but with social norms (see below) and everyday routines (see below) and thus present a formidable barrier to the imposition of inconvenient, albeit abstractly accepted, new values and behaviours. In some cases existing behaviours can be referred to as addictions. This can mean we would prefer to be free from them (we want what we crave but don't want to want it), but achieving this generally requires dramatic changes in circumstance or systematic outside interventions.

The second is the presence of attitudes and values that explicitly conflict with environmental values. One of the clearest examples is aspects of the religious right in the USA, but non-religiously fundamentalist Republicans, industrialists and free-market libertarians will also find the demands of climate change too contrary to their values and norms to accept its reality. Forms of psychological denial will often be employed to keep the evidence at arms-length (see below), and this is of course abetted by a partisan media that is largely dependent on commercial advertising (see Chapter 8).

A third way in which existing non-environmental attitudes, values and wants can demotivate environmentally friendly behaviours concerns the unfair distribution of effort and sacrifice that pro-environmental lifestyle changes tend to involve. This issue will because discussed under the 'ethics of nudge' in Chapter 6, and in terms of environmental justice in Chapter 2.

The fourth is presented at the end of the vignette and is the one we want to pay greatest attention to in this section. Recognising that something is the right thing to do, but being reluctant to do it because you cannot trust others to do the same, is the dynamic underpinning what has been referred to as the 'commons problem', 'prisoner's dilemma' or 'social dilemmas'. In his famous paper 'The tragedy of the commons' (originally published in 1968), Garrett Hardin's concern was world population growth, but the tragic dynamic he describes is relevant to analyses of numerous environmental and social problems, whether or not population control is the underlying theme. He explains how a common resource – free for all to use – can be destroyed by rational individual choices. Imagine a circumstance where common pastures are 'open to all' and ten herdsmen each have ten sheep grazing on them. If, however, an individual herdsman has the opportunity to add an extra animal to his flock then, acting rationally, he will do so. The utility of an extra animal (+1) is clear, and the disutility of there being slightly less grass per animal is shared by all the herdsmen, and therefore will not outweigh the utility of adding the further animal (approximately − 0.1). But, of course, if other herdsmen are thinking in the same way and have extra animals that would benefit from the common land, then 'at this point, the inherent logic of the commons remorselessly generates tragedy' (Hardin 1986, 313). The cumulative effect will be a degeneration of the pasture so that it can no longer serve anyone. The tragedy is that no one intended for this to happen. It is not the result of ill-will between herdsmen, it is simply the consequence of individually rational decision-making with respect to a free resource in a context of relative scarcity.

In the 'prisoner's dilemma' thought experiment two people are accused of a crime (say, armed robbery) and are being interrogated in separate cells. There is currently not enough evidence to make a conviction, so the police need at least one of them to testify against the other. Let's say you are one of the prisoners and you are made an offer: give evidence against your partner in crime and you get to go free while they go down for five years; remain loyal and you'll both get one year for possession of a firearm. It occurs to you, however, that it is in the interests of the police to make the same offer to the other prisoner. 'What if we both defect?' you ask. In this case, you'll both get three years because you were willing to cooperate. What should you do? Assuming that your aim is simply to spend as little time in jail as possible, the rational response is always to defect. No matter what the other person decides to do this will result in fewer years behind bars. If the other remains loyal you go free, if they defect you get three years whereas remaining loyal would have landed you with five.

Since the same is true for the other prisoner, then each individual finds himself in a trap that makes everyone worse off than they need to be. Had no one defected the prisoners would spend one year in jail rather than three. The scenario is, of course, making a number of assumptions, such as the prisoners not reaching a prior agreement not to defect, and trusting one another to stick to this.

In many situations, we cooperate with others because we know that that cooperation will be returned. In circumstances of mutual dependence – I need you to help me shear my sheep; you need me to help gather in your crops – the rule of reciprocation becomes fundamental, and has been identified as a heuristic (see Cialdini 2007). From a self-interested point of view, defecting will have very clear and quite swift negative consequences. There is a good argument (based partly on experimental evidence) for believing that an attitude towards cooperation based on the rule of tit-for-tat (be helpful at first, and then follow whatever the other person

Prisoner's Dilemma

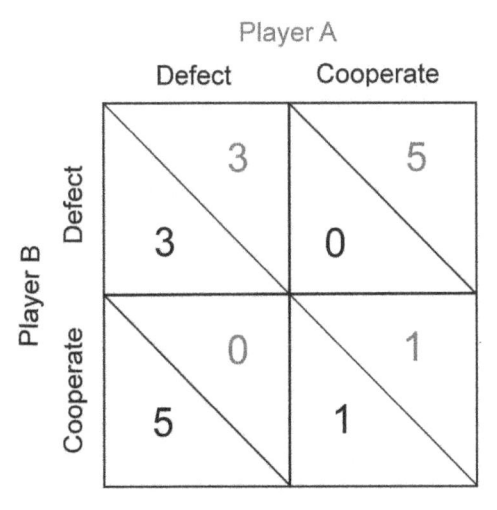

	Player A Defect	Player A Cooperate
Player B Defect	3 / 3	5 / 0
Player B Cooperate	0 / 5	1 / 1

FIGURE 5.3 The prisoner's dilemma. (Original by authors.)

does) is the one that will end up as dominant in small communities where at least some of the others have an inclination towards being cooperative. Moreover, a case can be made for the emotions and traits associated with this – such as fairness and friendship – being hard-wired because of their survival value for the individual (Kropotkin 1939; Axelrod 1984; Singer 1993).

So, knowing there will be repeated encounters with particular individuals and an understanding of mutual dependency can help ensure trust. Other factors that can explain why cooperation occurs in some situations and not others include the size of the group, the homogeneity of the group, relative sizes of the benefits of cooperation and of defecting ('free riding'), and past experience of how individuals in the group have behaved. A useful generalised finding is that in an open competitive market where participants are largely anonymous, 'rational egoists are the only type of players to survive', but in non-competitive situations in which those involved can identify those among them who adhere to social norms of cooperation, 'norm-users can survive and even flourish' (Ostrom 2014, 238).

According to Gardner and Stern (2002) the answer to the problem is to promote and make visible the right kind of environmental social norms through a combination of legislation, education (in the wider sense of the word), autonomous community action, and the appropriate framing of existing ethical principles. However, if the tragedy of the commons or the prisoner's dilemma is the most accurate way to frame our global environmental crisis, then a pessimistic conclusion is understandable. Research indicating conditions that will prevent tragedy occurring assume the existence of cohesive groups with high levels of trust generated by interpersonal familiarity, robust norms and shared knowledge of the nature and value of the resource(s) at stake. Even if a case can be made for an evolved disposition to cooperate under certain conditions, we also appear to have a deep-seated prejudice in favour of our in-group (Fiske 2005; Greene 2014). Reciprocity appears to be immensely important, and if we assume that someone in an out-group either cannot, or cannot be relied on, to provide and return favours, then there is no ground for a motivation for cooperation. The prediction is what we so often see – indifference or antagonism towards those not considered 'one of us'.

Stable examples of groups cooperating without enforceable punishments for transgressors are quite hard to find under relatively optimal conditions,[14] so how hopeful can we be with respect to a pollution problem that is both international and intergenerational?[15] This is the basis of Stephen Gardiner's argument in his book *The Perfect Moral Storm* (2011). The 'perfect storm' he identifies is the result of three individual storms: wealthy nations prioritising their particular concerns; our generational bias and the fact that future generations will have to deal with the worst consequences of climate change; and the absence of an adequate ethical framework (concerning, for example, international justice, intergenerational justice and environmental ethics) for motivating agreement and action. The way in which the last of these is problematic is made apparent if we see it in terms of Rittel and Webber's characteristics of 'wicked problems' (see above); in particular the indeterminacy surrounding these ideas and the 'essential uniqueness' of our climate crisis. We can make progress with wicked problems though, so long as we see them for what they are. However, considering the deep psychological biases underpinning the first two storms, Gardiner argues that 'even if the difficult ethical questions could be answered, we might still find it difficult to act. For the storm makes us extremely vulnerable to moral corruption' (2011, 22).

By 'moral corruption' he means self-deception, which is the focus of the next section. Research into public perceptions of climate change indicates that it is often seen as a social dilemma, and that this can be demotivating in terms of taking individual responsibility for environmentally friendly actions (Aitken et al. 2011; Capstick 2013). The emphasis is on not wanting to make sacrifices when others are not, but also on a sense of helplessness resulting from feeling like efforts made are insignificant if not mirrored by others. Ways to tackle both of these concerns will be discussed in Chapter 6.

5.2.4 Psychological denial

Hamilton and Kasser (2009) identify three broad 'coping strategies' that people employ to deal with the negative emotions caused by the truths of climate change: denial strategies, maladaptive strategies and adaptive strategies. Denial strategies aim at: 'suppressing anxiety associated with predictions of climate disruption by not allowing the facts to be accepted in the conscious mind. By denying the reality of the facts, no emotions need be felt' (2009, 2).

The desire for the world not to be this way combined with the overwhelming evidence that it is creates cognitive dissonance (anxiety). The dissonance is then soothed by making one side of the conflicting desires and beliefs go away through psychological suppression – in this case, the true belief that climate change is real and serious.

Far more common than outright denial are forms of half-recognising the problem that also instantiate well-known psychological defence mechanisms. Hamilton and Kasser refer to these as 'maladaptive' strategies, outlining five kinds:

1. 'Reinterpreting the threat' is the adoption of an understanding of the situation that plays down its scale and seriousness. Near the start of *This Changes Everything* Naomi Klein makes this confession:

    > I denied climate change for longer than I care to admit. I knew it was happening, sure. Not like Donald Trump and the Tea Partiers going on about how the continued existence of winter proves it's all a hoax. But I stayed pretty hazy on the details and only skimmed most of the news stories, especially the really scary ones. I told myself that the science was too complicated and that environmentalists were dealing with it. And I continued to behave as if there was nothing wrong with the shiny card in my wallet attesting to my "elite" flyer status.
    >
    > *(2015, 3.)*

She then lists the numerous strategies we have for 'looking away': escaping its gravity by joking about it; rationalising our disengagement by claiming that focusing on the economy is the best way to protect us from extreme weather; and downplaying the extent to which it is happening now (see also Gardiner 2011, 45).

One form of this strategy mentioned by Hamilton and Kasser is telling ourselves, 'If it were that big a threat the government would be doing something about it' (2009, 3). Previous discussions support what a powerful illusion this is, especially where governments are not doing enough, or are not seen to be doing enough. Climate crisis is an unprecedented global problem in which adequate government policy-based solutions are remarkably difficult to achieve. This realisation is itself hard to acknowledge – perhaps the hardest part of all – because it flirts so profoundly with the threat to 'ontological security'; defined by Anthony Giddens as 'the confidence most human beings have in the continuity of their self-identity and the constancy of the surrounding social and material environments of action' (1991, 92).

2. 'Diversionary strategies' shift our attention to activities that obscure the truth, and in Western cultures based on material acquisition and consumption fuelled by demanding and time-consuming jobs – 'this dazzling, exhausted life we lead' (Talen 2016, 14) – these are not difficult to find. The truth about climate change is not kept from us by a political or corporate conspiracy (despite the efforts of organised deniers): 'the censorship is our actual condition' (op cit.). Making reference to recent hurricanes in the US the Reverend Billy confesses:

> I am one of those people who believe that these storms are much deadlier because of us. But I suspect I am another progressive type who is still, at heart, a climate sceptic. I must be. What have I done for this storm? What do I owe this wind? It has gaseous acids in it. The bleached coral of the Caribbean is drumming on our house. But I keep my guilt nice and abstract. It is so easy to believe the climate science but then go about our digitalized day with the extreme weather and consumer culture in a desperate fight to the death, as if all that takes place in a separate world.
>
> *(Talen 2016, 35.)*

A now well-recognised diversion is known as the 'single action bias' – the maladaptive belief that engaging with one environmentally friendly behaviour is enough to 'do one's bit' (see section 7.7.2). This surprisingly common feature of our moral psychology is not only an erroneous belief, but conveniently takes the energy out of the motivational system – the need to take responsibility – that is the driver of the sustained and wide-ranging commitment required the tackle climate change and other environmental problems. Instead of helping, single actions can actually be counterproductive.

3. 'Blame-shifting' is the exaggerated belief that responding to climate change is more someone else's responsibility than our own. It is easy for members of small countries to scapegoat China or America (Norgaard 2009), and members

of the public can point to governments and corporations. This, of course, overlooks the fact that much of the time these institutions respond to voter or consumer pressure, and thus the individual's need not just to change their own behaviours, but to promote change more widely, and recognise the contexts in which these behaviours take place. In virtue ethics there is often an assumption that virtuous behaviours will have a degree of contagiousness, spreading to other individuals and groups (generating virtuous circles, or reinforcing loops of desirable action) and that this in turn serves to maintain the presence of the virtue in its originators (Hursthouse 1992, 226–8). However, for this 'virtuous circle' to emerge, someone, or some collective, has to first take responsibility.

4. 'Indifference strategies' are the opposite of full denial strategies in that they involve the suppression of our feelings rather than the facts. The reality of climate change and all it entails can be known to a person in the cognitive sense, but these implications are not felt and are instead greeted by apathy or indifference. What this amounts to is a de-personalisation; an abstract acknowledgement conditioned by a failure to engage with how this truth will matter to me (in the non-egoist sense of anything that I value, including family, humans, and other species). In a very important sense this compartmentalisation is far from the truth because experience of the world is normally and rightly infused with values. To abstract from them is to be disordered and even inhuman in the way Mersault in Albert Camus' novel *The Outsider* is. To be indifferent in the face of widespread harms is to become a nihilist. In the short term, this can be a comfortably numbing perspective, but it is not one we can or would normally wish to maintain.

   The documentary *The Age of Stupid* (Armstrong 2009) asks the question 'Are we worth saving?' but even if the answer is 'no' it is not an answer that can be authentically delivered with indifference. Instead, the dominating emotions are disappointment, anger, frustration and sadness. It is, in other words, a moral question, involving the relevant moral emotions.

5. 'Unrealistic optimism' or 'wishful thinking' rests on illusions that exaggerate the likelihood of changes being made in the absence of efforts by you or the institutions you represent. Unrealistic optimism has been identified as a widespread illusion (Taylor and Brown 1988), and it is one that is more easily supported than some others on the basis that the future, unlike the past or present, is a set of possibilities rather than actualities. Moreover, world powers have survived global crises in the past (the Cold War, ozone depletion), so why not this one? The hypothetical status of the future combined with loose but vivid inductive arguments and abetted by the confirmation bias all support wishful thinking.

Hamilton and Kasser offer the example of unrealistic hope in the outcomes of world climate conferences or the Kyoto Protocol (2009, 5), and a further case would be false confidence in technological fixes (see Chapter 4). Again, loose and selective inductive reasoning can bring to mind the extraordinary things we have achieved since the Industrial Revolution and in particular in the twentieth century, but this conveniently overlooks the fact that climate crisis is the result of technology-driven progress and (more importantly) the philosophical and political beliefs and values that have accompanied it. Not only is it highly conceivable that this is a problem that technology cannot fix, there are very good reasons for believing that a different way of understanding ourselves and our relationship with nature is primarily what is required. We can be hopeful about achieving this for sure, but crucially it is not a maladaptive hope derived from a desire not to fully engage with the problem. Fully engaging with the problem at the level of everyday routines and priorities, as well as policy, many would argue to be exactly what we need to do if we are to solve this climate crisis.

Among the 'adaptive coping strategies' Hamilton and Kasser consider is a 'new values orientation' that would be motivated by an honest engagement with the wider meanings of climate change; something that will be discussed in the next chapter in a specific discussion of shifting values in response to environmental issues. They also recommend a 'problem solving' frame of mind that helps people come to terms with the situation through overcoming helplessness. As previously discussed, however, there are real obstacles to attempting to conceive of climate change as a problem in the linear sense that individual efficacy requires, and the limitations on what a normal individual in the everyday business of life can actually achieve cast doubts on the value of this strategy. However, as the next section will discuss, problem solving does not need to be individual, and if a sense of collective efficacy can be generated then this could go further towards reducing the anxiety that motivates denial.

There is a rough causal sequence in Hamilton and Kasser's adaptive strategies, and their initial one is psychologically, and maybe logically, prior to the others. In the idea of 'expressing and controlling' emotions is a kind of therapeutic solution to the 'emotional engagement' barrier discussed above. If climate change is unconsciously perceived to be ontologically disturbing (they use the analogy of our own death to express its magnitude), then we need to achieve a hard-won acceptance of its reality. Fear, sadness and despair are 'natural' and 'healthy' reactions that shouldn't be repressed. However, nor can we live with these reactions indefinitely and maladaptive psychological defences will inevitably re-emerge. So, these feelings need to become part of a narrative that sees them replaced by empowering emotions. Along with the (still popular) 'mindfulness' (see also Jones et al. 2013), they refer us to the two further strategies already mentioned – problem solving and changing values.

Despite the limitations so far mentioned, the emphasis on this transformation and the difficulty of achieving it moves the discussion of emotions in climate change communication to a more enlightened level. We know that, unless correctly contextualised, fear and guilt can be counter-productive. This provides a sophisticated understanding of why this is the case – especially in terms of the overarching presence of the anxiety of helplessness – but also the possibility of devising new behavioural change strategies that could result in deep-seated attitude change. The message is: don't avoid negative emotions, but help people manage them so that their causes are addressed honestly and constructively.

The most convincing advice offered by Hamilton and Kasser is to help people not to feel isolated in their anxiety. Finding like-minded others and a visible recognition and response from governments and other institutions will not only assist with the efficacy issue, but it helps us cope with fear and therefore be less likely still to suppress its cause.

It seems likely that psychological denial is a significant barrier to appropriate responses to climate change. Moreover, it is not just something that limits individual behaviours, but Hamilton and Kasser quite reasonably argue that our 'hidden anxiety' is a well of energy that if released would mean much more public pressure would be brought to bear on policy makers and corporations (2009, 7).

Denial is all the more potent when socially reinforced. In terms of what she calls the 'sociology of denial', Kari Marie Norgaard argues that the gap between knowing about climate change and fully responding to it (so that it becomes something we significantly attend to and act on) is explained by social norms. From her ethnographic research in Norway and the US she found that 'people described a sense of knowing and not knowing about climate change, of having information but not thinking about it in their everyday lives' (2009, 26). What causes this 'double life' (as she calls it)? 'Information from climate science is known in the abstract, but disconnected from, and invisible within political, social or private life' (ibid).

This invisibility is the result of the suppression of negative emotions evoked by the topic (fear, guilt and helplessness), but importantly this is supported by social norms that, for example, make it a less than 'easy' topic of conversation. This, in turn, is conditioned by all the uncertainties surrounding the subject, along with 'emotional norms of toughness and maintaining control' (28). In the Norwegian case, sociological denial is exacerbated by a guilt-provoking contradiction between the country's self-image as 'humanitarian' and an international leader on environmental issues, and their emissions record (32).[16]

Insights like this remind us of ways in which beliefs (and their suppression) are partly a function of social norms and social dynamics. The practices that shape our daily lives are highly social in nature, and the conversations that take place within them will condition what we pay attention to. This will be especially true for issues where problems are perceived as being at a geographical and temporal distance, and where responsibility is diffused. In developed nations there are multiple issues where our responses are inadequate, but we only have what's been called a 'finite pool of worry'. Attention to global issues must be selective, and perhaps inevitably we take our cues as to what to pay attention to and commit to from the norms that surround us.

To the extent that psychological denial is a barrier to climate change engagement, it will give rise to sociological denial; a collective evasion of the topic. However, where individuals or cultures have yet to 'feel' the implications of climate change to the point where suppression is even necessary, social norms will also play a part in maintaining or changing levels of engagement. In other words, in a culture where our environmental crisis has low salience in the agendas and communications of government, media, religious institutions, schools and so on, individual awareness will, on the whole, be similarly muted.

Although a significant barrier, we would argue that psychological denial resulting from negative emotions in response to climate change is not as widespread as authors like Norgaard and Hamilton and Kasser are suggesting. Evidence that 'there is a great deal of unconscious anxiety about climate change in the community' (Hamilton and Kasser 2009, 6) is thin. Our point is not that the denial does not exist, but that, much of the time, this is not driven by profound anxiety that has been repressed, but by more superficial concerns about helplessness (not knowing how we can make a difference), climate change's low profile in our daily lives and social circles, the absence of a truly clear picture of what climate change means and entails, and a biological bias that makes us emotionally unresponsive to (what are perceived to be) long-term threats. The last two of these have already been discussed, the second will be addressed in the next section, and the first in the section after that.

Before moving on we will suggest a slight variation on Hamilton and Kasser's theory. If deep anxiety over climate change is not widespread in developed nations but its truth suppressed for other reasons, might the task of climate change communication be not to help people face up to their anxiety, but to create it? The message becomes: whether you like it or not the world is going to change over the next few generations, either because of climate change or because of the mitigation measures we take. In order, therefore, to cope better you need to start thinking deeply about the kind of sustainable world you would like to see. Technology alone is not the answer, we need to reconsider what is important to us – what makes us fulfilled and happy – and then we need to envision a match between this and what the planet permits. Those not already anxious should be now, but this kind of message is also empowering. It encourages reflection, conversation and imagination and, since so many people seem to be so unhappy anyway, it can be genuinely liberating. The anxiety in question is not simply a variation of fear, but a response to being reminded of some fundamentals of existence – mortality, contingency, and what makes a human life meaningful.

Put another way, the values associated with Hamilton and Kasser's adaptive coping strategies become subsumed under their 'new values' category. For most people, these disquieting emotions are not being managed but created, and created in a context in which they can find expression in appropriate values. And within that context problems to be solved begin to take form, as they are in the philosophies, campaigns and initiatives that define environmental movements. In the works of people like Leopold, Naess and Bookchin (but also any credible vision of the human condition that stresses the importance of intrinsic, largely non-materialist values) we find the bases of alternative forms of life that represent an antidote to the denial in which this new-born anxiety would otherwise seek refuge.

Climate change becomes an opportunity to create a different and hopefully better life. More on intrinsic values and their relationship to behavioural change can be found in the next chapter.

5.2.5 Social influence: norms, authority and trust

The science of climate change and other environmental issues can be difficult to understand, and the ethics and politics rarely present unified views on where the problem lies (or whether there is a problem in the first place) and what to do about it. The resulting confusion, along with the other barriers discussed here, mean that two sources of influence and guidance gain importance: social norms, and trusted authorities.

Social norms

What others are doing and how they perceive our behaviour is a well-recognised and important driver of behavioural change. One of the most influential behavioural change models – the Theory of Planned Behaviour (Ajzen 1991) – includes the opinions of relevant others among three predictors of forming an intention to act (the other predictors being the strength of one's current attitude towards the action and one's belief in one's ability to carry out the behaviour). It is one of Robert Cialdini's six 'universal' principles of compliance, basic to phenomena such as social identity, conformity, groupthink and group-polarisation, and features consistently in reports and other texts making recommendations for environmental behavioural change (for example: Shome and Marx 2009; Payne 2012; Markowitz and Shariff 2012; Darnton and Evans 2013; Marshall 2014).

Numerous studies in social psychology have demonstrated the powerful influence of conformity under conditions of uncertainty (Sherif 1936; Latané and Darley 1968; Janis 1982). When in doubt, we look to see what most others in the same situation are doing or thinking, and base our response on that; and this tendency is all the stronger if the 'others' in question are people we see as similar to ourselves (see the discussion of 'referent power' below).

We are profoundly habitual beings, and this goes a long way to explaining how difficult it is to change environmental behaviours. Daily routines are largely invisible and remain that way all the time there is no disruption to them. Disruption can come in several forms (some others are discussed under 'Habits'), but one of them is a perception that others are doing something differently, or have become critical of us for doing what we are doing.

The county of Dumfries and Galloway in South-West Scotland (where the authors live) is one of only two counties in the UK that use a system of centralised household waste recycling. Each household has only one bin for all waste, and this is then sorted into different recyclables at a central Eco Deco facility. Whether this leads to more efficient recycling is a matter of debate, but an indirect disadvantage of the system is that recycling in the region becomes invisible. Not only do we as residents not need to be conscious of it, we are not prompted to be conscious of it by the presence of recycling bins on the streets. Having to put waste in recycling bins makes sustainability more conspicuous and generates and maintains environmental virtues and habits, and clear evidence that others are doing the same reinforces this behaviour.

In an attempt to promote backyard composting in Nova Scotia (after a ban was imposed on organic waste going to landfill), Doug McKenzie-Mohr (2000, 549–50) explains how in one county the discovery that many more people than expected already composted allowed for the effective use of the influence of social norms.

> The program planners reasoned that one explanation for the absence of community norms supporting backyard composting was the relative invisibility of composting compared to other activities, such as curbside recycling. Accordingly, those who composted were asked to commit to placing a decal on the side of their blue box or garbage container indicating that they composted. As a form of commitment, the act of placing a decal on the side of their blue box or garbage container served to increase the likelihood that the household would compost more effectively, while at the same time fostering the development of ... social norms ... in which composting is seen as appropriate behaviour.

This form of public declaration is intended to persuade through commitment and consistency (see Chapter 6), and through what has been termed a 'descriptive' norm. In some circumstances, an 'injunctive' norm alongside the descriptive one can be more effective. The difference is one of evaluation: a descriptive norm merely demonstrates the commonality of an attitude or behaviour whereas an injunctive norm also makes a judgement on it (Cialdini 2003).

In an influential study on reducing energy consumption, a sample of residents of San Marco, California, were provided with information about their previous week's energy usage, along with the average consumption for their neighbourhood. When only a descriptive norm was provided, both those consuming below the average and those consuming above the average moved towards the middle, so mean usage didn't change. However, when an injunctive norm accompanied the descriptive norm (in the form of smiling or frowning emoticons) average consumption decreased significantly; high users reduced their consumption, but low users did not increase theirs (Schultz et al. 2007).

The US utilities company Opower have adopted this strategy by including injunctive norm information along with customer bills, and report consumption decreases of around 6 per cent for a significant segment of customers (Payne 2012, 98). On one level this shows that making norms conspicuous can affect people's behaviour, and that accompanying this information with an evaluation is sometimes also required. However, further investigation into the wider impact of this method revealed how 'core Republican voters' upped their usage in defiance of the value judgement. These are people who we would expect to be less likely to accept the ethos of the overtly green-minded Opower (who were later praised by President Obama) (Payne, op cit.). The implication is that for injunctive norms to be effective there must already exist a degree of respect for the authority (or the principle they embody) behind the value judgement. This way an internalised injunctive norm is made available to our awareness or 'nudged', and the behaviour change is not resisted. Otherwise, if we simply feel we are being told what to do, or being preached to, a 'boomerang effect' (where the effort to persuade ends up having not just no effect but the opposite effect) is likely.

With environmental issues the moral argument needs to be strong and it needs to be presented in a context that decreases the likelihood of individuals switching off or rationalising their existing behaviour. Descriptive norms are a vital feature of this presentation and, as the Opower example demonstrates, so is the source of the moral message. Message source will be discussed shortly, but beforehand it is important to reinforce the frustrating nature of social norms. They are without question one of the most powerful – if not the most powerful – of the behavioural influences. But if the norm does not exist in the first place then you cannot use the norm to create the norm. The situation with many environmental problems resembles the phenomenon of 'pluralistic ignorance' in which 'each person decides that since nobody is concerned, nothing is wrong' (Latané and Darley, cited in Cialdini 2007, 133):

> It has often been recognised ... that a crowd can cause contagion or panic, leading each person in the crowd to overreact to an emergency to the detriment of everyone's welfare. What is implied here is that a crowd can also force inaction on its members. It can suggest, implicitly but strongly, by its passive behaviour, that an event is not to be reacted to as an emergency, and it can make any individual uncomfortably aware of what a fool he will look for behaving as if it is.
>
> *(Latané and Darley 1968, 217.)*

Therefore we need to rely on the other levers to create a critical mass of engaged awareness among relevant groups. Once it exists, forms of exposure to the emerging norm can turbo-charge behaviour change, but the hard part is bringing it into existence in the first place.

The behaviour and policies of local and national government, corporations and other institutions help create the sense of norms, and the evidence is clear that citizens expect to see this if they are going to be prepared to make the necessary adjustments to their habits (e.g., Lorenzoni et al. 2007; Spence et al. 2010). It seems unlikely that the dramatic shift in one-use plastic bags in England since the 5p minimum charge was made law in 2015 (Defra 2016)[17] is simply about saving money (Convery et al. 2007). This intrusion into daily routines symbolises the government's recognition of the damaging environmental impact of the disposable bag habit, and the public has responded to an injunctive norm (as was so effective in Ireland, see Convery et al. 2007 and see also Carrigan et al. 2011).

The reduction made headline news in the UK when the figures were announced in late July 2016, and there were immediate calls from Friends of the Earth and other bodies not to think that this achievement is enough, and that attention should now be turned to plastic bottles, non-recyclable coffee cups and excess packaging (Smithers 2016). They are right to do so. For recycling or waste reduction to make headlines is highly unusual, and capitalising on it is all the more urgent since the message is such a positive one. Instead of guilt and helplessness, it is a story of collective success accompanied by accessible information on the kinds of environmental damage and financial impacts caused by plastic bags. On the basis of this, similar behavioural changes are suggested that, outside of this frame, would likely appear far less attainable or, crucially, less interesting.

Both the successes and failures of community initiatives can be explained in part by the influence of norms. Collective rather than individual efforts can have a normalising influence – both on other members of the community and the wider region or nation – by providing evidence that enough people are prepared to take responsibility for acting in environmentally friendly ways. However, these initiatives are also associated with factionalism in communities; being either representative of divisions or causing them. If, for example, those involved are seen by outsiders as middle-class liberals or 'not from around here' they will promote neither descriptive nor injunctive norms, and risk a boomerang effect (Pattie et al. 2003; Todhunter 2011; Aiken 2012).

Authority and trust

The trustworthiness of message sources will be explored through French and Raven's (1959) and Raven's (2008) influential categorisation of 'bases of social power'. They identify the following six forms of power (some of which we also refer to as 'authority'):

> **Legitimate power**: the authority derived from a position (politician, civil servant, CEO, priest, teacher and so on), or from the moral principles underpinning a person's commitments (such as someone defending their actions on the basis of human rights).
> **Reward power/coercive power**:[18] the power to influence people's actions through, say, financial rewards (such as a subsidy, bonus, low pricing, or a bribe) and penalties (such as taxes, fines, or late-comer disincentives); and other kinds of rewards and punishments, such as praise or criticism from a boss, teacher, parent or friend. That these incentives can be generated by people with no legitimate power over us helps to distinguish this category from the previous one.
> **Expert power**: the authority associated with someone's known (or assumed) expertise in a certain area.

Information power: the power that results from being in a position to know. This could be the result of being a witness to an event or, perhaps more commonly, having access to information as a result of one's position. This information could be classified or confidential, or one could withhold and release it in a way that deliberately empowers or disempowers others. The claim, among some organised deniers, that climate change is a conspiracy is an example of an (obviously untrue) allegation of abuse of information power.

Referent power: the influence of the views and actions of people we see as similar to us and whom we aspire to be like. Referent power is connected with social identity, and shares features with the power of social norms. Social norms, however, is a broader category that encompasses conformity with majority attitudes and behaviours. Referent power refers to the more specific appeal of groups that we, often unconsciously, identify with. In different contexts, it could be, for example, a political or ethical affiliation, a consumer 'tribe', ethnicity, age and class (and their associated struggles), devotion to a hobby. The success of the 'Don't mess with Texas' anti-littering campaign (from the 1980s) appears to be related to the referent power (Texan identity) implied by the strapline.

To these six types of power we will add what is elsewhere known as 'ethotic authority' (Aristotle 1991; Brinton 1986) – the influence associated with someone being regarded as a virtuous or 'good' person. In situations where we follow their lead this is not due to any position or moral principle they uphold,

FIGURE 5.4 Don't mess with Texas. (brionv photo, Creative Commons license: http://tinyurl.com/ya2ggksb.

or any specific expertise, but because they are people we trust to make sound judgements. In many respects, the distinctiveness of virtue ethics defines the distinctiveness of this form of authority. Over a period of time, the person possessing ethotic authority has consistently demonstrated virtues such as integrity, courage, self-knowledge and humility, indicating that their view on an issue is likely to have been arrived at in the right sorts of ways.

The role of authority in environmental behavioural change is considerable, and it was argued above that the legitimate power of government and employers needs to be more visible in order to promote and highlight changing social norms. The relative newness of climate change, combined with its hard-to-grasp scale and complexity, its social invisibility and source of easy-to-suppress negative emotions, amplifies the damaging effect on public engagement resulting from disagreement between perceived experts. Organised denial, though changing its focus, still exists, and therefore the right kind of authority is needed to diminish the salience of these voices in the public sphere.

Organised denial aside, the IPCC and other academics do not quite seem to be able to reach the general public. Although they provide background expertise, further platforms of communication are required to instil the urgency of climate change and its relevance to everyday life. To persuade people to make and prepare for major changes in their routines and outlook on the world the message needs to come from someone seen as sharing that world with them; who is somehow knowledgeable of and, in a sense, part of the business of everyday life as it is currently lived. Developing environmental awareness in general and climate change awareness in particular is a big ask, and a certain kind of trust is needed to motivate an appropriate response to it. This is not the trust that many or most of us have in the views of 97 per cent of climate scientists, but a trust that incorporates everyday familiarity with its source.

A reliable track record (including suitable expertise), combined with qualities needed to establish referent and ethotic power, seems to bring us close to the profile of someone who might increase public engagement with climate change. There seems little doubt that the success of *An Inconvenient Truth* is partly dependent on Gore being seen as trustworthy by much of its audience (and by that trustworthiness being deliberately and continually communicated to us during the film). Otherwise, though, it is hard to find many individuals who have the right profile to act as a trustworthy advocate. Several major celebrities – for example Arnold Schwarzenegger, Madonna and Cold Play – have thrown their weight behind climate change and other environmental issues; and sustained efforts have been made by Leonardo DiCaprio (who set up the Leonardo DiCaprio Foundation in 1998 with the aim of protecting wildlife and ecosystems, and co-wrote and produced the documentary *The 11th Hour* (Conners and Conners Petersen 2007)) and Daryl Hannah, an executive producer of the documentary exposé of corporate climate change denial *Greedy, Lying Bastards* (Rosebraugh 2012). Hannah's environmental activism also includes regular involvement with direct action and civil disobedience (see, for example, Gerkin 2011).

A drawback with celebrity environmentalists is that, as well-intentioned as they usually are, they are far from being experts or having the gravitas of intellectual impartiality. They can be viewed as gullible, bandwagon-jumping, obsessive, meddling, misusing their influence, as being an out of touch or a biased liberal elite, or even as being part of a hoax (Boykoff et al. 2010). For these reasons we would assume that the most effective environmental public advocates add expertise to charisma, ethotic and referent power. Figures like the late Australian naturalist and television personality Steve Irwin and, in particular, globally recognised and respected natural history broadcaster David Attenborough, create a credible bridge between science, entertainment and public engagement.

5.2.6 Enablers

An absence of know-how has been discussed under '5.2.1 Knowledge', but there is a different class of enablers – those external to an individual's skill set – that in many respects present a greater barrier to environmental behavioural change (Defra 2008; Moser and Dilling 2007, 2011; Shove et al. 2012). This includes limited accessibility to environmentally friendly technologies (such as recycling centres), an absence of eco-friendly services and products (and the poor labelling of those products), an absence of appropriate infrastructure (such as adequate bus services, cycle lanes, and showers at work to help encourage people to cycle), and an absence of adult education classes and other initiatives that can, among other things, provide advice and training. Alongside many of these goes an absence of financial incentives, and this is problematic for less wealthy people, not just because they do not have the resources for pricey initial investments, but because they would (rightly) see such demands as unfair.

Many of the emerging fundamentals of environmental behavioural change – providing knowledge and skills, aligning environmental issues with existing values and desires, making social norms visible, and combating a sense of helplessness – are things that community, or grassroots, initiatives have the potential to address. There are countless examples of these, including renewable energy projects, conservation projects, carbon neutral projects, information-sharing and advice groups (such as Carbon Conversations in the UK (originated by Cambridge Carbon Footprint), and Global Action Plan's EcoTeams), and more generalised set-ups such as the worldwide Transition Towns Network (Transition Network 2016; Aiken 2012). From an ethical perspective, they can be seen as, among other things, a deep and wide source of established and emerging environmental values and virtues. However, many also involve significant limitations and drawbacks, and there will be some consideration of both good and bad elements in Chapters 6 and 9.

5.2.7 Habits

Habits are characterised as behaviours carried out on a frequent routine basis, and which are automatic in their nature (Verplanken and Wood 2006; Darnton et al. 2011). Even quite skilful actions can become habits through practice and repetition;

a point being reached where minimal conscious effort is required to perform the behaviour. Along with this unconscious quality goes a reduced degree of control over the habitual action. They are characterised by their considerable momentum, which makes them relatively impervious to change via reasoned argument or self-reflection. When performing habitual actions we are very much 'in the world', operating in apparent harmony with our immediate environment whilst employing minimal mental effort. In this vein habits are remarkably effective all the time the individual's environment remains stable, and all the time they are working in accordance with the individual's goals. Good habits are, in short, a good thing. For Aristotle and others, virtuous behaviours are performed habitually; an indication of how they should be deeply integrated with an individual's personality and routine life. Good habits that are virtuous behaviours are therefore a good thing both for this reason and because they are relatively non-effortful. However, anti-virtuous (or vicious) habits are particularly bad for precisely the same reasons.

Many environmental behaviours are habitual: the food we buy and cook, how we deal with household waste, how we use energy and water, how we travel to work, and shopping behaviours (online and on the high street) including the use of bags. As several of these exemplify, habits can be changed, and in part this is due to some of the factors already discussed. In this section, however, we want to explore the challenges that emerge from the peculiarly entrenched nature of the habitual action.

There are broadly two approaches to changing and breaking habits: one that emphasises the experiences and choices of the individual, and one that emphasises the 'architecture' of daily life in terms of social and material structures, and associated skills and other competencies. These are, respectively, psychological and sociological approaches and, though some theorists see them as exclusive paradigms (e.g., Shove 2010), others (notably Darnton et al. 2011) see them as compatible and as necessary constituents of a complete account of how habits can be understood and altered.

One form of psychological intervention is derived from working with addictions. Individuals make a self-conscious effort to change their habits, sometimes in group settings such as WeightWatchers or, alternatively, through individual cognitive techniques. Habitual behaviours are picked out, made explicit, and replaced by new behaviours. The process has been conceptualised in terms of 'freezing' and 'unfreezing' behaviours, and involves a System 2 intervention based on exposure to group norms. With appropriate support, self-reflection and critical thinking are mustered to become aware of and, finally, acquire control over behaviours that are otherwise automatic responses to powerful internal desires and environmental triggers.

Group and other cognitive-based interventions have had some success in helping people overcome addictions, but the major drawback in terms of environmental behaviours is that the person needs to be strongly 'pre-motivated' in order for the process to be initiated and sustained. As we have seen, this degree of motivation will be lacking for many of us, and there is no strong analogue for Alcoholics Anonymous or WeightWatchers in the environmental sphere. As things stand, environmentally unfriendly behaviours do not cause personal discomfort, social disapproval or general life dysfunction in the way that alcoholism often does. And even in the case of personally dangerous or dysfunctional behaviours, the limitations of this approach are summed up by Verplanken and Wood (2006, 95) in this way:

> [T]he expectations established through behaviour repetition and the automaticity of habit performance are conservative forces that reduce openness to new information and that perpetuate well-practiced behaviours despite people's intentions to do otherwise. These aspects of habit performance significantly hinder the effectiveness of ... individually focused interventions, such as informational campaigns and self-help strategies. Interventions that provide people with information about the right thing to do or that increase their understanding about how to perform a behaviour are likely to be effective primarily with actions that are not practiced habitually. When the target behaviour is habitual, people's intentions, desires, and judgments do not easily overcome the practiced response that is cued automatically by the environment.

Also, to the extent that the changing of a habit requires intentions to change on behalf of individuals, we encounter the previously stated problem of environmental behaviours simply not having the salience and priority of, say, health related behaviours.

An alternative – and more promising – form of psychological (or more specifically social psychological) intervention involves the targeting of 'moments of change' (Wood et al. 2005; Thompson et al. 2011). Moments of change are life events such as retirement, pregnancy, moving home, leaving home, or starting a new job which disrupt routines and thus create a space for new forms of behaviour to be adopted and then settle as new habits. Take, for example, a student arriving at university for the first time. This world is unfamiliar, and many of the routine behaviours they have been used to are now either not available (such as having someone to cook their meals) or, where they are available (such as pursuing hobbies), efforts are needed in order to re-establish them. For a period of time System 2 is working hard and the person is in a reflective, anxious and potentially impressionable frame of mind. This usually won't last long, but while it does the people they meet and infrastructures in which they operate will have an uncharacteristically high degree of influence over their behaviours. If someone is learning to cook for themselves for the first time then a culture of healthy eating using ethically sourced ingredients can be encouraged by senior residents (in student houses and halls), information campaigns, and local shops selling appropriate goods at affordable prices. A first-time parent can be encouraged by local initiatives to consider the value of walking and the outdoors to help get the baby to sleep, and someone moving to a congested city might be more open to their new employer's 'cycle to work scheme' than someone established in that workplace and already habituated to using their car or public transport.

The evidence suggests that this approach is only usually successful under two conditions. The first is if a person already has an intention to change the habit in question (Bamberg 2006; Thompson et al. 2011). Under such circumstances interventions (such as a well-served and clearly timetabled bus route for a new housing estate) can be the final catalyst. The second is where the habit is weak (e.g., something that was contextually created and rarely a matter for reflective thought). Weak habits can be seen as those that co-opt a far smaller degree of a person's sense of identity or basic needs, and where their automaticity is more prone to being disrupted by contextual changes that can be externally manipulated. Strong habits, on the other hand, are things we must have a strong desire to change if change is going to happen. However, to return to where we began, since this strong desire by itself is often not enough to change the habit, the value of contextual approaches is that they provide external support for an otherwise weakened will (Wood et al. 2005).

Practice theory is the sociological approach to changing habits that has gained the most attention in recent years, and in particular the ideas of Elizabeth Shove and her colleagues (2010, 2012). In an expansion of MacIntyre's notion of practices (as discussed in Chapter 2), a practice in this context refers to most or all human activities, from feeding babies and washing clothes to attending festivals and parliamentary debates.

Shove understands everyday behaviours in terms of 'three elements': materials, procedures, and meanings. 'Materials' refers to physical objects, ranging from gadgets to roads and buildings. 'Procedures' includes competences (skills), but also to 'soft infrastructure' such as legislative frameworks and timetables. 'Meanings' refers to the connotations that various activities carry with them. So, the habit (or 'routine' as it is known in practice theory) of commuter cycling will be influenced by materials such as the design of bikes and the environments in which they are ridden (most obviously the presence or otherwise of cycle paths); by procedures like the ability to ride a bike safely and carry out maintenance and repairs; and meanings such as the odd, obsessive, cliquey or geeky connotations cycling can have in some cultures.

Practice theorists tend to be frank about the difficulty of attempting to influence particular practices, but they can inform us that in order for this to happen, these three features must be taken into consideration. To use one of Darnton et al.'s examples (op cit., 53–5), if the practice of line drying (as opposed to tumble drying) of clothes is to increase, a wide set of changes is needed. There is a competences aspect to it (constructing a washing line, knowing when to put out washing and when to bring it in, maybe even the acquisition and use of pegs), and a scheduling aspect (the time it takes in comparison to tumble drying). Having the right materials (e.g., design of yard or garden) can be a challenge that is relevant to planners and architects; and associated meanings can be quite significant. Clothes on a line can be considered ugly; in some cultures hanging out underwear is considered improper, and in others line drying in general diminishes someone's status, indicating, for example, an inability to afford a tumble dryer. In each case, it will be difficult to influence each of these elements of the practice, but the argument that these are the things that need to change if the habit is to change, is highly plausible.

As indicated, a distinctive feature of some practice theories is a rejection of psychological constructs as explanations of everyday activities. Individual humans are carriers of practices, and practices are the primary unit of analysis when it comes to understanding human behaviours. Practices change as the result of other practices, rather than because people decide they want to do things differently. Understood in this way psychological theories of habits are ruled out as irrelevant; as a category mistake in our attempts to make sense of human activity. A less reductive approach, however, allows for the basic model of materials, procedures and meanings to be fleshed out in a way that can incorporate cognitive aspects under 'meanings'. For example, the psychological theorizing of Bas Verplanken and others provides an invaluable explanation for why the System 1 operations of our psychology can make us relatively impervious to entertaining new ideas once a habit is established. This account is supported by a set of testable hypotheses concerning the conditions under which belief change can occur. These conditions dovetail quite well with the materials and procedures of practice theory, but practice theory by itself cannot provide a comprehensive account of the nature of habits or how to go about breaking them.

Crucial to Verplanken's 'habit discontinuity hypothesis' is that what he calls 'downstream' interventions – those directly communicating with individuals such as targeted information campaigns, encouraging self-control and targeting moments of change – are combined with background or indirect ('upstream') ones. These include taxation (such as London's congestion charge), infrastructural changes (such as cycle networks), technological changes (such as smart meters), policy changes (such as doorstep recycling), and the long-term educational effects of curriculum change and public information initiatives (which 'infuse the decisions of policy makers' (Verplanken and Wood 2006, 98)). Personal habit changes can be mediated by clear desires and intentions, but this is not a necessary feature of this importantly flexible approach.

The success, in many countries, of banning free plastic bags in shops is a good example of a successful mix of these interventions. In Ireland (for example) an information campaign explained the reasons for the ban and assured the public that taxes raised from their sale would go to environmental projects (Convery et al. 2007). The upstream intervention in this case is primarily the levy, but the way it impacts on shoppers is vital for understanding how this (for most people weak) habit is disrupted. All of a sudden, checkout operators are asking customers if they would like a bag (instead of just handing them over), and then informing people of the €0.15 (now €0.22) charge. Expectations are violated, and an automatic, non-effortful behaviour is conspicuously interfered with. As a result, a procedure that was firmly in the hands of System 1 processing shifts to System 2. Long-term behavioural change is then facilitated, not just by the expense, but by the availability of arguments for the new levy (in the information campaign), and made salient to individuals by the highly visible effects of plastic bag littering on the Irish countryside.

5.3 Conclusion

With a particular focus on public engagement with climate change, this chapter has looked at some fundamentals of the psychology of influence, and at barriers to environmental behavioural change along with some suggested solutions. The evidence is now overwhelming that human decision-making combines System 1 and System 2 processing, that certain kinds of issues or threats fail to engage System 1, and a failure to engage System 1 is a failure to engage in a way that will lead to committed action. A theme of the chapter has been the identification of virtues that have particular relevance to facing up to and overcoming global environmental crises. As indicated in the previous section, virtues are deep-seated features of an individual's personality that can often operate harmoniously with System 1 thinking. They are types of habit and, for this reason, slow to instil. Also, since habits are hard to change, dropping vices and replacing them with virtues can also be a slow and difficult process.

The situation we face is one in which some of those we would normally see as virtuous people are not environmentally virtuous. This is something that education and other broad cultural shifts can change (and arguably is changing), but the rate of change is important, and it appears that some fast-tracking of virtue-acquisition is required. In order to generate a virtuous circle, more of the population need to become environmental role models and be environmentally active in the broadest sense (for example, through political engagement). Environmental virtues with an epistemic orientation are perhaps, then, of paramount importance (see Leopold 1949; Hursthouse 2007; Swim et al. 2009) because they will continue to educate and transform a proportion of the population. These people then talk to, persuade, and put pressure on governments and other bodies, and a political agenda is established and maintained.

How this might be achieved remains a theme of subsequent chapters, but here it is worth pausing and summarising the main virtues of environmental behavioural change that have so far surfaced in this part of the book.

1. **Humility and tolerating uncertainty**. Most ethics requires us to move away from an egocentric focus, and several theorists – including Leopold and Singer – characterise post-enlightenment ethical theory in terms of successive attempts to widen our sphere of concern. Another relevant aspect of humility though is a realisation of the limitations of our reasoning abilities. This kind of self-awareness is of broad relevance to virtue theory, and the environmentally virtuous person in particular needs to be aware of the often misleading nature

of our emotional responses to climate change, and of the dangers of heuristic-based decision-making in what is a profoundly unfamiliar global context. A closely related virtue is tolerance of the uncertainty and complexity characteristic of wicked problems.
2. **Resilience**. Psychological denial can become a potent force should the enormity and complexity of the climate change problem trigger a sense of helplessness. Self-awareness is again important as a corrective to this, but so is the kind of resilience modelled by Al Gore in *An Inconvenient Truth*.
3. **Taking responsibility**. In situations of collective action 'taking responsibility' (van Hooft 2014) is an especially pertinent virtue. Citizens cannot expect governments or other institutions to adequately respond to climate change without public pressure, and politicians and other leaders must take responsibility for their part in fashioning and enacting a response at a global level.
4. **Virtues of cooperation**. Changing our own lifestyles is important, but usually we also need to work with others – both through practical necessity and because we often want to do more than individual change can accomplish. A wide range of virtues of cooperation therefore become relevant, including tolerance, trust, fairness and the 'group-deliberative virtues' (such as friendliness and courage) indicated in Chapter 2.
5. **Creative and imaginative thinking** (or openness to creative and imaginative thinking). Since enticement towards significant environmental behavioural change should not be framed in terms of sacrifice, positive alternatives for how to adjust to, and make the most of, a world that will either be significantly altered by climate change or by mitigation measures, are required.

A shift towards greater identification with non-human nature (as found in Schweitzer, Leopold and Naess – see Chapters 3 and 4) is likely to be important for taking the rights or interests of other species seriously, and for broadly improving human well-being. These ethics involve a paradigm shift that many have yet to make, and are for this reason a hard sell. An advantage of this list is that its stem virtues – humility, resilience, taking responsibility, cooperation and creativity and openness – are already familiar within many cultures and practices. Each, therefore, lends itself relatively easily to forms of moral framing that can contribute to a multi-dimensional approach to behaviour change (see Chapter 6).

In the next chapter, attention is turned to forms of intervention that primarily engage with System 1 thinking (social marketing and 'nudge'). The practical benefits of these approaches are discussed, along with an analysis of the ethical ramifications of methods that bypasses reasoned engagement and the self-conscious development of virtues.

Notes

1 See, for example, Seymour Epstein's (1998) 'experiential and 'rational' minds; Richard Thaler and Cass Sunstein's (2009) 'automatic system' and 'reflective system'.

2 This 'peripheral'/'central' distinction is basic to Petty and Cacioppo's (1996) influential 'Elaboration Likelihood Model' of persuasion.
3 Entman defines 'Salience' as 'making a piece of information more noticeable, meaningful, or memorable to audiences' (op cit., 53).
4 www.woodlandtrust.org.uk/support-us/support-an-appeal/arkaig-pinewoods/?gcli d=CjwKEAiAlZDFBRCKncm67qihiHwSJABtoNIgJlKQbX4UfyclosCdRos5WS-d636i2Eu5h5T18HmPhEhoCR-Dw_wcB&gclsrc=aw.ds.
5 Rosa Parks was the black American civil rights campaigner most famous for refusing to give up her bus seat to a white passenger in Montgomery, Alabama, in 1955.
6 In a tongue-in-cheek article in 2015 the Scottish version of *The Sun* newspaper argued that combatting climate change is important because rising temperatures will increase the prevalence of parasites that affect the health of sheep. Readers are therefore not being asked to care directly about global warming, but about the loss of their national dish.
7 For example, Shome and Marx (2009), Crompton (2010), Rose (2010), Darnton and Evans (2013), Marshall (2014, Ch. 42).
8 A point that is amusingly (and at times bizarrely) portrayed in the underground documentary film *Sizzle: A Global Warming Comedy* (Randy Olson, 2008).
9 www.bbc.co.uk/news/world-australia-37091391.
10 *Last Week Tonight* (HBO), broadcast May 2014.
11 In the House of Commons in 2013 the BBC were strongly criticised for using 'duelling experts' in their reporting of IPCC reports.
12 This point has been a long-standing criticism of technological fixes, as discussed in Chapter 4.
13 'Jubilee' in the sense of forgiving sins and releasing people from debts, rather than simply as an anniversary celebration as it is used with respect to, say, the monarch's jubilees in the UK.
14 Some social anthropologists and theorists argue that there are plenty of examples of communities operating in stable and co-operative ways, but these are largely outside of those structures that produce us as Hardin's rational egoist. These researchers suggest that the more the state and capital shapes individual psychology and group practices the harder it becomes (though not impossible) to develop uncoerced mutual aid (see, for instance, Kropotkin 1939, 183–4; Graeber 2012).
15 This, on the face of it, presents problems for Murray Bookchin's social ecology (Chapter 4), which relies on social cooperation to bring about sustainable societies and environments.
16 As George Marshall puts it, 'Everyone in Norway has a direct personal stake in this oil economy, thanks to the six hundred billion dollars saved in the state oil fund, which now includes a two-billion-dollar stake in Alberta's tar sands' (2014, 83).
17 From over 7.6 billion bags handed out by the seven main supermarkets in 2014, to 600 million in the first six months after the charge was introduced in October 2015 – a projected 85 per cent decrease.
18 Note that French and Raven (1959) treat these as two separate categories.

References

The 11th Hour (2007) directed by Nadia Conners and Leila Conners Petersen. USA: Warner Independent Pictures.
The Age of Stupid (2009) directed by Franny Armstrong. UK: Spanner Films.
Aiken, G. (2012) 'Community transitions to low carbon futures in the transition towns network', *Geography Compass*, 6(2): 89–99.
Aitken, C., Chapman, R. and McClure, J. (2011) 'Climate change, powerlessness and the commons dilemma: assessing New Zealanders' preparedness to act', *Global Environmental Change* 21.2: 752–60.

Aiken, G. (2012) 'Community transitions to low carbon futures in the transition towns network', *Geography Compass*, 6(2): 89–99.
Ajzen, I. (1991) 'The Theory of Planned Behaviour', *Organizational Behaviour and Human Decision Processes* 50: 179–211.
An Inconvenient Truth (2006) [documentary film] directed by Davis Guggenheim. USA: Lawrence Bender Productions.
Aristotle (1991) *The Art of Rhetoric*. London: Penguin.
Axelrod, R. (1984) *The Evolution of Cooperation*. London: Penguin.
Bamberg, S. (2006) 'Is a residential relocation a good opportunity to change people's travel behavior? Results from a theory-driven intervention study', *Environment and Behavior* 38.6: 820–840.
Bennie, L. (1998) 'Brent Spar, Atlantic Oil, and Greenpeace', *Parliamentary Affairs* 51.3: 397–411.
Boykoff, M. (2011) *Who Speaks for the Climate?* Cambridge: Cambridge University Press.
Boykoff, M., Goodman, M. and Littler, J. (2010) '"Charismatic megafauna": the growing power of celebrities and pop culture in climate change campaigns', *Environment, Politics and Development Working Paper Series*, WP: 28.
Brady, M. (2013) *Emotional Insight*. Oxford: Oxford University Press.
Brinton, A. (1986) 'Ethotic argument', *History of Philosophy Quarterly* 3.3: 245–58.
Campbell, J. (1949) *The Hero with a Thousand Faces*. New York: Pantheon Books.
Capstick, S.B. (2013) 'Public understanding of climate change as a social dilemma', *Sustainability* 5.8: 3484–501.
Carrigan, M., Moraes, C. and Leek, S. (2011) 'Fostering responsible communities: a community social marketing approach to sustainable living', *Journal of Business Ethics* 100.3: 515–34.
Cialdini, R. (2003) 'Crafting normative messages to protect the environment', *Current Directions in Psychological Science* 12.4: 105–9.
Cialdini, R. (2007) *Influence: The Psychology of Persuasion*. New York: Collins.
Convery, F., McDonnell, S. and Ferreira, S. (2007) 'The most popular tax in Europe? Lessons from the Irish plastic bags levy', *Environmental and Resource Economics* 38.1: 1–11.
Cook, J. and Lewandowsky, S. (2011) *The Debunking Handbook*. St. Lucia, Australia: University of Queensland.
Corner, A., Lewandowsky, S., Phillips, M. and Roberts, O. (2015) *The Uncertainty Handbook*. Bristol: University of Bristol.
Cox, R. and Pezzullo, P. (2015) *Environmental Communication and the Public Sphere*, Fourth Edition. Thousand Oaks CA: Sage.
Crompton, T. (2010). *Common Cause: The Case for Working with our Cultural Values*. WWF, Oxfam, Friends of the Earth, CPRE, Climate Outreach Information Network. Available at: www.foe.co.uk/sites/default/files/downloads/common_cause_report.pdf.
Damasio, A. (1994) *Descartes' Error*. New York: Putnam Publishing.
Damasio, A. (2000) *The Feeling of What Happens: Body, Emotion and the Making of Consciousness*. London: Vintage.
Darnton, A. and Evans, D. (2013) *Influencing Behaviours: A Technical Guide to the ISM Tool*. Scottish Government.
Darnton, A., Verplanken, B., White, P. and Whitmarsh, L. (2011) *Habits, Routines and Sustainable Lifestyles*. A summary report to Defra. AD Research & Analysis for Defra, London. Available at: www.defra.gov.uk.
Davis, H. (2009) *Caveman Logic*. Amherst NY: Prometheus Books.
Defra (2008) *A Framework for Pro-Environmental Behaviours*. Available at: www.defra.gov.uk/publications/files/pb13574-behaviours-report-080110.pdf.

Defra (2016) 'Single-use plastic carrier bags charge: data in England for 2015 to 2016'. Available at: www.gov.uk/government/publications/carrier-bag-charge-summary-of-data-in-england-for-2015-to-2016/single-use-plastic-carrier-bags-charge-data-in-england-for-2015-to-2016.

Demain (2015) directed by Cyril Dion and Mélanie Laurent. France: Mars Films.

DeSteno, D., Petty, R.E., Rucker, D.D., Wegener, D.T. and Braverman, J. (2004) 'Discrete emotions and persuasion: the role of emotion-induced expectancies', *Journal of Personality and Social Psychology* 86.1: 43–56.

Dunlap, R.E. and McCright, A.M. (2011) 'Organized climate change denial', in J. Dryzek, R.B. Norgaard and D. Schlosberg, eds, *The Oxford Handbook of Climate Change and Society*, 144–60. Oxford: Oxford University Press.

Entman, R. (1993) 'Framing: toward clarification of a fractured paradigm', *Journal of Communication* 43.4: 51–58.

Epstein, S. (1998) *Constructive Thinking: The Key to Emotional Intelligence*. Westport, CT: Praeger.

Facione, P.A., Sánchez, C.A., Facione, N.C. and Gainen, J. (1995) 'The disposition towards critical thinking', *The Journal of General Education* 44.1, 1–25.

Festinger, L. (1957) *A Theory of Cognitive Dissonance*. Stanford, CA: Stanford University Press.

Fiske, S. (2005) 'What's in a category?' In A.G. Miller, ed., *The Social Psychology of Good and Evil*. New York: Guildford Press.

French, J.R. and Raven, B. (1959) 'The bases of social power', *Classics of Organization Theory*, 7.

Gardiner, S. (2011) *The Perfect Moral Storm*. Oxford: Oxford University Press.

Gardner, G. and Stern, P. (2002) *Environmental Problems and Human Behaviour*, Second Edition. Boston: Pearson Custom Publishing.

Gasland (2010) directed by Josh Fox: USA New Video Group.

Gerkin, J. (2011) 'Daryl Hannah arrested at Keystone XL Pipeline Protest', *Huffington Post*. Available at: www.huffingtonpost.com/2011/08/30/daryl-hannah-arrested-keystone-protest_n_942072.html.

Giddens, A. (1991) *Modernity and Self-Identity*. Cambridge: Polity Press.

Gigerenzer, G., Todd, P. and the ABC Research Group (1999) *Simple Heuristics that Make Us Smart*. Oxford: Oxford University Press.

Graeber, D. (2012) *Debt: The First 5,000 Years*. New York: Melvillehouse.

Greedy, Lying Bastards (2012) directed by Craig Rosebraugh. UK: One Earth productions.

Greene, J. (2013) *Moral Tribes*. London: Atlantic Books.

Greenpeace (2013) *Dealing in Doubt: The Climate Denial Industry and Climate Science*. Available at: www.greenpeace.org/usa/en/campaigns/global-warming-and-energy/polluterwatch/Dealing-in-Doubt—-the-Climate-Denial-Machine-vs-Climate-Science/.

Hamilton, C. and Kasser, T. (2009) 'Psychological adaptation to the threats and stresses of a four degree world', *Four Degrees and Beyond* (conference held at Oxford University, 28–30 September 2009).

Hanscomb, S. (2017) *Critical Thinking: The Basics*. London: Routledge.

Hardin, G. (1986) 'The tragedy of the commons', in L.P. Pojman, ed., *Environmental Ethics: Readings in Theory and Application*. Belmont CA: Thomson Wadsworth. Ch. 46

Heidegger, M. (1962) *Being and Time*. Oxford: Blackwell.

Hovland, C., Janis, I. and Kelley, J. (1953) *Communication and Persuasion*. New Haven: Yale University Press.

Hulme, M. (2009) *Why We Disagree About Climate Change: Understanding Controversy, Inaction and Opportunity*. Cambridge: Cambridge University Press.

Hursthouse, R. (1992) *Beginning Lives*. Oxford: Blackwell.

Hursthouse, R. (2007) 'Environmental virtue ethics', in R.L. Walker and P.J. Ivanhoe, *Working Virtue: Virtue Ethics and Contemporary Moral Problems*, 155–71. Oxford: Oxford University Press.

IPCC (Intergovernmental Panel on Climate Change) (2007). *Climate Change 2007: The Physical Science Basis. Contribution of Working Group I to the Fourth Assessment Report of the Intergovernmental Panel on Climate Change* [Solomon, S., Qin, D., Manning, M., Chen, Z., Marquis, M., Avery, K.B., Tignor, M. and Miller, H.L. (eds)]. Cambridge University Press: Cambridge and New York.

IPCC (Intergovernmental Panel on Climate Change) (2013). *Climate Change 2013: The Physical Science Basis. Contribution of Working Group I to the Fifth Assessment Report of the Intergovernmental Panel on Climate Change* [Stocker, T.F., Qin, D., Plattner, G.-K., Tignor, M., Allen, S.K., Boschung, J., Nauels, A., Xia, Y., Bex, V. and Midgley, P.M. (eds)]. Cambridge University Press: Cambridge and New York.

IPCC (Intergovernmental Panel on Climate Change) (2014) *Climate Change 2014: Synthesis Report. Contribution of Working Groups I, II and III to the Fifth Assessment Report of the Intergovernmental Panel on Climate Change* [Core Writing Team, R.K. Pachauri and L.A. Meyer (eds)]. Geneva, Switzerland: IPCC.

Janis, I. (1982) *Groupthink*, Second Edition. Boston: Houghton Mifflin.

Jones, R., Pykett, J. and Whitehead, M. (2013) *Changing Behaviours*. Cheltenham: Edward Elgar.

Kahneman, D. (2012) *Thinking Fast and Slow*. London: Penguin.

Kearney, R. (2002) *On Stories*. London and New York: Routledge.

Kellstedt, P.M., Zahran, S. and Vedlitz, A. (2008) 'Personal efficacy, the information environment, and attitudes toward global warming and climate change in the United States', *Risk Analysis* 28.1, 113–26.

Keltner, D., Oatley, K. and Jenkins, J. (2013) *Understanding Emotions*, Third Edition. Hoboken, NJ: Wiley.

Klein, N. (2015) *This Changes Everything*. London: Penguin.

Kollmuss, A. and Agyeman, J. (2002) 'Mind the gap: why do people act environmentally and what are the barriers to pro-environmental behavior? *Environmental Education Research* 8.3, 239–60.

Kropotkin, P. (1939) *Mutual Aid*. London: Pelican.

Lasswell, H.D. (1948) 'The structure and function of communication in society', *The Communication of Ideas* 37: 215–28.

Latané, B. and Darley, J.M. (1968) 'Group inhibition of bystander intervention in emergencies'. *Journal of Personality and Social Psychology* 10.3: 215–21.

Leiserowitz, A., Maibach, E., Roser-Renouf, C., Feinberg, G. and Howe, P. (2013) *Global Warming's Six Americas, September 2012*. Yale University and George Mason University, New Haven, CT: Yale Project on Climate Change Communication.

Leopold, A. (1949) *A Sand County Almanac*. Oxford: Oxford University Press.

Levine, R. (2006) *The Power of Persuasion: How We're Bought and Sold*. Oxford: Oneworld.

Lorenzoni, I., Nicholson-Cole, S. and Whitmarsh, L. (2007) 'Barriers perceived to engaging with climate change among the UK public and their policy implications', *Global Environmental Change* 17: 445–59.

Louv, R. (2009) *Last Child in the Woods*. London: Atlantic Books.

MacGregor Burns, J. (1978) *Leadership*. New York: Harper Perennial.

Markowitz, E.M. and Shariff, A.F. (2012) 'Climate change and moral judgement', *Nature Climate Change* 2.4: 243–7.

Marshall, G. (2014) *Don't Even Think About It: Why Our Brains are Wired to Ignore Climate Change*. New York: Bloomsbury.

McKenzie-Mohr, D. (2000) 'Promoting sustainable behaviour: an introduction to community-based social marketing', *Journal of Social Issues* 56.3: 543–54.
Milgram, S. (1974) *Obedience to Authority*. London: Tavistock.
Moser, S.C. and Dilling, L. (2007). 'Toward the social tipping point: creating a climate for change', in *Creating a Climate for Change: Communicating Climate Change and Facilitating Social Change*, 491–516. Cambridge: Cambridge University Press.
Moser, S.C. and Dilling, L. (2011) 'Communicating climate change: closing the science-action gap', in J. Dryzek, D. Schlosberg and R.B. Norgaard, eds, *The Oxford Handbook of Climate Change and Society*, 161–74. Oxford: Oxford University Press.
Nicol, A. (2015) 'Save the haggis'. *The Sun*. Available at: www.thesun.co.uk/archives/news/873598/save-the-haggis/.
Nisbet, M. (2009) 'Communicating climate change: why frames matter for public engagement', *Environment: Science and Policy for Sustainable Development*, March–April. Available at: www.environmentmagazine.org/Archives.
No Impact Man (2009) directed by Laura Gabbert and Justin Schein. USA: Dogwoof.
Norgaard, K. (2009) 'Cognitive and behavioral challenges in responding to climate change', *World Bank Policy Research Working Paper Series*. World Development Report Team.
Nussbaum, M. (2001) *Upheavals of Thought*. Cambridge: Cambridge University Press.
O'Neill, S. and Nicholson-Cole, S. (2009). '"Fear won't do it". Promoting positive engagement with climate change through visual and iconic representations'. *Science Communication*, 30(3), 355–379.
Oreskes, N. and Conway, E. (2010) *Merchants of Doubt*. London: Bloomsbury.
Ostrom, E. (2014) 'Collective action and the evolution of social norms', *Journal of Natural Resources Policy Research* 6.4: 235–252.
Painter, J. (2013) *Climate Change in the Media*. London: I.B. Tauris.
Pattie, C., Seyd, P. and Whiteley, P. (2003) 'Citizenship and civic engagement: attitudes and behaviour in Britain', *Political Studies* 51: 443–68.
Payne, O. (2012) *Inspiring Sustainable Behaviour*. Abingdon: Routledge.
Petty, R.E. and Cacioppo, J.T. (1996) *Attitudes and Persuasion: Classic and Contemporary and Approaches*. New York: Westview Press.
Project Wild Thing (2013) directed by David Bond and Ashley Jones. UK: Green Lions.
Raven, B.H. (2008). 'The bases of power and the power/interaction model of interpersonal influence'. *Analyses of Social Issues and Public Policy*, 8(1): 1–22.
Rayner, S. (2006) 'Wicked problems: clumsy solutions–diagnoses and prescriptions for environmental ills', *Jack Beale Memorial Lecture on Global Environment*. Sydney, Australia.
Rittel, H.W. and Webber, M.M. (1973) 'Dilemmas in a general theory of planning', *Policy Sciences* 4.2: 155–69.
Rose, C. (2010) *How to Win Campaigns: Communications for Change*. London: Earthscan.
Rosteck, T. and Frentz, T. (2009) 'Myth and multiple readings in environmental rhetoric: the case of *An Inconvenient Truth*', *Quarterly Journal of Speech* 95.1: 1–19.
Sandler, R. (2007) *Character and Environment*. New York: Columbia University Press.
Schultz, P.W., Nolan, J.M., Cialdini, R.B., Goldstein, N.J. and Griskevicius, V. (2007) 'The constructive, destructive, and reconstructive power of social norms', *Psychological Science* 18.5: 429–34.
Sherif, M. (1936) *The Psychology of Social Norms*. Oxford: Harper.
Shome, D. and Marx, S. (2009) 'The psychology of climate change communication: a guide for scientists, journalists, educators, political aides, and the interested public'. New York: Centre for Research on Environmental Decisions.

Shove, E. (2010) 'Against the ABC: climate change policy and theories of social change', *Environment & Planning* 42: 1273–85.
Shove, E., Pantzar, M. and Watson, M. (2012) *The Dynamics of Social Practice*. London: Sage.
Sidahmed, M. (2016) 'Climate change denial in the Trump cabinet: where do his nominees stand?' *The Guardian*, 15 December. Available at: www.theguardian.com/environment/2016/dec/15/trump-cabinet-climate-change-deniers.
Singer, P. (1993) *How Are We to Live?* Oxford: Oxford University Press.
Smithers, R. (2016) 'England's plastic bag usage drops 85% since 5p charge is introduced', *The Guardian*, 30 July. Available at: www.theguardian.com/environment/2016/jul/30/england-plastic-bag-usage-drops-85-per-cent-since-5p-charged-introduced.
Spence, A., Venables, D., Pidgeon, N., Poortinga, W. and Demski, C. (2010) *Public Perceptions of Climate Change and Energy Futures in Britain: Summary Findings of a Survey Conducted in January-March 2010 Technical Report*. Cardiff University: School of Psychology.
Sunstein, C.R. (2015) 'Nudges, agency, and abstraction: a reply to critics', *Review of Philosophy and Psychology* 3.6: 511–529.
Swim, J., Clayton, S., Doherty, T., Gifford, R., Howard, G., Reser, J., Stern, P. and Weber, E. (2009) *Psychology and Global Climate Change: Addressing a Multi-Faceted Phenomenon and Set of Challenges: A Report by the American Psychological Association's Task Force on the Interface Between Psychology and Global Climate Change*. Washington: American Psychological Association.
Talen, Reverend B. (2016) *The Earth Wants You*. San Francisco: City Lights Books.
Taylor, S.E. and Brown, J.D. (1988) 'Illusion and well-being: a social psychological perspective on mental health'. *Psychological Bulletin*, 103(2): 193–210.
Thaler, R. and Sunstein, C. (2009) *Nudge*. London: Penguin.
Thompson, S., Michaelson, J., Abdallah, S., Johnson, V., Morris, D., Riley, K. and Simms, A. (2011) '"Moments of change" as opportunities for influencing behaviour'. London: Defra.
Todhunter, T. (2011) 'Low-carbon communities: a grassroots perspective on public engagement'. In Whitmarsh, L., O'Neill, S. and Lorenzoni, I. (Eds), *Engaging the Public with Climate Change*. London: Routledge.
Transition Network (2016) available at: https://transitionnetwork.org/.
Tversky, A. and Kahneman, D. (1974) 'Judgement under uncertainty: heuristics and biases', *Science* 185: 1124–1131.
Van Hooft, S. (2014). *Understanding Virtue Ethics*. London: Routledge.
Verplanken, B. and Wood, W. (2006) 'Interventions to break and create consumer habits', *Journal of Public Policy & Marketing*, 25.1: 90–103.
Washington, H. and Cook, J. (2011) *Climate Change Denial: Heads in the Sand*. London: Earthscan.
Wilson, E.O. (2006) *The Creation*. New York: Norton.
Wood, W., Tam, L. and Witt, M.G. (2005) 'Changing circumstances, disrupting habits', *Journal of Personality and Social Psychology* 88.6: 918–33.
Workman, L. and Reader, W. (2014) *Evolutionary Psychology: An Introduction*, Third Edition. Cambridge: Cambridge University Press.
Yukl, G. and Falbe, C.M. (1991) 'Importance of different power sources in downward and lateral relations', *Journal of Applied Psychology* 76.3: 416–23.

6

THE PRACTICAL AND MORAL LIMITATIONS OF THE PSYCHOLOGY OF INFLUENCE

The previous chapter discussed the psychosocial barriers to environmental behavioural change, along with some attempts to overcome these and a thematic focus on the virtues that would assist this process. This chapter presents an ethical analysis of interventions that base their methods on marketing know-how, and in particular the manipulation of habitual behaviours and System 1 thinking. To begin with, some history and basic principles of social marketing and nudge theory are set out, and then the central ethical issues generated by this approach to environmental behavioural change are explained and discussed. These fall under two headings, corresponding with two distinct sets of literature that have been critical of these approaches: the 'ethics of nudge' and 'Common Cause'.

6.1 Social marketing and nudge

6.1.1 Social marketing

Social marketing is the application of the insights of commercial marketing, along with non-commercial social scientific behavioural change research, to socially desirable goals (NSMC 2011). Commercial marketing has itself been an area of applied research since the 1940s (Packard 1957), and its insights have been used in attempts to generate behaviour change in health and environmental behaviours for a similar length of time. The US 'People Start Pollution, People Can Stop It' public information announcement, in which a Native American sadly witnesses industrial pollution and everyday littering, was influential in the 1970s and 80s[1] and has been rated among the best ads of all time (Cialdini 2003, 105). Another high-profile example is the successful 'Don't mess with Texas' campaign discussed briefly in the previous chapter.

It is, however, the 'below the line' behaviour-change techniques explored and adopted by various Western governments and other organisations since the 1990s that have become the particular focus of ethical scrutiny in recent years. The most distinctive feature of social marketing is what it shares with behavioural economics such as, for example, 'freakonomics' (Levitt and Dubner 2005), 'nudge' (Thaler and Sunstein 2009), and what is broadly termed the 'behaviour change agenda' (Jones et al. 2013, 1). In the UK Richard Thaler became an adviser to David Cameron's coalition government in 2010 and the Behavioural Insights Team (also known as the 'Nudge Unit') was set up under the leadership of civil servant David Halpern – a major figure in the psychological policy turn who was particularly influenced by the work of Tversky and Kahneman (see Chapter 5). The origins of this approach to health and environmental policy in the UK pre-dated Cameron and are traced by Jones et al. (ibid) to New Labour in the 1990s. It was under their leadership (1997–2010) that one of the first major experiments with behavioural psychology was undertaken by the Department for Energy, Food and Rural Affairs (Defra), resulting in their 2008 report *A Framework for Pro-Environmental Behaviours*.

In social marketing, the behaviour of individuals is changed through the exploitation of the kinds of psychological biases in decision-making that were explored in the previous chapter. Decisions are not directly coerced as they are with legal restrictions, nor are people incentivised via taxation, subsidies or other forms of reward and punishment. Behavioural change based on social marketing or 'nudge' is also to be contrasted with messages based primarily on the information deficit model, and also, for the nudge theorists at least, with subliminal advertising. The information deficit model is naïve in its reliance on System 2 processing, but the subliminal messaging goes too far in the other direction, undermining rather than merely biasing decision-making processes. From a government's point of view, social marketing makes sense in situations where legislation is not appropriate (for example, where it is felt to be an infringement on negative freedom – see Chapter 2), and where traditional forms of public information are limited in their effectiveness.

Since the principles of marketing encompass more or less whatever works to sell a product, idea or behaviour to an endless array of audiences, the practice of social marketing is broad and flexible. Everything discussed in the last chapter either has been, or could be, of interest to someone marketing environmentally friendly behaviours, and many of the examples found there result directly from its application. Since there is so much creativity and tacit knowledge in sales and marketing caution is needed when deriving principles from it, but these nevertheless have some explanatory value and, as is discussed shortly, social marketers themselves take them very seriously. They will also help provide an insight into the kind of thing social marketing is, and this will inform our analyses in terms of ethics and environmental behavioural change. It is worth noting at this stage as well that although other approaches criticise or reject some features and assumptions of social marketing, other aspects of it tend to be broadly accepted as necessary for effective communication. The difference can be an ethical one: 'you can use this strategy or tactic, but only if certain conditions are met' (see, for example, '6.3 Common Cause', discussed later in this chapter); or it can be an ontological one: 'This strategy or tactic can work, but only if understood in the context of a significantly (or radically) different understanding of what it is to be a human being' (as found in practice theory, see Chapter 5).

The National Social Marketing Centre (NSMC) – a UK-based company that specialises in providing social marketing information and training – has identified eight interconnected principles that typically underpin a social marketing campaign (2011, 39–78):

1. Understanding the people whose behaviour is being targeted.
2. Specific behaviour changes are sought, rather than (just) a change in knowledge and attitudes.
3. Approaches to behavioural change are guided by established theories, principally derived from psychology.
4. Interventions are informed by 'insight'; a deep-social-science-based account of barriers to changing specific behaviours (energy use, recycling and so on).
5. In what is referred to as 'the exchange', the benefits of new behaviours are maximised in the perceptions of target audiences, and their costs are minimised.
6. If principle 5 is to be achieved, then factors that compete for people's time and attention need to be understood ('the competition').
7. The people the campaign seeks to reach are divided into sub-groups who will be influenced by different motivational priorities or reached by different forms of content, style and media ('segmentation').
8. Where possible, multiple interventions should be employed to reach each segment; meaning not just different media and framing, but also factors such as financial incentives and practical advice.

Principles 3 and 4 involve the kind of knowledge discussed in Chapter 5; for example dual processing and social influence (norms and authority). Principles 1, 5, 6 and 7 all refer to the need for as much specific knowledge about target audiences as it is realistic to achieve given the time and other resources available. This feeds an understanding of the barriers to behavioural change that need to be overcome. Implied here is the requirement for the skilful framing of messages amongst a raft of other factors that determine the success of marketing communications: tone, narrative, genre, vocabulary, setting, characters (personality, virtues, demographic features), use of authorities, and so on. Major research projects in the UK and USA have attempted to make sense of public attitudes to climate change via segmentation. In the UK the government Department for Energy, Food and Rural Affairs (Defra 2008) identified seven groupings indicating varying levels of engagement. These are presented below, along with the percentage of the overall population, and quotations chosen by Defra that is representative of each:

Positive greens: 'I think we need to do some things differently to tackle climate change. I do what I can and I feel bad about the rest', 18 per cent.

Waste watchers: '"Waste not, want not" that's important, you should live life thinking about what you are doing and using', 12 per cent.

Concerned consumers: 'I think I do more than a lot of people. Still, going away is important, I'd find that hard to give up . . . well I wouldn't, so carbon offsetting would make me feel better', 14 per cent.

Sideline supporters: 'I think climate change is a big problem for us. I suppose I don't think much about how much water or electricity I use, and I forget to turn things off. I'd like to do a bit more', 14 per cent.

Cautious participants: 'I do a couple of things to help the environment. I'd really like to do more, well as long as I saw others were', 14 per cent.

Stalled starters: 'I don't know much about climate change. I can't afford a car so I use public transport . . . I'd like a car though', 10 per cent.

Honestly disengaged: 'Maybe there'll be an environmental disaster, maybe not. Makes no difference to me, I'm just living life the way I want to', 18 per cent.

In the US, the Yale Project on Climate Communication's *Global Warming's Six Americas* (Leiserowitz et al. 2013), has identified similar segments, which they name the 'alarmed', 'concerned', 'cautious', 'disengaged', 'doubtful' and 'dismissive'. The level of detail found in these reports, profiling not just different attitudes but also the demographic characteristics that tend to be associated with these attitudes, is very much what social marketers need in order to fashion and target their messages and other interventions (for example, Defra's 'Act on CO_2' campaigns around 2009).

Principle 2 indicates the target-driven nature of social marketing. Outcomes need to be both material and measurable: level of energy consumption, miles covered on foot or by bike instead of by car, number of hours spent in nature, volume of non-recycled household waste and so on. An ideal campaign should include a pilot study and an evaluation (McKenzie-Mohr 2000) so that relevant data is available for guiding future campaigns and policy decisions. Principle 8 also reiterates discussion from Chapter 5: whether from a social marketing perspective or some other approach to behavioural change, there is general agreement that, so long as they do not send contradictory messages, multiple interventions will be more effective than singular ones (Gardner and Stern 2002).

Interventions along the lines of the social marketing model have been shown to be effective (Jones et al. 2013, 152–3; Capstick et al. 2015), but in a highly qualified manner. First, in the UK, the behaviour change that takes place as a result of intervention amounts to, on average, around a 10 per cent reduction in carbon-intensive behaviours, which is not nearly enough to meet the country's 2050 target of 80 per cent reduction in greenhouse gases. Second, this figure is reduced enormously (perhaps to as low as 3 per cent) when indirect contributions to greenhouse gases (such as those 'embedded' in the consumption of meat and dairy products) are included in the calculations (Capstick et al. 2015, 3). Third, there is limited evidence for the long-term maintenance of the interventions that are studied by social scientists, and indeed for any 'spillover' effect – i.e., positive changes in one environmentally friendly behaviour transferring to other behaviours without the need for further interventions – that it is hoped would occur.

The reasons for this, along with further critiques of the application of social marketing to environmentally relevant behaviours, will be considered in Section 6.3.

Spillover: the term used to describe the transferral of a behaviour to other, similar, behaviours without the need to employ further methods of behavioural change. It has particular importance for climate change mitigation because such a wide variety of behaviours contribute to greenhouse gas emissions.

6.1.2 Nudge

Richard Thaler and Cass Sunstein's (2009) nudge approach draws on many of the insights employed by social marketing, and notably the biases and heuristics that are central to System 1 thinking. Using these insights, choices are 'shaped' (Hausman and Welch 2010, 128) in ways that benefit the individual or society. There are few if any clear differences between the two at the level of practice, but from its inception nudge has been explicitly politically contextualised in a way that social marketing has tended not to be. Its original name was 'libertarian paternalism', and if the intention is to improve the individual's welfare then this is indeed an example of paternalism (see Chapter 7).[2] If, however, it is primarily social benefits that are sought (as in the case of environmental behaviours) then a different terminology – 'behavioural welfarism' (Schubert 2017, 5) for example – is needed.

Whether understood as paternalism or welfarism, nudge, like social marketing, is ethically interesting because typical examples of it inhabit a grey area between clearly autonomous decisions made via rational reflection on accurate and sufficient information, and coercion through taxation or bans. Thaler and Sunstein name their approach 'libertarian paternalism' because individuals are not denied choices, only encouraged, through the 'gentle power of nudges' (Thaler and Sunstein 2009, 9) to make the right one. A nudge, they say, is

> any aspect of the choice architecture that alters people's behaviour in a predictable way without forbidding any options or significantly changing their economic incentives. To count as a mere nudge, the intervention must be easy and cheap to avoid. Nudges are not mandates. Putting the fruit at eye level counts as a nudge. Banning junk food does not.
>
> *(Thaler and Sunstein 2009, 6.)*

By 'choice architecture' they mean the context in which the choice is made. There seem to be few limits on what constitutes this context, but the distinctiveness of nudge is their emphasis on aspects that largely work below the radar of System 2 cognition. Some important categories are physical environment, defaults, framing and feedback.

The example mentioned in the quotation is an example of a nudge based on a change to the physical environment. On recognising that people in a canteen are more likely to choose food placed at eye level (rather than on higher or lower shelves), the food counter 'architecture' is designed so as to make the choice of the healthy dessert more likely. Where decisions are made quickly the cognitive (in this case perceptual) availability of options is important in determining what is chosen. The physical arrangement biases the individual towards what is healthier for them (or possibly towards what they rationally favour but find less appetising), that way helping to establish a positive habit, or perhaps assisting them in the resistance of temptation. An environmental example, which are often referred to as 'green nudges' might be the inconspicuousness of plastic bags in supermarket checkouts that has become the norm in the UK in recent years. In some cases these are literally 'under the counter', reducing their cognitive availability and implying a norm of using reusable bags.

Other kinds of example involve the default options on the machinery, software or official forms we use. Green nudges include an energy company's list of packages defaulting to green energy sources (Pichert and Katsikopoulos 2008), using lower (but not freezing) thermostat settings in the workplace, or a two-sided default on office printers (Schubert 2017). The effectiveness, at least to an extent, of such measures is now well established, and reasons for what has become known as the 'default bias' is in part based on giving the impression of a norm (see Chapter 5). Setting pro-environmental options as defaults sends the implicit message that this is the normal and quite possibly the right thing to do (Jones et al. 2013). In addition, and as the previous discussion of habits indicates (see Chapter 5), our behaviour comes with a certain inertia. We typically like to avoid cognitive effort and, other things being equal, tend to go along with what appears to be the status quo. As will be further considered below, nudges tend not to be effective where there is a strong desire in the opposite direction. Instead, they work well where we are in favour of or, very importantly, relatively indifferent to the encouraged behaviour (Sunstein and Reisch 2014, 142); and they work well where changes are small or incrementally introduced.

It can be said that the default frames choices in a certain way, but the nudge literature tends to apply the idea of framing in a more limited fashion, often referring to loss aversion. Loss aversion is our dislike of losing what we already possess in contrast to losing out on gaining the equivalent amount. One upshot is that pro-environmental behaviours are unlikely to be popular if people perceive they will be worse off than they currently are. Pichert and Katsikopoulos (2008) report a natural experiment in which the German utilities company Energiedienst GmbH advertised a shift from one to three possible tariffs. A green tariff was set as the default, and most customers (94 per cent) went with this 'no response needed' option, despite a non-green ('grey') alternative being offered that was 8 per cent cheaper. We cannot know for certain, but as well as this default, it is plausible to assume that framing played an important part in customers' choices: the green option was slightly cheaper than the previous single rate (so there was no off-putting loss involved), and was considerably cheaper than the third option – also green, but 23 per cent dearer. This latter factor generates what is known as the 'contrast effect', which describes how our evaluation of something is altered by the presence of an alternative that is significantly higher or lower on a scale of relevant attributes. For example, under experimental conditions applying 'self-stereotyping' theory, the 'centrality' of an individual's environmental values and their intentions to act environmentally can be increased by comparing their in-group to a less-well-performing out-group (UK to USA) and decreased by making a comparison in the opposite direction (UK to Sweden) (Rabinovich et al. 2011).

The use of feedback is also commonly cited as a form of nudge, and this again has particular relevance to energy consumption. UK law, for instance, stipulates that all households must be offered the chance of installing a smart meter by 2020. On the face of it constantly available information on rates of energy consumption appeals to System 2 rather than System 1 but, as Jones et al. (2013, 150) point out, 'by providing real-time, often colour-coded [red and green lights] signals on fluctuating energy use, smart meters are able to elicit moment-to-moment feelings of guilt and pride about our domestic behaviours'. Such feelings could be a result of moral principles (environmental or otherwise), or they could also be authority and social norm related, but either way they will function as heuristics.

According to Thaler and Sunstein the advantages of nudges, compared with taxation and bans, include lower complexity and cost (for example, not having to enforce behaviours), and their not being coercive. Also, as we have seen, they are more effective than relying solely upon neutrally presented messages aimed at reflective decision-making. In terms of the barriers identified in Chapter 5, nudges have been demonstrated to be effective in mitigating several of these, including complexity. With respect to using green energy defaults Sunstein and Reisch (2014, 142) argue:

> The choice of an electricity provider is not exactly intuitive; it may well be cognitively demanding and thus represent a nontrivial "effort tax." The default rule might stick simply because people do not want to engage in that thinking, take that risk, or make that tradeoff. . . . Even if people in some sense want to investigate the issue and possibly make a change, they might decide that they will do so tomorrow — and tomorrow never comes.

Nudge's congruence with the power of norms and authority has been mentioned; the impression that there is a green norm ought to mitigate the helplessness that can cause psychological denial, and they, of course, engage squarely with the habitual nature of behaviours, working with rather than against their momentum. Michiru Nagatsu (2015) has argued that nudges help overcome the prisoner's dilemma by reassuring enlightened egoists or 'conditional co-operators' (presumed to be the majority) – for whom the main motivation for free-riding is a distrust of others to cooperate – that the existence of nudge makes co-operation beyond the threshold needed for public benefits to be actualised a greater likelihood.

6.2 Challenges to using psychological influence (I): the ethics of nudge

In a recent paper Sunstein (2015) stresses that nudge refers not just to the exploitation of the behavioural biases associated with System 1 thinking but to any intervention that is non-coercive. This includes uncontroversial forms of communication that are primarily aimed at System 2 processing (so, for instance, any public information ad that relies on the information deficit model). His point is that with any type of advice or guidance there will be a default recommendation. In the case of GPS, for example, there are other routes we are free to take, and these might well be better for us, but the fact that we will tend to follow what the system recommends is not a cause of ethical disquiet (2015, 512). Sunstein's point is much the same as the one we made in Chapter 5 with respect to the ubiquitous nature of framing. If, as appears to be the case, framing is unavoidable, then ethics must accept this as a limiting condition of human knowledge and agency.

However, and as per the examples above, nudge becomes ethically significant when unconscious biases are knowingly exploited. In this vein, a recent and quite comprehensive taxonomy of ethical concerns can be found in Schubert (2017), and some of the headings below overlap with his (autonomy, self-development and fairness). Discussion under these and the other heading (relationship with government) are informed by what has been a growing literature on the ethics of nudge over the past decade (for example, Bovens 2009; Hausman and Welch 2010; Smith et al. 2013; Jones et al. 2013; Guala and Mittone 2015; Mills 2015; Nagatsu 2015).

6.2.1 Undermining autonomy in everyday choices

Nudge involves an apparent contradiction. It is supposed not to interfere with the choices available to people, and yet influences those choices at an unconscious level (Oliver 2013, 687). Using psychological insight, some options are made more salient than others, with the clear intention that this influences decisions in an automatic rather than reflective fashion. Viewed in one way, this seems to be no different to the manipulative methods of commercial marketing. In the words of Agnes Nairn:

> you can't take a technique that is slightly dodgy and just because you're using it for a good purpose that technique suddenly becomes okay. It's not. If you want to do this ethically you want people to make their own minds up [but with] a lot of the most effective marketing, you don't make your own mind up because it's happening on a subconscious level.
> *(Interview in Bond and Jones 2013 ('Bonus features').)*

There are, however, a couple of important differences. One is that nudge requires that governments are transparent with respect to the methods they are using and where and when they are using them. In commercial marketing, it is generally not in the interests of companies to make their persuasion tactics explicit, but in a sense this is true of nudge as well. However, the second difference explains why being explicit is less problematic for nudge. Unlike commercial marketing, the consumer is supposed to have tacitly agreed to, or at least understood, the reasoning behind the measures that the nudges support (Thaler and Sunstein 2009, 44–5). Under optimum conditions, it assumes a self-recognition that we are habitual beings who make many decisions quickly with minimal cognitive effort. While being accepting of this state of affairs – there seems little doubt, given the limitations of human psychology, that the capacity to act habitually is highly beneficial – we appreciate that it does not always lead to the best results (see Chapter 5). Luc Bovens (2009, 213) expresses this in terms of vices: inertia caused by laziness, temptation caused by weakness of the will (*Akrasia*), or the cognitive unavailability of relevant information caused by ignorance or self-deception. As cognitively and virtuously erratic beings we might welcome the existence of choice architectures that help us make the types of decision we would reflectively regard as right, but not always unreflectively opt for.

According to this reasoning, at the moment of decision our autonomy is impaired by nudges, but in the wider sense it is preserved. On the one hand what we choose is coherent with our overall 'preference structure' (Bovens 2009), and on the other we assent to the presence of nudges in order to facilitate us making that choice (Mills 2015).

Empirical evidence suggests that for 'green nudges' this supposition is born out. All the time environmental policies are seen as necessary and important, and so long as there is transparency about the employment of nudges by governments, people appear to welcome their presence (Hagman et al. 2015). Schubert (2017, 337), however, is cautious, pointing out that where a survey response reflects well on a person's self-image, what they say and what they actually want can be different things. As it happens, Thaler and Sunstein assume non-optimum conditions in which clarity of insight or agreement with the government's goals is often absent. The minimum requirement of their version of Rawls' 'publicity principle' – that the government be willing and able to publically defend its policy (2009, 244) – could nevertheless still be met under these circumstances. Thaler and Sunstein rule out subliminal advertising because the extent to which it undermines choice would not be defensible, but the use of nudges could be.

Moreover, nudge is argued to be preferable to coercive measures precisely because it recognises that not everyone will (reflectively) want what a nudge encourages, at least not on every occasion. It is important, then, that other choices are not prohibited, and also that we have the ability, time and energy to make the cognitive effort required to resist the momentum of cleverly designed choice architectures. Research suggests that people deeply opposed to the behaviour being encouraged will tend to be able to resist nudges (Gromet et al. 2013; Sunstein and Reisch 2014).

Nevertheless, because the evidence is not yet clear, and even if it were it would be probabilistic, the concern remains that 'people with exceptional preferences are not always exceptionally resistant to the influence of nudges' (Nagatsu 2015, 485). A set of individually negotiated nudges might provide a way around this problem, but three problems arise here. One is that nudges implemented on a large scale cannot reasonably be expected to be anything but generalised. Second, some nudges (such as those found on billboard advertisements) cannot, by their nature, be tailored. Third, even where tailored nudges are possible and desirable (Sunstein and Reisch (2014, 155) speculate about possible applications), the tailoring must be based on the individual's past behaviour, and is this not precisely what we want to change? In other words, short of presumably unfeasible research programmes, we cannot reliably identify the people who want to change their behaviours but who have so far lacked the effort or willpower to do so. That said, broad groups of vulnerable people (for example those with learning difficulties and other reasons for cognitive impairment) could perhaps be more realistically identified and, where possible, spared from nudges.

A further response to the autonomy problem is to remind ourselves that our choices are unavoidably shaped by biases and heuristics, whether or not they derive from government policy (Sunstein and Reisch 2014; Sunstein 2015). From this perspective, nudges can be viewed as a corrective to the tactics of commercial marketing and other message sources. The implication is that, if it wants to be effective, a government has no option but to design its interventions in accordance with heuristics-based decision-making. Fighting the insights of behavioural psychology with the information deficit model is an unfair playing field. On the face of it, this is not an unreasonable defence, but its adequacy will be further questioned below when we discuss the effect nudge might have on the individual's relationship with government.

Two further points help support the conclusion that nudge does not represent an undue infringement on autonomy. One is how the transparent existence, or for that matter proposed existence, of nudges helps raise reflective awareness of the 'typically hidden, problematic features of the institutional status quo' (Schubert 2017, 337). Otherwise put, if people are made aware of green nudges then, presumably, they have become, or are becoming aware of the reasons why these measures are felt to be necessary. This will include the seriousness of environmental issues like climate change, the hard-to-alter nature of many environmentally relevant behaviours, and the general prevalence of marketing tactics that seek to manipulate System 1 decision-making.

The second is that, as will be discussed later in this chapter with respect to the limitations of the spillover effect (and in the previous chapter with respect to habits), System 1 methods of persuasion are ineffectual if a person is ideologically opposed to the overall purpose of the persuasive measures. Rather than manipulating people to do things they otherwise find ethically or politically problematic or abhorrent, nudges appear to be most effective where attitudes are weak or where there's indifference and, in what is perhaps their most ethically acceptable form, they enable emerging pro-environmental values to become actions.

6.2.2 Undermining self-development

A second ethical consideration is the effect a regime of nudges might have on self-development, risking the creation of what Jones et al. call the 'citizen fool' (2013, 52). As Hausman and Welch (2010, 135) say:

> No matter how well intentioned government efforts to shape choices may be, one should be concerned about the risk that exploiting decision-making foibles will ultimately diminish people's autonomous decision-making capacities.

Instead of being encouraged or expected to reflect on democratic matters, people become accustomed to being nudged along in their lives, slowly turning into Homer Simpson (Thaler and Sunstein 2009, 45). In important senses persuasion through System 1 is disempowering: it plays to existing prejudices, and makes no attempt to educate. Instead, people are treated as passive consumers. Heuristics-drenched marketing may be acceptable in the worlds of soap powder and garden furniture sales, but the ethical implications are far more serious when these techniques are applied to the sorts of issues a person would be voting on.

It is certainly true that nudge, by itself, does not allow people to make mistakes and learn from them (Jones et al. 2013), and if political influence were entirely asserted via this approach we would be presented with a very serious problem. As Simone de Beauvoir put it, 'to want to prohibit a man from error is to forbid him to fulfil his own existence, it is to deprive him of life' (1994, 138). It is not just that particular lessons are not learned and personal responsibility not promoted, but a broad message is delivered that it is not important for the individual to do this. This contradicts what most virtue theorists advocate; that taking ownership of the direction of one's life is vitally important, both for individual happiness and for social progress.

One response is that nudges must sit alongside persistent efforts to provide information and arguments, and alongside attempts to engage the public in debate around environmental issues. All the time nudge is framed as a way to help us achieve what we reflectively desire, the problem of self-development ought to be mitigated. 'Whether an action was conscious or unconscious', Nagatsu argues,

> is not a relevant criterion for whether that action was delivered through practical reasoning. Although ample research suggests that most of our everyday choices are made unconsciously, we still consider ourselves as the authors of these choices, *post hoc*. What is relevant is rather whether the targeted mechanism can be, conscious or unconscious, characterized as reasoning of our own.
>
> *(2015, 489.)*

Similarly, several commentators (including Jones et al. 2013) propose that if nudge is to be employed then efforts should be made by government to enlighten the public with respect to the biased judgements of System 1. Even if this lessens its overall effect, nudge would still be effective and, arguably, especially so in cases where the citizen has made an active choice to allow herself to be manipulated in certain circumstances. System 1 and our habitual tendencies are powerful, and although education in relation to them can make us more rational, it will only ever be a matter of degree. Habituating ourselves not to turn on (or to keep dimmed) our self-surveillance under particular conditions seems readily achievable.

6.2.3 Undermining the individual's relationship with government

A third ethical concern has been expressed in this way:

> If a government is supposed to treat its citizens as agents who, within the limits that derive from the rights and interests of others, determine the direction of their own lives, then it should be reluctant to use means to influence them other than rational persuasion. Even if, as seems to us obviously the case, the decision-making abilities of citizens are flawed and might not be significantly diminished by concerted efforts to exploit these flaws, an organized effort to shape choices still appears to be a form of disrespectful social control.
>
> *(Hausman and Welch 2010, 134.)*

One response (which Hausman and Welch accept) is that in this respect nudge is nothing new. Not only have public information ads always employed non-rational forms of persuasion, but party political broadcasts, ministerial addresses, parliamentary debates, and so on, do as well. We might say, then, that so long as it remains contextualised in the way described in the previous sub-section, and so long as the methods employed are not excessively manipulative (such as subliminal persuasion), then nudge by itself is not altering the relationship between individual and government.

However, a remaining difference is the pervasive, frequent and systematic nature of nudge in comparison with these other examples of government communication. When a 'Behavioural Insights Team' is set up to manage this relationship, then here is perhaps precisely where we feel the bite of this criticism. It has an air of a 'ministry for propaganda' about it; a bureaucratic body that signifies a barrier of dubious legitimacy between those governing and those being governed.

Perhaps the best response to this concern is to invoke transparency. The UK's Behavioural Insights Team appears to go to great lengths to explain the work they are undertaking,[3] and in general it can be argued that all the time the other criteria emerging from this analysis are met (notably broad public consent) then a government's assuming this role should not necessarily be viewed as disrespectful.

What ought to be taken into consideration however is the possibility of a slippery slope; a largely unintentional slide from transparent and consensual endorsement of nudges, to hidden and non-consensual policies via careless neglect, rather than a desire to deceive, and an institutional forgetfulness of democratic principles, rather than anti-democratic motivations. It is clear enough how a commitment to nudge, rather than plain public information or financial incentives, runs a particular risk of becoming the thin end of such a wedge, and indeed the potential for this type of corruption should be taken very seriously. This, however, is not reason enough to dismiss nudge on ethical grounds all the time a government commits to appropriate checks and balances, and so long as other ethical doubts can be adequately addressed.

6.2.4 Issues of fairness

There are two broad arguments questioning the fairness of nudge. One concerns how members of underprivileged groups could be more susceptible to its influence, and the other queries the implication that individual citizens should be held accountable for national and global environmental crises.

With respect to the first of these, both Sunstein and Reisch (2014, 145–6) and Schubert (2017, 338–9) make the argument that due to having a higher 'cognitive load' (life is essentially more challenging), and typically lower levels of education and social capital, poorer people are less able to identify and resist nudges. If this is right they are therefore not only more disempowered as a result of nudge policies than wealthier people, they carry more of the burden as well – the rich get the social benefits whilst being more able to avoid making sacrifices.

One response to this is to point out that not all pro-environmental behaviours are necessarily sacrifices. Some, such as home insulation, will save money in the long run, and others, such as cycling to work, will likely benefit health and well-being. Nevertheless, cases of behaviour change will involve sacrifices, and even money-saving devices such as smart meters have been shown to generate particularly intense guilt and anxiety in fuel-poor households where putting the heating on can attain clear association with the 'money seeping out' (Hargreaves et al. 2010, 6114). Moreover, the well-being and personal and community growth benefits that can undoubtedly result from deeper environmental engagement are precisely the kinds of changes that nudge does not encourage. Arguably, in fact, and as we will proceed to discuss, the existence of nudge policies implicitly discourage such value-based shifts.

A second response concerns the tailored nudges previously discussed. To the extent that more vulnerable people and households can be spared nudges the social justice issue can be mitigated (Sunstein and Reisch 2014, 146) but, as we have seen, there are limits on the degree to which tailoring can take place. Short of progressive forms of environmental taxation that compensates the seemingly regressive effect of nudges on the less wealthy, the conclusion here seems to be then that unfairness remains a significant ethical issue for this approach to behavioural change.

6.3 Challenges to using psychological influence (II): 'Common Cause'

The 'ethics of nudge' literature sometimes hints at another form of concern about this approach to behavioural change. Schubert (2017, 339), for example, suggests that green nudges risk promoting an individualistic approach that overlooks the deeper socio-cultural roots of the environmental problems purportedly addressed, thereby relieving policymakers from the cumbersome task of actually fixing the flawed institutions at the heart of market failure, properly understood.

This issue has been best articulated by a climate change communication philosophy known as 'Common Cause'. In their 2011 article, 'Selling climate change? The limitations of social marketing as a strategy for climate change public engagement', Adam Corner and Alex Randall presented a set of arguments that contain some of the essential concerns of an influential movement among environmental communication academics and activists. The group also includes the WWF-UK strategist Tom Crompton and former Rainforest Foundation and Greenpeace campaigns director George Marshall. Marshall is a co-founder (in 2004) of the Oxford-based Climate Outreach and Information Network (now just known as Climate Outreach[4]), who conduct research and provide advice on climate change communication.

Corner and Randall argue that strategies that aim to generate immediate pro-environmental behavioural changes will tend to conflict with other (long-term) strategies that take a different approach. The different approach is broadly what Crompton had previously referred to as 'Common Cause' (2010), and the strategies they argue against are those employed by social marketing campaigns. They identify four problems with the use of social marketing in this context: 1) the problem of indiscriminate message tailoring; 2) a lack of evidence for spillover; 3) how segmentation reinforces an individualism that interferes with the collective response needed; and 4) how social marketing embodies aspects of the very political ideology that drives environmental destruction. Each of these claims will be analysed in turn.

6.3.1 Message tailoring

What Corner and Randall call 'indiscriminate message tailoring' refers to the tendency in social marketing to frame a message in any way that gives rise to a short-term behaviour change. In particular, there is a concern with the use of financial incentives. Whilst Common Cause accepts that to encourage a new attitude or behaviour it needs to be grounded in existing attitudes or behaviours, it argues that we must be discriminatory when deciding which existing attitudes and behaviours to select. A financial savings frame, in particular, unnecessarily limits the wider impact of a behavioural change and is thus seen as 'counterproductive' (Corner and Randall, 2011, 1008). Effective environmental intervention requires a broad range of behaviour changes, and this can happen in a couple of ways. One is through a spillover effect whereby the adoption of environmentally friendly behaviours in one domain (such as household recycling) leads to environmentally friendly behaviours in other domains (such a travel habits and energy efficiency) without the need for further interventions. The other is via a generalised attitude change, from environmental indifference to pro-environmental consciousness, that has an impact on a wide range of relevant behaviours. There is a clear link between these two processes in so far as a spillover effect can be mediated by an attitude change – the adoption of a single behaviour causing us to see ourselves as an environmentally concerned person – but in each case the route to the attitude change is considerably different (as will be discussed below).

Several limitations of the spillover effect will be addressed in the next subsection, and in the rest of this one we will explain the Common Cause reasoning that accounts for why framing environmentally relevant behaviours in terms of financial incentives will not prompt the kind of attitude change they claim is needed.

Common Cause's argument rests on Shalom Schwartz's (1994) well-tested Theory of Basic Values (listed in the box below).

Schwartz's basic values (1994, 22):

Power: social status and prestige, control or dominance over people and resources.

Achievement: personal success through demonstrating competence according to social standards.

Hedonism: pleasure and sensuous gratification for oneself.

Stimulation: excitement, novelty, and challenge in life.

Self-direction: independent thought and action; choosing, creating, exploring.

Universalism: understanding, appreciation, tolerance, and protection for the welfare of all people and for nature.

Benevolence: preserving and enhancing the welfare of those with whom one is in frequent personal contact (the 'in-group').

Tradition: respect, commitment, and acceptance of the customs and ideas that traditional culture or religion provide the self.

Conformity: restraint of actions, inclinations, and impulses likely to upset or harm others and violate social expectations or norms.

Security: safety, harmony, and stability of society, of relationships, and of self.

Among these, the theory identifies two fundamental and opposing sets of values motivating human behaviour: 'self-enhancing' (S-E) and 'self-transcendent' (S-T). Self-enhancing values concern the individual's own well-being (including achievements and their accumulation of wealth and social power), and self-transcendent values include compassion and ethical principles such as justice and equality. Intuitively we can perhaps recognise the personality types that Schwartz's model portrays, as expressed in people's virtues and political orientations. The depth of their temperamental origins notwithstanding, we can also see how it is psychologically difficult to switch between S-E and S-T values with ease. There is thus a basis for understanding people, in terms of their currently existing motivational set-up, as being dominated by either self-enhancing or self-transcendent values.

The significance of the openness to change–conservation dimension should be apparent from the figure (Figure 6.1 below). This interacts with the S-E–S-T dimension to produce what again seem to be recognisable sub-types; maybe the inspirational environmental activist (see Chapter 9 for examples) in the north–north west segment, or the religiously motivated Oxfam volunteer where the two eastern segments meet.

In terms of behavioural change, the crucial consideration is that although the value-sets are contradictory, most of us are flexible enough to be able change our orientation. In other words, currently S-E people have the potential to be S-T, and vice versa. The north-west–south-east diagonal represents the bridge, indicating how, even if this openness-conservation dimension of our psychology is fairly fixed, it has both S-E and S-T variations. For example, contrast the exciting and self-transcending Reverend Billy with the exciting and self-enhancing Donald Trump.

So, environmental interventions need to find a way of encouraging greater self-identification with S-T values, and less with S-E values. The means advocated

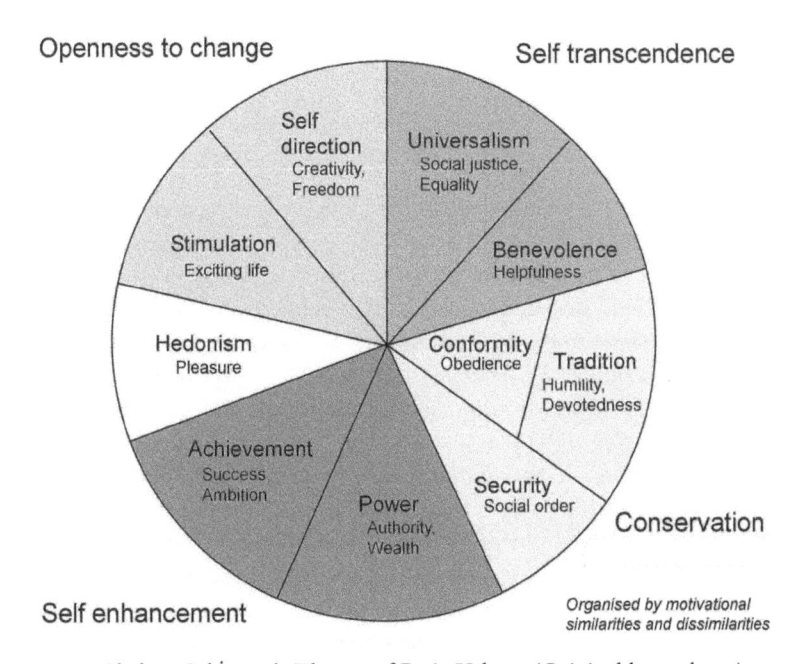

FIGURE 6.1 Shalom Schwartz's Theory of Basic Values. (Original by authors.)

by Crompton is the employment of 'deep' frames as opposed to 'cognitive' ones. While cognitive frames enable more superficial forms of understanding, deep frames are those that engage with fundamental values, and in this case values that are currently marginalised or dormant within an individual or community. Crompton's argument is that framing environmental behaviours in financial terms will fail to achieve the desired shift towards S-T values because the new behaviour is consistent with S-E values. A 'common-interest' frame on the other hand – based on compassion, duty, justice and so on – will encourage a holistic re-engagement with a set of neglected values that will have a widespread effect on environmentally relevant behaviours.

A social marketing strategy that assumes that any frame will do so long as the behaviour in question is changed will be ineffective. Instead:

> Fostering a sense of pro-environmental identity... among the general population is important if pro-environmental behavioural changes are to be embraced and maintained. Social marketing techniques may be able to play a role in achieving these aims, but they must be anchored in the deeper notions of identity and citizenship if they are to have a meaningful influence on promoting a proportional response to climate change.
>
> *(Corner and Randall 2011, 1012.)*

In an important sense this is an argument every bit as pragmatic as the social marketing approach (Capstick et al. 2015, 5): appealing to S-E values will not have the desired outcome. But it also seems from the Common Cause-related literature that there is an underlying ethical preference among these people for a more 'self-transcendent' society.

6.3.2 Spillover

The spillover effect is a variation on a now quite well-understood set of psychological principles associated with the need for 'cognitive consistency' (Petty and Cacioppo 1996). The best-known theory in this field is Leon Festinger's cognitive dissonance (1957), and in the context of its application to marketing Cialdini (2007) includes 'commitment and consistency' as one of his six principles of persuasion. In this section of his book Cialdini refers to a study by Freedman and Fraser (1966) in which people who had previously agreed to place a small sticker in their window saying 'DRIVE CAREFULLY' were far more likely to agree to a giant sign with the same message being placed in their garden than those who had not made the previous, very small, commitment (76 per cent vs 17 per cent). Even when the prior commitment was on a separate issue (signing a petition to 'Keep California Beautiful') the compliance rate for the large sign was 50 per cent.

This type of compliance is most commonly explained by self-perception theory whereby consenting to a small request alters self-perception, and the altered perception makes other behaviours that are consistent with this perception more likely. For it to work there must be no obvious external justification for the initial behaviour performed. Since it appears to be voluntary, the individual has to look to themselves for the justification, and typically this will be a positive social norm (that they are, say, charitable or civic-minded). Once this self-perception is established the norm of consistency makes future behaviours that fit with this self-perception far more probable. Not to behave in these ways is liable to cause 'cognitive dissonance' – the discomforting feeling created by inconsistency among one's beliefs and actions. This inconsistency can be between concurrent beliefs; beliefs and behaviours; behaviour and self-image; our attitudes and the attitudes of the people we are associated with (or like or respect); or between what we declare publically and what we do. The potency of the last on this list explains the common use of pledges and other publicly stated intentions in behavioural change interventions.

Being consistent is important to us in part for reasons that do not need spelling out, such as the desire to be rational and the fact that it means the credibility of one or other of the conflicting beliefs or behaviours is profoundly undermined. From an ethical perspective inconsistency calls us out as unreliable and therefore untrustworthy, perhaps a promise-breaker. In Cialdini's words 'inconsistency is commonly thought to be an undesirable personality trait' (2007, 60), and therefore 'once we have made a choice or taken a stand, we will encounter personal and interpersonal pressures to behave consistently with that commitment' (op cit., 57).

You would think then that commitment and consistency is a powerful compliance tactic, and indeed it is. However, in the context of environmental behaviours its efficacy has been found to be quite limited. Corner and Randall offer several reasons why, which we will briefly expand upon here.

First, and most obvious, if spillover is caused by self-identity, then the use of financial incentives, as the dominating frame at least, will fail to reveal an ethical identity because no further values-based self-justification is needed. Instead of, as in the Freedman and Fraser experiment, people being primed to see themselves as environmentally conscious, all they need to justify compliance is the environmentally irrelevant image of themselves as the 'sort of person who saves money' (Corner and Randall 2011, 1009).

Second, and more worrying, even if ethical self-identity is emphasised, cognitive dissonance still has significant limitations in relation to widespread and long-term environmental behavioural change. One reason for this is that performing some environmentally friendly behaviours is not obviously inconsistent with not doing others since it depends on how similar they are perceived to be, for example, buying organic milk vs cycling to work (Thøgersen 2004; Barnes Truelove et al. 2014). Spillover is thus in part dependent on knowledge, and often this knowledge will belong to people who are already environmentally engaged, which suggests a reduced need for a spillover effect. However, as has been argued in Chapter 5, there is a substantial difference between knowledge and action. The significance of spillover is that induced actions lead to other, related, actions because the need for consistency of behaviour is greater than the need for consistency of what are, after all, often only semi-articulated beliefs. Therefore, the pre-existence of a basic understanding of the range of environmentally relevant behaviours does not rule out the need for a spillover effect.

A further reason for the limitation of spillover however is that it is too easy to ignore or rationalise inconsistency when it comes to environmentally friendly behaviours. As John Thøgersen puts it:

> Inconsistency in a specific behavioural domain, such as . . . Environment-friendly behaviours, is less threatening to the self-concept of individuals who do not find these . . . morally important.
>
> *(2004, 101.)*

To make this worse, even as climate change becomes more important to people its abstractness (for many) still means that we can better 'endure' any inconsistencies we enact, especially when the associated behavioural changes are inconvenient. Helping this along is, of course, an absence of social norms to enforce behavioural consistency, and there will also be competing claims for (ethical) consistency, such as someone who prioritises their family's material status, or not being the 'sucker' who makes sacrifices whilst others choose not to.

A third consideration discussed by Corner and Randall for the limitations of spillover is increasing evidence for a 'negative spillover effect'. This means that the performing of a particular kind of action will decrease rather than increase the likelihood of performing similar actions. One suggested reason for this is the 'single action bias' (see Chapter 5), and another is the 'licensing effect' in which a sense of moral pride in one activity licenses other behaviours that are carbon-intensive (1009) – a phenomenon known as 'moral balancing'. Examples include owners of electric cars feeling less obligation to act in environmentally friendly ways than non-owners; and people who engaged in pro-environmental behaviours at home feeling less obligation to do so on holiday (Barnes Truelove et al. 2014, 130). This kind of pay-off makes sense if environmental values are not a deep part of one's identity. A person can be genuinely motivated to do their 'bit' and experience pride as a consequence, but if engagement with environmental issues is superficial then it is easy enough to see how their knowledge and motivational framework will lack resilience where there is an absence of environmental social norms or where other psychological and sociological barriers are present.

An interesting twist, however, is that where a behavior change is difficult or costly to achieve there is more evidence for a positive spillover effect (Barnes Truelove et al., op cit.). This would be predicted by self-perception theory because the added effort or cost should motivate a more pronounced reflection on one's pro-environmental identity. Whereas a more trivial behaviour can be taken in one's stride, a major one will more likely spark attempts at 'effort justification', including a shift towards seeing oneself as environmentally concerned. However, in the context of alternative (e.g. financial) justifications, the implication is that effort + encouragement towards recalling or nurturing environmental identity is the best approach for engendering positive spillover. As a recent review of research concludes:

> Although public commitment and consistency research suggests that positive spillover can occur even when no pre-existing environmental identity is triggered, there is extensive research to suggest that making an environmental identity salient could encourage positive spillover. This could either take the form of priming existing environmental identities or by framing initial behaviours in a way to encourage the development . . . of an environmental identity.
> (Barnes Truelove et al. 2014, 132.)

This contradicts Corner and Randall's criticism of a campaign placing faith in spillover, but in a way that offers broad support for the Common Cause approach. The general picture becomes: significant (difficult or costly) actions, framed in terms of environmental values, causes pro-environmental identity salience, and therefore a greater likelihood of the individual going on to perform other pro-environmental behaviours. Outside the scope of the Barnes Truelove et al. review, but within ours, is to add how dialogical intervention – also advocated by Common Cause – as well as encouraging reflection on one's identity, is the best means for educating people about environmental issues and the range of environmentally friendly behaviours that can be engaged with.

There is also evidence to suggest that a 'rule-based' (deontological) moral framework is more likely to generate spillover than one that is 'outcome-based' (consequentialist). The flexibility associated with the latter, it seems, makes people more prone to self-interested behaviour and therefore more likely to enact moral balancing rather than consistency (Cornelissen et al. 2013). The greater consistency of the deontologist, however, comes with a couple of caveats: the first is the issue of salience (as discussed above); and the second is that consistency can work against moral behaviours as well as for them. If a person starts to recognise that her past behaviours do not meet her ethical standards and would rather not acknowledge this, then remaining consistent with those past behaviours helps protect her from an uncomfortable truth. To change behaviour is to admit a wrong-doing.

A response to this tendency might be to promote the kind of moral maturity – involving flexibility, self-knowledge, self-forgiveness, humility and a recognition of the prevalence of moral luck – that is found in virtue ethics (Facione et al. 1995, 9; Naess et al. 2008, 81–2). However, this is to assume that people find environmental issues ethically relevant – or at least ethically important enough – in the first place. Whether you are a deontologist or a consequentialist you still need to navigate dilemmas, and as the '5.2.3 Existing values, attitudes and wants' section in the previous chapter shows, too often the environmental option, even if considered morally relevant, is easily deprioritised. A return is made, then, to the need for a salient environmental identity that will a) motivate consistency in pro-environmental behaviours, and b) mitigate against tendencies towards moral balancing and a 'slippery slope of moral decision making' (Cornelissen et al. 2013, 487) where self-protective motivations outweighs a desire to do the right thing.

6.3.3 Segmentation

Segmentation – as typically employed by social marketing – emphasises the differences between individuals and groups rather than their commonalities. Moreover, its neutrality means that it can only find and describe norms rather than create them out of dormant value-based sensitivities. The result is that one set of people are enticed towards behaviour change through their existing commitment to waste-watching, another through its health benefits, another through political allegiances, and so on. This, it is claimed, is a shallow and fragile basis for collective action. As well as the spillover limitations discussed, because the norms at play are other than environmental, they are less likely to nurture the sense that this is a shared concern based on some problematic attitudes and behaviours that everyone needs to address. Segmentation thus fails to engage existing community cohesion with respect to 'minor' behavioural change, and to the extent that it can be seen to impede collective support for 'more ambitious behavioural and policy changes . . . [it] may actually prove counterproductive' (op cit., 1010).

In place, therefore, of traditional approaches to segmentation, Corner and Randall propose that the targeting of 'social networks or communities' would be more beneficial. Framing in terms of locality has proven effective (Shome and Marx 2009), and 'social networks' suggests existing collectives associated with various practices (including hobbies) and causes (including grassroots initiatives). In the Common Cause report, Crompton recommends the forming of alliances with groups that may not be environmental, but whose concerns are self-transcending and who challenge the domination of self-enhancing values. For example, a group protesting against advertising to children could share sufficient ground with an environmental group (most obviously around issues of consumption) so as to campaign together against this practice (2010, 63–4). It might be added that through the bonds of collective action such allegiances could be mutually educative and thus swell support for both causes.

6.3.4 Ideology

This final argument put forward by Corner and Randall is in part a culmination of the previous three. Social marketing aims to sell environmental behaviours in a manner than affects individual decision-making via (ideally) individualised incentives. Social marketing is flexible enough for the 'selling' aspect to be deliberative and System 2-oriented, but it would only employ this method if the public were already primed to respond to it, which they are not (or are presumed not to be). Social marketing, as we have seen, has conservatism deeply rooted in its methodological assumptions. It claims to be ideologically neutral, but it strives to sell ideas to individuals that are then enacted at an individual (or perhaps family) level. We remain, in a crucial sense, passive consumers. Its subtext is the 'business as usual' of shallow ecology; that, with a few adjustments, our current way of life will again be sustainable. Even where other messages and policies have a more empowering approach, implicit contradictions between this and the marketing 'sell' will be enough for a continued under-appreciation of the gravity of the situation. The upshot, according to Common Cause, is that the kinds of changes that are needed will not be made all the time social marketing campaigns are the dominant public communication strategy.

Considered in light of the barriers analysed in Chapter 5 we can also see how an individualist approach is disempowering from the perspective of the individuals targeted. For example, it will exacerbate confusion through the disjunction between small changes to various consumption behaviours and the scale of the problem; and it beckons the prisoner's dilemma frame, motivating either free riding or the desire, not only to avoid being the sucker, but to avoid needless sacrifices for what looks like a hopeless cause.

Within the Common Cause agenda is a related but wider point concerning political participation. Social marketing is seen as one expression of a problem of democracy that is exacerbating climate change inaction. Among a handful of deep frames Crompton uses to exemplify this aspect of his theory is one that addresses the dichotomy of 'elite governance vs participative democracy' (2010, 55–7), and this is telling. It indicates both a fundamental Common Cause value and, for them, a practical requirement if climate change is to be adequately addressed. As we have seen, behavioural psychology has the potential to promote a more childlike attitude among citizens. Even if it is not the intention, it can create the impression that a benign government is in control of the environmental crisis and can guide us through it; and, of course, there is also a sense in which this is what many of us would like to believe. The opposite requires, among other things, cognitive effort, and an honest recognition that a democratic government, at best, represents us rather than just directs us, and indeed might not even do that (see Chapters 8 and 9). However, even if democratic government does fulfil a basic representative function, it still requires the citizenry to take more responsibility than it might be inclined to want, especially where political subjects are formed under an economy and polity that prizes efficiency over criticality.

6.4 Conclusion: the case for a collectivist frame

Referring to the paradigm case of climate change, the problem of engagement can be set out like this:

1. There are multiple disincentives for acting in direct response to climate change. For example:
    a) our individual efforts are seen as, at best, a drop in the ocean;
    b) if behavioural change is viewed or experienced as a sacrifice then we will be unwilling to do much unless we are sure others are as well.

2. However, this does not preclude the acceptance of nudges, prohibition or choice-editing (see Chapter 8); nor of initiatives organised by our pre-existing communities – such as our workplace, church or children's school.
3. Individual attitudes and their associated virtues remain important because attitude change across most institutions and individuals is required if the problem is to be solved. One reason is that our behaviour influences those around us (including any children we might have) through the various forms of authority and power each of us embody. Another reason is that some people are needed to be proactive in promoting pro-environmental behaviours within workplaces, local communities and the like, and these people need to care, not simply be appointed in a top-down fashion. If we rely on others to do this, then possibly no one will. A third reason is that excessive personal disengagement might end up making us reluctant to even vote for pro-environmental policies, let alone seek-out environmentally friendly products, or change other carbon-intensive behaviours.
4. Under these circumstances there remains a pressing need to enable personal engagement with climate change. A theory of how this might come about is provided by Paul Stern's 'value-belief-norm' theory (2000).

In figure 6.2 the notion of 'ecological worldview' (or New Ecological Paradigm (NEP)) encompasses any belief that recognises the extent of our interdependence with the natural world and the fragility of that world. As the diagram (Figure 6.2) shows, this can be rooted in a range of different types of value (with the 'egoistic' here including various forms of enlightened egoism), all of which share the goal of environmental sustainability, including stabilising the climate.

Someone who lacks this understanding does not figure in Stern's model but, as we have seen, to one degree or another most people nowadays do have this understanding, at least to the extent that they would in theory support some political measure to mitigate the situation.

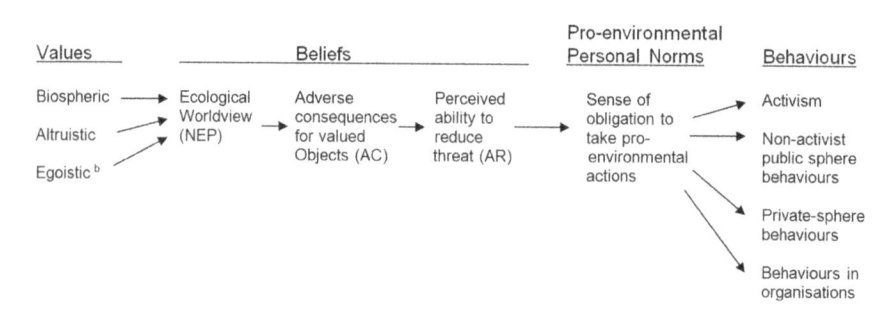

Values	Beliefs	Pro-environmental Personal Norms	Behaviours
Biospheric → Altruistic → Egoistic [b] →	Ecological Worldview (NEP) → Adverse consequences for valued Objects (AC) → Perceived ability to reduce threat (AR) →	Sense of obligation to take pro-environmental actions →	Activism Non-activist public sphere behaviours Private-sphere behaviours Behaviours in organisations

FIGURE 6.2 The 'value-beliefs-norm' theory of environmental behaviour. (Based on Stern 2000, 412 – original by authors.)

The real problem, as Chapter 5 explains, is engagement; turning abstract knowledge into attitudes, actions and virtues. Truly feeling the 'adverse consequences for valued objects' and being convinced of our 'ability to reduce the threat' are indeed vital constituents of a 'sense of obligation' to act. In both cases there are forces working on us, whether biological/emotional or rational in the sense of our limited impact on the world (an absence of the appropriate skills or material resources, limitations caused by social structures, or simply the scale of the issue) that reduce the likelihood of engagement.

There is little doubt that valuing the natural world – organisms, landscapes, species, ecosystems – will extend to valuing the preservation and sustainability of the planet as a whole. The trouble is that most people are anthropocentric rather than ecocentric. This is something that can maybe be changed, at least to a degree, via education and other practices – and there are several reasons why it is desirable to continue to attempt to do this – but we cannot be optimistic that most people can or should come to think this way.

Instead, practical and social reasons will be of greatest importance for making the general case for urgent and radical global responses, and in terms of personal engagement a range of virtues and practices must be promoted that make pro-environmental behaviours meaningful.

There is evidence that employing self-enhancing frames and competing social identities as behavioural change levers has some effect. The spectacle of US reality TV series *Energy Smackdown*, in which households compete to see who can save the most energy, makes for good entertainment. Also, as discussed, Rabinovich et al. (2011) have shown that an individual's environmental values and their intentions can be increased by comparing their in-group with a less-well-performing out-group. The policy implication is to make use of positive comparisons, rather than stimulating guilt through negative ones, and from a certain perspective this makes sense.

However, even if a version of this message could be reliably transmitted to the public, the limited and perhaps even counterproductive impacts of this kind of framing are becoming apparent. Overall the weight of argument and evidence is towards a collective response and a collectivist framing. George Marshall (2014, 233) makes the point that the hero quest (see Chapter 5) is a better narrative frame than (say) David and Goliath because it avoids the need for enemies. In particular, where our individual and collective weaknesses are foregrounded, the struggle is primarily with ourselves – our 'stupidity', our denial, our addictions, our systems – rather than with named individuals or organisations and their proxies.

The collectivist frame sits in the background, providing a backstop for when the question arises: 'Why am I making these changes, these sacrifices?' A dominant answer is voiced by those around us and local, national and international institutions: It is for the good of the planet and therefore it is for the good of us all. The logic of the commons is clear and not so hard to understand, so along with 'It's for the good of us all' must go 'And we can only solve this by working together'.

Working it out in practical terms is, of course, fraught, but a unanimous message of collective action must be endlessly repeated to lend coherency to all of the inevitably disparate actions being taken, and to help maintain motivation.

The importance of another dimension of collective action – the political realm – is the focus of the following three chapters.

Notes

1 This is referred to in Chapter 4 as the 'crying Indian campaign'.
2 Paternalism is an infringement of an individual's autonomy intended to be in their own best interests.
3 The BIT website documents all of their activities, including underlying rationales (www.behaviouralinsights.co.uk/); transparency with respect to their use of data is discussed at https://quarterly.blog.gov.uk/2017/02/21/transparency-and-evidence-show-your-workings/, and the Team's director, David Halpern, has published the accessible book *Inside the Nudge Unit* (Halpern 2016).
4 Possibly because the COIN acronym has connotations entirely at odds with what they stand for.

References

Barnes Truelove, H., Carrico, A.R., Weber, E.U., Raimi, K.T. and Vandenbergh, M.P. (2014) 'Positive and negative spillover of pro-environmental behaviour: an integrative review and theoretical framework', *Global Environmental Change* 29: 127–38.

Beauvoir, S. de (1994) *The Ethics of Ambiguity*. New York: Citadel Press.

Bovens, L. (2009) 'The ethics of nudge', in T. Grune-Yanoff and S. Hansson, eds, *Modelling Preference Change: Perspectives from Economics, Psychology and Philosophy*, 207–19. Berlin: Springer.

Capstick, S., Lorenzoni, I., Corner, A. and Whitmarsh, L. (2014) 'Prospects for radical emissions reduction through behavior and lifestyle change', *Carbon Management* 5.4: 429–45.

Cialdini, R.B. (2003) 'Crafting normative messages to protect the environment', *Current Directions in Psychological Science* 12.4: 105–9.

Cialdini, R. (2007) *Influence: The Psychology of Persuasion*. New York: Collins.

Corner, A. and Randall, A. (2011) 'Selling climate change? The limitations of social marketing as a strategy for climate change public engagement', *Global Environmental Change* 21: 1005–14.

Cornelissen, G., Bashshur, M.R., Rode, J. and Le Menestrel, M. (2013) 'Rules or consequences? The role of ethical mind-sets in moral dynamics', *Psychological Science* 24.4: 482–8.

Crompton, T. (2010) *Common Cause: The Case for Working with Our Cultural Values*. WWF. Available at: www.wwforg.uk/change.

Defra (2008) *A Framework for Pro-Environmental Behaviours*. Available at: www.defra.gov.uk/publications/files/pb13574-behaviours-report-080110.pdf.

Facione, P., Sanchez, C., Falione, N. and Gainen, J. (1995) 'The disposition towards critical thinking'. *The Journal of General Education*, 44.1: 1–25.

Festinger, L. (1957) *A Theory of Cognitive Dissonance*. Stanford, CA: Stanford University Press.

Freedman, J. and Fraser, S. (1966) 'Long-term behavioural effects of cognitive dissonance', *Journal of Experimental Social Psychology* 4: 195–203.

Gardner, G. and Stern, P. (2002) *Environmental Problems and Human Behaviour*, Second Edition. Boston: Pearson Custom Publishing.

Gromet, D.M., Kunreuther, H. and Larrick, R.P. (2013) 'Political ideology affects energy-efficiency attitudes and choices', *Proceedings of the National Academy of Sciences* 110.23: 9314–9.

Guala, F. and Mittone, L. (2015) 'A political justification of nudging', *Review of Philosophy and Psychology* 3.6: 385–95.

Hagman, W., Andersson, D., Västfjäll, D. and Tinghög, G. (2015) 'Public views on policies involving nudges', *Review of Philosophy and Psychology* 6: 439–53.

Halpern, D. (2016) *Inside the Nudge Unit*. London: WH Allen.

Hargreaves, T., Nye, M. and Burgess, J. (2010) 'Making energy visible: a qualitative field study of how householders interact with feedback from Smart Energy monitors', *Energy Policy* 38.10: 6111–9.

Hausman, D.M. and Welch, B. (2010) 'Debate: to nudge or not to nudge', *Journal of Political Philosophy* 18.1: 123–36.

Jones, R., Pykett, J. and Whitehead, M. (2013) *Changing Behaviours*. Cheltenham: Edward Elgar.

Leiserowitz, A., Maibach, E., Roser-Renouf, C., Feinberg, G. and Howe, P. (2013) *Global Warming's Six Americas, September 2012*. Yale University and George Mason University. New Haven, CT: Yale Project on Climate Change Communication, http://environment.yale.edu/climate/publications/Six-Americas-September-2012.

Levitt, S. and Dubner, S. (2005) *Freakonomics*. New York: William Morris.

Marshall, G. (2014) *Don't Even Think About It: Why Our Brains are Wired to Ignore Climate Change*. New York: Bloomsbury.

McKenzie-Mohr, D. (2000) 'Promoting sustainable behaviour: an introduction to community-based social marketing', *Journal of Social Issues* 56.3: 543–54.

Mills, C. (2015) 'The heteronomy of choice architecture', *Review of Philosophy and Psychology* 3.6: 495–509.

Naess, A., Drengson, A. R. and Devall, B. (2008) *Ecology of Wisdom: Writings by Arne Næss*. Berkeley: Counterpoint Press.

Nagatsu, M. (2015) 'Social nudges: their mechanisms and justification', *Review of Philosophy and Psychology* 6.3: 481–94.

National Centre for Social Marketing (2011) *Big Pocket Guide*. UK: NCSM.

Oliver, A. (2013) 'From nudging to budging: using behavioural economics to inform public sector policy'. *Journal of Social Policy*, 42.4: 685–700.

Packard, V. (1957) *The Hidden Persuaders*. New York: Ig Publishing.

Petty, R. and Cacioppo, J. (1996) *Attitudes and Persuasion: Classic and Contemporary Approaches*. Boulder, CO: Westview.

Pichert, D. and Katsikopoulos, K.V. (2008) 'Green defaults: information presentation and pro-environmental behaviour', *Journal of Environmental Psychology*, 28.1: 63–73.

Project Wild Thing (2013) [documentary film] directed by David Bond and Ashley Jones. UK: Green Lions.

Rabinovich, A., Morton, T. and Duke, C. (2011) 'Collective choice and individual self: the role of social comparisons in promoting public engagement with climate change', in L. Whitmarsh, S. O'Neill and I. Lorenzoni, eds, *Engaging the Public with Climate Change*. London: Routledge.

Schubert, C. (2017) 'Green nudges: do they work? Are they ethical?', *Ecological Economics* 132: 329–42.

Schwartz, S.H. (1994) 'Are there universal aspects in the structure and contents of human values?', *Journal of Social Issues* 50: 19–45.

Shome, D. and Marx, S. (2009) *The Psychology of Climate Change Communication*. New York: Centre for Research on Environmental Decisions.

Smith, N.C., Goldstein, D.G. and Johnson, E.J. (2013) 'Choice without awareness: ethical and policy implications of defaults', *Journal of Public Policy & Marketing* 32.2: 159–72.

Stern, P. (2000) 'Towards a coherent theory of environmentally significant behavior', *Journal of Social Issues* 56.3: 407–24.

Sunstein, C.R. (2015) 'Nudges, agency, and abstraction: a reply to critics', *Review of Philosophy and Psychology* 3.6: 511–29.

Sunstein, C.R. and Reisch, L.A. (2014) Automatically green: behavioral economics and environmental protection', *Harvard Environmental Law Review* 38: 127–58.

Thaler, R. and Sunstein, C. (2009) *Nudge*. London: Penguin.

Thøgersen, J. (2004) 'A cognitive dissonance interpretation of consistencies and inconsistencies in environmentally responsible behavior', *Journal of Environmental Psychology* 24.1: 93–103.

7

ECONOMIC CHANGE

Corporations and environmental responsibility[1]

7.1 Introduction

This chapter focusses on businesses, as these are key agents in creating environmental problems and many strategies involve them in generating potential solutions. These enterprises are collections of individuals, operating in a particular historical context, working to particular norms, with specific types of identity. As such, proponents of business-centred approaches regard them as useful institutions for collective action for the common good. Strategies that focus on business behaviour tend to be framed through particular core concepts that are attractive to commercial operators. Thus, the key questions of this chapter are: 1) to what extent can businesses generate environmentally benevolent behavioural change? and; 2) what are the strengths and weaknesses of alternative strategies for environmentally-sensitive production of goods and services.

Behavioural change is intimately connected to questions of power. Environmental behavioural change requires either maintaining or changing the ways in which people interrelate and how they interact, individually and collectively, with the natural world. As such, generating ecological practices and attitudes involves adopting or altering particular ways of seeing one another and accepting or rejecting particular types of ecological goal. However, ecologically-responsible behaviour does not take place in a vacuum but develops within the context of existing social structures, the dominant economic, political and social institutions, and the norms that govern them. For instance, if a core organisation considers short-term economic advantage as its overriding objective, it generates a particular way of viewing a social event (either as a cost or a benefit, an opportunity or a barrier) and produces particular types of social actor (for instance, the striving entrepreneur, characterised by Michael Douglas in *Wall Street* or the authoritative chairperson in the widely licensed TV programme *The Apprentice*). Different forms of power are involved in identifying and engaging with social institutions in order to sustain, change or undermine them.

Whilst power is sometimes reduced to a single form – that of coercion – it can also take other forms, such as 'constitutive power' – the ability to draw people together on shared enterprises. Economic power can be a form of constitutive power. Through making deals people can be encouraged to partake in a shared enterprise. Other forms of constitutive power arise without the influence of contractual obligation. These include finding shared aims to cooperate in a joint enterprise. This is often more benign than coercive power, but it can be the result of manipulative persuasion (see Chapter 5). Similarly, collaborative activities might not always have benevolent purpose or impacts. If people act without reflection, they may voluntarily reproduce forms of behaviour that mirror existing harmful norms.

> **Power**: the capability to bring about desired effects. It can be coercive, but it can also be co-operative and consensual. The ability to draw people together is called **constitutive power**.

The three main forms of power – ability to control (power over), the ability to make deals (contractual/economic power) and the ability to draw on commitment (soft power) – map closely onto three intersecting spheres of socio-political influence: 1) military and police; 2) business and corporate enterprise and 3) political and cultural (sometimes referred to as the ideological sphere). Military and judicial institutions, what Louis Althusser (1977) called repressive state apparatuses, operate largely through coercion. This is not to say that they do not also encourage collective sharing of values, but their main function is to ensure compliance by the use of force ranging from mild sanction (warnings, small fines) through to extreme interventions (imprisonment, exile, torture and execution).

The latter two forms of power cross over with the six forms of authority identified in Chapter 5. Reward and economically coercive power are forms of contractual power, whilst soft power includes claims to authority through expertise, access to information, appeals to shared values and identities, and claims to political or institutional legitimacy. These are often maintained by overt or covert force, highlighting how the main forms of power overlap. Economic contracts are enforced by law, with civil and then criminal legal sanction applied to malefactors. Security apparatuses gain consent not just through threats of coercion, but also by encouraging shared loyalties, exemplified in the encouragement of public participation in military ceremonies. Similarly, repressive functions are not solely limited to state bodies (the state being the ultimate arbiter on the legitimacy of the use of force within a fixed geographical area) but can be seen operating, sometimes at the micro-political level of mild threats and presumed sanction, across social institutions. Chapter 8 examines the democratic justifications for, and limitations to, using coercive power to achieve environmental goals.

> **The state** is standardly defined, following the German sociologist Max Weber, as the body that has final authority on whether physical coercion can be used over a fixed geographical area.

This chapter concentrates on economic power, which, in the Western world, largely operates under the principles of capitalism. It therefore starts with a definition of 'capitalism', because, while the term is widely used by proponents and opponents alike, its meaning can be opaque. The description, provided below, is not itself controversial, even though it comes from Karl Marx, a source that promotes strong reaction. However, Marx himself drew it from advocates of classical liberal economics (the people he was critiquing). In this instance, the disputes about capitalism surround the rival analyses that come from the definition, rather than the description itself. By looking at how and why capitalist enterprises generate and distribute commodities (goods made to be sold), this chapter examines how, if at all, these powerful institutions may be geared towards facilitating environmental change. It considers the arguments by those who advocate greater corporate freedom of the benefits of unrestricted capitalism (free enterprise), concentrating on the influential arguments of Milton Friedman and his followers. It then examines the arguments against Friedman's economic liberalism from proponents of 'corporate social responsibility' and 'corporate citizenship', and those who take a more critical stance against corporate power, such as Joel Bakan. Bakan, whose book (2004) and co-authored popular documentary-film *The Corporation* (Directed by Mark Achbar and Jennifer Abbott, 2003) gained much critical attention from radicals, suggests that corporations generate psychopathic behaviour. This chapter, thus, looks at proponents and opponents of corporations in order to assess the methods used to discipline these institutions into more environmentally sensitive activity, and considers alternative modes of production that are not reducible to capitalist exchange or state-centred production.

7.2 Capitalism: a brief introduction

Marx described capitalism using the following formula:

M — C ⟨ LP / MP ⟩ — W — C' — M'

FIGURE 7.1 The circuit of capital. (From Marx 1885; see also Cleaver 1979. Original by authors.)

M stands for Money available for investment, which is used to buy C (Commodities of Production), which are broken down into LP (Labour Power), which is usually thought of as physical labour, but can be mental labour too, and MP (Means of Production), such things as raw materials, machinery and types of energy. Means of Production and Labour Power are put together to Work (W) in order to produce C' (finished commodities for sale), which are then sold for M' (money), which should be – if you are a successful capitalist – a greater amount than the original M at the start. There is, thus, more money for investment in the next round of commodity production. If there isn't the likelihood of a higher amount of money at the end (M') than the initial money (M) at the start, then the capitalist will not invest.

> **Capitalism**: an economic system (with a corresponding stabilising political structure) in which goods are produced in order to provide a return on investment.

There are features of this description of capitalism that appear to be deeply attractive. The diagram explains why capitalism is a productive and dynamic system. It rewards successful investment and provides a motive for innovation. If an investor can find a way to produce more goods of the same quality with the same resources as their competitor then they will generate more profit and be in a stronger negotiating position when bidding for raw materials in the next round of commodity production. Inefficient or unnecessary production is punished by generating little or no profit. Capitalism provides a motive for technological innovation and developing new production methods, which can either produce new goods to satisfy needs better than alternatives or produce identical products more efficiently. In addition, at the end of the cycle, there is more money available for investment than at the start and thus capitalism constantly needs to find new markets.

Many people who would not class themselves as capitalists are nonetheless implicated in this circuit of capital. Investing money in a bank or building society, to earn interest on a deposit, involves the financial institution loaning money to entrepreneurs who invest the money in commodities of production and repay the loan and the interest out of the surplus. However, what marks a member of the class of capitalists from a person with a small savings account is that the capitalist gains the majority of their money from their investments in production, whilst the majority, even though they may have a savings account, must still meet their basic needs through selling their labour power to those who can profit from their labour.

For liberal environmentalists, capitalism has a number of advantages. First, it compels the most efficient use of resources (MP). Expending unnecessary costs on raw materials and energy will reduce the surplus (the difference between M' and M). Profligate entrepreneurs are vulnerable to losing markets to more efficient, and thereby either cheaper and/or more profitable, competitors (see Ruwart 2012). Second, it provides an impetus for investors to produce environmentally-friendly products where there is a market to do so.

For anti-capitalists there are two fundamental antagonisms at the heart of capitalism, which for a number of deep green and social ecologists (discussed in Chapter 4) cause significant social divisions. The first integral conflict is between the capitalist who wants as much effective labour power for their money as possible, whilst the supplier of labour power (the employee or worker) wants as much resource and as much autonomy as possible. For social ecologists like Bookchin (e.g., 1997, 97–8) this social cleavage between the employers with their specific interests and employees with conflicting interests requires significant systems of social control and psychological manipulation to prevent conflict. This social cleavage is the basis for human alienation from, and exploitation of, the natural environment (see Chapter 3).

The second antagonism is between use-value and exchange-value. For ecocentric and biocentric activists the circuit of capital highlights that ultimately capitalism is primarily concerned with exchange value: a single unitary and reductive account of what makes a good or service valuable, rather than myriad use-values. Use-values are the irreducible diverse things we value in themselves rather than for profit: such as the pleasures of friendship or seeing something beautiful or awe-inspiring. Every commodity has both a use-value and an exchange value. A loaf of bread, for instance, has many potential use-values: it can be eaten with butter, toasted with cheese, used as a punching bag or perhaps shaped into a fragile comedy hat to amuse young children. None of these is universally more important than any other. However, a loaf of bread, under capitalism, is a commodity. It can only be accessed if a customer can pay for it. If a customer cannot pay for the price of bread, it just grows mouldy on the shelf and none of its many use values are realised. Under capitalism, exchange value is supreme. This is problematic for non-anthropocentric ecologists who prioritise environmental values, or ecological laws, rather than exchange value and the laws that protect it (Humphreys 2013, 47).

> **Use Value** and **Exchange Value**: **use values** are the benefits to people in meeting individual or shared needs and desires. There are many different use values, and none takes priority in all instances. **Exchange value** is the price fixed to a commodity. In capitalism exchange value takes priority.

Capitalism is sometimes viewed as a universal feature of human society, as potentially hard-wired into the DNA of *homo sapiens*. William Wilkinson, from the influential US-based free-market think-tank the Cato Institute, whilst rightly warning against drawing 'positive political lessons from evolutionary psychology', nonetheless asserts that property rights and market exchange are natural ahistorical bases of human behaviour (Wilkinson 2005). The natural story of capitalism goes something like this: a caveman having a surfeit of picked berries then trades his surplus with a neighbour for her excess of mammoth meat and this bartering develops into a money system that allows for quantifying and storing exchange-value. As a society progresses, more established state-protected agreements arise with secured, sometimes virtual, currencies.

This narrative suggests that exchange and the development of trading systems are natural, universal, spontaneous and non-coercive in origin. One of the problems with such a narrative, as the anthropologist David Graeber (2011, 52) points out, is that it is a 'myth' with 'all the evidence against it'. Where surpluses were present they were not traded, but used in other ways, such as 'gifting'. Graeber's provocative and well-evidenced argument is that, where trading takes place, it is with strangers rather than neighbours, and currency acts as the mode of exchange (rather than appearing later). Within communities trade arose as a result of prior societal breakdown and with the imposition of state or state-like authority. Thus, for Graeber, capital and the social relations, categories of analysis and underlying principles (such as private property, profitability, self-interest) that underpin it, are not universal features of human society and are often the product of coercive intervention.

Identifying that production and allocation did operate on anti-hierarchical principles outside of exchange, opens up the possibility of production and circulation of goods based on norms other than capitalism. Initially, this might be hard to visualise – to use Frederick Jameson's (2003, 76) famous phrase – 'it is easier to imagine the end of the world than to imagine the end of capitalism'. However, even in societies that are largely structured on capitalist modes of production and exchange, alternatives exist. Some of these alternative forms of production, such those based on slavery, are clearly more pernicious than existing economic relations. However, production and distribution might be based on other, more benevolent (if still problematic) norms, like the allotment grower who produces goods for their family table and freely distributes the surplus to neighbours and food banks.

Despite capitalism operating by similar imperatives to increase money received, it does not operate in the same way across history and geographies. As Michael Hardt and Antonio Negri (2000), Simon Tormey (2004) and David Harvey (2007) argue, some countries, in certain epochs, have most production done by small-scale or micro-producers and have investment that is largely local and stable, while others have production centred on a few large corporations that is largely international and more fluid. The role of the state can alter too, from providing material resources to ensure an appropriately educated and healthy workforce, to more minimal functions of protecting private property and contractual obligations.

However, in recent years, a set of changes in global production have increasingly homogenised formerly disparate forms of production, producing an identifiably distinct new form of production, trade and social governance, referred to as neoliberalism.

> **Neoliberalism:** An economic and political system that asserts the primacy of market principles in co-ordinating the production and distribution of goods and services. These principles become the standard by which social institutions operate.

The key principles of neoliberalism include:

- increasingly interdependent rather than production based on national self-sufficiency (autarky);
- the reassertion of market principles as central to social regulation and the allocation of resources;
- the consolidation and extension of corporate institutions and enforcement regimes to protect corporate private property and contractual obligations owed to them.

These principles become integrated into the systems of production themselves and are ultimately imposed by particularly dominant national governments – such as the 'democratic' USA or 'Communist' China (Harvey 2005) – or through international bodies such as the International Monetary Fund and World Trade Organisation (Hardt and Negri 2000). Neoliberalism produces, its critics argue, a system in which corporations thrive at the expense of other entities, in particular environmental entities. Neoliberalism is not just anthropocentric, it is corporocentric as it prioritises benefits to particular types of humans and human-constructed institutions.

7.3 The corporation

Harvey (2007, 42–3, 48) associates the rise of the corporation with the ascent of neoliberalism.[2] A corporation is an institution structured by law to privilege the maximisation of M'-M (money received minus money invested), at the expense of all other considerations. It is the product of, and helps to produce, particular types of political and legal structures in order to operate. These stabilising institutions are necessary to enforce contracts, adjudicate on disputes, protect and extend private property and encourage popular acceptance of these principles.

> **Corporation:** a business that is legally obliged to maximise returns for its shareholders (referred to as 'stock-holders' in the US).

Neoliberalism, as the account above indicates, acts to protect and extend the power of corporations. It is based on a particular view of autonomy (see Chapter 2) predicated on individual property rights and consensual agreements. Neoliberals seek the eradication of barriers to individual contract making, such as government regulation (e.g., environmental law, health and safety legislation and minimum wage legislation) and taxation for social and environmental goals, as these interfere with property rights. If two individuals come to an agreement in which the one consents to a bare subsistence wage for a task that, at substantial personal risk, destroys the final breeding area of a highly endangered species that is owned by the other individual, then under neoliberal principles it would be illegitimate for the government to interfere.

Neoliberals acknowledge that free trade might enhance social inequalities and produce particularly powerful business entities, but they argue that these results are not an injustice as they are the product of the autonomous decisions of the people making the contract. Contractual freedom, as Adam Smith recognises, can lead to monopoly, but this is non-problematic for most neoliberals as private monopolies are still constrained by the possibility of rivals setting up in opposition. As a result their power is still non-coercive, so even anti-monopolistic law is viewed by many neoliberals as an illegitimate interference in contractual freedoms. The state does not disappear but it is restricted to protecting and extending property rights, defending contracts and promoting globally these principles as the universal codes of good conduct.

The principles of neoliberalism were initially advanced by influential philosophical and economic thinkers Robert Nozick, Friedrich von Hayek and Friedman, and by key post-war associations such as the Mont Pelerin Society, the Faculty of Economics at the University of Chicago, and think tanks aimed at influencing opinion-shapers and policy-makers like the Institute for Economic Affairs (IEA), Cato Institute and the Heritage Foundation. They found a receptive audience from a number of significant political players, like Keith Joseph, Margaret Thatcher and Ronald Reagan, as they appeared to have found policy solutions to the industrial unrest and economic stagnation of the 1970s, largely caused by the OPEC oil price shock (see, for instance, Harvey 2007, 22). From the 1970s onwards individual governments and transnational organisations, such as the International Monetary Fund, were influenced by Hayek and think-tanks supporting his ideas (such as the IEA) and by Friedman and his Chicago School. Neoliberal policies were first tried out in Chile under the dictatorship of Augusto Pinochet and then in the liberal democracies of the United Kingdom and the United States. These policies were based on replacing state and communal production and allocation of resources with private enterprise. Neoliberalism also re-shaped organisations that were not legally constituted as corporations to act as if they were. Schools, universities, national healthcare providers and even environmental agencies adopted many of the principles and structures of corporate governance. The norms by which institutions run are not the result of predetermined rules of nature, but develop in response to government, economic and social forces. These institutions can be preserved, altered, dismantled or radically transformed.

7.4 Milton Friedman and the rise of corporocentrism

Friedman's (2007) essay 'The social responsibility of business is to increase its profits' (henceforth 'The social responsibility'), originally published in 1970, captures the key features of 'corporocentric ethics' and highlights the possibilities and dilemmas for environmentalists engaging with business institutions to enact benign ecological change. Friedman's article epitomises the heroic neoliberalism of Nozick and Hayek with its prioritisation of market relations (and thus exchange values), embodied in a particular institutional form, that of the corporation. In addition, Friedman promotes a specific socio-political environment that supports corporate bodies over alternatives. Whilst he does refer to enterprises run for reasons other than profit ('eleemosynary') and the self-employed ('individual proprietors'), his principal focus is on 'business'; that is to say, an organisation run to maximise profits for its owners (Friedman 2007, 173). Ultimately these, and sole proprietors who are also profit-maximisers, are the main drivers of a successful economy.

> **Corporocentrism**: a legal, political and economic environment that enables corporations to thrive. It is often designed by corporate players to prioritise the interests of these organisations.

'The social responsibility' exemplifies corporocentric ethics. It promotes norms that structure an environment that prioritises the flourishing of corporations. This might initially seem odd, as Friedman's oft-cited text[3] is usually thought to illustrate an abandonment of business ethics (see, for instance, Duska 2000; Shepard et al. 1991), but a narrow ethic is identifiable in his work. Friedman argues that an employee of a corporation ('a businessman', to use his gender-partial language) has two moral responsibilities. The first duty is to obey the law and the second is to fulfil the contractual obligations into which he has freely entered. Friedman does not formally acknowledge an explicit ethical position, but these two principles provide a guide for action based on neo-Kantian deontology. These obligations are absolute, supreme and binding (Friedman 2007). So, other than obeying the law, an employee's supreme function is to maximise profits for their employers (the shareholders).

Friedman (2007, 173–4) offers a number of criticisms to those who argue that businesses should have other responsibilities, such as those of sustainability, or environmental or social justice. First that the term 'social responsibility' is too vague to provide proper guidance; second, that a business person does not have the proper skills to identify and therefore meet social justice considerations and that it is instead the proper function of government. The third and most important criticism argues that to act to meet social responsible goals, whether in terms of wider notions of social justice or environmental sustainability, damages the interests of the owners (the shareholders). Prioritising other goals that impinge on the primary objective of maximising corporate profits contravenes the employee's contract and is a form of theft.

The first objection is easily dealt with. The term 'social responsibility' does have fluid meanings but this does not make it meaningless. It simply requires careful contextualised clarification. Friedman himself provides a basic interpretation, which is clarified further by his critics, like Bakan (2004, 57) and Andrew Crane and Dirk Matten (2010, 48–9), in which corporate social responsibility (CSR) is identified in terms of the ethical principles of non-maleficence (limiting harm to others, including ecological damage) and beneficence (doing good for others), even when there is no contractual obligation to do so. It is the absence of this commitment to even non-malfeasance in Friedman's description of the corporate actor – a principle that is the cornerstone of benign professional codes of conduct dating back to the Hippocratic Oath ('first do no harm') – that becomes the start-point for Bakan's portrayal of corporations as psychopaths.

The second objection is that governments, rather than business people, are the appropriate agents for pursuing social goals like pollution reduction. Business people are not only ill-equipped to do so but are transgressing on the proper function of the state. It is up to the government, preferably a democratic one, to determine goals and then to apply these laws impartially to all parties (Friedman 2007, 176). The corporation has a duty to respect laws. The environmentalist should attempt to influence the democratic majority, not the corporate entity. This point, which appears unproblematic, becomes so as Friedman later rejects state intervention into the operations of corporations as socially damaging and a violation of individual liberty (Friedman 2007, 178).

Further, if businesses should pursue all legal routes to maximise profits, they would have an absolute duty to their shareholders to ensure that legislation that impacted on profits, such as legislation to prevent commercial exploitation of natural resources, was resisted. Hence, consistent with the growth of Friedman's liberalism, there has been increasing 'corporate capture' of government, where apparently competing political parties are dependent on corporate interests for campaign funding and thus beholden to these powerful groupings (Harvey 2005, 49). There is considerable debate about overt influence on environmental policy by corporate interests (see, for instance, Kamieniecki 2006 and Corporate Watch 2009) and how much of it is already internalised by policy makers who now embody the interests of business without requiring active pressure or overt threat (e.g., Campbell 2005).

The third criticism is that as an employee has signed a free contract to meet his employer's interests – which in the case of a successful business is to maximise profits – then it is impermissible to pursue other goals at the expense of this categorical duty. To use Friedman's (2007, 174) own example, if a manager sought to limit a company's pollution when there was no legal obligation or majority shareholder consent, then this environmental action would be ethically impermissible (and tantamount to theft).

For some environmentalists there is a possible hope for reconciliation with neoliberal organisations. First a company, according to Friedman, should pursue environmental goals, such as limiting pollution, where the law compels them. So, for instance, government-encouraged 'choice-editing' (as discussed alongside other state strategies in more detail in Chapter 8), in which certain ecologically-damaging goods were either prohibitively taxed or banned, would have to be complied with by corporate entities morally committed to obeying the law. The state as the ultimate protector of sovereign rights has to be respected.

> **Choice-editing**: the process by which consumers' choices are deliberately restricted to achieve a particular goal. It can be organised by governments or be a deliberate choice of retailers.

Secondly, and more significantly, a company might pursue socially or ecologically benevolent goals if it is likely to increase profit by enhancing consumer loyalty or attracting better job candidates (Friedman 2007, 177). Thirdly, markets provide a basis for free individuals to make contracts to meet their preferences. If environmentally-conscious customers desire non-polluting products or wish to buy up habitats in order to protect them, then the market will respond to these desires. There is nothing to prohibit campaigners from attempting to influence consumer preferences in more ecologically-sensitive directions. Friedman thus approves of CSR so long as it is done intentionally to maximise profits. This appeal to enlightened self-interest – that benevolent action will have better economic returns in the future – is, however, not without significant problems. Nonetheless, many, including many of Friedman's critics, turn to this solution.

7.5 Critics of Friedman

Friedman's essay has generated considerable critical response. This ranges from opponents, like R. Edward Freeman, who claim that Friedman's profit-orientated response ignores important duties to stakeholders, to those, like Robert Solomon (2002) and Bakan (2004), who argue that it ignores the virtues and instead generates psychopathic behaviour. Solomon (2002, 356), in his defence of business practice against the 'myth of amoral[ity]', argues that Friedman ignores the importance of corporate virtue. There are, however, problems with these responses to Friedman's corporocentrism. As is argued over the next few pages, many of them end up reasserting the primacy of neoliberal institutions and their core values.

7.5.1 Friedman, CSR and the role of stakeholders

Friedman's initial position is minimally ethical in that it prioritises respecting rights and keeping obligations that are freely made (contracts) over all other considerations. Using Adam Smith's (1776) concept of the invisible hand, Friedman (2007, 176) also smuggles in some utilitarian considerations, arguing that market economies produce best outcomes even if the good end comes about without anyone intending it. However, his defence that minimal CSR is possible where it maximises profit or is enforced by the state is principally non-ethical. Acting benevolently or non-malevolently because of compulsion (fear of government sanction) violates the principle that moral behaviour is freely chosen or willed (notwithstanding considerations discussed in Chapters 5 and 6). Further, to solely appeal to self-interest flouts the principle that ethical action is primarily concerned with the treatment of others.

Rogene Bucholz and Sandra Rosenthal (2002, 304) outline the apparent conflict between corporate social responsibility and Friedman's corporocentric ethics. Proponents of CSR argue that businesses have a responsibility to resolve social problems they can assist with and, in some cases, that they cause. Opponents of CSR take Friedman's position that imposing such obligations on corporations violates autonomy, undermines pluralism and leads to bad outcomes. They further argue that the scope of corporations' responsibilities would be unclear. To whom would duties, over-and-above legal and contractual ones, be owed?

In part, as Thomas Donaldson and Lee Preston (1995) and David Bevan and Patricia Werhane (2011) point out, stakeholder theory helps explain the ways in which CSR should play out. Businesses necessarily interact with a range of interest groups and institutions. Stakeholders include not just governments and investors, but also political groups, suppliers, customers, trade associations, employees and communities (Donaldson and Preston 1995, 69; Buchholz and Rosenthal 2002, 315). What is perhaps notable from an environmental point of view is that ecological entities are not included in the standard list of stakeholders; nonetheless, this could be modified. Stakeholder theory makes an empirical (factual) claim that more successful companies care about all the people who are influenced by the operation of the business, beyond those with formal contractual obligations (Q. Kotter and Haskett in Donaldson and Preston 1995, 71). There is, in addition, a normative (or ethical) feature to CSR that companies ought to act in a way that respects non-malfeasance and beneficence towards stakeholders (Donaldson and Preston 1995, 71; Freeman and Philips 1999, 10).

Friedman's response accommodates the normative (ethical) with the empirical (observable). Businesses should take into account their impact on stakeholders but only when it improves the bottom line. As R. Edward Freeman and Robert A. Phillips (1999) indicate, if stakeholder beneficence, such as being seen as communally and environmentally responsible, increases profits then this is precisely what the corporate employee should do. Similarly, if by 'harm' it means violating the negative rights of stakeholders (as in the case of theft), then Friedman's corporocentric ethics already rules out such forms of malfeasance. Imposing other restraints by taking into account other sorts of impediments would interfere with business efficiency, restricting economic development and thereby causing greater social disutility. Advocates of CSR, rather than being critics of Friedman, end up supporting his basic schema.

7.5.2 Corporations as non-virtuous agents

Virtue-orientated criticisms are raised by Solomon. He argues that neoliberals misconstrue the moral character of the corporation as one based solely on greed. Although Friedman is not specifically named, Solomon's (2002, 31–2) criticism of avaricious (self-interested alone) behaviour from those who follow Smith's economic analysis (in *The Wealth of Nations*) without his corresponding virtue theory (*Theory of Moral Sentiments*) appears to be aimed at Friedman and his Chicago School adherents. Solomon identifies neoliberal accounts of successful corporate practice with the traits of 'competitiveness, individualism, and economic self-interest'. These are viewed as destructive to harmonious social communities. Instead, Solomon argues, businesses require virtues that Friedman overlooks (2002, 33). Friedman, by concentrating on only one supreme virtue, turns it into a vice as it is not moderated by the other virtues essential to good business practice.

Similarly, propertarian advocates (see the box below) argue that Friedman's ethics do not undermine virtues, but are the basis for virtuous activity. Tibor Machan (2002, 93; see also Machan 2004) argues that virtuous self-reliant individuals are developed within the competitive structure of neoliberalism. Prudence and responsibility will be rewarded in the marketplace. However, there are a number of problems with Solomon's account of successful business eschewing selfishness and Machan's account of virtues being embodied in enlightened corporate self-interest. First, neither Solomon nor Machan take into account environmental virtues. The motivation is personal material advantage, not the development of ecological sensitivity and the flourishing of other forms of life. Second, the virtues are supposed to work in unity, but here a salesperson, for instance, is under no obligation to be honest or promote wisdom: they do not have to point out the commodity's weaknesses, only not to lie, if asked.[4] Finally, virtue theory does not promote one virtue as universally supreme (see Chapter 2), but for Machan in particular, justice (as understood in the limited terms of respect for property rights) is always and everywhere the most important value.

Libertarian or **Propertarian**: Since the 1970s, these terms have largely referred to a theory that gives supreme value to negative liberty (freedom from interference) and property rights and rejects all interference to individual contract-making. However, the term 'libertarian' originally referred to the anti-capitalist tradition and was deliberately co-opted by the free-market thinker and activist Murray Rothbard. In recent years anti-state socialists, like Iain McKay and Murray Bookchin, have attempted to regain the term 'libertarian' and label their free-market opponents as 'propertarians' or 'private-statists' because they privilege the freedom of owners of private property to use and distribute their goods irrespective of the outcomes and eventual freedoms of the property-deficient.

Michael Sandel (2012, 64) provides a forceful account of how market relationships undermine other important values and can erode important social practices. He uses the example of a kindergarten that had a problem with parents arriving a few minutes late to pick up their children. Their solution was to charge parents a penalty fine for late collection. From a neoliberal perspective, introducing a charge for a late pick-up when there was formerly no financial burden should result in a decrease in parental tardiness. However, instead, late pick-ups increased. The reason was that in the past parents recognised that arriving late was discourteous and inconvenient to the childcare professionals, but once it was turned into a financial relationship parents no longer felt a sense that their actions were wrong as it was now simply an additional service. When the childcare centre returned to the original 'honour' system, however, parents kept turning up late as the old norms and virtues had been undermined by being turned into a market relationship. Sandel suggests that once the virtues of a practice has been undermined by market reasoning it is fundamentally distorted, though they may return given time.

This is not to discount completely the role of financial incentives. Short-term financial incentives can assist people to overcome their reluctance to engage with benevolent practices with which they were otherwise unfamiliar. MacIntyre (1985, 188) gives the example of socialising a child into the practice of playing chess. Chess is a worthwhile pursuit, but a child might initially be encouraged to learn and play chess by being offering a small bribe or reward for learning and playing the game; but eventually the game is played not for the external reward but the internal goods. Similarly, short-term rewards might initiate people into environmental practices, such as walking to school or work rather than using the car. However, if the internal goods are insufficiently imbedded, when the financial reward is reduced or removed, the practice falls apart. Indeed, and as discussed in Chapters 5 and 6 with respect to the single action bias and the negative spillover effect, if monetary reasons become the only way to motivate commuters to adopt public transport over more carbon profligate forms of travel, then the financial reward for adopting the greener journey might be spent on even more carbon-excessive activities, like plane travel for another foreign holiday.

Bakan (2004, 37) also argues against strategies based on market reasoning, especially when embodied in the corporation. Encouraging behaviour change through commercial logic does not just distort ethical practice, but also encourages psychopathic behaviour. This is because a corporation is solely motivated by self-interest and is structurally incapable of taking into account the interests of others. These psychopathic organisations are especially dangerous as, according to Friedman's account, the only limit on this self-serving force is government control. However, as Bakan identifies (2004, 79–83), control by government is insufficient. Corporations are committed to self-interest and are in competition with other self-interested institutions; as a result, corporations have to undertake a cost–benefit analysis as to whether they comply with law. The commitment to legality is hypothetical rather than categorical.

Take a situation where there are two competing corporations. The first takes obedience to law as categorical (as Friedman seems to suggest) and ignores cost–benefit analysis and follows expensive legislative requirements when evasion would increase their profitability (taking into account the risk of successful prosecution). The second corporation acts self-interestedly on the same calculation. In this situation, the competitor is likely to gain advantage. In further competition for resources, the law-abiding corporation is at an economic disadvantage and will start to lose market share.

However, consistent with Friedman's account, corporations have a duty to influence governments to maximise return for investors, lobbying to nullify economically expensive environmental legislation (such as choice-editing). Psychopathic organisations, as Bakan points out, have been successful in this regard with corporate self-governance replacing the regulatory system; and where the regulatory system still exists, enforcement arms are denuded of resources leading to deliberately produced 'lax regulation and ineffectual enforcement' (Bakan 2004, 84). These lapses are not accidental but actively encouraged by corporate bodies (96–110).

Bakan advocates four main strategies to control corporate psychopathy and encourage greater ecological and social responsibility: 1) improve the regulatory system; 2) strengthen political democracy; 3) create a robust public sphere and 4) challenge international neoliberalism (161–7). The first two promote representative-democratic control of corporations through the constitutional process; the third and fourth are realised in ethical consumption and lifestyle change, and are subservient to the first two methods. So, although Bakan positions himself as a critic of Friedman, the strategy he proposes actually employs the methods Freidman endorses in his article.

Bakan's goal is to promote representative-democratic control of corporations, through the constitutional process: 'Government regulation, unlike market-based solutions, combines authority, capacity and democratic legitimacy to protect citizens from corporate misdeeds' (149). This, too, reiterates rather than challenges Friedman.

In his later work Friedman is much more overtly critical of interventionist governments but in 'The social responsibility' he argues that corporations should be subservient to the law, and that concerned individuals should pursue social goals through influencing the legislative process. Even in this more social-democratic piece however, Friedman (2007, 144–5) highlights the dangers to business, and thus to a successful and wealthy society, of government interference. Bakan's (2004, 104) state-centred tactic contradicts his findings earlier in his book, which detail how corporations manipulate representative government through lobbying and successfully transgressing laws if this is the most profitable action (2002, 80). Even with legislation specifically designed to limit corporate lobbying, other forms of corporate influence will be found as a corporation must do everything to maximise profits. Similarly, liberal states must accede to corporate power as these 'remarkably efficient wealth-creating machines' (159) provide the economic base for state activity. Yet for Bakan, statist control remains the most suitable method for controlling corporations, and without this tactic all other methods are redundant.

The movement against corporate rule would be impossible, even senseless, without robust nongovernmental institutions, community activism and political dissent; the belief that these can be a *substitute* for governmental regulation, rather than a necessary complement to it, is dangerously mistaken.

(151.)

To try to promote greater democratic control over corporations Bakan looks to his final two main tactics: 3) the creation of a robust public sphere not answerable to corporate interests or operating on business principles, which 4) challenges international neoliberalism (163–4). Yet these non-statist internationalist responses are structured back into corporate state activity. The radicalised citizenry's job is to influence rather than undermine or replace government, corporations and transnational institutions (such as the World Trade Organisation), which are predicated on maintaining capitalist production and prioritising exchange value over other values such as ecological concern (164).

7.6 Corporate citizenship

As Bakan describes, the rise of corporations was necessitated by the development of certain types of states, particularly those committed to free trade and the protection of individual property rights. Whilst these bodies have been ecologically damaging and repressive, their record is not necessarily poorer than other, more oppressive, state structures, which do not promote property rights. Crane and Matten (2010, 56, 68–9) discuss how corporations can act as benevolent agents by supplying goods that oppressive states are failing to provide to their subjects and encouraging the development of social, political and economic freedoms, especially where the state's ability to guarantee them has diminished (Matten and Crane 2005, 10–11). These freedoms are then used to promote ecological or social justice causes.

Advocates of corporate citizenship see it as a form of CSR, but the resources (which could go to shareholders) allocated to promoting social, political and economic rights have a bottom-line benefit for business. Corporate citizenship exists 'only if it is in their self-interest to do so' (Matten and Crane 2005, 15). It creates the corporocentric political economy by developing the structures for business efficacy. It seeks to establish the legal and social structures that can ensure a company's supply chain and the functioning social infrastructure of stable worker-citizens-consumers for future economic expansion (Valente and Crane 2009: 80–81). As such, corporate citizenship reinforces, rather than challenges, Friedman's account of corporate self-interest and hidden-hand benefits. Enhancing the power of corporations in this manner makes them 'more or less officially accepted player(s)' in the political arena (Matten and Crane 2005, 12). However, this embrace of the corporation into the main structures of the democratic state has been responsible for undermining the regulatory function of the state (10–11). Corporate citizenship reinforces the deceptive view that positive environmental change can only come through either the centralised state or corporate activism and it marginalises alternative, more responsive and potentially more ecologically sensitive, forms of political economy (such as those promoted by deep ecologists and social ecologists).

7.7 Corporate environmentalism

The idea of incorporating ecological principles, organisational practice or ethos into business practice is not new. Market environmentalism is a significant feature of the retail environment. The most obvious have been the largely superficial rebranding of products with green symbols to give their commodities some ecological cachet. Friedman (2007, 177) himself describes such 'window-dressing' as 'hypocritical', although he does not call for legal sanctions against it.

Even for companies whose products are not specifically designed for niche greenmarkets, sustainability has become a corporate catchword. But as President of the Society of Business Ethics, Joseph DesJardins (2015), points out, when the term 'sustainable' enters into the corporate sphere its meaning alters from its original ecological sense. He cites Ernst and Young and the Dow Jones Business Index that use notions of sustainability in a purely neoliberal way. They see sustainability simply in terms of maximising profits over the longer term, rather than seeking shorter-term gains (DesJardins 2015, 120–21).

DesJardins' point may find resonance amongst environmentalists who have sought to engage businesspeople in discussions about ecological issues. Corporate decision-makers often find it hard to integrate ecological thinking into their conceptual framework. The tendency is for the activist to reinterpret the green concern into a financial calculation that the businessperson is more familiar with. For example, the inherent value of a diverse eco-system threatened by rising sea level is given a monetary price. The risk is that such a strategy reduces ecological values to exchange values, and makes green principles secondary to achieving profitable goals. It reinforces a particular instrumental account of ecology.

Friedman and Nozick argue that free markets allow for the production of dissenting communities and distinctive modes of production. Those who wish to operate on the basis of a workers' cooperative or ecological commune can do so, so long as they can survive in a free market environment (see ethical consumption at 7.7.2 below). They either forego some profit for more expensive ecologically responsible production, or find customers who share green preferences and will pay extra for the product to support the environmental or social goal. Some enterprises, from small micro-businesses to larger corporations, operate in just such a way: these include artisan organic brewers and vegan food producers, international cosmetics companies like Body Shop and Lush and major renewable energy providers like EDF. However, these are not without substantial problems. First, even in ecological businesses, there are going to be times when ecological issues come into conflict with profit maximisation. It may be that the enterprise will choose to reduce profit (with the agreement of its shareholders), in which case it is no longer operating as a corporation in Friedman's sense of the term; alternatively, it relegates environmental values as secondary to exchange values.

According to Friedman (2007) and Nozick (1974) all groupings, even if they operate internally on different principles such as cooperation and usufruct (gaining benefit from something through use, but not having private ownership), have to interact with each other at least initially on the principles of market distribution and exchange. These take universal priority. Some ecological co-operatives cannot interfere with the property rights of competitors or suppliers even if they are ecologically damaging. Yet it is hard to provide non-circular arguments for why deontological property rights take such priority, especially when they are so damaging to benign social practices (MacIntyre 1985).

7.7.1 Monetarising the environment: carbon credits

Despite problems with neoliberalism, global policy-makers have adopted free market principles in an attempt to resolve environmental crises. Neoliberals, following Friedman, view environmental crises to be the result of inadequate property rights, not because of any deficiency in market principles. They encourage the enclosure of the natural environment into saleable and resalable entities. If an object is private property there is an incentive to protect it. The most significant of these developments, following the United Nations Conference on Climate Change (1992–97) that produced the Kyoto protocol, has been the formation of tradable pollution permits and carbon credits. Here countries are allocated a specific amount of greenhouse gas emission. Those that produce less than that amount can sell the surplus to those countries that would prefer to pay to maintain a high carbon dependent economy. Thus states that took carbon reduction seriously would be financially rewarded and the profligate would be taxed.

There are a number of criticisms concerning the operation of carbon credits in terms of measurement and enforcement mechanisms. There are also problems with the allocation of credits by nation states to particular industrial players, often at no charge, which provides these corporations with a competitive advantage against newcomers into the field who have no free carbon credits. Sandel (2012, 73) offers an ethical critique of carbon credits and the market thinking that lies behind it. By being able to buy their way out of environmental responsibility, rich countries are 'outsourcing . . . an obligation' (75). The credits system suggests that, collectively, producers do not need to embody an appropriate attitude to nature, but can continue to use it as a standing reserve. In addition, it encourages poorer countries to see the environment solely in instrumental terms. If credit values decrease or cease, then the motivation for environmental thinking diminishes. The credit system that ensures that the restrictions endured by poorer countries do not have to be experienced by the polluting richer ones undermines social solidarity (75–6). Financial incentives can provide short-term impetus to engage in unfamiliar environmental practices, but longer-term behavioural change requires practitioners to engage in it for its own sake. Action undertaken just for monetary reward means that the participants are likely to spend their windfall on other ecologically damaging activities.

Using markets to protect the environment faces another problem: the creation of ecological scarcity and production of environmental crises can maximise profits. Thus there are incentives towards undermining species and habitats in order to manufacture scarcity and raise prices or to create new markets to respond to emergencies (Chomsky and Achbar 2004, 195–6). Liberal economics concentrates on exchange value at the expense of the multiple and irreducible use-values (both intrinsic and instrumental) of nature (see Müller 2001). So when Mary Ruwart (2012) argues that private ownership of the forests protects them better than state ownership as 'industry grows 13 per cent more timber than it cuts in order to prepare for future needs', she not only creates a false dichotomy (state vs private commercial) – suggesting these are the only two options – but ignores the damage of monoculture that goes along with commercial logging. Ruwart sees forestry primarily in exchange terms as a resource for production; her ecological opponents place priority on use values over exchange values.

In addition, markets are not responsive to need, but to demand. A person reduced to begging has a desperate need for clean water and food but has no demand and thus their interests are ignored. The well-fed and watered wealthy, on the other hand, have high demand but less pressing needs. Entities that are external to the market economy, such as non-human animals, also have their interests similarly ignored as they too have no demand, unless they have their needs mediated through the economic activity of humans.

7.7.2 Ethical consumption

Before discussing the political constraints on corporations, Bakan discusses promotion of ethical consumption. He argues that consumers, as private citizens, should be encouraged to make retail decisions based on the corporation's social and environmental practices. Businesses, in order to protect their bottom line, will act to meet these ethically-concerned demands (Bakan 2004, 144–5). This position is perfectly consistent with Friedman's. A corporation should switch to producing environmentally sustainable goods through ecologically-responsible manufacturing methods if – and only if – it is the most profitable option.

Nonetheless, whilst welcoming and promoting consumers' power to economically punish corporate malevolence, Bakan (2004, 145) recognises that this response on its own is inadequate. A significant proportion of the public has little or no consumer power to undertake this tactic (146). Businesses, as has been pointed out elsewhere, are unlikely to make their ecologically destructive activities public and instead present their economically most effective production methods in the greenest possible light as a cheaper alternative to more ecologically-sensitive manufacture (Mitchell 2012; Lane 2013).

> **Ethical consumption**: making purchasing decisions motivated by moral principles, rather than price or immediate satisfaction.

As noted in Chapter 5, there is a further problem with ethical consumption, known as the 'single action bias'. By buying the occasional ecologically sensitive product, individuals feel that they have contributed to the reduction of greenhouse gases and thus fail to adequately engage in the more difficult and effective collective action that is necessary to address the wicked problem of climate change. For Bakan, viewing solutions to social and environmental problems as a matter of consumer choices, places corporations (the main producers of commodities) as the main institutions for resolving these problems, but once an enterprise operates as a business, its 'moral concerns and altruistic desires must succumb to [a] . . . corporation's overriding goal' (Bakan 2004, 53).

Environmental principles, when based on pure self-interest, are no longer part of the virtues but just a form of self-regard. The adoption of environmental principles within corporate strategies becomes a way for companies to integrate certain consumer and political concerns into their brand, building in value and helping to obscure other forms of ecological and social damage (Hanan 2013, 11–13). Bakan (2004, 147), like Friedman (2007, 177), recognises that if a corporation were to take more radical environmental action, prioritising ecological values over business principles, then in the absence of monopoly position their competitive position would be damaged and they would soon cease to exist. Thus, if the former is more profitable than the latter, a corporation has structural drive to appear to be acting in an environmentally-friendly manner rather than to actually behave in such a manner. This leads to greenwashing.

> **Greenwashing**: a term originated by Jay Westervelt to describe corporate marketing or PR strategies that deliberately deceive consumers into believing that a company is embracing environmentally-friendly practices.

As discussed earlier, Friedman (2007, 177) appears critical of those who engage in strategies akin to greenwashing but rejects state intervention to deal with bad business practice. For Friedman, the market alone is the best judge of corporate behaviour, even if it produces bad social and environmental outcomes.

7.8 Ecologically responsible alternatives

There are a range of ecological criticisms of Friedman's protection of the profit motive. Friedman's neoliberalism, like that of Rand, Nozick and Hayek, is based on the supreme value of protecting negative freedom. Ecologists, and others, consider other values to be more important and negative rights to be an inadequate account of freedom. Freedom is not just about freedom from interference, but also about freedom to do and to be; and this requires, as the radical geographer Elisée Reclus (2004, 158) identifies, access to resources that avaricious self-interest denies. People do not enter into important contracts without coercion but because of the enclosure or privatisation of the commons, in which communal resources are taken, often by force, into private hands, excluding others from using them. Thus, in order to meet material needs, many individuals who could have gained basic goods from the common grounds are now forced to sell their labour to survive – hence the notion of 'wage-slavery' (Graeber 2004, 70–1; see too Cohen 1983). Similarly, Bookchin (1997, 40–1) and Naess (2016, 218–20) may disagree on some important issues, but they are in agreement that individuals are not isolated and abstracted from one another and the natural world, but already and always implicated in each other's lives. Reducing complex diverse social relationships to contractual ones ignores the inequalities in contract making and undermines important forms of social solidarity and ecological concern.

Some ecological alternatives, as discussed in Chapter 8, are centred on constitutional methods for influencing a state's legislature and governmental, institutional arrangements. Chapter 9 looks at alternative, extra-constitutional and anti-capitalist methods for bringing about environmental change. But, in general, deep and social ecologists, rather than more anthropocentric environmentalists, tend to reject the false division found in neoliberals like Friedman, anarcho-capitalists like Ruwart and social democratic critics like Bakan: that the only two forms of production are either state ownership or private enterprise based on property rights. Critical management theorists (see Alveson and Wilmott 1992), anarchist geographers like Reclus (2004) and Peter Kropotkin (1939, 2013), and more contemporary radicals (such as Ward 1973 and Shantz 2010, 91–111), outline how goods can – and are – generated without the primacy of managerial hierarchy or structured around the law of value. Activities such as guerrilla gardening (using land, often without permission, to collectively grow and distribute crops freely), co-operative housing, direct action against littering and pollution, generate collective external and internal goods. Older traditions of land management and communal production still exist in the form of crofting communities in Scotland or are being revitalised and re-imagined in parts of Spain (Hancox 2013).

Environmentally sensitive production does not require a return to primitive or artisan production. As introduced in Chapter 4, Murray Bookchin (1997, 115–6) argues that democratic, inclusive and co-operative production can generate sophisticated supply chains necessary for contemporary large scale manufacture and give sufficient priority to ecological harms as local communities still have significant sway over decision making.

Autonomous production, which embodies environmental principles, has been a significant feature of alternative patterns of production in Latin America. Here notions of *Buen Vivir* – sometimes also referred to as *Vivir Bien* (and closely aligned to the Ecuadorian concept of *sumac kawsay*) – are significant. These seek to promote, protect and extend practices that embody 'a fullness [of] life in a community, together with other persons and Nature' (Gudynas 2011, 442). *Buen Vivir* thus shares significant similarities with the ecological *Eudaimonia* of virtue theory. Like practices based on environmental virtue, *Buen Vivir* is diverse in form and generates different practices in different contexts. This distinctive model of socio-economic activity stands in opposition to largely instrumentalist models of development.

Such green production is not immune to what is known as 'recuperation'. Recuperation is when a tactic or idea that intends to challenge the dominant social order is instead used to maintain that social order. For instance, environmental critics of large corporations who nonetheless publish their works through large publishing conglomerates. Businesses adopt some of the features of ecological activity and even market goods aimed at supporting ecological activity formally outside of the circuit of capital. So commercial firms offer goods to assist in autonomous production (such as aides derived from agribusiness targeted at allotment growers) or opportunities to travel to and participate in eco-tourism that helps preserve sustainable practices. But encroachment by corporate institutions alters these endeavours, turning them into commodified spectacles (Munt 1994; see too Urry 1992). Similarly autonomous production that is rich in ecological and social goods can be attractive for corporate capture and taken over by force. Nonetheless, the possibility of generating goods outside of the circuit of capital that prioritises ecological values instead of exchange value demonstrates a realm of possibilities for environmental behavioural change. These practices and values can sometimes be found subverting dominant modes of business behaviour, such as the subversive use of commercial property for ecological ends.

7.9 Conclusion

Claims about what is fundamental to ecologically-sensitive behavioural change are rarely uncontroversial, as explored in Chapters 3 and 4, but the ways in which needs and desires are generated and satisfied have long been recognised as having major impacts on natural environments. In many parts of the world, goods are produced and exchanged by institutions structured on the principles of neoliberalism, as exemplified by Friedman's corporocentric ethics. As a result, human labour, and non-human habitats and species, are viewed primarily as resources to be used instrumentally to maximise returns on investment. Other values are secondary to exchange-values. The relegation of environmental interests is a necessary feature of commercial practice that has to privilege economic returns. However, production based on this type of economy, although pervasive, is not necessary, nor is it universal. There are many communities in which production does give privileged positions to ecological values at the expense of greater profitability. These alternative ecologically-sensitive forms of production exist even in countries where neoliberal institutions are in ascendance. Sometimes these practices are so covert or marginal that they have not yet been encroached on by prevailing economic institutions; sometimes they challenge dominant practices and sometimes they are subsumed by them. Nonetheless, the existence and persistence of these non-statist environmental counter-examples to prevailing modes of production and distribution demonstrate that there can be – and are – practical alternatives to market-driven modes of production.

Notes

1 Elements of this chapter have appeared in the article Franks, B. (2014) 'The social responsibility of the anarchist is to destroy business', *Ephemera* 14.4, and the chapter (2017) 'Anarchist versus corporate ethics', in G. Baars and A. Spicer, eds, *The Critical Corporation Handbook*, 497–510, Cambridge University Press.
2 Tormey (2004, 181) also strongly identifies the corporation with neoliberalism hence the index entry: 'corporations *see* capitalism; neoliberalism'.
3 Google Scholar, as of 22 March 2016, lists over 11,000 citations of the text: http://scholar.google.co.uk/scholar?hl=en&q=the+Social+responsibility+of+The+Businessman&btnG=&as_sdt=1%2C5&as_sdtp=.
4 A different issue as to the legal and moral duty of warning of serious hazards, which Machan (2002, 93) raises and responds to.

References

Althusser, L. (1977) 'Ideology and ideological state apparatuses (notes towards an investigation', in *For Lenin and Philosophy and Other Essays*. New York: New Left Books.
Alvesson, M. and Wilmott, H. (1992) 'Critical theory and management studies: an introduction', in M. Alvesson and H. Wilmott (Eds), *Critical Management Studies*. London: Sage.
Bakan, J. (2004) *The Corporation*. London: Constable & Robinson.
Bevan, D. and Werhane, P. (2011) 'Stakeholder theory', in M. Painter-Morland and R. ten Bos, eds, *Business Ethics and Continental Philosophy*. Cambridge: Cambridge University Press.
Bookchin, M. (1997) *The Bookchin Reader*. London: Cassell.
Bulchhoz, R. and Rosenthal, S. (2002) 'Social responsibility and business ethics', in R.E. Frederick, ed., *A Companion to Business Ethics*, 303–21. Oxford: Blackwell.
Campbell, D. (2005) 'The biopolitics of empire: oil, empire and the Sports Utility Vehicle'. *American Quarterly* 57.3: 943–72.
Chomsky, N. and Achbar, M. (2004) 'Interview with Noam Chomsky, October 24, 2000', appendix to J. Bakan, *The Corporation*. London: Constable.
Cleaver, H. (1979) *Reading 'Capital' Politically*. Brighton: Harvester Press.
Cohen, G.A. (1983) 'The structure of proletarian unfreedom'. *Philosophy & Public Affairs* 12.1: 3–33.
Corporate Watch (2009) 'Listening to the siren's song: corporate lobbying at the UN climate talks', *Corporate Watch Magazine* 44: https://corporatewatch.org/magazine/44/augustseptember-2009/listening-sirens-song-corporate-lobbying-un-climate-talks.
Crane, A. and Matten, D. (2010) *Business Ethics*, Third Edition. Oxford: Oxford University Press.
DesJardins, J. (2015) 'Is it time to jump off the sustainability bandwagon'. *Business Ethics Quarterly* 26.1 (January): 117–35.
Donaldson T. and Preston L. (1995) 'The stakeholder theory of the corporation: concepts, evidence, and implications'. *Academy of Management Review* 20.1: 65–91.

Duska, R. (2000) 'Business ethics: oxymoron or good business?', *Business Ethics Quarterly* 10.1: 111–29.

Freeman, R.E. and Phillips, R.A. (1999) 'Stakeholder theory: a libertarian defense'. *Darden Graduate School of Business Administration working paper 1.3*, www.researchgate.net/profile/Robert_Phillips7/publication/228168804_Stakeholder_Theory_A_Libertarian_Defense/links/0c96051a3bbdb86e20000000.pdf. Also available as (2002) 'Stakeholder theory: a libertarian defense', *Business Ethics Quarterly* 12.3: 331–349.

Friedman, M. (2007) 'The social responsibility of business is to increase its profits', in W. Zimmerli, K. Richter and M. Holzinger, eds, *Corporate Ethics and Corporate Governance*. London: Springer.

Graeber, D. (2004) *Fragments of an Anarchist Anthropology*. Chicago, IL: Prickly Paradigm Press.

Graeber, D. (2011) *Debt: The First 5000 years*. New York: Melvillehouse.

Gudynas, E. (2011) '*Buen Vivir*: today's tomorrow', *Development* 54.4: 441–7.

Hanan, J. (2013) 'The ecology of empire: Wal-Mart's rhetoric of environmental stewardship and the constitutive power of the multitude', *Environmental Communication* 10: 1–19.

Hancox, D. (2013) 'Spain's communist model village', *The Guardian*, Sunday 20 October. Last modified on Friday 1 November: www.theguardian.com/world/2013/oct/20/marinaleda-spanish-communist-village-utopia.

Hardt, M. and Negri, T. (2000) *Empire*. London: Harvard University Press.

Harvey, D. (2005) *The New Imperialism*. Oxford: Oxford University Press.

Harvey, D. (2007) *A Brief History of Neoliberalism*. Oxford: Oxford University Press.

Humphreys, M. (2013) 'Green ideology', in M. Freeden, L.T. Sargent and M. Stears, eds, *The Oxford Handbook of Political Ideologies*, 422–438. Oxford: Oxford University Press.

Jameson, F. (2003) 'Future city', *New Left Review* 21: 65–9.

Kamieniecki, S. (2006) *Corporate America and Environmental Policy: How Often Does Business Get Its Way?* Palo Alto CA: Stanford University Press.

Kropotkin, P. (1939) *Mutual Aid*. London: Pelican.

Kropotkin, P. (2013) *The Conquest of Bread*. Edmonton: Black Cat.

Lane, E.L. (2013) 'Greenwashing 2.0', *Columbia Journal of Environmental Law*, 38.2: 279–331.

Machan, T. (2002) 'Business ethics in a free society', in R.E. Frederick, ed., *A Companion to Business Ethics*, 88–99. Oxford: Blackwell.

Machan, T. (2004) 'Aristotle and the moral status of business', *The Journal of Value Inquiry* 38.2: 203–23.

MacIntyre, A. (1985). *After Virtue*, Second Edition. London: Duckworth.

Marx, K. (1885) *Capital*, Volume 2. Available online at: www.marxists.org/archive/marx/works/1885-c2/.

Matten, D. and Crane, A. (2005) 'Corporate citizenship: toward an extended theoretical conceptualization', *Academy of Management Review* 30.1: 166–79.

Mitchell, S. (2012) *Walmart's Greenwash*. Institute for Local Self Reliance, internal report.

Müller, F. (2001) 'Environmental economics and ecological economics: antagonistic approaches?', *International Journal of Environmental Studies* 58.4: 415–44.

Munt, I. (1994) 'Eco-tourism or ego-tourism?', *Race & Class* 36.1, 49–60.

Naess, A. (2016) 'The shallow and the deep, long-range ecological movement', in L. Pojman, P. Pojman and K. McShane, eds, *Environmental Ethics*, Seventh Edition, 218–21. Wadsworth.

Nozick, R. (1974) *Anarchy, State and Utopia*. Oxford: Basil Blackwell.

Ruwart, M. (2012) 'Aggression and the environment', in G. Chartier and C.W. Johnston, eds, *Markets Not Capitalism*. Brooklyn: Autonomedia.

Reclus, E. (2004) 'Evolution, revolution and the anarchist idea', in J. C. Clark and C. Martin, eds, *Anarchy, Geography, Modernity: The Radical Social Thought of Elisee Reclus*. Lanham: Lexington.

Sandel, M. (2012) *What Money Can't Buy: The Moral Limits of Markets*. Harmondsworth: Penguin.

Shantz, J. (2010) *Constructive Anarchy: Building Infrastructures of Resistance*. Farnham: Ashgate.

Shepard, J.M., Shepard, J. and Wokutch, R. (1991) 'The problem of business ethics: oxymoron or inadequate vocabulary?' *Journal of Business and Psychology* 6.1: 9–23.

Smith, A. (1776) *An Inquiry into the Nature and Causes of The Wealth of Nations. Book IV: On Systems of Political Economy*, www.marxists.org/reference/archive/smith-adam/works/wealth-of-nations/book04/ch02.htm.

Solomon, R. (2002) 'Business ethics and virtue', in Frederick, ed., *A Companion to Business Ethics*, 30–7. Oxford: Blackwell.

Tormey, S. (2004) *Anti-Capitalisms: A Beginners Guide*. Oxford: Oneworld.

Urry, J. (1992) 'The tourist gaze and the "environment"', *Theory Culture & Society* 9.3: 1–26.

Valente, M. and Crane. A. (2009) 'Public not private', *Wall Street Journal*, reprinted in A. Crane and D. Matten (2010) *Business Ethics*, Third Edition, 80–1. Oxford: Oxford University Press.

Ward, C. (1973) *Anarchy in Action*. London: Freedom.

Wilkinson, W. (2005) 'Capitalism and human nature', *Cato Institute*, www.cato.org/policy-report/januaryfebruary-2005/capitalism-human-nature.

8
CONSTITUTIONAL POLITICAL CHANGE

Green votes and Green representation

8.1 Introduction

The previous chapter outlined how both advocates of neoliberalism like Milton Friedman and opponents like Joel Bakan identified the importance of government in formulating and enforcing regulation for the common good. For Friedman, ultimately best outcomes were achieved by governments limiting their role to protecting property rights and enforcing contracts; for Bakan, it is by restricting the power of economic oligarchies, enabling some degree of social provision and having an interventionist state to protect vulnerable ecological entities. This chapter describes and assesses the ways in which political activity through the nation-state can be used to bring about ecological behavioural change.

In liberal democratic states, like those in Europe, Canada, the United States, New Zealand and Australia, state-centred action has increasingly become the dominant model of bringing about environmentally desirable outcomes. Whilst Chapter 9 explores alternative models for generating environmental change, this chapter concentrates on how participation in electoral politics and practising constitutional freedoms (such as freedom of association and freedom of speech), in support of electoral activism, aims to bring about political change. It explores the many forms of participation in constitutional politics and the arguments for and against this form of environmental activism. It examines the main structures of the democratic state (the electorate, legislature, executive and judiciary/constitution), looking at international examples that illustrate important differences in their function, legitimacy and effectiveness, in order to assist those who wish to encourage environmental behavioural change through the political process.

8.2 Politics and the state: the basics

There are multiple interpretations of politics. The main one, even within academic circles, revolves around capturing and maintaining state power. Niccolò

Machiavelli's manual *The Prince* (1981, originally published in 1532) is an example, focussing as it does on the techniques for acquiring and keeping control of the state (princedoms and republics, in Machiavelli's case). In contemporary academic introductions to politics, the focus still tends to be on the structures of the state as the primary site of politics (e.g., Garner et al. 2016). Other studies initially acknowledge a wider definition of politics that deals with community decision-making; for instance, one standard textbook initially defines politics as 'human beings making important decisions for their communities and others' (Powell et al. 2011, 1). However, even this is later refined to mean authoritative decision-making through the structures of government (3).

> **The state** is standardly defined, following the German sociologist Max Weber, as the body that has final authority on whether physical coercion can be used over a fixed geographical area (Garner et al. 2016, 6).

The account of politics that is used here is much more extensive than simple statecraft or even the initially wider definition of community decision-making on behalf of others. Not only does this latter definition suggest that all politics is limited to representation rather than direct engagement, it also omits forms of politics that are not centrally about decision making but about influencing other peoples' realities either through coercive power, contractual/economic power or soft power (see Chapter 5). This more expansive account of politics involves decision-making not just through state structures (national, regional and local government) but decision-making in small groups. It thus becomes possible to talk of the 'politics of the allotment society'. It also includes more subtle micropolitics; the processes by which everyday social interactions and cultural activities influence a person's self-perception, understanding of other people and the way they view the world around them. Such approaches are considered 'micropolitical' because it is within small organisations, and everyday activities and relationships, that power and its embedded values operate (Portwood-Stacer 2018, forthcoming). Ecological micropolitics involves engaging in and altering everyday activities to more fully embody ecological principles rather than concentrating on making changes primarily through the macro- or state level.

> **Micropolitics** is concerned with the norms and power relations that structure everyday activities. It is contrasted with **macropolitics**, which concerns influencing decisions, policies and institutional norms at the international, state and federal level.

Micropolitics concerns individual and group norms and identities, and operates beyond the state; the power relationships and values that infuse everyday activities.

Thus, at this scale, it is possible to talk about the 'politics of fashion' or the 'politics of modern art' because the ways in which people dress or engage with a sculpture can alter the way they think about themselves and their sense of connection to others. If art never addresses ecological degradation, or if landscape is treated solely as a historic curio for elite consideration, then this will influence how people view the natural world and ecological concerns.

Micropolitics as 'the ability to influence other people's realities' is much more pervasive than macropolitics. However, these broader micro-definitions can still be brought back into the realm of constitutionalism. Especially at election time, politicians will, for example, become concerned with the potential impact on voters of the broadcast of a particular film or TV programme.

This chapter concentrates on political strategies based on influencing or capturing the state to effect environmental change. In so doing it focuses on the modern democratic form of the state. Wider forms of politics, including those outside of (and sometimes against) the state, are the focus of the next chapter. This book considers more formal political strategies, partly because many of the major ecological movements consider these types of representative political programmes to be the most efficient forms of environmental behavioural change (Porritt 1997, 65; Q. Saward in Davidson 2009, 47). In addition, alternative approaches to environmental political change discussed in the next chapter are often a response to the problems identified in the formal political process.

8.3 Greens politics and state institutions

As Michael Mason (1999, 31) argues, there is 'no simple correspondence between environmental politics and democracy', but 'shallower' anthropocentric political theory tends to be concerned with modifying liberal representative structures rather than abandoning them for alternatives. Green constitutional politics aims to engage with and use the structures of the democratic state to influence domestic environmental policy and promote international agreement. Through using the coercive and ideological features of the state, environmental parties aim to structure social, economic and political policy around the achievement of environmental targets. The state can use a broad range of instruments for bringing about behavioural change, from the extremely coercive such as banning ecologically-destructive practices and products (like energy-inefficient light bulbs), taxing undesirable activities (air travel) and subsidising sustainable ones (public transport), and constructing markets (such as carbon trading).

As ecosystems and greenhouse gases do not respect national borders, action on pollution, climate change and protection of endangered species often require international agreements. These are achieved through negotiation between national governments and are enforced by them as well. Engaging in state politics is thus part of, and requires, making environmental ideas dominant. Green parties seek to make ecological principles part of the 'common sense' of civil society; as such, they are incorporated within the guiding philosophy of the governing party or parties and are structured into legislation that is approved by the citizenry with little resistance.

> **Constitutional politics** involves utilising state-approved procedures for winning control of the organisations of government to formulate and pass laws. In democratic states, these legitimate methods are based around electoral activity and legally influencing political parties.

Whilst the state is viewed as the final arbiter for the legitimate use of coercive power within a given geographical region, other individuals or institutions may still use violence, but these acts are regarded as illegitimate and punishable, whilst those done with the approval of the state are acceptable and even rewarded. 'Government' is the term used for the decision-making bodies of the state that determine when, where and for what reasons force may be legitimately used. Threatening to lock someone up to gain money from them is usually considered a serious violation of rights, but if a governmental body does it to exact a democratically agreed tax then, under liberal democratic theory, such use of coercion is usually considered to be justified.

Within different types of state, there are distinctive (if overlapping) governmental structures to include some and exclude others from decision-making and policy enforcement. In tyrannies, the decision-making body is composed largely of the despot and his or her advisors; in democracies, the policy-forming body is selected by the people within the state.

There has been a significant move towards democratisation from 1974 to 2017, alongside a greater fragmentation (following the end of the Cold War) of states. In 2017, 45 per cent (87 out of 195) sovereign states (comprising 40 per cent of the global population) are full democratic (free) states; compared with 29 per cent (41 out of 152) of all states – containing less than a quarter of the world's population in 1974. In this year the majority of the global population were living in the

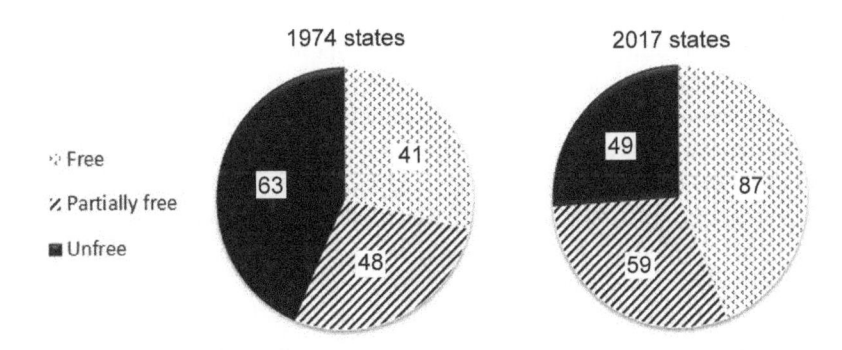

FIGURE 8.1 Global state structures in 1974 and 2017.[1] (Original by authors.)

44 per cent of states that were unfree (Freedom House 2014).[2] The substantial move towards greater democratisation during the period 1975–2005, which has made liberal democratic structures the most prominent, has seen a small reversal, with a slight slide back towards authoritarian governance (Freedom House 2016a).

There are four main bodies of the democratic state. First, there is the executive, the main policy-forming section. It determines the priorities of the state and steers the legislative programme, either through proposing new laws or amending or annulling old ones. In some countries, such as the United States, the executive (the President) is directly elected. In the UK the executive is elected by the legislature. Each voter has the chance to elect an MP. It is the candidate in the House of Commons (the United Kingdom's main legislature) who can command a majority of elected MPs who is chosen as Prime Minister. For effective green constitutional politics, the aim is to be involved in the executive in order to structure policy to support environmental legislation. The more power and influence green voices have in the executive, the greater influence they have over policy-setting.

The legislature is the body that meets to pass law. In most democratic countries this requires the support of a majority of the elected members, although in some states more than a bare majority is required, especially when constitutional matters are being discussed. Legislatures can be divided into two separate institutions (technically such legislatures are called bicameral). Bicameral systems are found in many states, for example, Germany (*Bundesrat* and *Bundestag*) and the Republic of Ireland (*Dáil Éireann* (Chamber of Deputies)) and *Seanad Éireann* (Senate). Other states have just a single legislative body (technically called unicameral), such as Israel's *Knesset* and the Maltese Parliament. Most bicameral systems give more authority to one particular chamber to prevent gridlock. For instance, in the UK, the House of Commons can eventually pass legislation whatever the opposition of the second chamber (House of Lords). The second chamber can, however, slow down the legislative process to encourage reflection and revision. Unusually, the UK's second chamber is little influenced by the electorate, being made up of appointees, bishops and a few landed aristocrats. This demonstrates that the categorisation of a state as a democracy is not precise but a continuum of particular characteristics. Problems can arise when a directly-elected president has different policy preferences to those of the elected legislature. Executive–legislature conflict, such as that between a Democratic US President (Bill Clinton and Barack Obama) and a Senate and Congress with a Republican majority, has led to policy inertia.

For constitutional politics, the more representation green parties have in the legislature the more likely they are to be part of the executive and the more easily they can influence policy proposals, rejecting those that are harmful and supporting those that protect and enhance the natural world. The wider political rights, necessary for a country to be a functioning democracy, also enables environmental viewpoints to influence debates.

The third feature of the democratic state is the electorate. The electorate are those people who can participate in the selection of representatives or (through referendum) directly make decisions. All democracies have rules to determine who has the right to vote and who is excluded. Criteria currently can include age (in most European countries the franchise has been set at 18, though some have experimented with 16), citizenship, or length of residence, and current legal status (some criminals serving long sentences and people sectioned with severe mental health problems are denied the vote). In previous eras whether a person could vote depended on gender, wealth and geographical location. Women were only fully enfranchised in the UK in 1928; full female enfranchisement did not occur in federal elections in Switzerland until 1971 and in some local elections Swiss women were still denied the vote until 1991.

The type of voting system has a significant impact on the effectiveness of green parties gaining constitutional influence. Assuming the same voting pattern, the

TABLE 8.1 UK Parliamentary Election 2015.[3] (Original by authors.)

Name of party	No. of votes in millions	Per cent of the vote	No. of seats	Per cent of the legislature
Conservative	11.3	36.9	331	50.9
Labour	9.3	30.4	232	35.7
Scottish National Party (SNP)	1.5	4.6	56	8.6
Liberal Democrat	2.4	7.9	8	1.2
UK Independence (UKIP)	3.9	12.6	1	0.2
Green	1.2	3.8	1	0.2
Other	1.1	3.6	21	3.2
Total	30.7 (66.1 per cent turnout)	100	650	100

TABLE 8.2 UK Parliamentary Elections 2017.[4] (Original by authors.)

Name of party	No. of votes in millions	Per cent of the vote	No. of seats	Per cent of the legislature
Conservative	13.7	42.4	318	48.9
Labour	12.9	40.0	262	40.3
Scottish National Party (SNP)	1.0	3.0	35	5.3
Liberal Democrat	2.3	7.4	12	1.8
UK Independence (UKIP)	0.6	1.8	0	0
Green	0.5	1.6	1	0.2
Other	1.2	3.7	22	3.4
Total	32.2 (68.7 per cent turnout)	100	650	100

voting formula (how votes are turned into representation) can result in significant differences in party representation within the legislature and thus the political make-up of the executive. The 2015 UK parliamentary election provides a good example.

The UK uses a system of running competitive elections in 650 geographically distinct areas (constituencies), each with approximately the same number of electors. The candidate with the most votes in each constituency becomes the Member of Parliament (MP). This system is known as 'first-past-the-post'. There is only one candidate per constituency, and most constituencies are won by candidates who receive less than 50 per cent of the vote. So, in a constituency contested by four more or less evenly-favoured parties, a person can be elected with 26 per cent of the vote.

The Conservative Party gained an absolute majority in the 2015 election (50.9 per cent of the seats) in the House of Commons but received less than 37 per cent of the vote. In first-past-the-post electoral systems it is quite common for a party to gain absolute majorities whilst only receiving a minority of the vote. Following the 2005 General Election the Labour Party had a very large majority of the MPs (around 60 per cent) in the House of Commons but Labour received barely more than 1 in 3 of the popular vote (35.3 per cent). Similar lopsided results occur in other first-past-the-post voting systems, such as in India and Pakistan.

With a majority of the MPs, the dominant party can choose the executive and pass legislation without recourse for support from any of the other political parties, so long as sufficient elected members of the main party stay loyal to the executive and its legislative programme. Supporters of this system of government argue that although it lacks representativeness (as the main party has less than majority public support for its policy platform) it has the advantage of stability and efficiency. The governing party can make law based on its manifesto without having to negotiate changes with other parties.

As Figure 8.2 demonstrates, minority parties, especially those with a geographically even but dispersed support like the Green Party, tend to do very badly under first-past the-post. In 2015 The Green Party received just under 4 per cent of the vote but gained only 1 MP (less than 0.2 per cent of the total). Other smaller

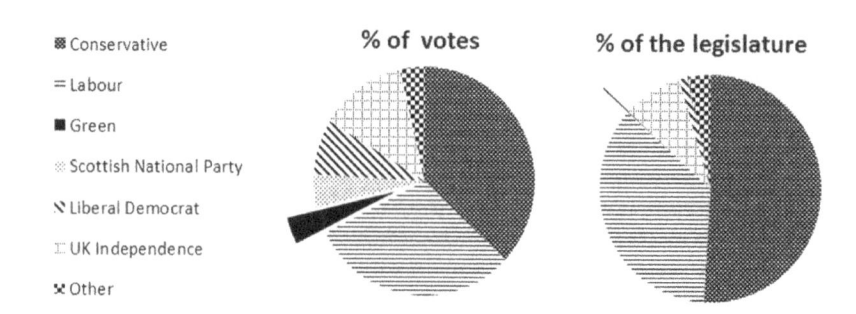

FIGURE 8.2 Percentage of the vote compared with percentage of representation under First-Past-the-Post in UK Parliamentary Elections 2015. (Original by authors.)

parties also fair badly under this voting system. The right-wing populist UKIP consistently finished second and third in many of the constituencies they competed in, however, for this they gained no representatives. They only finished first in one constituency. However, small parties with tighter geographical support, such the separatist social-democratic SNP, can do well under this voting system. The SNP gained 56 seats (out of Scotland's 59 parliamentary constituencies) in 2015 but overall gained far fewer votes in total than UKIP, and only a few hundred thousand more than the Greens. This was because the SNP's vote was concentrated in only the Scottish constituencies whilst UKIP and Green voters were more evenly – and thinly – distributed across the United Kingdom.

The 2017 election produced slightly more representative results as the electorate was more polarised into two opposing camps. Over 82 per cent of voters chose either the Labour or Conservative Party in the 2017 election as opposed to 67 per cent in 2015. Under first-past-the-post, a rational reaction by voters when there are two dominant parties with roughly equal support is to opt for the least worst option of the big two, rather than support a smaller party that has more desirable policy priorities. In 2017, smaller parties, such as Greens and UKIP, withdrew their candidates in some constituencies where they had little chance of winning but where their support could influence the election. By withdrawing their candidate they hoped that voters would prefer instead the more palatable contender from the two major parties and thus prevent the least preferred candidate from winning.

Most democracies, including more social democratic Scandinavian countries, use a different proportional system. Here representation in the legislature deliberately – and more accurately – reflects the proportion of votes cast. At the minimum it requires multiple representatives per constituency, with representation per constituency based on proportion of votes in support. In some systems, like Israel, there is just one national constituency.

In the vast majority of places that have proportional systems, no single party can govern alone as it is rare for any party to achieve over 50 per cent support amongst the electorate; backing tends to be required from at least one other political party. Most proportional systems produce coalition governments made up of two or more political parties. When green parties have been parties of government – such as in Germany (1998–2005) and the Republic of Ireland (2007–11) – it has been in proportional systems with the Green Party as the minority partner in the executive. Green parties thus tend to have more influence in proportional systems. Green parties in countries without proportional systems make reforming the first-past-the-post electoral system a key policy demand.

Because they require a government made up of parties representing at least 50 per cent of the voters, proportional systems are considered by theorists of comparative politics (such as Arendt Lijphardt 2012) to be much more representative and legitimate. However, because they include more than one party in policy formation and the legislative processes, they tend to be slower (less effective) and less stable, with governing coalitions falling apart over policy difference and new coalitions forming or elections being called. This is particularly true in systems that elect many different parties to the legislature, none of which have substantial support, meaning that the government requires a large number of coalition partners. Negotiations to create coalition governments are secretive and can take a long time (it took over a year for a coalition government to form following Belgium's 2010 General Election). Radical change is often hard as it requires the support of all the coalition partners.

Different modifications have been made to mitigate against some of the problems of proportional systems. Different types of proportional system can give bigger rewards to larger parties over smaller ones.[5] Having fewer representatives per constituency means that a higher proportion of votes is needed to elect an MP than in constituencies with a large representation to be divided up. Similarly, some systems build in a deliberate voter threshold to reduce the influence of very small parties. In a strictly proportional system with 500 seats in the parliament up for election, a party would need only 0.2 per cent of the vote to guarantee representation. This might mean that fringe parties with extreme and destabilising views could be elected despite being deeply detested by 99.8 per cent of the electorate. Some proportional systems, like Israel, set an initial threshold of 3.25 per cent of the vote before a party is allocated any seats. This reduces the number and influence of very small minority parties and encourages party loyalty. Without such a threshold, a well-known dissenter of a major party could gain a small percentage of the popular vote and thus retain their place in the parliament as an independent agent, but they would be unlikely to gain the popular support to overcome a high threshold without the assistance of a major party.

Some countries combine proportional and first-past-the-post in various ways: for instance, electing one part of the legislature through one method and the other house through another method, or combining the methods in mixed-member proportional systems, where there is a direct constituency vote for one candidate and a list choice across a region for proportional votes. Again greens tend to be badly underrepresented in single-person constituencies and gain elected representatives in the multi-party proportional systems (for instance Scotland and Germany).

The final feature of the democratic state is the judiciary and constitution. The constitution is the rules by which officials operate and the judiciary is the final authority on such rules. In order to create a supposed neutral set of arbiters, in most liberal democracies the judiciary is independent of political parties, although in the US vacancies to the Supreme Court are subject to political approval (proposed by the President and confirmed by the Senate). The constitution offers a general framework for government, protecting particular liberties from interference by elected officials. Rights to political free speech are, for example, protected under the US constitution. A majority of Americans and their elected officials may support, for instance, a ban on burning the national flag, for sincerely-held patriotic reasons, but as long as the flag is legitimately-owned private property and burning it is not placing anyone's body or property in danger, then this confrontational and strident piece of political theatre is constitutionally-protected free speech.

There is some disagreement about whether judges ultimately make the law or are just interpreters of the law. There have been instances where law seems to have been deliberately interpreted by judges to make the legislation ineffective; similarly, changes in the personnel of judges has meant radical reinterpretations of law to make major political change. In *Brown* v *Tapeka* (1954) the Supreme Court ruling outlawed racial segregation when previous rulings from the same body had held that 'separate but equal' for black people had been constitutionally acceptable and thus legitimised discrimination (Hague and Harrop 2010, 254–5). Opponents of environmental legislation have sought judicial review of green legislative proposals claiming that such legislation contravenes existing law or constitutional protections. Similarly, green activists hope to extend constitutional protections to environmental entities; examples include the Balearic Islands and Germany extending personhood rights to all great apes and not just humans.

The constitution usually includes the guarantees for a fully functioning democracy: including free speech, a free press, freedom of assembly, (near) universal suffrage with (near) equality of voting, and officials subject to the law. These constitutional protections are not absolute. Not all speech is protected, with certain forms of pornography, libel and harassment being examples of sanctioned speech. The press also faces some control in the form of privacy bills, D-notices or DA-notices (requests from government to editors to withhold publication on the grounds of national security) and copyright protection. Some assemblies, especially in public spaces, can meet legal restrictions. However, the relative freedoms offered by liberal democracies can be utilised by green parties to promote environmental issues amongst the electorate and to provoke further reflection on economic and social behaviour outside of the formal legislative arena. Green parties, environmental pressure groups and ecological direct action organisations also use these freedoms to coordinate and promote their activities inside and outside of parliaments.

8.4 State effectiveness and legitimacy

The standard position is that majoritarian systems – those with first-past-the-post voting, unicameral or heavily asymmetric bicameral legislatures, strong executives with little interference from a judiciary and highly limited constitution – are more efficient and stable governments but less legitimate, as they represent smaller sections of the public. Consensual democracies – with proportional governments, multi-party and dependent executives and more symmetric bicameral structures, an independent and interventionist judiciary and strong written constitutions – are less effective and stable but more representative (Lijphart 2012). It is standardly accepted that green constitutional politics has more success operating through consensual systems than majoritarian ones.

An alternative view holds that in majoritarian systems a swing of a few per cent can be the difference between a major party being in opposition and having a workable majority. As a result, major parties have an interest in taking on ecological concerns to win a majority. In consensual systems, greens as specific parties might have won a degree of representation and even governmental power, but they have been the minor party in the government and developments in environmental law have been insubstantial and piecemeal. Governments run by parties that are not specifically green have also introduced green legislation in order to capitalise on the votes of the green-leaning electorate. Similarly, consensual electoral systems also create room for radical anti-environmental parties who can also become minor parties in government. UKIP, which gained significant representation in the proportionally-elected Welsh Assembly, has a number of major figures who are climate change sceptics (Bawden 2014).

8.5 Constitutional green politics

Liberal democratic theory dominates Anglo-American political thought. Even those standing outside of that tradition, such as conservative, Marxist, environmentalist, anarchist and feminist practitioners, largely locate themselves in opposition to – or advances on – liberal theory. Liberalism, as discussed in earlier chapters, is primarily based on the free individual; it justifies the existence of the coercive state as being based on consent, albeit tacit (Locke 2000). The coercive state is further legitimised by liberals because it provides the best protection of individual freedoms (Locke 2000). The model of the liberal state is about ensuring the rights of the citizenry as far as possible (Figure 8.3).

In this simple model, the citizenry elect representatives to the legislature and they in turn select the executive. If the executive formulates plans that are illegitimate or undesirable, then the legislature can choose to replace them; and if

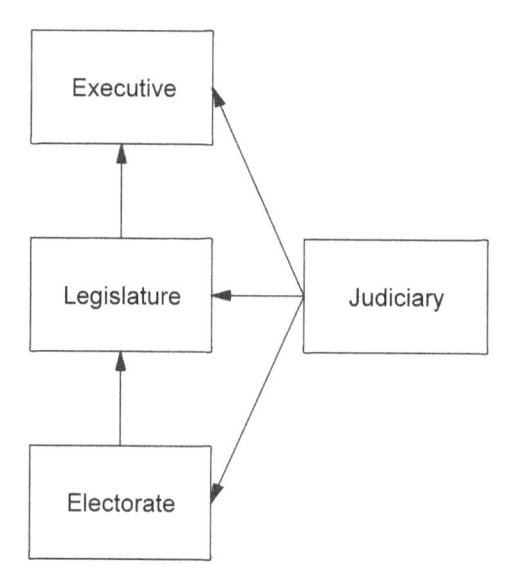

FIGURE 8.3 Simple model of the representative democratic state. (Original by authors.)

the legislature acts in ways that violate the wishes and interests of the electorate then they can be replaced at the next election. According to this model, ultimate authority lies with the electorate. The independent judiciary acts to ensure that the laws passed are impartially applied and constitutionally sound. For Kant (1991, 73–9), law exists to protect the rights of individuals to freely pursue their goals and it can only use coercion to prevent or punish overt violations of other people's freedoms. Laws apply equally to all regardless of the citizen's wealth or social status. In addition, all citizens have an equal say in the making of law, for instance where there are decisions to be made on which rights to prioritise in cases of conflict: an example might be whether noise abatement laws constitute a restriction on free speech or a legitimate protection for an undisturbed family life. For Kant, even if a law is not to the individual citizen's liking, it is still binding. This is because of a principle of legislative reciprocity: the dissenter equally participates in the law-making process and would expect the law to be obeyed by her opponents if it was framed in the alternative way she preferred (77).

In this simple model if citizens have particularly pressing political goals, such as a wish to see environmental policies enacted, then this can be facilitated through the structures of the state. Sufficiently motivated green electors will result in the election of a green legislature who can choose an executive to formulate effective environmental policy that the legislature will then pass into law. Power lies with the citizenry, which raises the question: why do so many citizens feel powerless?

One answer is that the simple model omits too much, ignoring other groups that significantly affect the political process. As shown below (Figure 8.4), the executive tries to influence the legislature and – by manipulating or reforming the voting formula – to influence the electorate too, in order to keep their loyalty. Other institutions play a significant role in the operation of the state and the policy-forming structure. Chapter 7 discussed how businesses – legitimately for neo-liberals like Friedman, illegitimately for social democrats like Bakan – try to influence politicians through lobbying and donations. Businesses can threaten to disinvest or withdraw from a particular nation's economy if the law is not to its liking, or use its financing to support a particular party or its rival in order to gain the most favourable legislative environment for its activities. Extensive environmental protection that might reduce profits and restrict the freedom of corporations to trade as they wish would meet opposition, with overt or implied threats to withdraw and instead invest in more receptive competing states.

Corporations sponsor organisations like the Heartland Institute (2015, 2016), who claim to have won the debate on behalf of climate change sceptics. The Heartland Institute boast that they have decisively altered the minds, not just of the main policymakers, but the general public as well through lobbying and extensive marketing. Similarly, environmental pressure groups like Greenpeace, Animal Aid, Sierra Club and PETA (People for the Ethical Treatment of Animals) attempt to influence government directly, and through the electorate, to pursue legislation that is consistent with their cause.

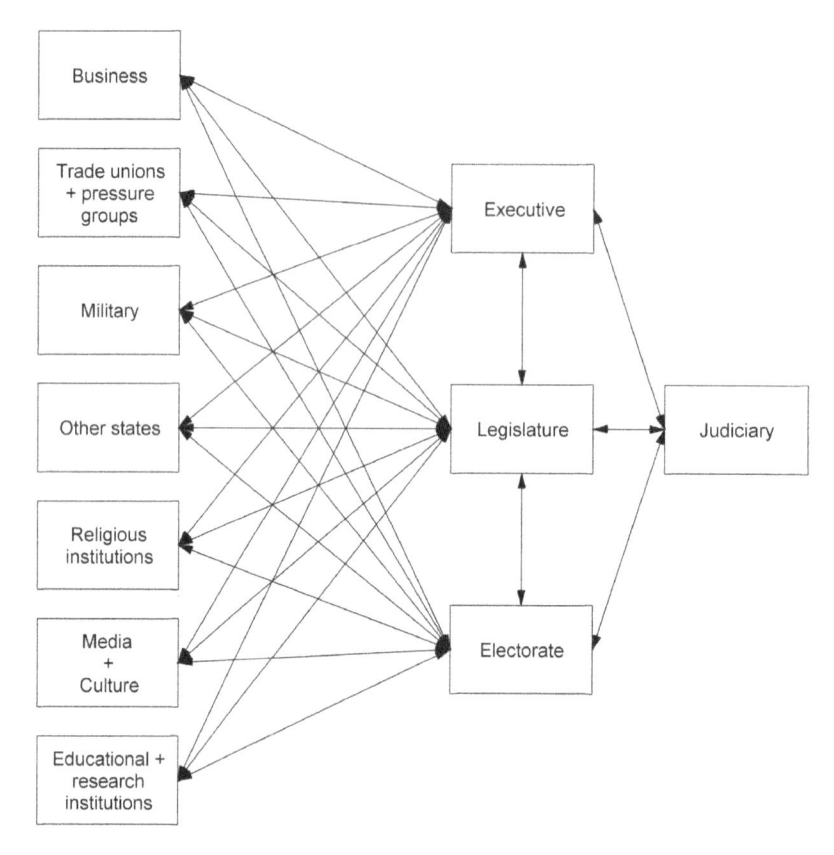

FIGURE 8.4 Sophisticated model of the representative democratic state. (Original by authors.)

The influence of the media is most significant here too. Various claims and counter-claims are made about the impact of mainstream media (largely run by, and as, large-scale corporations), especially with the rise of the internet and citizen journalism. But even with the rise of electronic social media (see Chapter 9) the mass media still does have influence in highlighting and prioritising some issues and marginalising others. Noam Chomsky and Edward Herman (1998) argue that the media deliberately distorts information in order to serve and protect the interests of dominant groups within society. Nick Davies (2008) suggests that distortion is not intentional but simply the product of news media's primary corporate responsibility to make as much money for investors as possible. Thus, cheaper domestic stories and the 'churning' of press releases take precedence over more expensive foreign news and investigative reporting. Nor is the influence one-way. Governments influence the media either through financial contracts (public sector advertising) or through direct coercion. In the UK the latter includes D- (or DA-) notices, which involves seizing journalists and their notes and banning publication of stories that are damaging to national security. Governments also infiltrate news teams and plant false stories (Davies 2008, 247–8). In less democratic countries, measures are more extreme including the imprisonment, torture and assassination of journalists (Freedom House 2016b). Usually, though, the main interests of liberal democratic government and the owners of media are compatible.

As much of the corporate news media's income comes from advertising, the tendency is to create a print or aural (in the case of radio) landscape conducive to the dissemination and reception of commercial advertising. Discordant voices and radical opinion, such as those coming from radical ecologists, are likely to disrupt the medium for commercial advertising unless they are carefully framed. Thus there is a tendency to prioritise other sorts of stories that will attract advertisers and steer readers towards consumption.

Elitist political theorists argue that power becomes concentrated in tight self-supporting networks that become self-serving and mutually sustaining. Having access to specialist contacts within the group gives insiders advantages that outsiders will lack. Hence political, business and military dynasties develop as the previous generation provides specialist access to the new generation. Informal and formal social networks, from geographical neighbourliness, attendance at charity dinners, old school and alumni associations to formal events like the World Economic Forum and the Bilderberg Group, provide opportunities for elites to privately negotiate and co-operate. Non-elites try to build their own alternative networks of support and co-operation through formal and informal networks.

8.6 Specialist green parties

The standard, if flawed, traditional liberal account of democracy suggests individual voters select representatives on the basis of their relative personal merits and policy positions. However, much voter behaviour is influenced by the candidates' political party. Political parties play five important roles in constitutional politics in general and green politics in particular: 1) interest aggregation, 2) implementation, 3) channels of expression, 4) elite recruitment and socialisation, and 5) emotional attachment (see Hague and Harrop 2010, 203–25). The example of the German Green Party (*Die Grünen*) – the most successful of the specialist constitutional organisations in terms of party size and influence over time in the executive of a state – provides good illustrations of these features and the ways in which different tendencies within political movements view them. *Die Grünen* experienced a notable and persistent schism between the *realos* and the *fundis*, who interpreted these party roles in distinct ways (Connelly and Smith 1999, 88–91; Blüdhorn 2009). This schism also appeared in other European green parties, including in the UK. It shares similarities, but is not identical with, the division between deep and shallow greens (Porritt 1997, 63) (see Chapter 4). The *fundis* wanted to remain loyal to deep green principles, which they considered were best exemplified and protected in decentred Green Party structures, whilst the *realos* sought greater Green Party electoral success by having a more centrally-administered structure to offer clear policy positions with a leadership recognisable to the wider electorate (Burchell 2000; Blüdhorn and Szarka 2004).

Interest aggregation

Large parties are ways of combining people with the same interests to find common solutions. In order to facilitate collective action, these organisations also need to identify actual or potential areas of conflict in order to reduce or marginalise them. The structure of the party allows for decisions on party principles and policy priorities. Even in democratic parties such decisions can be managed and curtailed, with resolutions taken at gatherings of the membership vetoed, marginalised or heavily amended by the leadership. Green parties tend to prioritise democratic engagement and have in place organisational principles to limit the influence of the leadership. However, this has led to conflict between the elected leaders who gain legislative posts and gain expertise in *realpolitik*, and the administratively inexperienced but committed membership. *Realos* prioritised the importance of more generally acceptable and electorally attractive principles, as determined by the knowledgeable leadership; *fundis* wanted to remain committed to core principles and decentred practices, regardless of electoral outcome.

Implementing collective goals

Political parties do not just identify what needs to be done and gain agreement across the organisation, they also provide an apparatus for bringing about social change. For constitutional parties this can still sometimes extend beyond the state mechanisms; for instance, many European Labour and Socialist Parties (including the UK's Labour Party) were originally engaged in supporting and building trade unions as well as building electoral support. Green parties too, especially amongst the *fundi* wing, consider their role to include coordinating support for environmental direct action (Connelly et al. 1999, 88). In the limited context of state activism, a government needs an energised party to provide researchers, strategists and managers for developing and implementing policy, such as building, restructuring or decommissioning a national health service.

Channels of expression

Political parties provide an organisational structure with associated media (newsgroups, electronic bulletin boards, printed party literature) for communicating desires and goals between party members and party leaders. In successful parties, they provide a mechanism for linking the rulers with the ruled. There are different structures for connecting the leadership to the membership; a few are overtly autocratic, with decisions made by the leadership and passed down to the members. Most appeal to democratic participation as this maintains party loyalty and enthusiasm for the party programme. Some leaders feel that too great a democratic engagement can lead to division and confusion. Party democracy might prioritise the narrow vision of the party activists, but does not attract sufficient electoral support from outside of the party. On the other side, ordinary party members can feel that representatives and leaders have become isolated from the base and have different interests and priorities to the membership. So *Realos* argue that decentred organisation cannot provide clear policy positions to the electorate, whilst *fundis* favoured *Die Grünen*'s original less-hierarchical forms of party management. The latter also feared that party restructuring favoured by the *realos* gave greater influence to the opinions of the leadership and would result in diluting the Party's distinctive policies and political approach (Blüdhorn and Szarka 2004, 305–7).

Elite recruitment and socialisation

Parties help to normalise new ideas amongst the membership and provide a sense of loyalty and belonging. Parties also provide an important function for choosing candidates for different offices of the state, from local councillors to legislators and members of the executive. They control the flow of personnel and ideas up the offices of state. Even in democratically structured parties, however, this can lead to a restrictive group of candidates and representatives. Even with quotas to allow for greater parity in female representation – and green parties historically have a good record of gender-inclusion – inequalities and exclusions occur. *Fundis*, in particular, were critical of the prioritisation of recognisable, media-friendly and articulate candidates, who under more centralised party structures were given greater control. This seemed to privilege those with greatest social capital (strong networks of influence and high educational access), thereby reinforcing rather than challenging divisions in social power.

Emotional attachment

People have strong positive feelings about the political parties they join. They provide a sense of identity, and are places in which friendships (and enmities) are formed. Because of their social as well as political functions they are repositories of memory and, in some cases, provide some of the social architecture of a community. Conservative, Liberal and Labour clubs used to provide venues for many non-party-political social occasions. Green Party activities provide participants with a sense of worth and largely pleasant inter-personal relationships, and these help the organisation to persist in an otherwise hostile political environment.

To summarise these five points, specialist green parties are a way of expressing and influencing the political agenda. Their presence in a community and their electoral impact are indicators of the influence of environmental issues and policies throughout the social arena. Falling green party membership and electoral support is often, perhaps unfairly, seen as indicative of a waning of interest in green issues. Greater electoral success is seen as giving additional legitimacy to green activism inside and outside of the state apparatus. The existence of specialist ecological parties also points to a perceived inadequacy in the existing parties. Standard social democratic, liberal and conservative parties are viewed as prioritising short-term issues that reflect their histories and main electoral bases. These tend to downgrade environment concerns and the interests of non-human entities.

It should be noted that not all political organisations are political parties. Alternative ecological groupings – such as Greenpeace – perform many of the roles identified above, but without participating in electoral activism. Green pressure groups and direct action organisations (see Chapter 9) also identify and aggregate interests, communicate across the group and beyond, assist in identifying people to carry out particular tasks, and provide people with important social interaction and a sense of identity. However, as these groups operate with only indirect influence on, or completely outside of, the governmental framework, they have no direct role in policy formation or law-making.

For supporters of environmental democratic participation, the fact that multiple institutions impact on the activities of the state (pluralism) is a strength rather than a weakness. It allows for multiple interests to be represented in the process of government planning, ensuring that legislation is as informed, non-coercive and legitimate as possible (Giddens 2009, 8–13, 106–10). The development of green parties' and mainstream parties' interest in environmental policies shows, for the social democratic sociologist Anthony Giddens, that liberal democratic structures are receptive (56). While Giddens is aware of the problems of corporate lobbying on the democratic process, he is nonetheless a passionate advocate of democratic environmentalism (119–23) and supportive of green groups that engage with corporations and governments (120, 123–8). Conversely, he is largely critical of anti-state green actors (53, 56–7).

8.7 Democratic state methods of behavioural change

Giddens identifies specific policy apparatuses that democratic institutions can use to respond to the causes of climate change and to counter or reduce their impacts. These include encouraging markets in environmental goods and mitigating the harms of externalities (5). Unlike some critics, Giddens believes a properly-regulated market in carbon credits, policed through appropriate state and inter-governmental apparatuses, can assist in producing significant environmental benefits.

Governments have a range of legislative mechanisms at their disposal. The main ones are prohibition, choice-editing, taxation and nudges. The ethics of nudge was discussed in Chapter 6, and the other three will be analysed here. Prohibition is the most aggressive of the policy options, but is widely employed. Governments have banned a range of chemicals and once-prolific pesticides from production because of their wider impacts on the environment and health. Polychlorinated biphenyl, which was used as a coolant, has been banned in many countries, including the UK and the USA, because of its carcinogenic qualities. Rachel Carson's *The Silent Spring* (see Chapter 3) identified the toxic build-up caused by the insecticide DDT, which led to bans across the industrialised world and its use restricted to reduction of malarial mosquitos elsewhere. Giddens (109–10) defends outright prohibitions on energy-profligate light bulbs on utilitarian grounds, whilst neoliberal deontologists consider it an unjustified restriction on consumer autonomy. Amongst the reasons why Paul Nuttall, at the time a senior UKIP politician, opposed the ban on energy inefficient lightbulbs was because it 'had no regard for people's right to choose' (Q. in UKIP 2013).

Not only can liberal democracies pass laws to prohibit forms of corporate environmental damage, they also have the infrastructure to legitimately and effectively enforce these bans. Few other bodies in civil society, argues Giddens (2009, 109) have such strength, co-ordination and legitimacy.

Slightly less prescriptive than outright prohibition is the use of taxation to manipulate production and consumption. Taxation can increase the costs of polluting production to encourage more cost-efficient and sustainable forms and prompt consumers to select greener products (Giddens 2009, 108–9). For neo-liberals, such statist intervention is an unacceptable disruption of consensual agreements. Some radical greens also oppose the imposition of taxes, but for different reasons. For them, these taxes still permit wealthier consumers to pay for ecologically damaging activities. Rather than providing incentives to end ecologically damaging practices, it provides a basis for states to maintain them at maximum tax-raising levels. It also 'monetarises the environment', placing an exchange value on ecological goods that, for ecologists, like those from the anti-air transport expansion group Plane Stupid, have more important and complex uses and meanings (Richard 2009).

Giddens (2009, 131–3) also points to successful government green intervention in the form of providing financial support (subsidy) for new eco-technologies. For neoliberals, subsidies distort market relationships and they also require raising tax to pay for them, which violates negative liberty. There have also been significant examples of subsidies being used for political favours to assist industries and industrialists sympathetic to the government, and being targeted in areas that will boost electoral support. However, such corrupt practices do not completely detract from the effective use of subsidies. For instance, Giddens (79) suggests that government grants were a vital part of developing the infrastructure for renewable energy in Iceland, when producers were too small and geographically diverse to fund and co-ordinate it effectively on their own.

The strategy of choice-editing (see Chapter 7) includes elements of prohibition and price-manipulation. It involves 'eliminating the option of buying products with a poor environmental or social record – [it] is . . . [a] progressive strategy taken by retailers that does not rely on consumer behaviour change, but instead mainstreams sustainable products as default options' (Gunn and Mont 2014, 464). Whilst there are forms of governmental choice-editing, in many forms it is largely organised by retailers and producers rather than governments. However, even in retailer-organised choice-editing, governments might be encouraging these commercial bodies to adopt the strategy 'voluntarily' by threatening more direct intervention. Sometimes commercial bodies might freely employ choice-editing when there is consumer demand. For instance, some supermarket chains voluntarily choice-edited genetically-modified products off their shelves because many consumers wished to avoid them and not have to carry the costs of having to check every label. Others are willing to forego some commercially desirable but environmentally damaging products in order to attract higher-paying customers looking to support green enterprise. Through prohibition, however, governments remain, ultimately, the most powerful available choice editors (467).

A further environmental function of the democratic state is to negotiate with other states (democratic, partly free and unfree) to create international environmental regulation. There is little point in one country acting to reduce greenhouse gases if other countries take no action: environmental legislation has to be at an international scale, as well as responsive to local national differences (Connelly and Smith 1999, 218). Giddens (2009, 186–7) points to the successful Montreal Protocol to phase out atmospheric-ozone-depleting CFCs, and the setting up of the Intergovernmental Panel on Climate Change (IPCC) and the Kyoto Protocol as examples of international action on climate change. Even if there are significant potential signatories absent from the Kyoto Protocol, by 2004 'it [had] received support from countries that were, between them, producing 61 per cent of world emissions' (187). The Paris Climate Agreement is a voluntary accord to reduce carbon emissions in order to hold the rise in the global average temperature to below 2°C and assist in developing mechanisms to adapt to climate change. It has been signed by 195 nations, although one of the largest global polluters, the United States, in 2017 signalled its intention to withdraw from the Agreement.

8.8 Non-democracies and environmental policy

As indicated in Figure 8.1 above, whilst representative democracies are, globally at present, the main form of state organisation and provide the model for many partially free states, many countries are non-democracies. There is a great diversity of non-democracies: theocracy, absolute monarchy, military dictatorship, state-socialist and free-market or modernising authoritarian regimes to name but a few. Rather than being three discrete categories of state as in Freedom House's classification (free, partially free and unfree), the relationships between authoritarian and democratic states are more complex and fluid. Some democracies have features of non-democracy (constitutional bans on particular parties such as overt Nazi parties in Germany and Israel or the Communist Party of the Basque Homelands by the Spanish state) and restrictions on freedom of assembly. Some authoritarian governments have a few democratic features such as a relatively free press. So, too, do democratic states and authoritarian regimes mutually assist one another. Democracies like the United States and the United Kingdom historically have been actively involved in undermining anti-authoritarian movements in states whose dictatorial leader supports their interests (see, for instance, Herman and Chomsky 1994; Murray 2007).

On the face of it, authoritarian regimes could be more efficient in turning environmental policy into practical action as there are fewer checks on executive power. Authoritarian governments already have systems to control people, and some have institutions to coerce populations into ecologically beneficial outcomes. As political scientist Mark Beeson identifies:

> China, an authoritarian regime, has arguably done more to mitigate environmental problems than any other government on earth: without the one-child policy instigated in the 1970s, it is estimated that there would already be another 400 million Chinese.
> *(Beeson 2010, 289.)*

Such a policy would have been far harder to implement without its coercive systems of governance and control of the media.

Like many industrialising countries, China formerly had an environmentally destructive approach to economic development (Carter 2007, 358). More recently, however, it has pursued a more ecologically sensitive set of policies, encouraging environmental NGOs to operate in the state. The central government – dominated by the Chinese Communist Party – is developing and imposing environmental policies onto its regions (Beeson 2010; Gilley 2012). However, there are significant problems for an authoritarian approach to environmental politics.

First, as Bruce Gilley (2012, 296–7) indicates, the efficiency of authoritarian states can be overstated. Whilst political elites do not have democratic checks and balances to contend with, they nonetheless have to maintain support of interest groups (such as the military, economic sectors, main religious institutions and foreign states) as well as rival factions within the same party. Cultures of corruption and nepotism develop to maintain support for the ruling sub-group.

Second, ruling authoritarian states, in order to provide a sense of legitimacy, tend to rely on traditional beliefs and institutions as the central stabilising myth (see Weber 1949). These unifying fictions of fulfilling a predetermined national destiny or superiority to – and fear of – outsiders and neighbours are considered more important than ecological policies and are often antipathetic to green values and goals. The development of nuclear production facilities in the USSR and USA were environmentally catastrophic and predicated on the priority given to national defence during the Cold War (1947–91). Authoritarian leadership generates an alienating social cleavage between the ruler and the ruled that for deep and social ecology lead to ecologically destructive behaviour. Authoritarian institutions also have corrupting impacts on virtue-rich social activities as explained earlier (see Chapters 2, 6 and 7). Undermining active reflective participation leads to less enthusiastic and shallower engagement in environmental activities, and limits the possibility for greater experimentation and imaginative environmental problem-solving. For instance, a dictator may make appointments to important environmental ministries and scientific research posts not on the basis of the specialist knowledge, ecological sensitivities and creative problem-solving abilities of the possible candidates, but their role in supporting the governing family, party or ethnic bloc.

8.9 Evaluating constitutionalism

There are considerable strengths to environmentalist engagements in liberal democracies, which result in 'an overwhelming majority of environmental activists, writers and philosophers . . . [being] staunch defenders' of its values (Porritt 1997, 65). Green politics, for Porritt, is now overwhelmingly tied to liberal democratic institutions and principles. The advantages of green constitutionalism are that it provides a stable and largely peaceful way to bring about policy change (Porritt 1997, 65–6; Giddens 2009, 6–7, 115). Liberal institutions, claim supporters, encourage largely non-coercive and reflective decision-making. Green constitutionalism offers a range of options for engagement from mere voting to setting up or electioneering for a specific ecological political grouping, and standing for election and representing that group in the democratic structure. It provides a mechanism for engaging with other, currently uncommitted, publics.

Green constitutionalism has also brought about significant pieces of legislation. Giddens points to numerous policies in the UK (81–7) and across the globe that have contributed to a reduction in carbon as a result of democratic action (88–90). The links between democracy and green policy performance are strongly correlated (though that does not prove causation). The best performing countries, according to Yale and Columbia Universities Environmental Performance Index (EPI), are those that have a relatively wealthy populace and stable democratic institutions (EPI 2016) such as Finland, Iceland, Croatia and Costa Rica.

Porritt, like Giddens, is committed to the centrality of constitutionalism to green politics. He considers the role of micropolitics to be overplayed, and considers direct action and civil disobedience to be only effective in support of constitutional change (66–7). Porritt sees some opportunities for co-option of green values into more standard social democracy (73). Bruce Pilbeam (2003) similarly considers that, despite obstacles, there is considerable potential for democratic interchange between constitutional conservatives and environmentalists. Porritt (1997, 62) confirms that there were 'surprisingly cordial relationships between environmental campaigners and [Conservative] governmental Ministers and officials'. Through constitutional engagement, core environmental values become entrenched within the policy frameworks of the major political parties.

However, a number of criticisms have been advanced against constitutional environmentalism from a range of critical perspectives. Radical conservative critics like David Shearman and Joseph Wayne Smith (2007) argue that constitutional parties, in order to be electorally successful, need to mobilise support from a significant minority of the population. Because of the electorate's lack of sophistication this is best done by appealing to their immediate material desires rather than to wider long-term interests, such as ecological considerations. Giddens also identifies a number of potential problems for constitutional green politics, which echo those of Smith. These include the possibility that environmental catastrophes can only be resolved by quick authoritarian action, the failure of markets, the impact of lobbyists on governments (119–23) and the limitation of governments pursuing national self-interest when international agreement is needed to resolve climate crises (219–20). Nonetheless, Giddens remains optimistic about the possibility of liberal democratic solutions to environmental problems.

Despite the policy levers identified by Giddens, the track record of green political change is not impressive. Perhaps it is because they have only been minority parties; greens in government have succeeded only in achieving minor reforms with deeper structural problems that cause ecological degradation going unresolved (Dobson 1990, 134; Blüdhorn 2009). When swift extra-governmental action is required to prevent imminent environmental degradation, constitutional governments have largely either been responsible for the environmental harms or attempted to prevent swift autonomous action. This is because such action challenges the ultimate authority of the state and is viewed as illegitimate. Thus successful environmental campaigns often triumph after facing and overcoming opposition from democratic governments, such as the Tasmanian Franklin River dam in Australia in the 1980s (Singer 2011, 257-8) and the anti-roads protests in the UK in the 1990s (see McKay 1996).

Peter Singer (2011, 266) largely defends constitutional democratic activism on rule utilitarian grounds (introduced in Chapter 2) as providing a peaceful way to resolve potentially violent conflicts. However, Singer also accepts that liberal democracy, even when working honestly, is slow moving and can be unresponsive to pressing ecological disaster. It is particularly unresponsive to non-humans because they lie outside of the constitutional process (265). As a result, Singer argues that certain forms of ecological direct action, even when they are illegal and damage private property, can be legitimate if democratic resolution is not possible and the ecological and social benefits are sufficiently high (267–71).

Radical eco-critics have a much more extensive critique of constitutionalism. They regard the modern state as being intimately bound up with capitalism. This is not to say that the state and corporations always have identical interests (Carter 1989, 183–5) – for instance, the state might wish to tax corporations to have greater resources, whilst corporations wish to keep their resources unencumbered – but the two are nonetheless symbiotic or at least strongly entangled and convergent. States have a material interest in not harming the economic base of their country by over-taxation ('parasitism') as they will lose future resources and face international competition (Bookchin 1997, 89); whilst corporations require an active agency for effective dispute resolution and enforcement, and the extension and defence of property rights.

For political theorists like Michael Hardt and Antonio Negri (2000), modern states were developed to resolve the internal conflicts that arise out of capitalism. The modern political identity of the productive national citizen developed as a way of generating loyalty to a system that necessary exploits and oppresses labour (95, 105) and nature. A system of administration develops to enforce decisions and end conflicts but keeps the current economic system of profit maximisation intact (99). The rules governing international trade lie outside of the sovereign nation-state and are located in transnational bodies such as the World Trade Organisation and the International Monetary Fund. Individual countries are not redundant however; they are still the main bodies that facilitate and enforce these regulations – what Hardt and Negri call 'imperial administration' (339–41).

Such critics are aware that democratic institutions allow for the expression of discontent and radical alternatives, such as the zero growth policies associated with many green parties. However, these conflicting interests are incorporated into capitalist administrative structures (311–12). By operating through constitutional liberal institutions, green critics raise issues and concerns currently not met, and thus indicate potential new markets for goods, such as innovatively green-branded products and novel technological fixes. Alternatively, effort that could be spent directly resisting ecological problems at their source becomes instead concentrated on attempts to win state power, often in vain. However, constitutional political action, through lobbying, electoralism and concerted action outside of the electoral system (see the next chapter) can and does influence government policy. Even when non-constitutional action is not primarily concerned with influencing government policy, politicians will be swayed by public pressure or attempts to stabilise the political process from extra-parliamentary movements by co-opting popular movements, though on occasions this may amount to little more than greenwashing.

Thus green and other apparently oppositional parties, by participating in the state, start to ape the behaviours of the main constitutional parties they were supposed to oppose. Consistent with some of the *fundi* criticisms of the *realos*, radical parties attempt to sell themselves to the electorate to increase their representation in the legislature. To do this they require the support of significant social players, such as the mainstream media, and sponsorship from asset-rich organisations, with a necessary restructuring of the message to fit in with the media template (see symbolic action in Chapter 9). The terms in which environmental political messages are delivered and received are structured by the constitutional process. They appeal to the national sovereign subject, to issues of rights and welfare protection guaranteed through the state (313); as a result, multifaceted ecological problems are distorted to ones that are conceived of as soluble within the framework of the capitalist-state (Doherty et al. 2000, 7).

Within states, legislators make the decisions, even though they are geographically and socially disconnected from the places their policies impact. This is also true of the majority of the voting population, who in principle have ultimate sovereignty. As a result, radical ecologists like Murray Bookchin, eco-anarchists, socialists, feminists and syndicalists, seek decentralised – and often fluid – decision-making, such that there is not the alienation between those making decisions and the communities impacted by that judgement (see for instance Bookchin 1997, 32; Clark 2013, 160–2, Biehl 1991; Shantz 2002, 38).

Green parties are often split between the effectiveness of *realpolitik* by engaging with and supporting centralised state-centred decision-making and their acknowledgement, on the other hand, that such structures for making policy are insensitive to site-specific issues and disempowering for local communities. *Realpolitik* has brought some successes. Greens have gained significant electoral positions in local and state elections. Greens won the governorship in Baden-Württemberg (2011-) in Germany and control of Brighton and Hove Council in the UK (2011–15) as well as positions within national coalition governments. Alexander Van der Bellen, the former Green Party leader, was elected the Austrian President in 2016. However, like other radical parties who have had major electoral success winning state and local power, the Green's record in government has not been impressive. Whilst the Green Party in Ireland introduced minor reforms in planning law to subsidise energy conservation and promote renewables, it did little to fundamentally alter the economy and its imperative of ecological exploitation. As part of their alliance with the Social Democrats, the Greens in Germany (1998–2005) successfully resisted the reintroduction of nuclear power generation, but there was little significant structural change. Similarly, the Austrian Presidency has little executive power (as this lies with the Austrian Federal Chancellor) although it is symbolically important, especially as Van der Bellen narrowly beat a far-right anti-immigrant candidate. In Britain, local Greens have largely acted in accordance with the priorities of the national government, leading to social welfare cutbacks and wage reductions for council refuse and recycling workers. As a local Green Party parliamentary candidate Davy Jones (2013) explains, there were divisions within the local Green Party itself about the council's policies between those 'who want to manage the system better, and those who want to change the system altogether'.

Constitutional action is structurally constrained. Constitutional and international agreements protect international property from state seizure or competition, meaning that radical action that curtails corporate activity leads to capital flight as investors move their assets out of the country. This leaves the government without the resources for social restructuring. If radical governments take over major parts of the economy, as, for instance, the oil industry in Venezuela under their late President Hugo Chavez, then the state becomes a manager: the nationalised industry operates like any other, with the state seeking to maximise outcomes (usually financial) and treating the state employee as just an instrument to that end. Bookchin (1997, 128), for instance, claims that nationalisation has tended to recreate the social schisms and alienation that are the cause of, and embedded within, the conquest of nature.

8.10 Constitutionalism and non-constitutionalism

As it is predicated on some basic freedoms of conscience, speech and assembly, constitutional democratic parties can work, at least initially, with extra-parliamentary activism. In countries like Switzerland and some individual states within the US (notably California), legislation allows referendums to be called by the public.[6] In Switzerland, 100,000 electors can propose a new law if it is supported by a sizeable majority of voters in a sufficient majority of voting districts (cantons) (Hague and Harrop 2010, 194). The wider political campaign to gather signatures is also intended to mobilise popular support against fracking companies.

Green parties have traditionally had a foot in both environmental protest movements and constitutional politics (Doherty 2000), though even here the non-parliamentary activity is largely one of demonstration and symbolic revolt rather than environmental direct action (Rootes 2000, 43). However a tension persists, consistent with Kant's 'legislative reciprocity'; namely, it is hard for activists within constitutional parties to support actions that break the law and expect others to obey the laws they make on acceding to power. Thus, there is a general reluctance to support direct action that often breaks the law, even when it provides quick, effective, just and socially equitable responses to environmental crises. This unwillingness to engage in extra-parliamentary action is overcome only in some extraordinary circumstances. So engagement in the wider Green protest movements is often in support of constitutional activity: raising the party's profile, engaging potential voters and electoral campaigners (electioneers), rather than promoting an alternative form of politics. Even when Green Party activists support extra-parliamentary activities, a crunch point invariably comes, especially at key moments in the electoral cycle, where constitutional activists have to prioritise their time to either electioneering or direct action. The more they tend towards the latter, the further they move away from state-centred approaches to politics to alternative micropolitical forms of behavioural change.

8.11 Conclusion

Eco-political behavioural change in recent years has been increasingly focussed on the macropolitical. The democratic state is made up of four main institutions that can all impact on the efficiency and legitimacy of green legislation. Although these four institutions – legislature, executive, electorate/electoral system and judicial structures – are common across liberal democracies, there are differences in their norms and structures that impact on the effectiveness of Green electoral activists. Constitutional arrangements that are based on proportional representation, coalition governments and more than one legislative assembly, and having an activist and ecologically-sensitive judiciary, provide more opportunities for effective green influence on policymaking.

Shallower green goals are more likely to be successfully achieved through constitutional activism as these do not require substantive systematic change and provide opportunities for piecemeal reform. At least initially, these reforms will be viewed as legitimate by the bulk of the national population. However, more radical change is structurally restricted by the multiple barriers in the electoral system that limits radical groups' electoral success and governmental effectiveness. Political parties require exposure (preferably positive) in mainstream media to assist voter-recognition. They need resources to compete against significant corporate material support for rivals. Even when radical parties gain electoral majorities they are constrained by liberal constitutional protections of commercial interests and international trade agreements that invalidate substantive economic restructuring. Competition from other states means that resources can quickly flow from one country to another, causing poverty and instability should restructuring threaten commercial advantage.

The chapter has concluded by looking at the interactions between constitutional and non-constitutional behaviour – a theme that is developed further in the next chapter. Many green groups do engage in both. However, since limited resources and legislative reciprocity mean that it is hard for constitutionally-orientated groupings to commit to both constitutional and non-constitutional action, the former usually takes precedence.

Notes

1 Figures from Freedom House 2014 and Freedom House 2017a.
2 There are some problems with Freedom House's methodology, categorisation and application, which might reflect a specific foreign policy bias. For instance, Freedom House listed Apartheid South Africa as 'partly free' despite the vast majority of the citizens being disenfranchised. Israel is categorised as 'free' despite, so critics contend, having disenfranchised people who under international law should be allowed to enter and be recognised as citizens. Russia in 2016 is listed as 'unfree' even though they have multi-party competitive elections and some small, albeit heavily embattled, free press (Freedom House 2017b).
3 Source BBC Politics, Election 2015, www.bbc.co.uk/news/election/2015/results.
4 Source BBC Politics, Election 2017, www.bbc.co.uk/news/election/2017/results.
5 See, for instance, the difference between Hare and Droop largest remainder proportional formulas and D'Hondt and Sainte-Laguë highest average methods.
6 Referendums tend to be called by governments to legitimate policy or resolve conflicts between competing sections of the political class. Pier Uleri (1996) provides a detailed typology of referendums covering the originator of the vote, whether it is legally obligated (such as amending the Constitution), whether the voters' decision is binding or advisory and to whom it applies.

References

Bawden, T. (2014) 'Ukip green policy: climate change "open to question" says energy spokesman Roger Helmer'. *The Independent*, 30 December 2014, www.independent.co.uk/news/uk/politics/ukip-green-policy-climate-change-is-open-to-question-says-energy-spokesman-roger-helmer-9949125.html.
Beeson, M. (2010) 'The coming of environmental authoritarianism'. *Environmental Politics* 19.2, 276–94.
Behavioural Insights Team (2016), www.behaviouralinsights.co.uk/.
Biehl, J. (1991) *Rethinking Ecofeminist Politics*. Boston: South End.
Blüdhorn, I. (2009) 'Reinventing Green politics: on the strategic repositioning of the German Green Party', *German Politics* 18.1: 36–54.
Blüdhorn, I. and Szarka, J. (2004). 'Managing strategic positioning choices: a reappraisal of the development paths of the French and German Green Parties', *Journal of Contemporary European Studies* 12.3: 303–19.
Bookchin, M. (1997) *The Murray Bookchin Reader*. London: Cassell.
Burchell, J. (2000) 'Here come the Greens (again): The Green Party in Britain during the 1990s', *Environmental Politics* 9:3: 145–50.
Carter, A. (1989) 'Outline of an anarchist theory of history', in D. Goodway, ed., *For Anarchism: History, Theory and Practice*, 176–97. London: Routledge.

Carter, N. (2007) *The Politics of the Environment: Ideas, Activism, Policy*, Second Edition. Cambridge: Cambridge University Press.
Chomsky, N. and Herman, E. (1998) *Manufacturing Consent: The Political Economy of the Mass Media*. London: Vintage.
Clark, J.P. (2013) *The Impossible Community: Realizing Communitarian Anarchism*. London: Bloomsbury.
Connelly, J., Smith, G., Benson, D. and Saunders, C. (1999) *Politics and the Environment: From Theory to Practice*. London: Routledge.
Davidson, S. (2009) 'Ecoanarchism: a critical defence', *Journal of Political Ideologies* 14.1: 47–67.
Davies, N. (2008) *Flat Earth News*. London: Chatto & Windus.
Dobson, A. (1990). *Green Political Thought: An Introduction*. London: Unwin Hyman.
Doherty, B. (2000) 'Environmental protests in Britain 1988–1997', in B. Seel, M. Patterson and B. Doherty, eds, *Direct Action in British Environmentalism*, 25–61. London: Routledge.
Doherty, B., Paterson, M. and Seel, B. (2000) 'Direct action in British environmentalism', in B. Seel, M. Patterson and B. Doherty, eds, *Direct Action in British Environmentalism*, 1–24. London: Routledge.
EPI (Environmental Performance Index) (2016) *2016 Report*, http://epi.yale.edu/mwg-internal/de5fs23hu73ds/progress?id=YBZaeAfeuGCdZVG9D1OCE9mtpnkYhvcPt8LxkDvP3RQ.
Freedom House (2014) *Freedom in the World Country Ratings*, https://freedomhouse.org/sites/default/files/Country%20Status%20%26%20Ratings%20Overview%2C%201973-2014.pdf.
Freedom House (2016a) *Freedom in the World 2016*, www.freedomhouse.org/sites/default/files/FH_FITW_Report_2016.pdf.
Freedom House (2016b) *Freedom of the Press 2016*, https://freedomhouse.org/report/freedom-press/freedom-press-2016.
Freedom House (2017a) *Freedom in the World 2017: Populists and Autocrats – The Dual Threat to Global Democracy*, https://freedomhouse.org/report/freedom-world/freedom-world-2017.
Freedom House (2017b) *Russia*, https://freedomhouse.org/country/russia.
Garner, R., Ferdinand, P. and Lawson, S. (2016) *Introduction to Politics*. Oxford: Oxford University Press.
Giddens, A. (2009) *The Politics of Climate Change*. Cambridge: Polity.
Gilley B. (2012) 'Authoritarian environmentalism and China's response to climate change', *Environmental Politics* 21.2: 287–307.
Gunn, M. and Mont, O. (2014) 'Choice editing as a retailers' tool for sustainable consumption', *International Journal of Retail & Distribution Management* 42.6: 464–81.
Hague, R. and Harrop, M. (2010) *Comparative Government and Politics: An Introduction*, Eighth Edition. Basingstoke: Palgrave Macmillan.
Hardt, M. and Negri, T. (2000) *Empire*. London: Harvard University Press.
Heartland Institute (2015) *Winning the Global Warming Debate*. Youtube, www.youtube.com/watch?feature=player_embedded&v=EnrroptHcu8.
Heartland Institute (2016), www.heartland.org/.
Herman, E. and Chomsky, N. (1994) *Manufacturing Consent: The Political Economy of the Mass Media*. London: Vintage.
Jones, D. (2013) 'The pay dispute at Brighton Council: a Green view', *Red Pepper* (May), www.redpepper.org.uk/the-pay-dispute-at-brighton-council-a-green-view/.
Kant, I. (1991) 'On the common saying: "this may be true in theory, but it does not apply in practice"', in H. Reiss, ed, *Political Writings*, 61–92. Cambridge: Cambridge University Press.

Lijphardt, A. (2012) *Patterns of Democracy*, Second Edition. London: Yale University Press.
Locke, J. (2000) *Two Treatises on Government*. Cambridge: Cambridge University Press.
McKay, G. (1996) *Senseless Acts of Beauty*. London: Verso.
Machiavelli, N. (1981) *The Prince*. Harmondsworth: Penguin.
Mason, M. (1999) *Environmental Democracy*. London: Earthscan.
Murray, C. (2007) *Murder in Samarkand – A British Ambassador's Controversial Defiance of Tyranny in the War on Terror*. London: Mainstream.
Pilbeam, B. (2003) 'Natural allies? Mapping the relationship between conservatism and environmentalism', *Political Studies* 51: 490–508.
Porritt, J. (1997) 'Environmental politics: the old and the new', *The Political Quarterly* 68: 62–73.
Portwood-Stacer, L. (2018, publication forthcoming) 'Micropolitics', in L. Williams, N. Jun and B. Franks, eds, *Anarchism: A Conceptual Approach*. London: Routledge.
Powell Jr, G.B.J., Strømand, K.J. and Dalton, R.J. (2011) *Comparative Politics Today: A Theoretical Framework*. London: Pearson Higher Ed.
Richard (2009) 'Green taxes. Don't believe airline whinging over air passenger duty'. *Plane Stupid*, 24 July, www.planestupid.com/category/blog-tags/green-taxes.
Rootes, C. (2000) 'Environmental protest in Britain 1998–1997', in B. Seel, M. Patterson and B. Doherty, eds, *Direct Action in British Environmentalism*, 25–61. London: Routledge.
Shantz, J. (2002) 'Green syndicalism: an alternative Red-Green vision', *Environmental Politics* 11.44: 21–41.
Shearman, D.J. and Smith, J.W. (2007) *The Climate Change Challenge and the Failure of Democracy*. California: Greenwood Publishing Group.
Singer, P. (2011) *Practical Ethics*, Third Edition. Cambridge: Cambridge University Press.
Sunstein, C.R. and Thaler, R.H. (2003) 'Libertarian paternalism is not an oxymoron', *The University of Chicago Law Review* 70.4: 1159–202.
Uleri, P. (1996) 'Introduction', in M. Gallagher and P. Uleri, eds, *The Referendum Experience in Europe*, 8–19. Basingstoke: Macmillan.
United Kingdom Independence Party (UKIP) (2013) 'New EU ban could be a "lightbulb moment"'. *United Kingdom Independence Party in the European Parliament* 15 August, www.ukipmeps.org/news_334_New-EU-ban-could-be-a-%60lightbulb-moment%60.html.
Weber, M. (1949) *The Theory of Social and Economic Organisation*. Glasgow: William Hodge and Company.

9

NON-CONSTITUTIONAL POLITICAL CHANGE

Green direct action, civil disobedience and symbolic activity

9.1 Introduction

The previous chapter concentrates on a standard but rather minimal account of politics (macropolitics), which focuses on statecraft. It examined how winning and controlling the state could advance green behavioural change. Using this state-centred politics as a focus, more micro-forms of politics – the way in which decisions are made in everyday activities or the ways people interpret the world around them – are marginalised or only become significant when they impact on state power. The previous chapter, as a result, explored the role of Green constitutional parties in influencing state institutions and the policy-making process. It examined some of the different policy instruments available, including prohibition and financial incentives. It explored arguments in favour of behavioural change being initiated through the constitutional process and some of the criticisms raised by conservative and radical critics. This chapter, by contrast, classifies and assesses environmental tactics that are non-constitutional; that is to say operating outside the familiar mechanisms of standing for election, supporting candidates, starting new or assisting existing electoral parties, voting, or seeking to influence elected representatives through existing lawful means, such as petitions and letter-writing campaigns. It identifies the distinctive place of ecological values in unconventional green political tactics and considers the moral arguments for and against these micropolitical methods.

Constitutional supporters like Porritt (1997, 65) consider non-constitutional methods to be of secondary importance to behavioural change achieved through the electoral system. He is critical of academic and political commentators who place greater emphasis on green direct action in their accounts of environmental politics. Nonetheless, historically these non-constitutional tactics have been strongly identified with green politics (Davidson 2009, 47) and they still inspire contemporary activists across the globe.

Proponents of non-constitutional direct action are broadly drawn from overlapping sections of eco-socialism, in particular from anarchism, heterodox Marxism and syndicalism, rather than from social democratic or orthodox Marxist (Leninist) traditions. What these groupings share in common is a rejection of capitalism. They, like constitutional versions of Green socialism, consider ecological exploitation to be largely the result of capitalism (see Pepper 1993; Keefer 2008–9); however, whereas constitutionalists hope to use the state to reform the economy, anti-constitutionalists seek a fundamentally different set of solutions and practices.

The circuit of capital (see Chapter 7) describes how capitalism structures production in order to maximise exchange value, and this, argue critics, diminishes concern for other principles, such as intrinsic ecological values. Classical and redistributive modern liberals concentrate on maximising instrumental values, with ecologically-minded modern liberals aiming to use some of the economic wealth generated by capitalism to alleviate harms and minimise externalities. Radical ecologists, by contrast, prioritise the generation and maintenance of intrinsically valuable relationships with other people and the natural world. 'Valorisation' refers to the ways in which activities under capitalism are given a value because they help sustain this particular economic system, a value often cast in terms of exchangeable prices (Weekes 2011, 6 and 18; Cleaver 1992). Thus the police force and criminal justice system are highly esteemed when they effectively protect private property. 'Auto-valorisation' or 'self-valorisation' refers to the process by which people act together to produce activities that have their own norms and identities separate to, and often in conflict with, capitalist values (Weekes 2011, 32; Cleaver 1992).

Valorisation: the process by which activities within a particular type of economy are given a value because of the role they play in securing and extending this system of production and distribution. **Auto-valorisation** or **self-valorisation** refers to the process by which people collectively develop their own system of values, often in conflict with dominant notions of worth.

Anti-constitutionalist green politics developed as a set of responses to the processes and impacts of capitalist methods of production. Resistance to capitalism occurs at the micropolitical level as people emphasise other values at the expense of those of capitalism. Collectively, the assumption by proponents is that as these micropolitical practices increase in magnitude, extent and regularity, they intersect with each other to promote more environmentally virtuous activities and, in turn, diminish the frequency of hierarchical and destructive activities.

This form of micropolitical analysis originates from social anarchisms and dissident forms of open or autonomist Marxism (a non-Leninist revolutionary socialism that is critical of orthodox Marxism's hierarchical political strategies, and is associated with Harry Cleaver, Silvia Federici, John Holloway and Antonio Negri). As such it does not concentrate on the standard socialist agent for change – 'the worker' at the point of production – as the primary and universal agent for transforming society. Instead, resistance to the micropolitics of capitalism occurs across diverse social activities and consequently engages many different types of person. The notion that there is a diverse and ever-changing set of people engaged in contesting hierarchies of wealth and power is often referred to as 'the multitude' (Hardt and Negri 2011). The multitude does not ignore the worker at the point of production, but it is not the only place and the only location in which different non-exploitative social activity takes place. The multitude is a set of evolving and overlapping identities, and is thus different to constitutionalism in which the democratic citizen is the main agent for political change.

9.2 Green direct action and civil disobedience

In many circumstances, the terms 'direct action' and 'civil disobedience' are used interchangeably, largely because there is significant overlap between the two as they both act outside of the electoral process. However, the two terms are not identical. 'Civil disobedience' necessarily requires breaking the law (it has to be civilly disobedient), and it also makes claims to be 'non-violent'. These claims can be problematic as even tactics usually covered by the term 'pacifist', such as work stoppages (De Ligt 1989) or road blockades of nuclear weapons sites (Carter 1973, 9), can be construed as causing deliberate economic and psychological harm to the victims or third parties (see Niebuhr 1942; Bufacchi 2005). Nonetheless, proponents of civil disobedience are concerned with using methods that peacefully break the law, even if 'non-violence' itself is a problematic term.

> **Civil disobedience** is a purportedly peaceful, but illegal, political act carried out to protest and often to reform existing structures. In its classical form the participants are willing to accept punishment for transgressing the law.

Civil disobedience, at least in its classical form, (for example, the cases of Rosa Parks, Mahatma Gandhi and Martin Luther King) involves dissenters accepting judgement through the courts, in an effort to show that the law or policy they oppose is flawed (Doherty et al. 2000, 1; Rawls 1971, 365, 367). However, in recent times, not all acts referred to as civil disobedience involve the perpetrators accepting punishment from the authorities. Instead, some may seek to evade capture. Civil disobedience is distinguished by Rawls from more 'militant action', as civil disobedience may break the law, but does so in order to reform the legal framework of the state (Rawls 1971, 66–7) rather than to radically overhaul, negate or replace it. Civil disobedience is also morally motivated (366), but its motivation is either the consequentialist objective of bringing about a more desirable legislative framework or because rights are being violated (365 and 369).

Although both civil disobedience and direct action are political in the broadest sense of the word, there are a number of significant differences. First, direct action makes no claims to be 'non-violent'. There are forms that announce themselves as 'non-violent direct action' and manuals and groups dedicated to this subcategory (Doherty et al. 2000, 2),[1] but the fact that the prefix 'non-violent' is required indicates that of itself 'direct action' can be violent or non-violent. The second distinguishing feature is that direct action is not necessarily illegal. Whilst most forms do involve civil or criminal transgression, there are forms of direct action that are perfectly legal. Autonomous groups of citizens who organise litter patrols to clear up plastics and other debris from shorelines in order to protect wildlife and improve the aesthetic environment is an example of legal direct action.[2] Some actions are both civil disobedience and direct action, such as Rosa Park's powerful resistance to racial segregation on Alabama buses. Her act was peaceful, illegal and did not resist going to trial, so it is often used as a prime example of civil disobedience (see Chapter 5). It was also direct action, as her act flouting the discrimination against black passengers prefigured her goal, which was the desegregation of bus travel in particular and wider North American society in general.

Direct action is a political action that attempts to bring about resolution in full or part immediately. It prefigures the goals it wishes to achieve through the act itself. It can be legal and some forms make no claim to be non-violent.

Prefiguration occurs in many political behaviours but is a particular feature of direct action. It involves the values embedded in a practice foreshadowing the desired values embedded in future types of relationship or activity. So if the goal is an egalitarian society then the methods and organisation to bring about this goal should be as egalitarian as possible.

The most striking feature of direct action is that it is 'characterised by an intention to affect social and ecological conditions *directly*' (Doherty et al. 2000, 1). Whilst there are problems with Brian Doherty, Matthew Paterson and Benjamin Seel's definition of direct action in that it uses the word being defined in its description, it nonetheless points to the unmediated feature of direct action. A person or group who uses direct action seeks an immediate full or partial solution to a problem themselves, rather than going through a series of institutions. Direct action is 'prefigurative' in that the methods foreshadow in some small way the desired outcome (Franks 2003). In pursuing ecological goals then, these should be embodied in the means. Direct action thus appears closer to virtue theory; it is goal directed, but also seeks to generate goods immediately that prefigure and help to achieve these goals.

Many noticeable environmental activities are not direct action. For instance, Earth Day demonstrations, which have been organised since 1970 to raise public awareness of the need for environmental protection, are not in themselves direct action, although they can give rise to them. These demonstrations do not immediately prevent any environmentally damaging activity, and indeed some celebratory events involve considerable ecological resources. Civil disobedience and constitutional action can be consequentialist – dividing the eventual goals from the methods – but direct action, which is prefigurative, rejects this separation. Ecological direct action aims to consistently embody its goals in methods. An activity geared towards protecting the environment that left excessive pollution behind would not be considered prefigurative. Because prefiguration stands opposed to the separation of means and ends found in consequentialist and deontological (rights-based) ethics and seeks to generate immediate goods, it has strong parallels with virtue ethics (Franks 2010).

There have been a considerable number of eye-catching incidents of direct action across the globe. Agricultural workers in Dachuan (Gansu province), China, frustrated at the contamination coming from a factory that was poisoning their water supply and damaging agricultural land, drove tractors with tankers full of the contaminated water to the factory. The farmers sprayed it over the factory's walls through rubber hoses to disrupt production and highlight the harm it was causing. As a result of this protest, and others mounted by affected citizens, the factory paid compensation and made significant efforts to reduce pollution (Jing 2000, 212–3). In the United States, anti-logging protestors have controversially 'spiked' trees. 'Spiking' involves hammering a large metal spike into the base of a threatened tree. If loggers start to cut a protected tree down the spike damages the blade and can cause injury to the lumberjack. Because of this tactic's potential for injury it is rejected by proponents of civil disobedience and other proponents of direct action, who consider the harm to timber workers to be inconsistent with their goals. As a result, this effective tactic for forest protection was largely replaced by other methods in the 1990s, although it has recently reappeared in Oregon, with notices warning loggers of the presence of spikes (RT 2016).

Other forms of environmental direct action include protestors who oppose genetic modification of fruit and vegetable seedlings by destroying experimental plots (Bodiguel and Cardwell 2010, 375, 380), and anti-fracking campaigners in Australia, United States and the UK blockading fracking sites to prevent further carbon fuel extractions and inhibit local pollution.[3] As ecological damage takes multiple forms, direct action to oppose is similarly diverse. In the 1990s anti-road campaigners occupied land to prevent construction of new highways (McKay 1996 and McGregor 2011). Similar methods have been used by Plane Stupid to frustrate airport expansion. Environmental protestors in these instances use the occupied land to experiment in sustainable and egalitarian forms of living. This is a model borrowed from the annual Climate Camps (started in 2006 and themselves an adaptation from earlier Peace Camps). Climate Camps were open and free international gatherings of environmental activists to share knowledge and engage in collective direct action to interrupt climate-endangering activities including coal-powered power stations (Drax in 2006, Kingsnorth in 2008), coal terminals (Antwerp Bulk terminal in 2009) and airports (Heathrow in 2007 and Aéroport du Grand Ouest in 2009) (see, for instance, van der Zee 2011; Wainright 2006).

Direct action's international profile was raised most significantly by Greenpeace and later by Paul Watson's *Sea Shepherd* Conservation Trust. Greenpeace's boat, the *Rainbow Warrior*, was such an impediment to French attempts to dump nuclear waste at sea that its agents blew up the ship when in harbour in New Zealand in 1985. The boat was scuttled and Fernando Pereira, a photographer, was killed. Paul Watson's campaigning vessel the *Sea Shepherd* deliberately interfered with whaling ships, seal hunters and tuna fisherman who negligently catching dolphin too (Watson 2008) and continues to use direct action to protect oceanic wildlife (*Sea Shepherd* 2017).

Direct action has its roots in the radical labour movements (Flynn et al. 2014), however there are forms of direct action that emanate from other political traditions. Business owners who want to repel rough sleepers because their presence might put off customers have instigated a range of strategies that directly dissuade the homeless, without going through the constitutional process, such as erecting spikes to prevent them from settling, to outright assaults on the displaced and dispossessed. However, the direct action discussed here involves the prefiguring of environmental goals, often framed in anti-hierarchical political forms, rather than those, like the initiatives targeting homeless people, which enhance and protect social and economic divisions.

There are four main benefits, raised by advocates of green direct action: diversity of form, immediacy of impact and empowerment for participants, the pleasurable features (and other inherent goods) of direct participation and its '*Demoi*-cratic' ethos.

9.2.1 Diversity

The first benefit, its diversity, is clear by the number of different methods used by groups committed to direct action. New practices, or twists on older forms, evolve as standard ones become known and controlled by the institutions they challenge. Amongst the main forms (used in environmental protest since the fall of the Berlin Wall) have been: cooperative production, squatting and occupation, resistance to enclosure, selective vandalism and 'pixieing' (stealing the tools of opponents in order to use them against the owners), consumer boycott, the producer boycott and in particular the green strike. Co-operative production attempts to build ecologically-sensitive forms of production and communal living that, where possible, evade engaging with hierarchical and environmentally damaging institutions (going 'off grid') (Plows 1998; Aufheben 1998; Jordan 2002; Trapese Collective 2007). Squatting and occupation involve taking over disused property or the land owned by corporations that is used – or intended to be used – in an ecologically damaging manner. Examples include preventing road building by taking over abandoned houses that were on the new route and thus prevent or slow down demolition, and building protest camps on fracking sites. Resistance to enclosure involves protecting common goods from being taken into private hands. Examples range from the Zapatista rebels in Mexico protecting communal grounds from being sold off by the state to private investors (Federici 2010) to disrupting the sale of community playing fields to property developers.

Another form of ecological direct action is selective vandalism or ecotage (environmentally-motivated sabotage) – also known as 'monkey-wrenching'. Named after Edward Abbey's (2004) novel, this involves activists destroying the industrialists' tools in order to limit, slow down or prevent damage to habitats. It is closely linked to theft or pixieing. Here the contractors' tools and materials are (re)appropriated for conservation purposes. For example, the materials brought by contractors to build roads have been used by protesters to build shelters and barricades. This method equalises the apparent disparity in resources between well-funded commercial operators and the relatively impoverished green campaigners.

The consumer boycott involves refusing to buy goods from companies with a poor environmental record and urging others to do the same. The producer boycott involves employees refusing to engage with ecologically destructive products or processes and is a return to the origins of direct action in the labour movement. The most significant form of the producer boycott is environmental strike action. Green syndicalists such as Judi Bari (1992) and Jeff Shantz (2002) have highlighted how ecologically restructuring requires the co-operation of the general employed workforce if it is not to be a form of authoritarianism. Thus, democratic labour organisation plays a significant role in advancing green production and distribution and to conserve threatened environments (see IWW Environmental Union Caucus 2016). Examples include the Australian Builders and Labourers Federation's (BLF) members in the 1970s taking industrial action, against their own immediate economic interests, by refusing to build new developments on forest and island reserves (Shantz 2002, 22–3),

The wide variety of direct action contrasts with the reasonably constrained number of options available in constitutional politics; the occasional vote, party member then activist and ultimately to candidate and elected representative. Nonetheless, these provide a more limited set of activities than direct action, which also allows for degrees of involvement and commitment. The green activist need not be a permanent member of a protest camp, and levels of engagement alter as opportunities for participation wane or grow and can occur in many different aspects of life, for instance in the workplace as well as through community action.

9.2.2. Immediacy and empowerment

Ecological direct action stands out as its methods embody the conflict between the current, largely economic, values of continued environmental exploitation, and the self-valorisation of the green activists (Aufheben 1998, 108). The tactics used make an immediate impact, albeit sometimes only on a small scale. By contrast constitutional action, as even its supporters identify (Singer 2011, 263–5), can be bureaucratic and slow-moving. Direct action involves people in the here-and-now attempting to bring about immediate change that prefigures their values. Even if the action is ultimately unsuccessful, they still provide opportunities for behaviours based on ecological and anti-hierarchical values to be put into practice. As Porritt notes (1997, 67) critics of the anti-roads protests in the late 1980s and early 1990s claim that these protests did not prevent a single planned road being built. However, leaving aside the fact that the protests did increase road-building costs such that future highway expansion plans were curtailed (67), there are other important grounds for defending these forms of direct action. Participants who engaged in the large anti-road occupations at Newbury, Pollock and Leytonstone found a sense of self-empowerment and communal engagement that inspired them. Indeed, whilst it is possible to see successful consequences of some forms of direct action, such as construction firms pulling out of ecologically damaging hydro-electric schemes and disinvestment campaigns against tyrannical governments (Doherty et al. 2003, 676), some of the intrinsic benefits are often only obvious to those engaged or adjacent to an action. The way these inspire, sustain and shape future ecological practices is not something that can be predicted or easily identified, especially as some forms of direct action (such as pixieing) are deliberately and necessarily covert.

Direct action is viewed as empowering because in constitutional politics the ordinary citizen has little direct power; their vote is sought only intermittently with few parties, who often share core ideological features, to choose between. By contrast, direct action, because the impacts are immediate and unmediated by representatives, provides people with a sense of engagement often lacking in constitutional activity. Wendy Maples (2000, 134–5 and 145–6), for instance, discusses her early disappointment and sense of powerlessness when lobbying a politician compared with recognising and developing different aspects of her character when involved in immediate challenges to the balance of power. Feelings of helplessness, which often arise in situations dealing with environmental crises (see Chapter 5) are, at least temporarily, overcome by engaging in activities that embody the values the activist wishes to see more widely accepted. It is transformative, altering the perceptions of activists about what is possible and it opens up avenues for forms of solidarity that were not previously imaginable (Dudouet 2008, 13–4 and 18–9).

9.2.3 Satisfaction

With the sense of empowerment there also comes moments of satisfaction, pleasure and even elation. Whilst mainstream constitutional politics is often seen as a tedious grind of committee meetings, minute-taking and leafleting, there are conscious efforts to make environmental direct action as enjoyable and carnivalesque as possible. Anti-roads protestors turned the squatted streets that blocked the progress of a proposed new link road into sculpture parks and play areas (Jordan 1998, 131–3); whilst anti-fracking campaigners at Balcombe used sound systems, clowns as well as protestors high-up on tripods to block the energy firm Cuadrilla from carrying out exploratory drillings on the site (BBC 2013). Even supporters of direct action Brian Doherty, Alexandra Plows and Derek Wall (2003, 674, 682) recognise that the diversity of forms and the pleasure gained by participants can make direct action sometimes appear as a self-indulgence. Their more positive accounts contrast with those of critics like Avner De-Shalit (2001, 117–8) who see direct action as often too full of despair.

9.2.4 Demoi-cratic

As David Graeber (2013, 150–207) explains, 'democracy' is much wider than the centralising majority-vote-measuring process with which the term has now become standardly associated. To differentiate the distinctiveness of direct action's democratic feature the term '*demoi*-cratic' is preferred. *Demoi*-cratic activity differs from constitutional democracy because the latter is ultimately based on the sovereignty of the single agent, the citizen, unified within a state (the *demos*). By contrast, direct action involves and invites participation of the multitude: diverse people in various roles and with different identities (*demoi*), without any identity being always and everywhere the most important. There is direct action undertaken by workers, neighbours, parents, as well as the variety of overt 'environmentalist' identities.

Demoi-cracy often involves democratically organised decision-making. In planning direct action, people are free to participate or refuse as they wish. Meetings are advertised in which ideas for forms of action are openly and freely discussed and people opt to undertake those that meet their interests and desires. Different decision-making processes are used in different settings (Clark 2013, 186). Sometimes it is informal and amiable discussion between individuals. In others consensus decision-making is preferred. No single form of decision-making is sufficient to cover the different forms of co-ordinating the myriad types of direct action. Sometimes, as critics within the direct action movement indicate (Earth First! 1998, 10–13), patriarchal (and class) assumptions can go unchallenged and dominant male privileged voices take priority in the debates, with others marginalised and belittled. Such patronising and elitist behaviour does not originate in the protest site, although they can be brought to the fore: 'there is something about sites that brings out the caveman in some men' (13). Nonetheless, the Earth First! writer who recognises and challenges patriarchal behaviour argues that the values inherent in ecological direct action provide a strong basis for challenging sexism and other forms of hierarchical behaviour (13).

9.2.5 Criticism and replies

However, such apparent pluralism is not without its difficulties. Sometimes particular identities emerge that are closed and alienating. De-Shalit (2001, 129–33) points to how activists who strongly identify with their own particular environmental organisation undermine routes for co-operation, placing group loyalty over the generation of effective tactics (rebuilding a singular dominant identity). He also highlights how this activist group identity can lead to elitist attitudes towards members of the community who were not experienced campaigners. Clare Saunders (2007, 231) also suggests that those who eschew constitutionalism are more prone to elitism, finding it hard to collaborate with others. Because anti-constitutionalists reject engaging with the state at the local level this 'leads to counter-cultural networks that develop strong collective identities and become cliquey by virtue of their beliefs'. This potential elitism is reinforced by standard media portrayals of ecological direct action. As Matthew Paterson (2000, 152) notes, mainstream media associates activists with 'a small minority of extremists rejecting "normal" society'. Framed in these ways direct action can generate antipathy, especially amongst those unfamiliar with these movements or tactics, and defensive elitist attitudes by practitioners in response.

Some sections of the environmental protest movement have been conscious that there are risks of producing a new type of social hierarchy based on a class of experts who are specialists in direct action. Their skills and experience makes them appear superior to other populations (see Anonymous 2000a). Forms of ecological direct action that require significant skills and commitment, such as squatting in – and locking on to – threatened trees runs the risk of producing a vanguard group at the head of the struggle. This is a problem with experienced activists acting arrogantly or paternalistically to those with other backgrounds.

The growth of expertise is not in itself a problem. Skill-sharing and co-operation are core features of enlightened environmental activism and these help to lessen hierarchies of expertise. Similarly, just because some people necessarily take a lead in a particular context is not the same as claiming that this group or action should always and everywhere take priority (Anonymous 2000b). Ecological direct action recognises that there are many different forms of environmental and social exploitation. Forms of resistance to these generate prefigurative practices that intersect with each other. In some locations, one group and its particular micropolitical tactics will take priority, in another geographical or historical context another group comes to the fore. These struggles intersect with each other; a point affirmed by Plows (1998, 161) who argues that there are in practice no 'single issues'. In developing direct action against ecological deterioration, issues of social justice are inevitably highlighted and vice-versa. Building new bypasses to speed the distribution of commodities invariably means health damage to local people and social alienation as neighbourhoods are cut off by the dangerous arterial road, as well as damage to local habitats.

Such interweaving of social and ecological issues challenges a further criticism advanced by De-Shalit (2001, 118–9), that proponents of direct action are too biocentric and thus incapable of engaging with the anthropocentric concerns of ordinary citizens. Non-constitutional campaigners do, however, recognise and raise sophisticated and compassionate anthropocentric concerns in their campaigns and by engaging with wider constituencies introduce them to principles and perspectives that are not solely human-centred.

Other theorists from radical political backgrounds, such as the Marxist virtue theorist Paul Blackledge (2010), argue that prefigurative micropolitics is insufficient.

There is, they argue, a clear central site of conflict and that requires the most efficient organisation possible to overcome this oppressive and exploitative system. This is a view shared by David Pepper (1993, 227) who argues that a globally co-ordinated response to climate change is unlikely to be generated from networked groups and instead efficient state action is require to co-ordinate international responses to ecological crises and to meet human needs (233–34). For Pepper, state seizure, in a non-violent manner (234), is a necessary strategy for implementing effective environmental change.

Orthodox Marxist and eco-Marxist approaches, such as Blackledge's and Pepper's, have similarities with the other consequentialist approaches to environmental change identified throughout the book. They are attractive as they recognise the immediacy of ecological threats and have a clear strategy for their resolution. However, consequentialist political responses also fall foul of the criticisms raised of instrumentalist approaches (covered in Chapter 2 and 4), namely the development of inequalities between order-givers and order-takers, hubristic understanding of ultimate goals that can be imposed upon wide populations, the impacts on individual and collective autonomy, and the undermining of virtue-rich practices.

Whilst direct action is often portrayed negatively, it does not follow that it is necessarily unpopular or alien to people's usual practices. Even in the usually conservative mainstream media supportive coverage can be found and counter-narratives emerge stressing such things as 'youthful idealism' (Paterson 2000, 152–3), consistent with desirable social attributes (153, 160–1). Radical action is not necessarily unpopular with the public. Doherty, Plows and Wall (2003, 684) cited a United Kingdom opinion poll in 2000 that found majority support for particular types of environmental direct action. Because of the pervasiveness of micropolitics, even those who claim to reject radical action have usually partaken in it to some degree, even if they have not acknowledged it. For instance, it is not unusual for colleagues to assert their own needs (auto-valorisation) over the priorities of management by taking illicit additional breaks at work, with fellow employees covering for each other, or using work equipment for their private needs (for more examples see, for instance, Sprouse 1992).[4] When environmental direct action is addressed in terms of everyday subversions that are part of existing, if little spoken about, customs and practices, it seems less 'extreme' and abnormal.

9.3 Combining direct action and constitutional action

As discussed in Chapter 8, some groups use constitutional processes, like calling for referendums, as part of direct-action campaigns. Similarly, many environmental groups who do not formally engage in electoral politics may still engage in the constitutional process by lobbying governments to change legislation. Greenpeace (2010), for instance, run a 'political unit' that is aimed directly at making 'sure that our campaign demands are clearly heard by decision-makers, and we ask them to translate these demands into real action that protects the environment'. They then give examples of how they use actions like 'blocking Downing Street with tonnes of coal' to highlight 'environmental crimes' they wish to pressure the government to legislate against. The obstruction of the UK Prime Minister's residence, in a manoeuvre that looks like direct action, is undertaken, though, to promote constitutional action. It is only an 'appearance' of direct action because the dumped coal does not directly interfere with the crime, as Greenpeace identify it, that they wish to prevent; it is more a piece of symbolic action (what they call 'direct communication') rather than direct action, as discussed below.

Other groups and individuals are involved in both constitutional politics and direct action. Doherty, Plows and Wall (2003, 678–9) discuss the significant overlaps between members of Earth First!, members of the Green Party and the ecological-social justice sections of the Welsh nationalist Plaid Cymru. The Green Party itself has been actively involved in some protests that intersect with direct action, such as occupations and protest camps (see, too, Rootes 2000). Many of the original founders of constitutional ecology parties were drawn from the anti-consumerist 'social movement culture' (Blüdhorn 2009, 39). Even Porritt (1997, 63 and 66), a great defender of the institutions of liberal democracy to co-ordinate necessary ecological change, recognises that it is the 'values-driven voice' found in the direct action movement that is important to the constitutional Green movement and, for Porritt, more important than the virtues of direct action itself.

There are undoubtedly some intersections between direct action and constitutional action, however the two tend to be in tension rather than symbiotic. Direct action to be properly immediate is antipathetic to the representative and mediating institutions of government. Similarly, government considers legitimacy for action to come through the representative process rather than from autonomous institutions and communities and thus is largely antipathetic to direct action as it undermines legislative reciprocity. As discussed in the previous chapter, people in the Green Party and other ecologically-minded representative groupings inevitably face a choice, especially when elections arise: do they dedicate their time and resources to direct action or to constitutional action? Largely the Green Party prioritises the latter at the expense of the former

9.4 Symbolic action

Some purely symbolic actions, like public demonstrations, are often confused with direct action. The differences are important. Symbolic action's primary function is to raise awareness of a problem or campaign promoting a solution, but the symbolic tactic itself does not attempt to resolve it (Carter 1983, 16). Dropping politically provocative banners against fracking outside of a legislature, or the blockage to the entry of Downing Street by coal in order to get publicity for reducing carbon emissions from fossil-fuel power generation, do not themselves interfere with the contentious practice. Thus protest marches, vigils, production of information sheets, websites and Facebook 'likes' are symbolic.

There is significant overlap between symbolic actions and constitutional activities and forms of direct action. Planning and promoting direct action requires symbolic action. Similarly, ecologically damaging activities are maintained by forms of communication that attempt to justify such activities or placate potentially disruptive audiences. Direct actions can be read symbolically. Because they are prefigurative they are a synecdoche; a small part that represents the whole. Standard examples might be the individual soldier standing for the army or, in ecological terms, a sustainably-run, jovial and democratically organised protest site standing for the possibility of more carnivalesque, ecologically-sensitive and participatory social arrangements.

Green symbolic action takes different forms. The first is consciousness-raising about a particular issue by introducing, to particular or general audiences, a topic or concept that has been ignored or marginalised. Some groups deliberately target major commercial and state broadcasters, generating media events or spectacles that will be delivered by mainstream media. People for the Ethical Treatment of Animals (PETA) have gained significant attention for their campaigns against the cruelty of fur farming by using famous actresses and models in states of undress to highlight their slogan: 'I'd Rather Go Naked Than Wear Fur'. PETA's symbolic strategies, however, have earned considerable criticism; for example in highlighting abuse of non-human animals they are accused of playing on standard sexist tropes. Also, engaging with the mainstream media means assisting deeply hierarchical commercial institutions that support ecologically damaging practices. Advertising is a major revenue source for newspapers and magazines that not only promote specific environmentally contentious activities as private car ownership and regular aviation travel but a consumer society in general. As such, these media tend to be antipathetic to green protests and will record them in a distorted manner. Other groups, by contrast, concentrate on producing their own promotional materials, utilising methods that are more prefigurative of their wider goals (see, for instance, Atton 1999; Trapese Collective 2007). They regard the production of spectacles to feed into the mainstream media as a way of giving up power to socially pernicious institutions, especially as resources exist for more direct forms of communication. Instead they prioritise direct communication and dialogue.

A second feature of symbolic action is its aim to contest and undermine the ways in which a major institution's ecologically destructive activity is normalised, legitimised and even cast in a positive light. This process of 'subvertising' involves undermining the positive associations that companies try to develop for their brand through advertising (see Ottery 2011). It borrows from the concept of *détournement* (Debord and Wolman 1989) in which cultural provocateurs interfere with a dominant message or sign in order to reveal its seduction and disingenuous features.

Take, for example, the two logos of the oil company BP (formerly British Petroleum).

The first depicts the standard BP logo (Figure 9.1) which in the original uses the green colour usually associated with the environmental movement. It suggests an ecological focus further emphasised by the sun-cum-flower logo with its association with solar power and the natural environment. The latter, designed

FIGURE 9.1 Wikipedia Commons picture of BP garage. (Creative Commons license: https://upload.wikimedia.org/wikipedia/commons/0/08/A_BP_Prices_Sign_Outside_A_BP.jpg.)

for Greenpeace UK's BP logo competition (Figure 9.2), was launched in response to the Deepwater Horizon oil spill which began on 20 April 2010 in the Gulf of Mexico. BP were responsible for the pipeline breach that heavily polluted the ecology of the Gulf of Mexico, and with continuing negative health (Peres et al. 2016) and ecological (Beyer et al. 2016) impacts in the area. Eleven people were also directly killed. Tweaking the logo so that the green is swamped with dripping oil – emphasising the company's main enterprise – also suggests blood and hints at its ecological impact. As such, the logo carries not only different associations than BP's original design, but also highlights the deceptiveness of the symbolism deployed by the company's design team.

The conflict over the production, distribution and interpretation of signs highlights an area of overlap between symbolic and direct action. There is often a financial value attached to brands, so undermining companies' carefully constructed consumer-friendly image is a form of economic sabotage, something that both original proponents of sabotage to promote social values (Flynn 2014, 101–03) and defenders of corporate immaterial property are aware (Kähr et al. 2016).

FIGURE 9.2 BP oil slick, designed for the Greenpeace UK BP logo competition. (With permission from Greenpeace.)

All political behaviour, whether it is direct action, civil disobedience or constitutional action also carry a symbolic meaning. There is often a gap between how activists view their activities, how they imagine non-participants perceive their activities and how they are actually viewed. Activist-geographer Anthony Ince (2010, 11) provides an example of the distinction. He was involved in protests to close down a gathering of the political leaders of the main economically dominant countries, the G8, in Geneva in 2003. These protests were intended to 'prevent business as usual; to protest their [the G8 leaders] illegitimate claims to control the world, its people and resources for their own benefit'. It was to show solidarity for the economically oppressed and the ecologically vulnerable. However, as Ince reports, for some local people the activist protests simply transmitted a message of incoherence, self-indulgence and paternalism. Too often actions that appear to be direct action are instead ineffective and reduced to just symbolic action. What it communicates is often distinct from the participants' intended message.

9.5 Eco-terrorism

Is there a case for green terrorism? The question itself is deeply problematic. First, few terms in politics have such contested interpretations as 'terrorism', such that the question runs the risk of being simply too vague to answer. Thus, for the sake of brevity, this section does not attempt to describe or assess the evolving and competing definitions of terrorism that have emerged since the nineteenth century, but takes the basics of the UN Ad Hoc Committee on Terrorism's (UNAHCT) draft of the Comprehensive Convention on International Terrorism definition:

> Any person commits an offence within the meaning of this Convention if that person, by any means, unlawfully and intentionally, causes:
> (a) death or serious bodily injury to any person; or
> (b) serious damage to public or private property, including a place of public use, a state or government facility, a public transportation system, an infrastructure facility or the environment; or
> (c) damage to property, places, facilities, or systems referred to in paragraph 1 (b) of this article, resulting or likely to result in major economic loss, when the purpose of the conduct, by its nature or context, is to intimidate a population, or to compel a government or an international organization to do or abstain from doing any act.
> *(Quoted in Schmid 2004, 198–9.)*

Thus terrorism is the deliberate generation of fear amongst governments or the general population through illegal, seriously damaging and coercive violence for political goals. Note that deliberate threats or actual damage to natural ecologies, that are carried out in order to pressurise governments or coerce populations, are considered terrorism – but only if they are illegal. Severe ecological damage done by, or with the approval of, governments does not constitute terrorism under the UNAHCT's definition unless such damage violates international law.

There are other reasons why the question of eco-terrorism is so problematic to address. The term 'terrorism' has such pejorative implications that anything with that label is likely to be rejected out-of-hand. Public concerns are understandable (though they may be exaggerated).[5] There are numerous groupings that have perpetrated acts of extreme violence against powerless populations throughout the world, whether it is youngsters attending a social democratic political camp in Buskerud, attendees at music venues in Paris and Manchester, shoppers in markets in Nice, Berlin, Tikrit or Stockholm or worshippers in Tanta and Alexandria in Egypt. The exaggeration of risk is a key function of terrorism, through spectacular acts of destruction the power of the group and its political cause is amplified.

Third, as a result of the negative associations of the term, there are individual risks with even raising the question of legitimate use of terror for ecologically desirable goals. Democratic countries have instigated harsh measures on individuals or groups for discussing terrorism in ways that are regarded as approval and advocacy, if it could be considered to be incitement. Prosecutions and in some cases assassinations of those considered to be supporting terrorism makes even raising (albeit critically) the question of justified green terrorism a slightly risky undertaking. The small risk of punitive action increases when governments extend the definition of terrorism to penalise opponents (see, for instance, Loadenthal 2013; Sanguinetti 1982; Welsh 2007). For instance, the editors of *Green Anarchist* magazine in 1997 were prosecuted, and initially convicted and sentenced for three years, for supportive reporting of Animal Liberation Front (ALF) activities, though the conviction was later overturned.

States and security-centred institutions have, for political reasons, tended to broaden the definition of terrorism to include Green movements. Ian Welsh (2007) argues that as society's main institutions and the natural environment are increasingly regarded in neoliberal terms as resources for securing private profit, any form of political disruption, like direct action, that damages private property is likely to be framed as terrorism. The RAND Corporation (2005), which offers research and analysis to the US military, listed direct-action groups like Earth Liberation Front (ELF) and the ALF alongside Aum Shinrikyo, Hizbollah, Provisional Irish Republican Army (IRA) and Jemaah Islamiyah, despite these latter being involved in attacks on civilians that have cost tens of thousands of lives between them whilst the environmental groups have killed no one. Green syndicalists Bari and her partner Darryl Cherney (see 9.2.1) were viewed as domestic extremists and targeted by the FBI and blown up by a bomb placed in their car.[6] The FBI considered ALF and ELF to be terrorist groups because of their advocacy of direct action (Trujillo 2005, 144).

The extension of the concept of 'terrorism' by agencies like the FBI to cover any form of illegal politically-motivated activity that seeks to 'coerce governments, populations or a segment thereof' (ibid), downplays the notion that terrorism is 'significant' activity, and primarily intended to coerce populations and governments. Green direct action (as described above) and terrorism can usually be distinguished as the first tends to inflict lesser harms (largely property damage and minor inconvenience) in pursuit of producing immediate benefits, whereas UNAHCT's terrorism involves severe harms. The intention behind direct action is to produce immediate benefit not to generate generalised fear and is thus justified using prefigurative reasoning; terrorism is primarily aimed at producing fear and intimidation and justifications are sought through consequentialist reasoning.

Peter Singer, too, identifies that terrorists often use consequentialist reasoning in support of their tactics. However, he argues that given the certainty of the harms committed and the unlikelihood that these actions will lead to the positive goals (where they are positive) then 'for sound practical reasons, terrorism is never justified' (Singer 2011, 274). Singer's absolutist position on terrorism is attractive, but not without problems. First, his examples of terrorism are those of the spectacular and murderous: hijackings, indiscriminate bombings and targeted assassinations, whilst the FBI and others extend the definition of terrorism to the sorts of property-destructive direct action that he considers in some circumstances to be justifiable (Singer 2011, 268–70).

A second reason for questioning Singer's absolutist rejection of eco-terrorism is that it is not consistent with his utilitarian position. Utilitarianism seems to provide a key rationale for justifying even spectacular forms of eco-terrorism. As

Singer reports, using WHO data, anthropogenic climate change is already causing significant human harms in terms of new malaria outbreaks, loss of agriculture and fisheries as habitats change '140,000 deaths in 2004, compared with the number of deaths there would have been had average global temperatures remained as they were during the period 1961 to 1990' (Singer 2011, 216–7). Projections for future outcomes are even more devastating with rises in heat-related deaths, disease and famine. If eco-terrorism that aimed at physically harming citizens rather than simple property destruction generated a positive outcome, then on utilitarianism's consequentialist reasoning it would be justified.

Arguments in favour of spectacular acts of violence to produce changes in social attitudes were promoted by propagandists – by deed in the late nineteenth century and anti-colonial movements in the twentieth century. These advocates of terror argued that whilst it was hoped that their actions would have immediate social benefits (consistent with direct action), even if they failed they would 'carry a powerful symbolic meaning' (Kinna 2006). As outlined in Chapters 5 and 6 System 1 thinking is hard to shift, especially if environmentalists look insincere or the threat looks distant. Eco-terrorism might be a way of forcing the issue onto the public consciousness and demonstrates the commitment of those professing concern for climate change. Thus eco-terrorism might have the types of positive outcomes utilitarians, like Singer, promote.

However, Singer's conclusion, rather than his reasons, is probably correct. Elsewhere (see, for instance, Chapters 2 and 4) the weaknesses of utilitarianism as a guiding framework have been described, in terms of extending inequalities, undermining autonomy and damaging virtuous social practices. Further, a justification for eco-terrorism based on its symbolic impact requires the use of intermediaries for carrying that symbolic message. In democratic societies these are usually the institutions of the mass media, which as discussed in the sections above, tend to reframe even less confrontational green activities in a distorted and antipathetic manner. Terrorist action, especially if it physically harms innocent civilians, is unlikely to be reported sympathetically and make green issues seem even more remote. Because of the shocking symbolic power of terrorist action, the character of the terrorist can dominate public discourse and marginalise other benevolent ecological activities and identities.

This is not to say that green activism can entirely disassociate itself from terrorism. As mentioned above, many forms of green protest and direct action that conflict with current economic and political practice will be framed by opponents as 'terrorism', just as some green activists frame environmental destruction as forms of 'state terrorism'. Nonetheless, whilst the frustration that leads to terrorism maybe understandable, the 'quick fix' it is supposed to provide falls foul of many of the same problems that other 'quick fixes' like geo-engineering suffers from: it can be indiscriminate, producing unintended outcomes and being so coercive as to undermine important rights and weaken self-development. Responsibility for social change lies more with the vanguard terrorist group, and less on individual and collective action.

9.6 Organisation: social networks and electronic communications

In contrast to previous discussions, more accessible and everyday political actions take place through electronic internet-enabled communication and organising ('social networks'). It is pertinent to point out, however, that despite the growth of Information and Communications Technologies (ICT) based communications and activism, ecological organisation is still significant in real (or non-virtual) spaces.

An organisation's identity is shaped by the material resources at the disposal of the collective, and the values embodied in members' interactions with each other and with different groups. These also impact on a group's effectiveness (Saunders 2007). One assumption is that environmental groups that are able to engage with numerous partners will be more effective than isolated groups. This is broadly correct but, for certain forms of direct action, small immediate actions can be more effective than the longer drawn-out negotiations with multiple parties. Similarly, the involvement of some groups might be counter-productive. For instance, some radical environmentalists reject negotiation with state or corporate bodies as these bodies must prioritise protection of private property rights and in doing so compromise effective action based on environmental values.

There are multiple types of ecological organisation, and they each operate by different norms. Some are similar to commercial organisations in which consumers buy green products or an environmental experience for a regular subscription, and the goal is to grow the commercial and membership base. Whilst these are seen as a means to the end of generating more effective environmental lobbying, the means often become the ends, with ever greater resources going on advertising for and retaining membership rather than on pursuing ecological activities. Others are more federated or networked in a way that is consistent with more *demoi*-cratic forms of organisation.

Some employ at the local level consensus decision-making, other prefer more informal and personal group dynamics based on pre-existing friendships. As discussed in the previous chapter, tactics and organisations are co-produced. Political parties usually require a hierarchical structure to be effective and provide voter-accountability. Local groups co-ordinating action against open cast mining, for instance, use a mixture of established personal contacts (affinity) and direct democracy. Neil Gavin (2010, 463) points out that groups with fluid 'flattened, dispersed, organisational structures' have less control over their members, and thus can engage in tactics that can be more easily portrayed negatively by the mainstream press. Gavin's immediate point about the negative symbolic impact of ill-disciplined direct action would be rejected by those groups unconcerned at the approval or otherwise of corporate media. Instead, they judge forms of direct action by whether the values it embodies reflects the group's goals. It is, nonetheless, a problem for those groups, largely from deep and social ecology backgrounds who consider horizontal, informal and open organisation as best embodying their social goals, to deal with anti-social and disruptive behaviours, without recreating damaging social hierarchies (Aufheben 1998, 116–20). Small and larger groups have used a range of methods for ensuring that those seeking to disrupt mutual aid or place others in danger are challenged, invited to reflect on their behaviour, have co-operation withdrawn or are forcibly excluded from the group.

Initially, the widespread adoption of computer-mediated communication in the late 1990s was greeted by environmental groups positively as it made them less reliant on the older forms of corporately structured and resource-expensive media for distributing their ideas, contacting potential allies and coordinating activities (Diani 2000). The internet shares some of the positive characteristics of the more fluid democratic ecological networks: being decentred, open access and participatory. However, as Gavin (2010) indicates, electronic communication nevertheless still has its distortions. First, people are only likely to access a group's website if they have already heard of it. Coverage by conventional media is likely to expose a wider public to a group's existence (465–7). Second, the influence of corporations has not been challenged by the internet of search engines and ICT industries still play vital gatekeeper roles. Google has come under increasing critical attention for the algorithm it uses for listing search answers. Being placed high up in a Google search significantly increases the chances of visitors to that site, and a low listing (especially one that does not appear in the first page) makes it unlikely for a new visitor to find that site. Prosperous organisations have the skills and finance to ensure higher placing for their sites containing a group's name than the activist group itself (467–8). Finally, as the web and web-users have become more sophisticated, the quality of the group's website interface and media becomes increasingly important. Hard to navigate and unattractive sites are unlikely to become well used, and corporate media can afford better writers, designers and technicians and more bandwidth: 'professionalism and money count, on the web as they do elsewhere' (468). As Gavin concludes 'the web is not as open a field as some might wish' (468).

Peter Wilkin (2016), in his analysis of virtual organisation in East European civil society, identifies some of the benefits and disadvantages of web-based activism. ICT cheaply and swiftly enabled protest movements to emerge and co-ordinate activity, such as the Occupy movement and the Arab Spring. However, it also makes electronic surveillance much easier. State and quasi-state bodies, who have greater resources at their disposal, can survey and control activists much more effectively and use electronic resources to propagate their own worldview (142–4).

Nonetheless, corporate and state control is rarely complete, especially given the enormity of electronic traffic. Personal website domains and social media sites, such as Facebook, allow direct communications at little cost. It also provides access to a new form of campaigning. The UK citizen's movement *38 Degrees*, America's *Moveon* and Australia's *GetUp!* and the transnational *Avazz* are networks of internet-enabled citizens engaged in a broad range of progressive, social democratic and anthropocentric environmental campaigns (Chadwick and Dennis 2017, 1–3). *38 Degrees* has a membership of over 3 million (1) who, alongside its professional staff acting in 'gatekeeping roles' (13), choose through online polling which campaign to concentrate upon. These campaigns have tended to cover a broad spectrum of concerns covering social democratic protection, civil liberties and consumer rights. It has been involved in successful environmental lobbying of national, devolved and government organisations to prevent ecologically damaging forms of fracking (Stewart 2015) and planned destruction of woodlands (Priestly 2016). Its main form of operation is providing a platform for online petitions, with links to other social media outlets and professional advice on how to promote the interest shown in the petition to local and national media (Chadwick and Dennis 2017, 5–12) to put pressure on politicians. As such *38 Degrees* operate almost exclusively through the constitutional process. Its symbolic activities are used to influence macropolitics, utilising and supporting corporate media and state structures, with little or no engagement with direct action.

Environmental direct action groups use ICT to promote and co-ordinate their actions. Not only are climate camps and anti-fracking disruptions advertised through group websites, Facebook pages and Twitter accounts, but information of police activity is distributed through mobile telephone communications. Policing is digitally recorded to try and reduce excessive (and illegal) security operations (see, for instance, Carroll 2002; Taylor 2004). Talks justifying and teaching techniques for eco-direct action are recorded and available on a range of ICT platforms. However, Wilkin (2016, 143) also points to 'pessimist' criticisms of new social media that, rather than encouraging wisdom and collegiality, they give rise to 'ignorance and bigotry', where 'online search engines [provide] . . . read-made answers'. Answers to difficult multifaceted dilemmas ('wicked problems' as discussed in Chapter 5) are expected in less than 140 characters, thereby misrepresenting the nature of the problem and/or generating facile or dangerous solutions. Rather than promoting collegiality, shaming, bullying and groupthink are common. However, these vices also pervade non-electronic forums. In addition, as Wilkin explores, there are significant examples of democratic and anti-hierarchical electronic media, which encourage respectful discussion within their sites and provide a bridge to collective respectful real (non-virtual) communities. These new media sites provide access to information that assist transparency and the undermining of oppressive elites are possible and effective (145–6).

Electronic activism, however, carries environmental costs. Various studies (e.g., Plepys 2002, Williams et al. 2008; Walsh 2015; Bekaroo et al. 2016) have been made of the toxic components of personal computers that leach into the general atmosphere on disposal, the damage done to the environment through mining raw materials, and the water and energy use in production of ICT.

> This growth in carbon emission by ICT from 530 $MtCO_2e$ [metric tonnes of carbon dioxide or equivalent greenhouse gas] in 2002 to 1430 $MtCO_2e$ as expected in 2020 is a growing concern to both the natural environment and the climatic conditions, which also impacts human beings and the society at large.
>
> *(Bekaroo et al. 2016.)*

In contrast, the airline industry by 2020 is expected to emit around 1,100 MtCO$_2$e (Q. Climate Group, SMART 2020 in Bekaroo et al. 2016). Offsetting some of the ecological harms of ICT is its role in potentially reducing emissions from commuting as homeworking increases and from more efficient logistics. Nonetheless, electronic activism is not an environmentally neutral activity.

9.7 Lifestyles

Environmental micropolitical action involves transforming lifestyles. 'Lifestyle is a set of routine choices an individual makes about practices such as dress, diet, housing, leisure activities and more' (Portwood-Stacer 2013, 4). They are material expressions of a political position in everyday activities (42). Such lifestyle changes can be just a form of ethical consumption (see Chapter 7). Examples include ecologically-minded customers opting for a product whose manufacture or disposal generates less harmful environmental outcomes, or whose parent company fund green social and political schemes even if these come at a higher price. However, environmental lifestyle politics is not reducible to consumer activism alone and some are actively antipathetic to consumerism (25–50).

9.7.1 Ecological communes

One area in which ecological prefigurative activity is foregrounded is in generating intentional communities (communes) whose members are dedicated to embracing environmental values in their everyday living (see Meijering et al. 2007). This includes experimenting with living arrangements to generate ecologically harmonious forms of living based on values different to those that dominate in the wider society. Some still use consumer durables like 'refrigerators, microwaves, washing machines, and cars, but attempt to limit their use of these' (43), and still engage in capitalist enterprise, selling their labour or products of their labour and buying commodities from retail stores (43, 45). Others are much more radical, attempting a more self-sufficient and abstentious existence, with a more critical stance towards dominant industrial living practices (46–7).

As Louise Meijering, Paulus Huigen and Bettina van Hoven (2007) note, communes are often exclusionary. Historically they have tended to draw membership from white and moderately financially secure sections of the community and, by design or omission, exclude the very young, the elderly and those with disabilities (43, 47). From the outside the methods employed by some communes seem off-putting. For instance, at a Colorado commune members are encouraged to urinate onto the compound's bushes rather than into a toilet in order to prevent water being diverted from a river into the flush toilet and to provide hydration to the plants (Portwood-Spacer 2013, 28–9). To outsiders (and especially neighbours) this seems idiosyncratic and anti-social. This individualist response also seems to do little to prevent heavy industry from using the river water commune members have saved.

Nonetheless, even eccentric 'outsider' groups, unconcerned by how others view them, can be inspiring, generating strong collective identities and innovative forms of living (Bey 2003, 95–106), even if they intentionally isolate or unintentionally alienate themselves from others (Clark 2013, 184–5). Some intentional communities are viewed as an attempt to 'drop out' of society (Portwood-Stacer 2013, 147), where people live 'ethically' in isolation from the rest of (a corrupt) society. Isolated lifestyle activism is criticised because ecological damage and institutions seeking exploitative advantage do not cease at the commune wall (147). Also, the social division between the ethical commune-dwellers and the non-membership can lead to elitist behaviour with a negligent or abusive attitude towards outsiders. Because of mutual hostility, a commune may become an exclusionary community, making its ecological practices unlikely to be more widely adopted in the wider locale in which the commune resides (Meijering et al. 2007, 49).

9.7.2 Lifestyles and the community

As Laura Portwood-Spacer notes, terms like 'lifestyle politics' suggest an individualist approach, consistent with the belief that 'one person can make a difference', which tends to be integrated into the politics of neoliberalism (9). Many criticisms of lifestyle politics, such as those from Murray Bookchin (1995, 6–8, 11–12), associate it with a neoliberal version of individual autonomy and egoistic mysticism at the expense of collective freedom. Whilst some lifestyle green politics is consumerist and individualist, many others tie themselves explicitly into a wider social politics. Paul Chatterton's (2014) *Low Impact Living* (based on the Low Impact Living Affordable Community LILAC) project makes explicit links between democratic participatory communal ownership and organisation and environmentally harmonious housing. Chatterton links the development of low impact living with affordability and the development of communal virtues (wisdom or 'learning', 'self-reliance', fairness or 'equality') and with enhancing ecological virtuous practices (9, 11), in an adaptation of the virtuous circle (9).

Although ecofeminist writer and activist Starhawk's (2005) writings occasionally stray into the irrational mysticism rejected by Bookchin, she nonetheless identifies how setting up ecological communities, even if they are only temporary, can help develop communal and environmental skills that are personally and collectively empowering. Collaborating in building an eco-village, clearing industrially despoiled land or developing permaculture gardens and compost toilets, develops participants' understanding of the complexity of eco-systems and develops technical knowledge and competencies for enhancing collegial working. They also provide a material resource for other anti-hierarchical and environmental practices. As John P. Clark (2013, 210–3) identifies in the aftermath of Hurricane Katrina, a community builds resilience by developing and sharing practical skills. It makes these social groups less dependent on states and corporations and this allows for the development of a critical autonomy that further encourages communal development and virtuous interactions.

A recurrent feature of radical movements for expansive socio-economic change is how they become side-tracked into producing marketable products (t-shirts with militant slogans emblazoned upon them, or radical books sold by multinational corporations) or become insulated into their own small communities (Clark 2013, 1984–5). But the inclusion of overt eco-values into everyday practices normalises these values and introduces them to people not previously unfamiliar to them (Portwood-Stacer 2013, 150).

9.8 Conclusion

This chapter looked at eco-political behaviour change beyond the state. It concentrated on micropolitical forms, in particular direct action and symbolic action. Direct action is prefigurative. It tries to bring about, albeit in a small or temporary way, immediate change that foreshadows the wider ecological goal. Unlike constitutional action, which is often consequentialist and works through layers of representatives, social change is unmediated. Whilst constitutional change is primarily about the citizen acting through the constitutional process to alter government policy, direct action involves loss of different types of overlapping agency (for instance employee, family member, musician, neighbour, gardener, squatter and saboteur) making immediate interventions to challenge environmentally destructive activity.

Direct action takes multiple, evolving forms. Some of them are overt and eye-catching, such as the eco-occupations of commercially-owned land to prevent the destruction of wilderness or the poisoning of the water table. Other micropolitical ecological behaviours are pervasive and often no longer recognised as political or ecological. They can become so ingrained into everyday activities that they are simply part of that practice. Walking or cycling to work or school with friends might not be a conscious environmental choice and just part of a family's routine, although the original, long-forgotten motivation might have been ecologically-inspired.

Direct action is not without dangers of rebuilding elites and hierarchies, either between current participants and non-participants or experienced versus novice members. However, a sense of critical reflection and openness to others can do much to reduce this tendency. The virtues inherent in eco-direct action, whilst they do not guarantee critical reflection to prevent vices developing, are nonetheless likely to generate it. Direct action requires a sense of modesty, seeing no site of struggle as being universal or sufficient on its own to resolve ecological problems; like other virtuous practices they should encourage the maintenance and growth (spillover) of other ecologically-sensitive practices.

Notes

1 See, for instance, Greenpeace's (2016) 'Nonviolent direct action' training and activist network and the Peace News/Campaign for Nuclear Disarmament's (1984) *Preparing for Non-Violent Direct Action*.
2 See, for instance, the beach patrol networks in Melbourne, Australia, www.beachpatrol.com.au/About-Us.
3 See Frack Off: http://frack-off.org.uk/.
4 It should be stressed that, should any of the authors' line-managers being reading this, none of the authors have ever engaged in these activities. Honest boss.
5 For instance, the most extensive single act of terrorism so far in the twenty-first century, the September 11 2001 attacks, killed just short of 3000 people and, since then until December 2014, fewer than 60 Americans were killed domestically through terrorism (START 2015). During the same period approximately 400,000 Americans were killed on the roads. Globally over a million people die in road traffic accidents (WHO 2015), compared with around 30,000 who in 2014 lost their lives directly through terrorism (Institute for Economics and Peace and START 2016). To say nothing of the many more who die from heart disease, cancer or poverty-related diseases.
6 Cherney and Bari's estate (she later died of cancer) received $4 million in damages having successfully sued the FBI (see Democracy Now 2012 and the documentary *Who Bombed Judi Bari*).

References

Abbey, E. (2004) *The Monkey Wrench Gang*. Harmondsworth: Penguin.
Anonymous (2000a) 'Give up activism', *Do or Die: Voices from the Ecological Resistance* 9: 160–6.
Anonymous (2000b) 'Postscript', *Do or Die: Voices from the Ecological Resistance* 9: 166–70.
Atton, C. (1999) 'Green anarchist: a case study of collective action in the radical media', *Anarchist Studies* 7.3: 25–50.
Aufheben (1998) 'The politics of anti-road struggle and the struggle of anti-road politics: the case of the No M11 Link Road campaign', in G. McKay, ed., *DiY Culture: Party and Protest in Nineties Britain*, 100–28. London: Verso.
Bari. J. (1992) 'Judi Bari interviews Louisiana Pacific Mill Workers', *IWW Environmental Unionism Caucus*. Placed online 9 June 2013: http://ecology.iww.org/texts/JudiBari/Judi%20Bari%20interviews%20Louisiana%20Pacific%20Mill%20Workers.
BBC (2013) 'Balcombe anti-fracking camp: activists train for direct action'. *BBC News* 18 August 2013, www.bbc.co.uk/news/uk-england-sussex-23744365.
Beeson, M. (2010) 'The coming of environmental authoritarianism', *Environmental Politics* 19.2: 276–94.
Bekaroo, G., Bokhoree, C. and Pattinson, C. (2016) 'Impacts of ICT on the natural ecosystem: a grassroot analysis for promoting socio-environmental sustainability', *Renewable and Sustainable Energy Reviews* 57: 1580–95.
Bey, H. (2003) *T.A.Z.: The Temporary Autonomous Zone, Ontological Anarchy, Poetic Terrorism*. Brooklyn: Autonomedia.
Beyer, J., Trannum, H.C., Bakke, T., Hodsonand, P.V. and Collier, T.K. (2016) 'Environmental effects of the Deepwater Horizon oil spill: a review', *Marine Pollution Bulletin* 110.1: 28–51.
Blackledge, P. (2010) 'Marxism and Anarchism', *International Socialism* 125 (10 January), www.isj.org.uk/?id=616.
Blühdorn, I. (2009) 'Reinventing Green politics: on the strategic repositioning of the German Green Party', *German Politics* 18.1: 36–54.

Bodiguel, L. and Cardwell, M. (2010) *The Regulation of Genetically Modified Organisms: Comparative Approaches*. Oxford: Oxford University Press.

Bookchin, M. (1995) *Social Anarchism or Lifestyle Anarchism: An Unbridgeable Chasm*. Edinburgh: AK Press.

Bufacchi, V. (2005) 'Two concepts of violence', *Political Studies Review* 3.2: 193–204.

Carroll, R. (2002) 'Italian police "framed G8 protesters"', *The Guardian* 22 June, www.theguardian.com/world/2002/jun/22/globalisation.rorycarroll.

Carter, A. (1973) *Direct Action and Liberal Democracy*. London: Routledge & Kegan Paul.

Carter, A. (1983) *Direct Action*. npl: CND.

Chadwick, A. and Dennis, J. (2017) 'Social media, professional media and mobilisation in contemporary Britain: explaining the strengths and weaknesses of the citizens' movement 38 degrees', *Political Studies* 65.1: 42–60.

Chatterton, P. (2014) *Low Impact Living: A Field Guide to Ecological, Affordable Community Building*. London: Routledge.

Clark, J.P. (2013) *The Impossible Community: Realizing Communitarian Anarchism*. London: Bloomsbury.

Cleaver, H. (1992) 'The inversion of class perspective in Marxian theory: from valorisation to self-valorisation', in W. Bonefield, R. Gunn and K. Psychopedis, eds, *Open Marxism*, Volume 2, 106–44. London: Pluto.

Davidson, S. (2009) 'Ecoanarchism: a critical defence', *Journal of Political Ideologies* 14.1: 47–67.

De Ligt, B. (1989) *The Conquest of Violence*. London: Pluto.

De-Shalit, A. (2001) 'Ten commandments of how to fail in an environmental campaign', *Environmental Politics* 10.1: 111–37.

Debord, G. and Wolman, G. (1989) 'Methods of detournement', in K. Knabb, ed., *Situationist International Anthology*, 8–13. California: Bureau of Public Secrets.

Democracy Now (2012) 'Judi Bari revisited: new film exposes FBI coverup of 1990 car bombing of California environmentalist', *Democracy Now*, www.democracynow.org/2012/3/27/judi_bari_revisited_new_film_exposes.

Diani, M. (2000) 'Social movement networks: virtual and real', *Information, Communication and Society* 3.3: 386–401.

Doherty, B., Paterson, M. and Seel, B. (2000). 'Direct action in British environmentalism', in B. Seel, M. Patterson and B. Doherty, eds, *Direct Action in British Environmentalism*, 1–24. London: Routledge.

Doherty, B., Plows, A. and Wall, D. (2003) 'The preferred way of doing things: the British direct action movement', *Parliamentary Affairs* 56.4: 669–86.

Dudouet, V. (2008) *Nonviolent Resistance and Conflict Transformation in Power Asymmetries*. Gerghof Research Centre for Constructive Conflict Management, http://edoc.vifapol.de/opus/volltexte/2011/2586/pdf/dudouet_handbook.pdf.

Earth First! (1998) 'No escape from patriarchy: male dominance on site', *Do or Die: Voices from Earth First!* 7: 10–13.

Federici, S. (2010) 'Feminism and the politics of the commons in an era of primitive accumulation', in Team Colors Collective, ed., *Uses of a Whirlwind*. Edinburgh: AK.

Flynn. E. (2014) 'Sabotage the conscious withdrawal of the workers' industrial efficiency (1916)', in E. Flynn, W. Smith and W. Trautmann, eds, *Direct Action and Sabotage: Three Classic IWW Pamphlets from the 1910s*. Oakland/Chicago: PM Press and C.H. Kerr.

Flynn, E., Smith, W. and Trautmann, W. (2014) *Direct Action and Sabotage: Three Classic IWW Pamphlets from the 1910s*. Oakland/Chicago: PM Press and C.H. Kerr.

Franks, B. (2003) 'The direct action ethic', *Anarchist Studies* 11.1. 13–41.
Franks, B. (2010) 'Anarchism and the virtues', in B. Franks and M. Wilson, eds, *Anarchism and Moral Philosophy*. Basingstoke: Macmillan.
Gavin, N. (2010) 'Pressure group direct action on climate change: the role of the media and web in Britain – a case study', *The British Journal of Politics and International Relations* 12: 459–75.
Graeber, D. (2013) *The Democracy Project*. Harmondsworth: Penguin.
Greenpeace (2010) 'Lobbying'. *Greenpeace*, 9 December. www.greenpeace.org.uk/about/lobbying.
Greenpeace (2016) 'Take nonviolent direct action'. *Greenpeace*. Last edited 29 February, www.greenpeace.org.uk/active-supporters/forms/non-violent-direct-action-network-application-form.
Greenpeace (nd) 'Behind the logo: about the tar sands'. *Greenpeace*, www.greenpeace.org.uk/files/tarsands/tar-sands.html.
Hardt, M. and Negri, A. (2011) *Commonwealth*. London: Harvard University Press.
Ince, A. (2010) *Organising Anarchy Spatial Strategy Prefiguration and the Politics of Everyday Life*, doctoral dissertation. Department of Geography, Queen Mary, University of London. Online at: https://qmro.qmul.ac.uk/xmlui/bitstream/handle/123456789/496/INCEOrganisingAnarchy2010.pdf?sequence=1.
IWW Environmental Unionism Caucus (2016) 'About the Environmental Unionist Caucus', http://ecology.iww.org/about.
Jing, J. (2000) 'Environmental protests in rural China', in E. Perry and M. Selden, eds, *Chinese Society: Change, Conflict and Resistance*, 143–60. London: Routledge.
Jordan, J. (1998) 'The art of necessity: the subversive imagination of anti-road protest and Reclaim the Streets', in G. McKay, ed., *DiY Culture: Party and Protest in Nineties Britain*, 129–51. London: Verso.
Jordan, T. (2002) *Activism! Direct Action, Hacktivism and the Future of Society*. London: Reaktion.
Kähr, A., Nyffenegger, B., Krohmer, H. and Hoyer, W.D. (2016) 'When hostile consumers wreak havoc on your brand: the phenomenon of consumer brand sabotage', *Journal of Marketing*, 80.3: 25–41.
Keefer, T. (2008–9) 'Fossil fuels, capitalism, and class struggle', *The Commoner* 13: 15–21, available online at: www.commoner.org.uk/N13/01-Keefer.pdf.
Kinna, R. (2006) 'Introduction', in R. Kinna, ed., *Early Writings on Terrorism*. London: Routledge.
Lenin, V. (1975) *'Left Wing' Communism: An Infantile Disorder*. Peking: Foreign Language.
Loadenthal, M. (2013) 'Deconstructing "eco-terrorism": rhetoric, framing and statecraft as seen through the Insight approach', *Critical Studies on Terrorism*, 6:1, 92–117.
Maples, W. (2000) 'It's just not natural'? Queer insights on eco action', in B. Seel, M. Paterson and B. Doherty, eds, *Direct Action in British Environmentalism*, 133–50. London: Routledge.
McGregor, J. (2011) 'Once upon a life', in *The Observer Magazine* 13 Feb, 16–7.
McKay, G. (1996) *Senseless Acts of Beauty*. London: Verso.
Meijering, L., Huigenand, P. and Van Hoven, B. (2007) 'Intentional communities in rural spaces', *Tijdschrift voor economische en sociale geografie* 98.1: 42–52.
Niebuhr, R. (1942) *Moral Man and Immoral Society*. London: Charles Scribner's Sons.
Ottery, C. (2011) 'Subvertising: billboard ads for the public interest', *Ecologist* 10 May, www.theecologist.org/campaigning/culture_change/881357/subvertising_billboard_ads_for_the_public_interest.html.

Paterson, M. (2000) 'Swampy fever: media constructions and direct action politics', in B. Seel, M. Paterson and B. Doherty, eds, *Direct Action in British Environmentalism*, 151–66. London: Routledge.

Pepper, D. (1993) *Eco-Socialism: From Deep Ecology to Social Justice*. London: Routledge.

Peres, L.C., Trapido, E., Rung, A., Harrington, D., Oral, E., Fang, Z., Fontham, E. and Peters, E. (2016) 'The Deepwater Horizon oil spill and physical health among adult women in southern Louisiana: the women and their children's health (WaTCH) study', *Environmental Health Perspectives*, http://dx.doi.org/10.1289/ehp.1510348.

Plepys A. (2002) 'The grey side of ICT', *Environmental Impact Assessment Review*, 22.5: 509–23.

Plows, A. (1998) 'Earth First! Defending mother earth direct style', in G. McKay, (Ed.), *DiY Culture: Party and Protest in Nineties Britain*, 152–173. London: Verso.

Porritt, J. (1997) 'Environmental politics: the old and the new', *The Political Quarterly* 68: 62–73.

Portwood-Stacer, L. (2013) *Lifestyle Politics and Radical Activism*. London: Bloomsbury.

Priestly, R. (2016) 'We saved the Blakes Walk poplars!', *38 Degrees* 26 April, https://home.38degrees.org.uk/2016/04/26/we-saved-the-blakes-walk-poplars/.

RAND (2005) *Aptitude for Destruction: Case Studies of Organizational Learning in Five Terrorist Groups*, Volume 2. Santa Monica: RAND.

Rawls, J. (1972) *A Theory of Justice*. Oxford: Oxford University Press.

Rootes, C. (2000) 'Environmental protest in Britain 1988–1997', in B. Seel, M. Paterson and B. Doherty, eds, *Direct Action in British Environmentalism*, 25–61. London: Routledge.

RT (2016) 'Old growth trees spiked by eco-warriors in Oregon to stop logging', *RT*, 13 June, www.rt.com/usa/346434-tree-spikes-protest-oregon/.

Sanguinetti, G. (1982) *On terrorism and the State: The Theory and Practice of Terrorism Divulged for the First Time*. London: Chronos.

Saunders, C. (2007) 'Using social network analysis to explore social movements: a relational approach', *Social Movement Studies* 6:3: 227–43.

Schmid, A. (2004) 'Frameworks for conceptualising terrorism', *Terrorism and Political Violence*, 16:2: 197–221.

Sea Shepherd (2017) 'Who we are'. *Sea Shepherd*, www.seashepherdglobal.org/who-we-are/.

Shantz, J. (2002) 'Green syndicalism: an alternative red-green vision', *Environmental Politics* 11.4, 21–41.

Singer, P. (2011) *Practical Ethics*, Third Edition. Cambridge: Cambridge University Press.

Sprouse, M. (Ed.) (1992) *Sabotage in the American Workplace*. Edinburgh: AK.

Starhawk, (2005) 'Diary of a compost toilet queen', in D. Harvie, K. Milburn, B. Trott and D. Watts, eds, *Shut Them Down! The G8, Gleneagles 2055 and the Movement of Movements*. Leeds, Brooklyn: Dissent! and Autonomedia.

START (National Consortium for the Study of Terrorism and Assorted Responses to Terrorism) (2015). *American Deaths in Terrorist Attacks: Fact Sheet*, www.start.umd.edu/pubs/START_AmericanTerrorismDeaths_FactSheet_Oct2015.pdf.

Stewart, K. (2015) We've beaten fracking's more evil twin'. *38 Degrees*, 8 October, https://home.38degrees.org.uk/2015/10/08/weve-beaten-frackings-more-evil-twin/.

Taylor, M. (2004) 'Protester released after eight months in Greek jail', *The Guardian* 14 February, www.theguardian.com/uk/2004/feb/14/globalisation.world.

Trapese Collective (2007) *Do It Yourself: A Handbook for Changing our World*. London: Pluto.

Trujillo, H. (2005) 'The radical environmentalist movement', in B.A. Jackson, J.C. Baker, K. Cragin, J. Parachini, H.R. Trujillo, P. Chalk, eds, *Aptitude for Destruction: Case Studies of Organizational Learning in Five Terrorist Groups* Volume 2, 141–75. Santa Monica: RAND.

Van der Zee, B. (2011) 'Climate camp disbanded', *The Guardian* 2 March, www.theguardian.com/environment/2011/mar/02/climate-camp-disbanded.

Wainright, W. (2006) 'In the shadow of Drax, not so much a fight as a festival', *The Guardian* 1 September, www.theguardian.com/environment/2006/sep/01/energy.activists.

Walsh, B. (2015) 'The surprisingly large energy footprint of the digital economy', *Time Magazine*, 14 August.

Watson, P. (2008) 'Sea Shepherd and Greenpeace – an unfortunate conflict', *Sea Shepherd*, 31 January, www.seashepherd.org.uk/news-and-commentary/commentary/sea-shepherd-and-greenpeace-an-unfortunate-conflict.html.

Weekes, K. (2011) *The Problem with Work*. London: Duke University Press.

Welsh, I. (2007) 'In defence of civilisation: terrorism and environmental politics in the 21st century', *Environmental Politics* 16:2, 356–75.

WHO (World Health Organization) (2015) 'Road traffic deaths and proportion of road users by country/area', www.who.int/violence_injury_prevention/road_safety_status/2015/TableA2.pdf?ua=1.

Wilkin, P. (2016) *Hungary's Crisis of Democracy: The Roads to Serfdom*. London: Lexington.

Williams, E., Kahhat, R., Allenby, B., Kavazanjian, E., Kim, J. and Xu, M. (2008) 'Environmental, social, and economic implications of global reuse and recycling of personal computers', *Environmental Science & Technology* 42 (17): 6446–54.

10
CONCLUSION
Integration without reduction

10.1 Coexistence at every scale

In this final chapter, we will attempt to articulate the book's arguments and themes in terms of some values and virtues that have emerged as central to environmental behavioural change.

Chapters 2, 3 and 4 survey the variety of value systems that have evolved regarding environmental questions. This exploration reveals distinct viewpoints at particular times and in specific cultural contexts. The variety of views and behaviours has been shaped by diverse human experiences: varied cultural contexts, accumulating knowledge about the natural world, growing human powers and periodic awareness of undesirable outcomes.

Three points are worth emphasising here. First, there has been a long-standing and continuing dialogue about notions of connectedness or community. Most challenges to conventional thought (and ethical norms) were triggered by confrontations. Europeans exploring Africa and the New World encountered new peoples, new species and new resources (and sometimes understood them as the same thing). Theological guidance proved difficult to adapt to these new circumstances, and viewpoints and consequent actions were diverse. Close association with unfamiliar environments also encouraged close examination of how they functioned. Careful observers such as Albert Schweitzer in Gabon, Aldo Leopold in wilderness regions of the American southwest, and marine biologists trying to understand the near-loss of species as a result of the whaling and cod-fishing industries, generally concluded that human actions need to be constrained in favour of less-powerful life forms.

Second, such questions have been closely allied with recognitions of harm. A sense of empathy and compassion for suffering is a common factor in motivating questions of community. Identifying harm and reasons to oppose it have motivated ethicists towards wider notions of kinship.

Third, the themes of community and harm have mutated in specific contexts. There have been distinct social and cultural niches that preserve or challenge particular modes of thought and lifestyle. Questions of human equality and human suffering, for example, have been raised in eighteenth-century slave-trade debates, nineteenth-century feminism, twentieth-century social segregation and twenty-first-century consideration of issues as distinct as national immigration policies and transgender equality. Each has been channelled by a combination of attitudinal transformations, media attention, public protests, legislative changes and economic accommodations.

In recent decades, such concerns have been extended episodically to non-humans and their environments through the activities of conservation groups, humane societies, anti-pollution campaigns, animal rights activists, and so on. Contemporary environmental concerns are often sharpened by specific threats to the welfare of other life forms, such as, for example, the plight of polar bears in the rapidly changing Arctic environment, or of mountain gorillas facing encroaching human activities. The harpooning of a killer whale that survived briefly in captivity (Moby Doll) transformed public perceptions of the species. In such circumstances, the biocentric sentiments described by Albert Schweitzer may bolster our commitments to more abstract causes such as actions to protect endangered species or to counteract climate change. These nevertheless represent the minority of cases. Most human activities continue to put people first and certain favoured species above wider concerns. In Britain, for instance, the definition of a Site of Special Scientific Interest (SSSI) is often required to legally protect environments that might otherwise be dedicated to providing economic benefits. Anthropocentric values confront biocentrism and ecocentrism regularly in the courts and in popular media.

These perspectives raise awareness of the interconnection and interdependence of species, but scarcely hint at the complexity of ecosystems and climate systems. Modern scientific research has been essential in revealing these deeper connections and in motivating greater caution in human behaviours. Ecology, earth satellites, atmospheric chemistry and climate simulations have merged scientific knowledge with ethical sensibilities in modern biospheric ethics.

Readers of this book have access to a perspective unavailable to previous generations. At several levels, this contemporary perspective illustrates co-existence. Biocentrism calls attention to the fact that as human beings we share our environments with other beings that have value in themselves. Ecocentrism provides scientific evidence for this mutual interdependence of life forms and of the non-animate components that sustain them. And more recent biospheric perspectives extend these symbiotic links to the global scale. Awareness of coexistence provides reasons for altering modern human behaviours: those other elements of our environments may be identified as worthy in themselves; recognised as 'like us'; or seen as important to human prospering or survival.

These living systems can also be recognised to have similarities with human-made systems. In the modern world, economics and technological systems are complex and mutually dependent. Insights have developed over the past few decades about how such entwined systems carry considerable momentum and restrict transitions to other ways of life.

A final dimension of co-existence concerns the systems of values themselves. A crude evolutionary analogy can be suggested. Environmental value systems co-exist and compete in modern societies, finding expression in stable niches. Thus far, environmental ethics provides heterogeneous solutions that suit particular contexts.

Common to modern environmentalisms, however, is the notion of integrity. Ecologists highlight the need to understand ecosystems 'in the round', as a whole rather than as discrete parts. Deep and social ecologies emphasise a holistic view of environmental issues that transcends disciplines. A principled approach, basing scientific, political, behavioural and economic actions on ethical foundations, offers a consistent method for tackling global environmental issues.

10.2 Virtues and empowerment

If climate change is a wicked problem, the temptation is to treat it as a tame one. For example, it has been argued that understanding it in terms of the tragedy of the commons or prisoner's dilemma (see Chapter 5) is an inaccurate frame that fails to do justice to climate change's wicked nature. This form of criticism parallels the book's cautionary attitude towards utilitarian and deontological ethics. Exclusive reference to these moral theories is to impose a false order on something inherently complex and slippery. Practice theories and virtue ethics, on the other hand, are designed to accommodate the contextualised and multifaceted nature of our moral lives.

Two broad notions of social practice have been referred to in this book:

1. Alasdair MacIntyre's more limited definition that views practices as activities that are complex and challenging enough to purposefully engage the individual with an ever-developing set of knowledge and skills, and
2. approaches, often from within sociology, in which all aspects of human existence – from daily routine to the enacting of demanding professional skills – are seen as practices.

Rather than viewing the rational autonomous decision-making individual as the focus of analysis, both share a commitment to human activity as best understood in terms of socio-historically situated activities that shape our knowledge and values. From MacIntyre we take practices to be central to the idea of a purposeful and therefore flourishing human existence, and from sociological theorists can be garnered an appreciation that the majority of what we do in our lives – including most of our environmentally relevant behaviours – is habitual. Habits are maintained by factors such as social norms, competences and physical infrastrucure that are external to what is traditionally viewed as the self.

The inadequacy of the information deficit model of behaviour change shows that something is amiss with certain – perhaps commonsensical – assumptions about human functioning. In part, this is rectified by dual process theories, but the social, skills-based, everyday/routine, and material circumstances of behaviours must all be reckoned with if we are to gain a more complete understanding of how people operate in the world. While recognising that not all aspects of the self and of behaviour are explained in terms of practices, it can be argued that they provide important perspectives for making sense of everyday human existence.

Humans are in the world, but also have transcendent powers of reason and imagination – albeit ones that are intermittent and unreliable. Accounts of practice theory that allow for a degree of compatibility with psychological accounts of the self – for example, ones that acknowledge the significant potential of reflective (System 2) thinking for influencing the direction of an individual life – provide us with a suitably well-informed and multi-dimensional account of human identity and behaviour.

Individual virtues are never finally defined and, as we have seen, they are endlessly intertwined. The exploration of a virtue should be transparently understood as a portal to the rich and diverse nature of the human condition: motivations, emotions, rationality, culture (practices, social norms, values), biology, and ontological fundamentals such as death and contingency. Chapter 5 concluded with a briefly articulated list of five important environmental behaviour change virtues: humility, resilience, taking responsibility, virtues of cooperation, and creative and imaginative thinking. Here we add further detail to these, making explicit their links to the book as a whole.

Humility and tolerating uncertainty

Climate change is unengaging because of its perceived spacial or temporal distance, and unpalatable because of the contradictions in our values and lifestyles that it exposes. Its uncertain and changing physical and political implications also make it impossible to fully cognitively digest, so that along with struggling to gain and maintain the attention of System 1, it leaves System 2 unsatisfied as well. Climate change is complex, uncanny and frustrating. Human beings have a strong dislike of feeling helpless and out of control, and climate change is a symbol for just that.

At this juncture, two virtues become salient: humility and tolerance of uncertainty. Usually, humility in environmental ethics refers to recognition of our dependence upon nature, our smallness, and the extraordinary complexity and beauty of the natural world. Here though we have in mind an epistemological humility, along with the virtue of being able to accept uncertainty. Even though our understanding of the global human problem of climate change is necessarily limited, we must nevertheless act on the basis of the knowledge we have and in the ways in which we are able.

Changes need to emerge from (or at least have a strong connection with) existing practices, and thus virtues must as well. Respect for nature and wonder at nature cannot be grafted on, but fortunately, this is not necessary because they already exist. When David Attenborough or Brian Cox inspire TV audiences, they are not giving them something they did not have before, but awakening frames of mind and attendant virtues that have been marginalised and suppressed.

Moreover, these frames of mind represent pinnacles of human happiness. It is now well recognised (in virtue theory and elsewhere) that active and skilled engagement with challenging activities is fundamental to human happiness. Through scientific and leisure pursuits, nature has enormous potential as a source of such engagement. Encouraging people into nature in the first place is the harder task, and this is where not just the System 1 persuasion represented by Attenborough's social powers become relevant, but forms of legislation as well (for example, a requirement for outdoor learning in schools). Once this initial step is achieved, we can more easily imagine the resulting energy and self-relevance spilling over into the establishment of broader values in a way that installing smart meters will not.

In this respect, Schwartz's model (see Chapter 6) is the one we would endorse. It maps out possibilities of human concern, recognising that the vast majority of us can be more or less 'self-transcendent' or more or less 'self-enhancing'. The 'more or less' will be partially determined by individual differences linked to innate temperament and early experiences, but also significantly determined by the social and material structures of a human life: daily routines, social dynamics, competences and infrastructure. Virtues – their meaning and expression – are located within this broad framework.

Resilience

Humility – whether instilled by exposure to nature and ecological learning or by some other means – ought to help us be more resilient in the face of the scale of contemporary environmental crises. Our expectations of understanding and control should be more realistic, making us less prone to seeking escape from these problems through psychological denial. Resilience is also needed because we will often, initially at least, need to work hard to resist temptations and to successfully break environmentally unfriendly habits. To the extent that these behaviours impact on the people around us, or that we choose to be environmental activists, we will also need to be resilient in the face of confused or uncooperative friends and colleagues, and in the face of slow social progress.

Taking responsibility

Of the negative emotions associated with global environmental issues (including fear and guilt), a sense of helplessness is the most damaging. Helplessness can be the result of the knowledge, skills and resources needed to live a low-carbon lifestyle, but it is also directly linked to the collective nature of solutions to problems like climate change.

When donating to charities that save lives through relieving poverty it can feel like a drop in the ocean, but in these cases our help does at least make a meaningful difference, if only a small one. For this reason, an individual, even if they see themselves as part of a tiny minority, should continue to be motivated to contribute. Unfortunately, though, this argument will not work for attempts to combat climate change. Here our efforts will make no difference whatsoever unless enough others do the same, and evidence suggests that significant sections of the public see the problem in this way. Often then, in terms of environmental behaviours, taking responsibility means hoping others will do the same, and the need to encourage others to do the same becomes all the more relevant.

Virtues of cooperation

For many who are willing to change behaviours in the face of collective problems of this sort, evidence of appropriate actions being taken by national and global bodies will be necessary to sustain their motivation. The typically group-based nature of direct action also makes a difference to real and perceived efficacy and, as discussed in Chapter 9, there are a range of positive side-effects to do with friendship, bonding, and a sense of common purpose that often accompany collective action.

The organisation of effective group working is not easy to get right, but possession of a number of what might be called 'virtues of cooperation' will increase the likelihood of success. These include attitudes and abilities relating to genuine inclusiveness, facilitating constructive discussions, and the courage and will to confront difficult people. As indicated (see Chapter 2), epistemic virtues – especially those associated with our handling of complex problems involving multiple stakeholders and that lack optimal solutions – are also important. Often overlooked in the literature on environmental virtue ethics is this set of virtues, but it has profound importance for tackling our climate crisis.

Creative and imaginative thinking

Practices can and, of course, do change, but success in this respect is difficult to predict. What is clear is that multiple events and interventions are usually required for change to happen, and this is almost certainly the case with many of those practices relating to our global environmental crises. This book has explained and analysed a range of these, and some must inevitably be top-down and feel like sacrifices. However, all the time that these are seen to be towards a common good that is attainable – and therefore clearly and consistently supported by national and international institutions – the evidence is that enough people across the globe will support them.

However, to date, and even including the 2016 Paris Climate Agreement, these efforts have not been enough. Continued grassroots pressure must be maintained, and here is where the virtue of creative and imaginative thinking (or an openness to the creative and imaginative thinking of others) is constantly required. On the one hand, this applies to new ways of framing and forming messages and, on the other, it applies to longer-term transitions towards sustainable forms of life.

A defining and distinctive feature of virtue theory is that ethical values are contextualised among the broad set of motivations that define a typical human life. If acting in the right way does not feel like an obligation we are more likely to do it, but as things stand pro-environmental behaviours tend to not only feel like obligations, they are ones that can easily be rationalised away. Personal integration is needed, and thus both sustainable lifestyles and the communicative and transformative actions taken to reach these need to sometimes be sources of pleasure, and always sources of meaning. Meaning comes from a sense of purpose and connectedness with the world, and thus an accurate and effective understanding of environmental behavioural change must acknowledge not just its duty-based, but also its historical, personal, cultural, economic and political dimensions. A social practice-based virtue ethics can provide this integrative ethical framework.

10.3 Promoting economic and political change

The different ethical traditions that inform and structure environmental debates have developed out of historical events and social conflicts. The wickedness of environmental problems, which are bound up in the intersections of historical and social conflict, technological change and economic struggles, requires humility in theoretical and practical responses. This book's anti-reductivism supports the idea that there are multiple causes and scales for interpreting these problems and so there is no supreme strategy or methodology. Various disciplinary approaches have been addressed (though not all can be covered adequately) from ecology, history, politics, sociology, psychology, economics and philosophy (especially ethics).

Practice-based virtue theory is consistent with this interdisciplinary method. It integrates many of these different theoretical approaches, whilst – through humility – also recognising its limits and the importance of insights from other perspectives. It also identifies the possibility of transcendence, through which new methods can arise that supersede our current understanding. Virtue theory also incorporates important features of deontology and utilitarianism without being reduced to either. In addition, virtue theory also has the advantage of being adaptive to social activities, privileging some virtues above others or generating new ones depending on the activity and its historical and geographical location.

Because of this book's core concern with rejecting reductivism it supports multiple responses to wicked environmental problems like climate change. It thus highlights and celebrates forms of micropolitics that are consistent with green virtues. It is similarly critical of economic and political programmes based on singular strategies (such as absolute free markets or constitutionalism), unique and supreme actors (for instance entrepreneurs, geo-engineers or national citizens) and monopolising power (like states or corporations). This is not to completely rule out engaging with state power through the constitutional process or offering economic incentives to achieve environmental goals, but suggests that such tactics can only be provisional and should be supplanted by more ethical responses where possible.

The book discusses a large spectrum of possibilities for making ecologically-sensitive change. In Chapters 7 and 8 it documents major features of the economic and political world that restrains environmentally responsible thinking and action. Economic considerations that are predicated on the supremacy of exchange value are inevitably going to limit critical thinking about, and social activities based on, other values (like intrinsic ecological goods). Similarly, constitutional methods are ultimately based on the security of the state and garnering votes sufficient to control the legislature and executive. Also discussed are ways to critically engage with hierarchical institutions to limit these constraints, such as participation in electoral activity. It also raises the possibility of breaking with dominant economic and political institutions completely and pursuing other forms of social organisation, and of economic production and distribution.

Thus, the tendency has been to favour grassroots *demoi*-cratic methods (see Chapter 9) over engagement in hierarchical economic and political structures. Communal practices that are responsive to their environment and then spill over into other socially and environmentally virtuous activities are preferred over policy intervention and executive action. These diverse mutual enterprises tend to be more accessible, empowering and immediate for individuals and thus more satisfying and transformative to participants and their wider social networks.

The dual impulses of complacency and despair in the face of ecological crises have been covered in the book. However, apparently overwhelming obstacles have been overcome before. Dramatic improvements were achieved in political and civil equality resulting from diverse collective action carried out by virtuous individuals and inspired groups capable of motivating others. What were once fringe ecological concerns are influencing social activities as never before. Change is on its way: the question for us all is how will we most positively influence it?

APPENDIX

Reflections on teaching

The perspectives and content of this book have evolved over a number of years and via courses taught separately and in combination by the three authors. Our initial undergraduate liberal arts students were succeeded by Masters-level students with first degrees – and often employment – in the environmental sciences, humanities, engineering and social sciences. The original cohorts of British students were later joined by international counterparts from five continents. In the most recent implementations, the teaching has extended to distant campuses (notably University of Nankai, China) and supported by online components and resources.

This diverse student population has been valuable in shaping the analytical and pedagogical approaches adopted in the courses and book. Unlike teaching an established subject to a disciplinary audience, the subjects of environmental ethics and behavioural change are challenged by rapidly evolving scientific knowledge, analytical perspectives and cultural values. The varied backgrounds and goals of our students consequently have shaped how we motivate, explore and defend our topic coverage.

Students' initial assumptions and expectations are markedly different and encourage lively classes. Our experiences suggest that ethical exploration and application demand personal engagement and dialogue in both individual and group settings. Teaching methods have ranged from traditional lectures (sometimes via video-link or recorded for online viewing) to small-group discussions and one-to-one online or face-to-face dialogue. Our preferred format is assigned reading from this book and online questions for reflection, followed by seminar discussions.

The unfamiliarity of many students to ethical questions can be unsettling and intimidating for their class contributions. Language proficiency, deference to authority or lack of confidence in articulate verbal argumentation can also be inhibiting in some cultural contexts. We have found that online open-ended questions early in the course, followed by timely online individual feedback from course leaders, can help uncertain students gain confidence and explore their moral compass. For example:

- Give an example of an ethical concern that may arise in the practice of environmental management, either as a professional (engineer, manager, communicator) or as a citizen.
- Which environments could be used most freely (i.e., without significant ethical concerns) as resources by humans? Give an example, and explain why they are acceptable. Could other planets, for instance, be such an environment?
- Are there any potential drawbacks – ethical, social, scientific or otherwise – of the following technological fixes? Explain.
    - Production of genetically-engineered food supplements for an impoverished community blighted by annual crop failures and vitamin deficiency.
    - Siting of unshielded radiation sources in rainforests to prevent illegal logging operations.

Lengthier and more complex out-of-class exercises can be tackled by individuals, and picked up for in-class development by small groups of students. For example:

- Company X's deep-sea oil-storage tank is no longer required following the completion of a pipeline. Company X has two options for disposal: dismantling on-shore at huge expense and with a better-known degree of environmental damage, or deep-sea disposal, in which environmental harms are less well known and potentially far more hazardous. The first option is ten times more expensive than the first, running into tens of millions of pounds. If the more expensive first option is preferred, the company would ask for the additional costs to come from government expenditure. In order to demonstrate your understanding of ethical theory, discuss how
    - a utilitarian,
    - a deontologist, and
    - a virtue ethicist
    - might go about assessing this case; e.g., suggest what questions they would ask and how they might justify one or both options.

The varied environments and practices experienced by our students are a fertile resource for class discussions. Sharing their distinct national or disciplinary worldviews and moral assumptions early in the course builds their confidence as independent contributors to class explorations. This can range from the personal (e.g., comparing the qualities of preferred pets) to international (e.g., who should pay for environmental remediation of the seas).

These relatively brief reflections, problem-solving exercises and group interactions are underpinned by forms of assessment that seek to monitor and extend competences. A traditional essay allows students to carefully analyse the implications of, for example, an ethical framework, psychological approach or political strategy to an environmental problem. Alternatively, a report to an imagined organisation (e.g., an engineering firm, heritage organisation, legislative body or activist group) serves to highlight pragmatic action, encouraging students to evaluate and justify a selection of methods to achieve an environmental goal for a particular audience.

Problem-Based Learning

These multiple aims are embedded in a Problem-Based Learning (PBL) task towards the end of the teaching term. Such activities encourage students to learn independently and via peer-tutoring to apply theory to novel situations. As environmental issues are typically both unexpected and have contentious solutions, they are ideal topics for this kind of learning-on-the-fly.

The 'mechanics' of the PBL involve:

- Some 3–4 weeks out-of-class time, in parallel with class work.
- Small groups consisting of some 3–5 contributors to ensure individual engagement with the problem, but not necessarily a division of labour into isolated parts.
- Some 3–5 groups, each tasked with adopting distinct ethical values (e.g., anthropocentric, ecocentric or 'deep green').
- An end-of-project presentation involving all group members to the full class, followed by questions.

Group members are typically selected by the class leaders to require role-playing of challenging positions, in order to encourage understanding of conflicting environmental perspectives.

This PBL task represents a small portion of the course grade. The low weighting is intended to avoid disadvantaging students who are unfamiliar with either group work or public presentations. It is nevertheless a feature of our course as it provides skills essential to professionals involved with environmental change.

The selected PBL tasks typically change year by year, and are chosen to be issues not yet resolved by policy-makers or by public consensus. Similarly, their scope should include a local or regional issue having global significance.

The topics typically are amenable to local or regional data-gathering of secondary sources (e.g., journal, newspaper and blog accounts, but no archival research, surveys or interviews, which require university ethical approval).

In past years candidate topics have included:

- Effective ethical arguments for encouraging carbon management by businesses.
- A low-carbon aviation strategy.

- Dumping disused oil platforms at sea.
- Windfarms for remote Scottish islands.
- Hydraulic fracturing ('fracking') for gas recovery in Scotland.

The briefing for the fifth topic was as follows:

Task

Your team are a sub-committee of a Scottish-based action group [*ethical orientation to be assigned to each group separately*] who have been asked to make recommendations on the group's position with respect to lifting of the moratorium on commercial fracking (hydraulic fracturing) in Scotland.

Your task is to outline and justify your organisation's **policy** and **strategy** in terms of:

- Whether, in principle, fracking should be supported or not.
- If you are pro-fracking in principle, relevant criteria for determining whether, in specific cases, fracking should be supported or not.
- The broad communication strategy your organisation should employ in order to get your message across to relevant stakeholders in the fracking debate. Importantly, this strategy must itself be shown to be consistent with the ethical orientation of your organisation.

The case you make will relate directly to the issue of commercial fracking in Scotland, but you can of course draw on examples from other countries to provide inspiration and support for your arguments, and your arguments will themselves be generalisable beyond the Scottish context.

Group presentation

The group presentation will require you to collaborate with the other members of your group (group membership will be assigned by the course convenors) and then to present your findings to the lecturers during the final class. The members need to work together to create a cohesive and well-rehearsed presentation that does justice to your efforts and that will convince the audience in question.

Each group presentation should be between 15 and 20 minutes long, and based on the contributions of the entire group. All members of the group should speak, but not everyone needs to speak for an equal length of time. No PowerPoint or other energy-consuming presentation media are required, but neither are they discouraged.

Please note that there is no need to explain the basic process of fracking at the start of your presentation. It is assumed your audience knows what this is, and you should only make reference to its technicalities where these become relevant to explaining your ethical position on the issue, and to how you will communicate this to relevant stakeholders.

Summary

This Appendix illustrates how the perspectives, positions and principles of this book have been informed by the course topics and wider discussions between the authors and our students. The book itself can serve as a unitary source for learners and teachers elsewhere, and for practitioners and activists inside and outside of academia. Our aim is to open up some of our approaches to critical evaluation from others, which can only help assist the education, dialogue and action on environmental change.

INDEX

38 Degrees 251-2

Abbey, Edward 238
abolition movement 58, 87, 109
acid rain 86
act utilitarianism 21; *see also* utilitarianism
action, direct *see* direct action
action, symbolic *see* symbolic action
activism 139, 194-, 204, 218-20, 225, 227-8, 241, 249-54
activists i, ix, 13, 27, 165, 167, 183, 191, 195, 213, 219, 224, 228, 232, 236, 238-41, 246, 249, 251, 254, 256n1.
advertisements 46n2, 99n5, 103, 107-8, 124, 153, 157, 160-1, 172, 216-7, 244, 250, 252
aesthetics 2, 33, 56, 69, 78, 86, 235
Africa 57, 59, 87, 93, 229n2, 261
agency 14, 19, 20, 24-4, 35, 119, 159, 225, 255; *see also* activist, autonomy, citizen, consumer, practitioner *and* voter
The Age of Stupid 109, 129
agenda setting 108
agents, non-virtuous 191-4
agriculture 5, 57, 58, 67, 70, 73n5, 236, 249
Akrasia 160
Alaska 72
Alberta 146n16
ALF: See Animal Liberation Front
algorithm, ethical: *see* hedonic calculus
allotments 11, 22, 92, 184, 200, 205
Althusser, Louis 180

America, Latin 57, 58, 107, 199
American Civil War 5
Amoco Cadiz oil spill 7
anarchism 199, 201n1, 214, 226, 233; anarchism, green *see* eco-anarchism
anarchist geographers 199
anarcho-capitalism *see* propertarianism
anarcho-primitivism 89, 199
androcentrism 87
Animal Aid 215
Animal Liberation Front (ALF) 248
animal liberation movement 64-5, 248
animal rights 14, 23, 34, 56-7, 75, 145
animal rights movement 14, 56, 262
animal protection organisations 62-4
animals; domesticated 52, 62, 63, 68; livestock 23 50, 68; marine 8, 42, 51-2, 53, 54, 55, 63, 72, 73n2, 80, 237, 262; wildlife; 5, 22, 42, 50, 51, 52, 53, 55, 60, 62, 64, 65, 67-8, 70-3, 76, 83, 99n1, 110, 112, 262 working 3, 62
Anscombe, G. E. M. 37-8
anthropocentrism *see* ethics, anthropocentric
anthropogenic climate change 5, 8, 98, 112, 114, 115, 249
anti-fracking campaigns 236, 239, 252
anti-roads protests 225, 236, 239
anti-vivisection movement 53, 58, 64, 108
appliances, energy-saving 70, 78
Apollo programme 109
Apprentice, The 179
aquariums 51

Index

aquifers 36, 81
Arctic 262
argument 107-8
Aristotelianism *see* virtue theory
Aristotle 37-42
arrogance 16, 71, 241
Asia 23, 23, 63, 107, 128, 185, 223, 269
Atlantic slave trade 57-8, 87, 262
atmosphere 76, 89, 90, 98, 252
Attenborough, David 139, 265
audience 8, 13, 103, 108, 244, 271-2
Audubon Society 70
Aum Shinrikyo 248
Australia 115, 139, 204, 236, 238, 251, 256n2
Australian Builders and Labourers Federation (BLF) 238
Austria 227
autarky 185
authority *see* power
autonomism *see* Marxism, heterodox (autonomism)
autonomy x, 9, 17-18, 20-1, 25-33, 36, 45, 54, 81, 94, 99, 106, 159-61, 176n, 183, 185-6, 190, 221, 242, 249, 254-5
autovalorisation 233, 238, 242
Avazz 251

Bakan, Joel 181, 188, 189, 192-4, 197-9, 204, 215
Bari, Judi 238, 248, 256n6
Beauvoir, Simone de 162
Beeson, Mark 223
'behaviour change agenda' 153
behavioural change, barriers 114
behavioural change, defined 10-11
Behavioural Insight Team 10, 153, 163
'behavioural welfarism' 156
behaviourism 10
beneficence 40, 43, 54, 166, 188, 190
benevolence *see* beneficence
Bentham, Jeremy 19-21, 55
Berlin, Isaiah 31
Bevan, David 190
Bilderberg Group 217
biocentrism, popular 62-3
biocentrism, radical 64-5
bioconcentration 71
biodiversity 3, 118
biosphere 5, 76, 83-4
biotic community: *see* community, biotic
biotic pyramid 81
Blackledge, Paul 38, 41, 241
Blackstone, William T. 34

Body Shopbeauty 4, 55, 69, 264
Bookchin, Murray 85-9, 93, 95, 97, 99n5, 132, 146n15, 183, 191, 199, 226-7, 254
boomerang effect 135-6
boycott 237-8
BP *see* British Petroleum (BP)
Brand, Stewart 97
Brave New World 97
Brazil 57, 58, 107
Brent Spar 111
Britain 7, 11, 57-8, 62, 84, 93, 227, 262, 269; *see also* UK
British National Social Marketing Centre (BNSMC) 154
British Petroleum (BP) 111, 244-6; *see also Deepwater Horizon* oil spill
Brittany 72
Buchholz, Rogene 190
Buen Vivir 199-200
Burns, Eugene 97
businesses ix, 55, 73, 75, 103, 111, 179- 201, 215, 217, 237, 271; *see also* corporations

California 67, 87, 107, 134, 168, 227
Cambridge Carbon Footprint 139
campaigning 111, 251-2
Campbell, Joseph 110
Canada 51, 204
canyons 35, 67
capitalism 109, 181-4, 191, 194, 199, 201n2, 225-6, 233-4, 253; *see also* capital, circuit of *and* value, exchange
captive animals 72-3, 73n2
carbon based society 16, 25-7, 36, 114, 117, 118, 139, 155, 170, 174, 192, 222, 224, 236, 243, 252, 265, 271
carbon capture 90, 98-9, 99n1
Carbon Conversations 139
carbon trading 90, 155, 196-7, 206, 220
Carlyle, Thomas 50
cars 16, 33, 94, 98, 122, 170, 253
Carson, Rachel 70-1, 77, 79, 93, 220
Cato Institute 183, 186
CFCs: *see* chlorofluorocarbons
character 15, 19, 28, 37-41, 43, 54
charisma 113, 139
Chatterton, Paul 254
Chavez, Hugo 227
Chernobyl nuclear accident 72
Chicago School 186, 191
China 23, 128, 185, 223, 269
Chinese Animal Protection Network 63
Chomsky, Noam 216

chlorofluorocarbons (CFCs) 90, 222
choice-editing 173, 189, 193, 220-2
Cialdini, Robert 106, 125, 133-5, 152, 168-9
circuit of capital 181-3, 200, 233
citizens i, ix, 7, 8, 12, 15-16, 26, 44, 51, 69, 80, 85, 109, 135, 145, 162-4, 168, 173, 193, 194, 197, 207, 209, 214-6, 225, 229n2, 235-6, 230-41, 249, 251, 255, 267, 270
citizens, corporate 181, 194-5
civil disobedience 10, 109, 139, 224, 234-6, 246
civilisation 59, 89
Clark, John P. 254-5
Clark, Stephen 68
clean-up campaigns 36, 72, 78, 86
Cleaver, Harry 181, 233
Climate Camps 236, 252
climate change i, ix, 5, 8, 18-19, 26-7, 35-6, 41, 45, 96-8, 99n2, 102, 104, 106, 109-10, 112-33, 138-9, 145, 146n6, 155-6, 161, 165, 168, 170, 173-4, 198, 206, 214-5, 220, 222, 242, 249, 262-7
Climate Outreach 165
Clinton, Bill 208
Clinton, Hilary 110
coercion 23, 29, 136, 156, 158-60, 180-1, 184, 199, 205-7, 214-6, 223, 247, 249
co-existence 49, 69, 80, 89, 105, 262-3
cognitive dissonance 104-5, 127, 168-9
Cold War 129, 207, 223
collaboration 80, 88, 180, 241, 254, 272
collectivist frame 173-5
colonialism 28, 57-9, 249
commitment and consistency 134, 171
commodities 20, 90, 97, 181-3, 191, 195, 198, 242, 253
Common Cause 152, 164-8, 171, 173
communes: see community, intentional
communication 102-3
Communist parties 222-3
Communist Party, China 223
communitarianism 88-9
communities ix, x, 2, 43, 48, 72, 77-9, 102-3, 110, 119, 132, 164, 168, 190-1, 219, 226, 241, 255, 270
community activities x, 7-8, 10-11, 23, 36, 89, 92, 113, 121, 126, 136, 139, 146n14, 184, 194-5, 199-200, 205, 238, 254
community, biotic 57, 61, 66, 68-9, 72, 83, 87

community identity 4, 12-13, 15-16, 18, 75, 88-90, 92, 134, 172-4, 243, 261-2
community, intentional 10, 88, 195, 253-4
commuters 142, 192
compassion 4
competences 11
confederation 88-9
confidence 7, 12, 70, 78, 89, 90, 98, 99, 128-9, 269, 270
confirmation bias 113, 116, 129
Confucianism 37
consciousness-raising 244
consensus 115
consequentialism 3, 13, 19-20, 26-8, 33, 36, 45, 54-5, 66, 75, 84, 98, 171, 234, 236, 242, 248-9, 255
conservation 4, 92, 139, 227, 238, 262
Conservation Commission 68
conservatism 38, 41, 110, 112, 123, 141, 167, 172, 214, 220, 224, 232, 242
Conservative Party 209-11, 219, 224
constitution 193, 204, 212-4, 267
constitutionalism x, 10-11, 58, 193, 199, 204-29, 232-4, 236-40, 242-3, 246, 252, 255, 267-8
consumer x, 6-7, 20, 25, 29, 78, 97, 99n5, 129, 137, 155, 160, 162, 172, 189, 194, 197-8, 221-2, 237, 245, 250, 252-3
consumer culture *see* consumerism
consumer products *see* commodities
consumer society *see* consumerism
consumerism 9, 20, 25, 70-1, 77, 86, 90, 109, 128, 172, 243-4, 253-4
consumption, ethical x, 193, 195, 197-8, 253
contrast effect 158
cooperation 8, 87, 89-90, 92, 121, 125-6, 145, 146n15, 196, 256, 264
corporocentricism 185, 187-9, 190, 194, 200
corporate citizenship 7, 181, 194-5
corporate social responsibility (CSR) 187-90, 194
Corporation, The (film) 181
corporations 6-7, 9, 18, 97, 99n4 and n5, 102, 128-9, 131, 135, 138, 179-201, 221, 225, 227, 245, 250-2, 255, 267
corporations and climate change denial 139
corporations and the democratic process 215-7, 220, 227-8
cost-benefit analysis 192-3
counterculture 94, 241
courage *see* virtues, courage
Cox, Brian 115, 265

Crane, Andrew 188, 194
creativity 145
Crisp, Roger 22
critical management theory 199
Crompton, Tom 165, 168, 172-3
cruelty 62-4, 108, 244
'Crying Indian' campaign 99n5, 176
Cuadrilla 239
culture 3, 8, 16, 37, 48, 53, 70, 73, 76, 80, 83, 86, 89, 94-5, 109-10, 112, 116, 121, 128, 132, 141-3, 145, 166, 223, 243, 264
cultural relativism 16
customers 7, 15, 18, 134, 143, 158, 183, 189-90, 195, 222, 237, 253

David and Goliath frame 111, 175
Davies, Nick 216
DDT 70-1, 220
Deep Ecology 5, 76, 79-86, 88, 90, 93
deep green ecology 183, 217, 271
Deepwater Horizon oil spill 72, 245
default bias 157
Demain 109, 111, 122
democracy 173, 186, 193, 206-22, 224-8, 240, 243
democracy, direct 88, 173, 251
democracy, liberal 186, 204, 212-3, 221, 224-5, 228, 243
democracy, participatory *see* democracy, direct
democratisation 207-8
demoi-cratic action 237, 240, 250, 268
denial, organised climate 10, 115-6, 138-9, 214, 215
denial, psychological 127-32
deontology x, 1, 13, 25, 27-35, 36-7, 40-45, 54, 75, 98, 106, 110, 122, 163, 171, 187, 196, 221, 236, 263, 267, 270
deontology, neo-Kantian 187
Department for Energy, Food and Rural Affairs (Defra, UK) 135, 139, 153-5
deserts 76
De-Shalit, Avner 240-1
Desjardins, Joseph 195
détournement 244
Devall, Bill 82
'developing' countries 99n6
DiCaprio, Leonardo 138
diet: *see* vegetarianism and veganism
direct action x,10, 58, 64, 71, 109, 111, 121, 139, 199, 213, 218, 220, 224-5, 228, 232-46, 248-50, 252, 255, 256n1, 266

dissent, political 194-5, 215, 235
diversity, biological 69, 80, 82, 92, 118
diversity, cultural 12, 40
diversity, political 222, 237-8
diversity, technological 95
Doherty, Brian 235, 240, 242-3
DNA 52, 183
Donaldson, Thomas 190
Dow Jones Business Index 195
Drengson, Alan 97
Driver, Julie 38
Dryzek, John 35
dual process theory 8, 105, 113
duck-rabbit illusion 112
dust bowl 70
duties 1, 5, 28-9, 32, 35, 37, 40, 54, 57-8, 75-6, 79, 88, 168, 174, 188-90, 193, 201n4, 267

Earth Day 71, 78, 86, 99n5, 235
Earth Liberation Front (ELF) 248
earthworms 52, 60, 71
eco-anarchism 226, 248
ecocentrism: *see* ethics, ecocentric
eco-communities 92
eco-fascism 85
eco-friendly products 78, 139
eco-socialism 233
EcoTeams 139
eco-terrorism 10, 246-50
ecology, deep: *see* Deep Ecology
ecology, science of 4
ecology, shallow: *see* Shallow Ecology
ecology, social: *see* Social Ecology
economics 3, 6, 55, 86, 90, 93, 99n4, 114, 153, 181, 186, 197, 262, 267
economists 12, 93
economy, market 11, 197 *see too* capitalism
ecosophy 81, 82
ecosystems 3-6, 8, 13, 18, 33, 43, 48, 55, 66, 68, 72-3, 76, 79-82, 86, 89, 95, 98, 106, 118, 138, 175, 206, 262, 263,
ecosystem services 99n1
Ecuador 107, 199
EDF (Électricité de France) 195
egalitarianism, biological 24, 26, 80, 94
egalitarianism, biospherical 80, 82, 84
egalitarianism, social 23-4, 26, 61, 79, 80, 83-4, 89, 92, 94, 235-6
electorate 204, 208, 211-9, 224, 226, 228
ELF: See Earth Liberation Front
elites 57, 98, 127, 206, 217, 254-5
elitism 173, 219, 223, 241
Ellul, Jacques 96

emotional engagement 120
empowerment 238-9, 263-6
enablers 139
enclosure (primitive accumulation) 196, 199, 237
endangered species *see* species, endangered
energy production 5, 139, 195
engagement 8
engineers 6-7, 12, 84, 95, 96, 98, 269-71
Enlightenment 1, 15, 21, 28, 41, 44, 52-3, 86-7, 102
entrepreneur 179, 182, 267
environment ix, 1, 2, 3-4, 10, 16, 34, 50, 69-70, 76, 87, 141, 196-7, 221, 236, 243, 247, 252
environmental communication 104, 109
environmentalism 5, 13, 77, 85, 97, 195-6, 220, 224, 263
environmentalists 9, 15-17, 25-6, 71-2, 99, 127, 139, 182, 187-8, 199, 214, 224, 240, 250
Ernst and Young 195
essentialism 42-3
ethics: anthropocentric x, 4, 13, 28, 42, 48, 49-51, 53-5, 84-7, 92-3,109, 175, 183, 185, 199, 206, 241, 251, 262, 271; applied 15, 17-9; biocentric x, 4, 13, 24, 56-62, 71-3, 75-6, 79, 83, 108, 183, 241, 262; biospheric 80, 82, 84 *see also* Deep Ecology *and* Social Ecology; consequentialist *see* consequentialism; corporocentric *see* corporocentricism; deontological *see* deontology; deep ecology *see* Deep Ecology; ecocentric 5; meta- *see* meta-ethics; neo-Aristotelian *see* virtue theory; normative 15, 17, 190; popular 55; professional ix, 2, 7-8, 12, 18, 42, 44, 80, 188, 263, 270-1; rights-based: *see* deontology; shallow ecology *see* Shallow Ecology' social ecology: *see* Social Ecology; utilitarian *see* utilitarianism; virtue *see* virtue theory *and* virtues
ethnocentrism 87
Eudaimonia 39-40, 42-3, 200
evolutionary psychology 120-1
executive 204, 208, 210-11, 213-7, 219, 222, 227-8, 268
expertise 7
externalities 90, 220, 233
extinctions i, ix, 3, 5, 8, 71-2, 107
Exxon Valdez oil spill 72, 87

faith 12
farms 6, 43, 52, 55, 61, 68, 70, 72, 73, 76, 81, 92, 93, 98, 118, 236, 244
FBI: See Federal Bureau of Investigation
fear 107, 115, 119-20, 122, 130-2, 248, 265
fecundity 20
Federal Bureau of Investigation (FBI) 248, 256n6
Federici, Silvia 233
feedback 157, 158, 270
feedback loops 84, 270
feminism 109, 262
feminist 38, 87, 214, 226, 254
financial incentives 139, 154, 164-6, 169, 192, 196
finite pool of worry 131
fisheries 8, 69, 107, 249
fishermen 55, 68, 237
fluorocarbons 86
forestry 54, 66, 67. 197
forests 21, 32, 67, 68, 86, 87, 99n1, 108-9, 165, 197, 236, 238, 284
fossil fuels 5, 243
fox hunting 41, 50
fracking: *see* hydraulic fracturing
framing 7, 103, 108-114, 119
France 71, 72
Franklin, Benjamin 38
free market x, 89, 90, 124, 183, 191, 195-6, 222, 267; *see also* capitalism *and* value, exchange
freedom 4, 25 28-9, 31-3, 37, 52, 68, 85, 90, 213-5, 254; *see also* autonomy *and* rights; economic *see* rights, property; negative *see* rights, negative; positive *see* rights, positive
freedom of assembly *see* freedom of association
freedom of association 204, 213, 222, 227
freedom of speech, 26, 204, 213, 216-7 , 227
Freeman, R. Edward 189-90
French, John and Raven, Bertrand *see* social power
Friedman, Milton 181, 186-200, 204, 215
Friends of the Earth 71, 92, 136
frugality 78
fur trading 54, 72
future generations 5, 15, 126

G8 meetings 91, 246
Gabon 261
Gaia theory 84, 87

Gaian movements: *see* Green movements
Gandhi, Mohandas 38, 93, 235
Gasland 111
Gavin, Neil 250-1
geo-engineering x, 98, 249, 267
gender 4, 13, 23, 37, 80, 88, 187, 209, 219, 262
genetic engineering 12, 236, 270
Germany 208, 211-3, 222, 227
GetUp! 251
geysers 67
GHG: *see* greenhouse gases
Giddens, Anthony 128, 220-2, 224-5
Gila Wilderness Area 67
Gilley, Bruce 223
Global Action Plan 139
global contexts 145
global warming: *see* climate change
globalisation 90-92
goals, environmental 11, 15, 25, 27, 33, 88, 99, 102, 152, 160, 180, 186-9, 193, 215, 218, 223, 235-7, 242, 250, 268 *see too* targets, environmental
Google 201n3, 251,
Gore, Al 38, 109-10, 138, 145
government ix, 2, 9, 11, 25, 85, 94, 96, 102, 109, 116, 128-9, 131-2, 138, 144-5, 153, 159-64, 173, 185-90, 192-4, 199, 204-29, 243, 247-8, 255, 270
government, authoritarian/non-democratic 208, 222-4, 238; local 92, 135, 219, 227; devolved 113, 214, 252; national 10, 23, 67-8, 99n4, 116, 153-4, 185, 210-2, 220, 225, 227, 229n2, 243
Graeber, David 184, 240
Grand Canyon 35, 67
grassroots 139, 172, 266, 268
Great Chain of Being 49, 50, 53, 55, 57, 66
greatest good 55, 77; *see also* utilitarianism
greatest number 19, 55, 77; *see also* utilitarianism
Greedy, Lying Bastards 139
Greek philosophy 1, 49, 60, 73n1, 84, 105
Green Anarchist 248
green movements 10, 87, 92, 243, 248
Green parties 206, 208-11,213, 217-220, 226-8, 243; *Fundis* 217-9, 236; *Realos* 217-9, 23; local 226-7; national 210-11, 217, 219, 227, 243
Green, T. H. 32
greenhouse gases (GHG) 46, 90, 106, 155-6, 196, 198, 206, 222, 252

Greenpeace 71, 92, 111m 165, 215, 220, 237, 242, 243, 245-6, 256n1
greenwashing 99n7, 198, 226
group presentation 272
Grünen, Die see Green Party (Germany)
guerrilla gardening 199
guilt 107, 109, 115, 122, 128, 130-1, 136, 158, 164, 265
Gulf of Mexico 72, 245

Habits 140-4
Hannah, Daryl 139
Hardin, Garrett 124, 146n14
Hardt, Michael 184, 225-6
harm, 2, 4-7, 9-10, 12, 17-18, 21-2, 26-7, 31, 36, 40, 52-4, 60, 63-4, 71-2, 75-8, 84-5, 87, 94, 99n5, 121, 129, 166, 188, 190, 199, 220, 225, 233-4, 236, 248-9, 253, 261-2, 270
harmony 140, 144, 167, 191, 253-4
Harris, Paul 35
Harvey, David 184-5
Heartland Institute 215
hedonic calculus 20
hedonism 20, 166
helplessness 115, 127, 130-2, 136, 139, 145, 158, 265, 239
Heritage Foundation 186
Herman, Edward 216
hero quest frame 110, 175
herons 61, 68, 83
Hetch Hetchy Valley 73n6
heuristics 105-7, 112, 120
hierarchies, biological 56-9
hierarchies, social 9
hierarchies, value
hikers 67, 83
Hippocratic Oath 188
historians 49, 89
Hizbollah 248
holism 8, 66, 69, 77, 81, 88, 93, 113, 118, 168, 263
Holloway, John 233
honesty 2-3
Hovland, Carl 102, 104-5
hubris 96-7, 242
Huigen, Paulus 253
Hulme, Mike 118-19
humane societies 4, 62-3, 262
humane treatment 52, 54, 64, 72
humanism 1
Humanitarian League 58
Hume, David 44-5
humility *see* virtues, humility

hunting 4, 41, 50-1, 55, 58, 67-8, 72-3, 83, 99n1, 237
Hursthouse, Rosalind 38, 40, 42
Huxley, Aldous 97
hydraulic fracturing ('fracking') x, 227, 236-7, 239, 243, 252, 272
hydroelectric power 3, 87, 239
hydrosphere 76

ICT *see* Information and Communications Technologies (ICT)
ideological sphere 180
immigration policy 85, 262
imperative, categorical 30-1, 192
imperative, hypothetical 29, 192
imperial administration 226
inclusiveness 4, 13, 76, 83, 266
An Inconvenient Truth 109-10, 113, 122, 138, 145
independence 28, 54, 113
independence movements 28, 57
indigenous peoples 49, 87, 89
individualism 38, 61, 165, 173, 191, 253-4,
industrial revolution 1, 8, 130
industry, petrochemical 70
inequality 4
Information and Communications Technologies (ICT) 250-3
information deficit model 114, 153, 159
inherent value: *see* intrinsic value
injustice 59, 88, 90, 94, 118, 120, 186
innovation 5, 7, 68, 78, 93-7, 182
insecticide 70, 220
insects 60-1
instinct 2, 15, 28-9, 42-3, 54, 119
Institute for Economic Affairs (IEA) 186, 256n5
instrumental value 3-4, 34, 38-9, 57, 73n8, 195-7, 200, 233,
instrumentalism 3, 28, 195-7, 200, 242
   see too values, instrumental
integrity 8, 20, 37, 41, 43-5, 69, 86, 111, 138, 263
interdisciplinarity 12, 66, 80-1, 267
Intergovernmental Panel on Climate Change (IPCC) 27, 107, 115, 138, 146n11, 222
International Monetary Fund 185, 186, 225
interventionism, governmental 193, 204
interventionism, judicial 213
intrinsic value 3
intuitions 82-3, 88
invisible hand 32, 189-90
Ireland 136, 143, 208, 211, 227

Irwin, Steve 139
Islands, Faroe 51
islands 32, 68, 107, 238

James Bay hydroelectric project 87
Jameson, Frederick 184
Jenaah Islamiyah 248
Jesus 38, 110
Jones, Davy 227
Joseph, Keith 186
judiciary 204, 212-6, 228, 233
justice 4, 32, 41, 43, 58, 98, 167-8, 191
justice, climate 35
justice, environmental 35-6, 43, 124, 243, 263
justice, intergenerational 126
justice, international 126
justice, instinct for 119-20
justice, social 36, 88, 119, 164, 167-8, 187, 194, 241, 243

Kahneman, Daniel 105, 153
Kant, Immanuel 28-31, 33-4, 37-8, 42, 44-5, 52-5, 72, 92, 215, 228
Keep America Beautiful campaign 99n5
Keynes, John Maynard 32
kinship 4, 56-7, 62, 64-5, 75-6, 83, 261
Klein, Naomi 107, 122, 127
Knight, Kelvin 38
Know-how 120
Kropotkin, Peter 146n14, 199
Kyoto Protocol 129, 196, 222

Labour movement 36, 237-8
Labour Party (UK) 153, 209-11, 218-9
labour parties 218
labour power *see* power, labour
Land Ethic 66-9, 80-1, 93
Lasswell, Harold 102
legislation 6, 9, 18, 33, 44, 89-90, 126, 153, 186, 188, 193, 207-8, 210, 213-5, 220, 222, 224, 228, 242, 265
legislators 7, 10, 67, 208-10, 219, 226
legislature 199, 204, 208-15, 226, 228, 243, 268; and bicameral 208, 213; unicameral 208, 213
legitimacy 9, 163, 181, 193, 204, 211, 213-4, 219, 221, 223, 228, 243,
Leninism *see* Marxism, orthodox (Leninism)
leopards 63
Leopold, Aldo 38, 43, 66-71, 73, 76-7, 79-81, 83, 93, 95, 99n1, 132, 144-5, 261
liberal arts 269

liberalism 31, 34, 36, 42, 112, 121, 123, 136, 139, 182, 193, 217, 224, 226 ; classical 31-34, 42, 45, 181; economic *see* liberalism, classical; modern 32-33, 36, 42, 45, 233; neo- *see* neoliberalism
libertarian *see* propertarian
libertarian paternalism *see* nudge theory
liberty *see* freedom
licencing effect 170
life, instance of 61
lifestyle ix, 3, 7, 11, 26, 76, 78, 90, 93, 98-9, 109, 114, 124, 145, 193, 253-4, 262, 264-5, 267
lithosphere 76
littering 31, 33, 78, 99n5, 137, 144, 152, 199, 235
livestock 7, 67, 70
lobbying 193, 215-6, 220, 224, 226, 239, 242, 250, 252
local contexts 3, 95
Locke, John 28-31
loop, closed 95
loop, feedback: *see* feedback loop
loss aversion 157-8
Love Canal 72
Lovelock, James 84
Low Impact Living Affordable Community (LILAC) 254
Lush 195
Lynas, Mark 27

Machan, Tibor 191, 201n4
Machiavelli, Niccolò 205
MacIntyre, Alasdair 36-9, 41-2, 142, 192, 263
macropolitics 205-6, 228, 232, 252
maker communities 92
management, environmental 5, 51, 67-9, 71, 99n1, 270-1
management, organisational 27, 199, 219, 242,
Manhattan Project 95
manipulation 9-10, 32, 106, 108, 112, 116, 142, 153, 159,161, 163, 180, 183
Maples, Wendy 239
Marcuse, Herbert 96
markets x, 81, 90, 182, 189, 195, 197, 206, 220, 224, 226, 247, 267; *see also* value, exchange.
Marshall, George 119, 121, 165, 175
Marx, Karl 181
Marxism 214, 241; heterodox (autonomism) 233-4; orthodox (Leninism) 233, 242

Mason, Michael 206
Matten, Dirk 188, 194
meanings, shared 11
media 5, 58, 62, 97, 102-3, 108-9, 112-17, 123-4, 132, 154, 216-9, 223, 226, 228, 241-2, 244, 249-252; *see also* social media
medieval period 49, 79
Meijering, Louise 253
meta-ethics 15-17
Mexico 49, 72, 238, 245
microbes 76, 97
micropolitics 180, 205-6, 224, 228, 232-4, 241-2, 253, 255, 267
Middle Ages 51
Mill, James 19
Mill, John Stuart 19-20, 22, 24, 26, 44
mining 54, 67, 73, 250, 252
Moby Doll 73, 262
modernity 1, 6
momentum, technological: *see* technological momentum
Monbiot, George 27
monitarisation 196-7, 221
monkey-wrenching 238; *see also* direct action
monomyth 110
monopoly 186, 198
Mont Pelerin Society 186
Montreal Protocol 89, 222
Moorland 21
moral corruption 127
moral philosophy: *see* ethics
moralism 44-5
morality: *see* ethics
Mother Earth News 84
mountains 67, 73, 76, 82, 262
Moveon 251
Mowat, Farley 68
Muir, John 67
Mumford, Lewis 96
municipality 88

Nader, Ralph 97
Naess, Arne 38, 76-86, 88, 93, 95, 97-8, 132, 145, 199
nanotechnology 12
narrative 109, 111, 121, 130
nation-states *see* states, constitutional
National Assembly for Wales *see* Welsh Assembly
National Parks 67, 73, 73n6
nationalisation 227
native Americans 67, 89

naturalists 56, 83, 139
nature 3, 34, 40, 43, 49, 50, 57, 60-1, 66-7, 93, 97-8, 102, 119, 123, 130, 155, 166, 196-7, 200, 225, 227, 264-5
Negri, Antonio 184, 233
Neo-Aristotelianism *see* virtue theory
neo-Kantian *see* deontology, neo-Kantian
neoliberalism 184-9, 191-201, 204, 215, 221, 248, 254
Netherlands 107
networks, social 63, 68, 70, 88, 113, 139, 172, 217, 219, 241-2, 256, 268
networks, socio-technical 6, 98, 113, 139, 143, 250-1
networks, species 68, 81, 89
New Ecological Paradigm (NEP) 174
New Mexico 67
New World 49-50, 261
newsworthiness 121
NIMBY (Not In My Back Yard) 99n2
No Impact Man 109
non-coercive 159, 184, 186, 220, 224
non-constitutionalism 10, 58, 232-56
non-maleficience 17, 188
Non-Governmental Organisations (NGOs) 102, 194, 223
norms 2, 7-8, 10-11, 15, 17-18, 26-7, 29, 35, 39, 42-5, 82-3, 111-12, 119, 121, 123-4, 126, 131, 133-40, 154, 158, 166, 170, 172, 179, 180, 184, 186-7, 192, 205, 228, 233, 250, 261, 263-4
norms, descriptive and injunctive 134-5
Norway 76, 82, 131, 146n16
Nozick, Robert 24-5, 31, 186-7, 195-6, 198
nuclear waste 71, 237
nudge, theory of 9-10, 102, 104, 124, 135, 145, 152-3, 156-9, 220; *see also* Behavioural Insight Team
nudge, ethics of 159-65, 220
Nussbaum, Martha 37, 38
Nuttall, Paul 221

Obama, Barack 135, 208
obligation, contractual 32-3, 35, 180, 184-91, 199, 204-5
Obomsawin, Alanis 27
Occupy movement 251
Oelschlaeger, Max 97
oil spills 5, 72, 87, 245
Oliver, John 115
OPEC (Organization of the Petroleum Exporting Countries) 78, 186

Opower 134-5
Oregon 236
Organisation of Petroleum Exporting Countries (OPEC) 78, 186
organisations, animal rights 14, 64-5, 215, 244, 248, 262
organisations, conservation 63, 67-8, 70-1, 237, 262
organisations, environmental 2, 240
ornithologists 68
outcomes *see* consequequentialism
over-grazing 70
ozone depletion 86, 89, 117-8, 129, 222

Paris Climate Agreement 222, 266
Parks, Rosa 109, 234
paternalism 156, 176n1, 246
paternalism, libertarian *see* nudge theory
Paterson, Matthew, 235, 241
patriarchy 240; *see also* sexism
People for the Ethical Treatment of Animals (PETA) 215, 244
Pereira, Fernando 237
persuasion 103-5, 110, 112, 146n1, 160-3, 168, 180, 265
pesticide 11, 42, 70, 220
pets 52, 56, 62, 270
Phillips, Robert A. 190
philosophy, ecological 81-2; *see also* deep ecology
Pilbeam, Bruce 224
Pinochet, Augusto 186
Plaid Cymru 243
Plane Stupid 221, 236
platform, deep ecology 82, 85
platform, oil 18, 72, 272
Plato 37, 49
Plows, Alexandra 240-3
pluralistic ignorance 135
policy-makers 7, 10, 12, 81, 96, 99, 186, 196, 271
policy-making 9, 55, 232
politics ix; constitutional *see constitutionalism*; defined 205; non-constitutional *see* direct-action
polluter pays principle 36
pollution 6, 8, 19, 23, 36, 71-2, 77-8, 80, 97, 126, 152, 188-9, 196, 199, 206, 236, 262
population, human 4, 16, 35, 54, 84-5, 107, 124
power: coercive 136, 180-1, 205, 207; constitutive 180; contractual 180-1, 205; economic *see* contractual; expert 136;

labour 10, 29, 57, 182-3,199-200, 253; legitimate 136, 138; over 180; referent 133, 137, 139; reward and coercive 136; social 9-10, 136, 166, 219, 265; soft 180, 205.
practice theory x, 142-3
practices ix, 1-2, 9-13, 16-17, 24, 27, 35, 38-40, 42-5, 48, 64, 71, 73, 76, 79, 93, 98, 102, 113, 115, 131, 133, 142-3, 145, 172, 175, 179, 192, 196-8, 200, 206, 218, 221, 233, 237, 239, 241-4, 249, 253-5, 263-4, 266, 268, 270
practitioner, x, 17, 44, 197, 214, 241, 273; *see also* agency, practices
pragmatism, environmental 13, 13n2
precautionary principle 73, 81
predators 61, 67, 73
prefiguration 235-7, 239, 241, 244, 248, 253, 255
pressure groups 102, 213. 215-6, 220
Preston, Lee 190
prey 61
Prince, The 205
principles, ethical ix-x, 1, 4, 14-15, 17, 19-46, 62, 75, 79-84, 92, 126, 136, 158, 167, 184-8, 195-6, 198-200, 206, 217-8, 224, 233, 241, 273
prisoner's dilemma 124-6, 158, 173, 263
problem-based learning (PBL) 271-2
production, cooperative 88-9, 126, 180, 195-6, 199, 237, 265
productivism 20
profit 6, 22, 55, 57, 72, 182-4, 187-90, 193, 195-8, 200, 215, 225, 248; *see also* capital, circuit of
progress, moral 87
progress, social 52, 96, 113, 162, 184, 265
progress, technological 7, 12, 70, 78, 90, 109, 130
Project Wild Thing 111
propertarianism 24-5, 31, 46n1, 124, 191, 199
propinquity 20
Provisional Irish Republican Army (IRA) 248
proximity 81, 114, 121
psychology ix, 8
psychology of influence 102-45
psychopathy 181, 188-9, 192-3
public sphere 138, 193-4

Quakers 57
quality of life 9, 82, 113
Quebec 87

racism 16, 22-3, 109
Rand, Ayn 31
RAND Corporation 248
ranking of life 48-50, 52
ranking of values 75
rationality 17, 34, 53, 61, 86, 113-4, 264
Rawls, John 32, 35, 160, 234
Ray, John 56-7
Reagan, Ronald 33, 99n4, 186
realpolitik 218, 226
reason *see* rationality
reciprocation 18, 26, 125-6, 215, 228-9, 243
Reclus, Elisée 199
recreation 51, 67-8, 73, 99
recuperation 200
recycling 78, 95, 120, 133-4, 136, 139, 143, 165, 227
redwood forests 87
reductionism 66, 261, 267
reflexivity 52-3, 72, 92
Regan, Tom 34, 56
regulation ix, 9
representation, electoral 208-22, 226, 229
resilience *see* virtues, resilience
resource depletion i, ix, 17, 77-8, 80
resources, material 10
responsibility 5, 7, 9, 26, 33, 45, 54, 64, 97-9, 120, 123, 127-29, 131, 136, 145, 162, 175
responsibility, corporate social *see* corporate social responsibility (CSR)
Reverence for Life ethic 59-62, 65, 69, 75, 80, 83, 93, 102, 191, 193, 196, 217, 249, 265-6
Reverend Billy (Talen) 109, 128, 167
rights 18, 27-32 *see also* deontology; animal *see* animal rights movement *and* speciesism; -based ethics: *see* deontology; consumer 252; negative 28, 31-3, 45, 46n1, 153, 190, 198-9, 215; political and civil 4, 28, 87, 146n5, 208, 212, 214; positive 28, 31, 45, 215, 226, 249; property, 10, 18, 27, 31, 33-4, 46n2, 181, 184, 186, 191, 194, 196, 205, 225, 250; utilitarian defence of 25-6; 36
Rolston III, Holmes 38
Rose, Chris 111
Rosenthal, Sandra 190
Rothbard, Murray 191
Royal Society for the Prevention of Cruelty to Animals (RSPCA) 62
Rule utilitarianism 26, 36, 225
Ruwart, Mary 197, 199

A Sand County Almanac 68-9
sabotage 238, 245; *see also* direct action
Salt, Henry Stephens 58-9, 61-2, 64, 79
Sandel, Michael 192, 196
Scandinavia 211
Schlosberg, David 35
Schumacher, Ernst 93-4
Schweitzer, Albert 59-66, 69, 73, 75-6, 79-80, 82-3, 93, 145, 261-2
sciences, natural 2, 57
scientific revolution 57
Scotland 108, 133, 199, 211-2, 272
Scottish National Party (SNP) 209, 211
Scruton, Roger 37, 38, 41
Sea Shepherd 237
secular arguments 44, 52-4, 58
Seel, Benjamin 235
segmentation 154-5, 172
segregation 213, 235, 262
self-awareness 53-5
self-development 162
self-enhancing values 166-7
self-interest 90
self-knowledge 9
self-perception theory 168, 70
self-transcendent values 166-7
self-valorization *see* autovalorization
sentience 34, 52-4, 75, 84
Sessions, George 82
sexism 22-3, 240, 244
shallow ecology 76-9, 81, 85, 98, 172
Shantz, Jeff 238
shared meanings 11
shareholder *see* stakeholder
Shearman, David 224
Silent Spring 70, 220
Singer, Peter 14-15, 20, 22-4, 55-6, 62, 144, 225, 248-9
single action bias 128, 170, 192, 198
Site of Special Scientific Interest (SSSI) 262
slavery 3, 4, 23, 28, 3, 37, 57-9, 62, 64, 87, 109, 184, 262
Slote, Michael 38
Small is Beautiful 93
Smith, Adam 32, 36, 186, 188, 191
Smith, Joseph Wayne 224
Social Ecology x, 5, 13, 76, 85-92, 93-4, 99, 146n15, 183, 195, 199, 206, 223, 250, 263
social capital 164, 219
social marketing x, 9, 58, 152-6
social media 216, 251-2
social power 9-10, 104, 136-8, 166, 219
socialism 38, 41, 191, 222, 226, 233

socialism, green *see* eco-socialism
Socialist parties 218
Society of Business Ethics 195
sociological denial 131
solidarity 196, 199, 239, 246
Solomon, Robert 189, 191
species, companion 56
species, endangered 26, 64, 83, 98, 186, 206, 262
speciesism 23
spillover 156, 165-6, 168-71
spirituality 43, 60, 83, 85, 93, 109, 119, 123
squatting 237-8, 241
stability 69, 84, 89, 110, 166, 210, 229
stakeholders ix, 75, 189-90, 266, 272
standard of living 55, 77, 82, 84
Starhawk 254
state, constitutional 3, 11, 57-8, 88, 180-1, 184, 186, 188-99, 201-28, 233-4, 236, 240-2, 244, 247-2, 255, 256n6, 267-8
statecraft 205, 258; *see also* realpolitik
stewardship 32
strike, environmental 237-8
Studer, Kenneth 97
subjectivism 15
sublime experience 67, 83
subliminal advertising 153
subsidy 136, 221
suffering 4, 36, 52-4, 61-5, 71, 73, 108, 261-2
Sunstein, Cass 156, 158-60, 164
survival of the fittest 89
sustainability ix, 12, 41, 55, 69, 78, 82, 84, 86, 90, 94, 99n7, 134, 147, 174-5, 187, 195
symbiosis 5, 18, 69, 80
symbolic action x, 71, 226, 243-6, 255
System 1 and System 2 thinking 105, 107, 116, 143-4
syndicalism 226, 233, 248
syndicalism, green 238, 248
systems, ecological *see* ecosystems
systems, economic 12, 182, 225, 233
systems, planetary 80, 83-4, 98
systems, technological 6, 95, 97, 262
systems, voting 210; *and* first-past-the-post 211-3; proportional representation, 211-4, 228, 229n5

taking responsibility 145
targets, environmental 10, 206; *see also* goals, environmental

taxation 6, 25, 143, 153, 156, 158, 164, 186, 220-1
technocracy 7, 96
technological fix i, ix-x, 95-9, 109, 129, 146n12, 226, 270
technological momentum 95
technology, appropriate 81, 93-101
technology, intermediate 93-4
technology, sustainable 99n7
telos 42; *see also* goals
terrorism 121, 247-9, 256n5; green *see* eco-terrorism
Thaler, Richard 156, 158-60
Thatcher, Margaret 33, 99n4, 186
theologians 56, 59
theology 4, 37, 44, 49, 52, 54, 56, 58, 84, 261
theory of basic values 166-7
Theory of Moral Sentiments 37, 191
This Changes Everything 107, 122, 127
Tormey, Simon 184
tourism 5, 72, 200
trade, slave 57-8, 87, 262
traditions; religious 37, 40, 49, 60, 73n1, 79, 85, 93; shared 11; Western 3, 49-51, 62, 70, 73n1, 99, 128n2
tragedy of the commons 7, 124, 126, 263
transition towns ix, 113, 122, 139
transparency 9, 45, 160-1, 163, 252, 264
trees 51, 65, 68-9, 99n1, 109, 236, 241
Trump, Donald 127, 167
trust 110, 123, 126, 138
trustworthiness *see* trust
Tvergastein 82
Tversky, Amos *see* Kahneman, Daniel

UNAHCT (United Nations Ad Hoc Committee on Terrorism) 247-8
uncanny, climate change as 119
uncertainty 112, 115-8, 133, 145, 264
United Kingdom (UK) 10, 17, 99n4, 108, 115-6, 133, 136, 139, 153-5, 157-8, 163, 165, 208-11, 214, 216, 218, 220-1, 224-5, 227, 236, 243, 245-6, 251
United Kingdom Independence Party (UKIP) 209, 211, 214, 221
United States of America (USA) 1, 3,4, 11, 49, 57-8, 66-7, 69-71, 73n1, 84, 85, 87, 89, 93-4, 96-7, 99n5, 103, 109-10, 116, 121, 128, 146n5, 152, 212, 214, 235, 251, 256n5, 261

University of Chicago 186, 191
urban life 4
utilitarianism x, 1, 15, 18, 19-27, 28, 31-32, 35-36, 37, 41-4, 55-7, 61, 66, 69, 77, 88, 99n, 110, 122, 189, 190, 221, 225, 248-9, 263, 267, 270
utility 18-19, 21-4, 26, 28, 52, 55, 57, 64, 124, 190

Valadés, Diego 49
valleys 67, 73n6, 76
valorisation 233-4, 238, 242
value-belief-norm theory 174
value, circuit of *see* circuit of capital
value, circuit of capital 181-3, 200, 233
values, environmental 2, 123-4, 139, 158, 161, 170-1, 175, 183, 196, 224, 250, 253, 263
value, exchange 183-4, 187, 194-7, 200, 221, 223, 268
value, instrumental 3-4, 34-5, 57, 233; *see also* exchange value
value, intrinsic 3-4, 34, 38-9, 56, 69, 75, 80, 82, 132-3, 183, 197, 233
value, moral 3
value system ix, 5, 48, 58, 66, 72, 75-6, 261, 263
value, use 183-4, 197; *see also* intrinsic value
Van der Bellen, Alexander 227
van Hogen, Bettina 253
veganism 64, 73, 195
vegetarianism 23, 58, 64
veneration 83
Venezuela 227
vices 38, 106, 144, 160, 192, 198, 252, 255
vicious cycle 40
virtues 1, 6, 8, 37-44, 54, 72, 75-6, 99, 102, 104, 106, 114, 134, 138-9, 144-5, 152, 154, 167, 174-5, 189, 191-2, 198, 243, 254-5, 261, 263-7; chastity 41; cooperation as 145, 264, 266; courage 37-40, 43, 109, 120, 138, 145, 266; epistemic 41, 106, 266; fairness as 43, 126, 145, 164, 254; friendliness (liberality) 40, 44, 122-4, 127, 145; frugality 78; humility 81, 138, 144-5, 171, 264-5; integrity 264; modesty as 256; resilience 9, 41, 120, 145, 170, 254, 264-5; self-reliance 191, 254; tolerance of uncertainty 264; wisdom as 38, 40-1, 111, 191, 252, 254; wonder and respect for nature as 35, 40, 183, 264

virtue theory x, 34, 37-44, 110, 122-3, 145, 191, 200, 235, 265, 267
virtuous circle 40, 129
Vivir Bien see *Buen Vivir*
von Hayek, Friedrich 31, 186-7, 198
voter 11, 51, 129, 135, 174, 206-18, 227-8, 229n, 238-40, 250

Wall, Derek 240, 242-3
Wall Street
waste, chemical 72
waste, nuclear 71, 237
Watson, John B. 10
Watson, Paul 237
Watson, Richard 84-5
Wealth of Nations, The 37, 191
Weinberg, Alvin 95-7, 99n8
well-being 3, 18, 24, 42-3, 49, 56, 60, 66, 70, 75-7, 79, 90, 110, 145, 164, 166
Welsh Assembly 215
Welsh, Ian 248
Werhane, Patricia 190
Western traditions *see* traditions, Western
Westervelt, Jay 198

Whale and Dolphin Conservation Society 63
White Jr, Lynn 49, 73n8, 79
wicked problem 4, 35, 117-8, 126-7, 145, 198, 252, 263, 267
wilderness 3, 4, 67, 83, 108, 255, 261
Wilkin, Peter 251-2
Wilkinson, William 183
will to live 64, 73, 75
windfarms x, 118, 272
wind turbines ix, 5, 92, 94
Wisconsin 68
Woodland Trust 108
World Economic Forum 217
World Horse Welfare Society 63
World Trade Organization 185, 194, 225
worldview 3, 9, 49, 82, 87, 174, 270

Yale and Columbia Universities Environmental Performance Index 224
Yellowstone National Park 67-8, 73

Zerzan, John 89
zoo 51